Max Egremont was born in 1948 and stu[...]
Oxford University. As well as four novels, ne is tne author of two
biographical studies, *The Cousins*, which won the Yorkshire Post
First Book Award, and *Under Two Flags: The Life of Major General
Sir Edward Spears*.

Max Egremont lives in West Sussex with his wife and four
children.

BALFOUR

A Life of
Arthur James Balfour

MAX EGREMONT

A PHOENIX GIANT PAPERBACK

First published in Great Britain
by William Collins Sons & Co Ltd in 1980
This paperback edition published in 1998
by Phoenix, a division of Orion Books Ltd,
Orion House, 5 Upper St Martin's Lane,
London WC2H 9EA

A CIP catalogue record for this book is available
from the British Library.

ISBN: 0 75380 146 9

Printed and bound in Great Britain by
Butler & Tanner Ltd, Frome and London

FOR CAROLINE

CONTENTS

LIST OF ILLUSTRATIONS

INTRODUCTION

Arthur Balfour fascinated and eluded his contemporaries. His tall, etiolated, elegant figure was a familiar political landmark for some forty years, yet he defied analysis or easy intimacy. Few people could resist his charm and urbanity: few felt that they really understood him. Balfour himself disliked attempts to explain his character or behaviour. He preferred to remain remote, set apart a little from the rest of humanity, isolated from its irrational passions and ignorant curiosity.

If Balfour scarcely ever indulged in personal revelation or self-justification, others have gone in search of him. This is not the first study of his life. In 1936, Balfour's niece, Blanche Dugdale, produced a two volume biography. This was followed, in 1962, by Kenneth Young's fine book, and in 1973 Sydney Zebel published a work devoted to Balfour's long political career.

Why then embark upon another life of Arthur Balfour? My first excuse must be a deep interest in both the man and his time; my second, new material and fresh sources. Mrs Dugdale's work bore the marks of family piety and reticence, although it was a pioneering study; Mr Young, as he himself admits, was the victim of the fifty year rule regarding access to public documents (including the later years of the Balfour papers in the British Museum); Professor Zebel ventures hardly at all into his subject's personal life. I have tried to combine concisely the personal and the political, and provide new insight into both. Inevitably there will be other biographies of Balfour. If I succeed in illuminating even a part of this extraordinary and tantalizing figure, this book will not have been written in vain.

I am profoundly indebted to the Earl of Balfour for allowing me to make use of the Balfour papers and welcoming me with such kindness on my visits to Whittingehame. Others whom I thank for permission to consult papers in their possession are the Duke of Westminster (George Wyndham's papers in the Grosvenor Estate Office); the Marquis of Lansdowne and the Earl of Shelburne (the Lansdowne papers); the Marquis of Salisbury (the papers of the 3rd and 4th Marquises of Salisbury,

Lord Quickswood's papers, Lady Gwendolen Cecil's papers); the Earl of Wemyss (the Balfour-Wemyss correspondence); Viscount Cobham (the Hagley papers); Lord Rayleigh and the Hon: Charles Strutt (Lady Rayleigh's papers); Frances, Lady Fergusson (the Dugdale papers); Professor Michael Jaffé and the Syndics of the Fitzwilliam Museum, Cambridge (the Wilfrid Scawen Blunt papers); Mr Philip Mallet (Bernard Mallet's diary); Mrs John Maxse (the Maxse papers); Viscount Bridgeman (Diary of the 1st Viscount Bridgeman).

I have received much generous help from Mr J. K. Bates and his staff at the Scottish Record Office; the staff of the British Museum Library and Department of Manuscripts; the staffs of the Bodleian Library, Oxford, the London Library and the Public Record Office. Others who have guided, assisted and encouraged me include the Dowager Duchess of Devonshire; Elizabeth, Marchioness of Salisbury; the Dowager Countess of Balfour; the Countess of Longford; Irene, Countess of Plymouth; the Earl and Countess of Wemyss; Viscount Gage; the Dowager Lady Harlech; Diana, Lady Avebury; Lord Neidpath; Lord Ravensdale; Lady Eve Balfour; Mr Michael and Lady Evelyn Brander; Lady Alison Kremer; Lady Lang; Lady Mary Lyon; Sir Tatton Sykes, Bart:; Sir John Balfour; the Rt Hon: Sir Alan Lascelles; the Hon: Charles Strutt; the Hon: Guy Strutt; Mrs Sheila Allen; Dr John Campbell; Mrs Irene Cox; Mrs Barbara Draper; Mr Roger Fulford; Mr Robin Harcourt Williams; Dr Ruddock Mackay; Mrs Alison McCann; the Hon. Mrs Betty Miller-Jones; Mr Walter Scott; Mr Michael Vyvyan; Mr Paul Woudhuysen; the Society for Psychical Research.

To Dr Hugh Cecil I owe an especial debt, for he read through my manuscript and undoubtedly brought about its improvement. My editor, Mr Philip Ziegler, as usual provided perceptive and sure guidance. Finally, throughout the writing of this book my wife has endured the enigmatic, occasionally exasperating, presence of Arthur James Balfour in her life with great patience and understanding. I doubt if she realizes how much she has contributed to whatever merits this study of his life may have.

1

Childhood and Early Youth

On 6 October 1848, Lady Blanche Balfour confided her principal faults to her journal. She wrote of 'worldliness, self-conceit, want of devotional feeling, indolence',[1] yet comforted herself with the year's greatest blessing: a son, her first male child. The boy was named Arthur, after his godfather the Duke of Wellington, and James, after his father and Balfour grandfather.

The journal entries were characteristic, for their religious piety and consciousness of personal imperfection. Lady Blanche was the daughter of the second Marquis of Salisbury. At the age of eighteen she married James Maitland Balfour, eldest son of James and Lady Eleanor Balfour of Whittingehame in East Lothian. Her husband's father, after making his fortune in India as a contractor for the East India Company, had bought the Whittingehame estate from the Hay family, having Robert Smirke, architect of the British Museum, build him a house there at the foot of the Lammermuir Hills.

Old James Balfour was the founder of his family's fortune. His descent was distinguished, stretching back to Siward of Northumbria who is said to have first come to Scotland in the eleventh century. In Macbeth, Duncan's avenger is perhaps this Siward, who claimed descent from a fairy bear or 'union of a white bear with a lady'[2] as a recent mythologist has remarked. The name Balfour originates from the Gaelic 'balfoidh or' or village at the foot or end of the River Or in Fife where the Balfours set themselves up as bonnet lairds. From this region George Balfour, younger son of the Balfour of Dovan and Lawlethan, left for London in the seventeenth century to make his fortune as a linen draper. By 1642 he had succeeded enough to be able to buy the estate of Balbirnie near Markinch.

James Balfour, or 'the Nabob' as his descendants referred to him, left Balbirnie as a younger son for India. He returned rich, his contracting business having dealt in military material, victuals for the Navy, even the building of railways. However, there seems to have been something of the penny-pinching Scot about him, a contemporary remarking that 'Mr. Balfour's predecessor in the purveying business had kept open house, but the windows and doors appear to have been the only part of his house which were kept open'.[3] Balfour had begun service as a clerk in the East India Company, but was asked to leave for accepting gifts. Then, turning to business, he amassed a small fortune.

James Balfour clearly regarded India as the key to a better life at home. In 1815, soon after his return, he married Lady Eleanor Maitland, daughter of 'Citizen Maitland' the eighth Earl of Lauderdale, renowned for his Jacobin sympathies. After marriage Balfour established himself as a country gentleman, buying estates in Fife (at Balgonie, near his elder brother's home), in Ross-shire (at Strathconan) and at Whittingehame. Family legend has it that James Balfour originally wanted to settle in Fife but, during the journey to Balgonie, Lady Eleanor was so seasick on the Firth of Forth that she vowed never to live on its northern side. At any rate Whittingehame was chosen as his main residence and by 1827 Smirke's neo-classical mansion was ready for occupation, James Balfour having given up his idea of enlarging the old peel tower into a suitably grand country house.

At Whittingehame in 1820 the Balfours' eldest son James had been born. In all they had five children, four surviving to adulthood of which the first two were sons and the second two daughters. James Maitland Balfour carried his parents' hope of developing his newly established patrimony and in 1843 seemed to be following the directions they wished by marrying Lady Blanche Cecil.

Lady Blanche, sister of a future Prime Minister, came from a family as distinguished as the Balfours could have wanted. Attaining prominence in the sixteenth and seventeenth centuries at the courts of Queen Elizabeth and James I, the Cecils later became still richer through the marriage of Lady Blanche's father to Miss Gascoyne, heiress to estates in Lancashire and Essex. If their political power had waned, the force of the Cecil name was still strong and this Lord Salisbury, by holding office in two Tory governments, restored the family tradition of public service. James Maitland Balfour was twenty-two and his bride eighteen at the time of their marriage. Over the next eleven years nine children were born to them, the 'Nabob' dying in 1848, the year of his oldest Balfour grandson's birth.

Arthur Balfour's parents brought up their young family at Whittingehame, imbuing in the children a lifelong love of lowland Scotland. James Maitland Balfour was not to live long enough to leave much of a personal legacy. 'My father,' his eldest daughter Evelyn remembers, 'was fond of hunting, golf and shooting,'[4] and this is an appropriate epitaph for a life chiefly devoted to those activities. There was one excursion into a wider world. The 'Nabob' had briefly represented the County of Haddington in Parliament from 1831 to 1835; James Maitland Balfour was, from 1841 to 1847, Conservative member for the Burghs of Haddington, Dunbar, North Berwick, Lauder and Jedburgh. Apart from this he served in the East Lothian yeomanry and developed his estates.

Lady Blanche's part in her son's life was to be greater. 'Our debt to her,' he acknowledged, 'is incalculable.'[5] She was a remarkable woman, of strong faith, courage and resolution; but to say this is not enough. After her death the Presbyterian minister at Whittingehame, Dr. Robertson, wrote a cloying memoir of which Arthur Balfour observed to his niece and biographer: 'It's all quite true of course, but for Heaven's sake don't get the idea she was a goody!'[6] In 1861, echoing this, Arthur Balfour's aunt Adelaide Balfour wrote to Lady Blanche of 'your dear brown eyes and singing laugh – I love your laugh – what do I not love about you?'[7]

Lady Blanche was a devout religious believer, but she never lost touch with the ways and humour of the world. Brought up at Hatfield, sister of a future Prime Minister, daughter of a Conservative politician, god-daughter of the Duke of Wellington, there was nothing cloistered about her early life. As a girl she was short but handsome and the Duke of Wellington enjoyed escorting her at balls in London. With the Duke, indeed, she was clearly a special favourite; he gave her a copy of the map of the field of Waterloo he had had made before the day of the battle and lent her Stratfield Saye for her honeymoon.

The marriage was ill-fated. First there were difficulties with her mother-in-law. Lady Eleanor was as imperious as her father was egalitarian, and often reduced Lady Blanche to tears with criticisms of her management of Whittingehame. After the Nabob's death she continued to take an interest in the place, even though full provision had been made for her to live with her other son Charles at Newton Don in Berwickshire, and, tired and lame, would be pushed about her old home by a servant or relation, commenting severely on the alterations. In the evenings of such visits Lady Eleanor appeared for dinner 'in full panoply of bare shoulders, diamonds, crinoline and lace flounces'. 'I wonder,' another guest once nervously asked Lady Blanche, 'am I smart enough?' To which the answer came: 'Quite. She is always so ridiculous.'[8] Then there was the character of James Maitland Balfour himself. They had been married young, because, it is said, Lord Salisbury, anxious to re-marry, wished to rid himself of his daughters. James was supposed to have had a violent temper and to have been out of sympathy with Lady Blanche's religion. Yet their daughter Evelyn remembers her mother's devotion to him and her misery at his early death.

Arthur Balfour's first memory was of watching the victory fireworks from the Turf Club at the conclusion of the Crimean War. This, taking place in the latter part of 1856, precludes any recollection of his father; thus he was not conscious of the greatest tragedy of his mother's life. In 1854 James Maitland Balfour fell ill with tuberculosis which the doctors attributed to a broken blood vessel. For the next two years Lady Blanche nursed her husband, staying devotedly near, creeping into his bedroom at night while he slept to put coal on the fire, travelling to Madeira with him and their oldest children in winter across the perilous Bay of Biscay, crying out to those who would comfort her, 'what is all the world to me if my husband is dying?'[9] In the process of this labour and grief she broke her own health, already damaged by bearing eight children. Later Arthur Balfour was to remember little of these first years yet they forced from his mother a strength she had never previously needed. In February 1856 James Maitland Balfour died in Madeira, leaving his eight children to the care of his wife.

Henceforth Lady Blanche, chastened by this appalling loss, involved herself almost wholly in her family and her religion. She continued to live at Whittingehame where, with the help of her old friend, Miss Emily Faithfull (daughter of the vicar of Hatfield), she brought up her children, attempting to inculcate in them her own cherished Christian virtues. There was about her an energy, a power which left in them feelings compounded of admiration and awe. 'You felt,' her daughter Evelyn wrote, 'you had to do right when with her' and commented on her mother's facility for commanding immediate obedience. This power caused the children to compete for her attention, to long for her praise. In 1856 on Evelyn's birthday, the girl was asked what particular treat she would like and answered, a long walk alone with Lady Blanche. Years later another of Arthur Balfour's sisters was asked by her niece what Lady Blanche would have thought of her grandchildren and answered, 'It is quite impossible to tell you that. If any of you had known her you would all have been so different from what you are that I really cannot say.'[11]

Lady Blanche's strength and her capacity for inspiring her children to try to please her, to live up to an abstract idea of what they imagined she wished them to be, moulded the Balfour family. There were, among her children, startling successes: Arthur Balfour became Prime Minister, Eleanor the Principal of Newnham College, Frank had a professorial chair of morphology created for him at Cambridge, Gerald reached the cabinet; yet there were failures as well. Before the glaring light of Lady Blanche's example, some turned away, dazzled, conscious of weakness and inadequacy, despairingly searching for other ways of life and sources of comfort. Cecil Balfour gambled, forged a cheque in his brother Arthur's name, left for Australia, was shunned by his family and killed from a fall from a horse; Eustace Balfour married the domineering Lady Frances Campbell, turned to drink and died a hopeless alcoholic; Alice Balfour, after an early trip by wagon through South Africa, devoted her life to housekeeping for Arthur, preoccupied with petty domestic economies, apologizing often for herself and her chronic shyness.

But for her oldest son Lady Blanche was adored and adoring. Almost the earliest record of Balfour is of him astride his mother's knee asking: 'Can you tell me why I love you so much?'[12] Lady Blanche was no distant half-known figure occasionally, out of duty, visiting the nurseries, but an ever-present force in her small childrens' lives. She taught them to read, gave them the first rudiments of education, passed on to them her strong low church faith, being, as Dr Robertson observed, 'Both father and mother to her large family'.[13] There were helpers, such as Miss Emily Faithfull and a German governess, but it was Lady Blanche who ruled.

The tone of her rule was a mixture of Christian dedication and good humour. There were daily Bible classes and the children were always plainly dressed to avoid unnecessary ostentation. She believed, too, in demonstrating the practical side of charity. Lady Blanche would distribute religious tracts at East Linton railway station and during the cotton distresses of 1862 and 1863, caused by the American Civil War, two girls from Lancashire were taken in at Whittingehame. She told her daughter Eleanor that after the family had grown up she planned to move to the East End of London and devote the rest of her life to the poor. Yet another daughter, Alice, remembers her laughing until the tears coursed down her cheeks and Arthur Balfour told his niece: 'She was very amusing. She was brilliant. Looking back now I can see she was one of the most brilliant talkers I ever knew.'[14]

It was a formidable combination. By turns austere, demanding, affectionate and lighthearted, Lady Blanche was to be the strongest single influence on the young Balfours. From her they received encouragement and praise for successes, blame and retribution for failure. Her personal dominance, the way she ruled her large and close family, inspired not so much a spirit of competitiveness as a jostling for her goodwill, a feeling that to please her was the highest reward for any endeavour. There was no adolescent rebellion against Lady Blanche, no collective family despair at the unreason of her dictates. Throughout, as the lone parent, she kept the admiration and respect of her children. The scars of those who felt they had failed were, as with Cecil and Eustace, long-lasting, yet for the favoured there was a confidence born of early happiness, a serenity springing from those first contented Whittingehame days when the person who mattered most to them had seemed pleased. All this, together with material advantages, gave Arthur Balfour a fine start to life.

The early death of his father had left Balfour a great inheritance. Strathconan, the large property in Ross-shire bought by his grandfather, was let during his minority. Many improvements were carried out at Strathconan by Balfour's parents, the chronic overcrowding remedied by assisted emigration to Canada, yet on the occasion of the first visit the Balfours made there with the family, they transferred the children to a second carriage for fear that the first would be mobbed by the angry tenantry. In fact, they were welcomed by cheering crowds, the terrible highland poverty having been alleviated by a decrease in the population.

Whittingehame was the Balfours' real home. Apart from Smirke's impressive house with landscaped grounds, there was an estate of some ten thousand acres on East Lothian farming land, some of the best in Britain. In addition there came a large port-folio of investments, started by the 'Nabob', all of which were steadily gaining ground during Balfour's long minority. On his twenty-first birthday, he was said to be one of the richest young men in the country, worth over a million pounds, his inheritance having been carefully tended by Lady Blanche and trustees amongst whom was his uncle, the Prime Minister Lord Salisbury. Later, as we shall see, much of this was to be frittered away through bad judgement and incompetence.

Balfour's childhood was not cossetted. In 1862 an effort was made to contribute further to those hit by the cotton depression. The Whittingehame staff was reduced, the saved wages given to the Lancashire Relief Fund and the children set to work at domestic chores. Arthur Balfour blacked the boots, the other boys swept and the girls cooked. One morning the minister visited Lady Blanche and was told she would like to invite him to lunch 'but my daughters are doubtful if the steak will be rightly done'.[15] Such behaviour was looked upon as strange by the locals who came to realise that Lady Blanche was, in the words of a con-temporary observer, 'a person whose thoughts were not like other people's thoughts, and who could do things which other people could not do'.[16]

Then there were the illnesses which were so permanent a

feature of Whittingehame life. Lady Blanche had ruined her own
health and the children, growing up in the harsh East Lothian
climate, were often sick, Gerald nearly dying of diptheria which,
at one stage, struck the entire family down. Arthur Balfour was
always regarded as 'delicate' and suffered a succession of colds
often breaking into influenza. This resulted in a sapping of
vitality, a superficial absence of youth's usual quickness. In
1859, on arrival at his Preparatory School at the Grange, Hoddesdon, in Hertfordshire, the Headmaster, the Reverend C. H.
Chittenden, later remembered that the boy's health had been 'far
from strong, not from any definite tendency to disease as far as
appeared but from lack of vital energy'.[17]

This characteristic was to be much identifed with Balfour
throughout his life. People would mark the languor, the exhausted exterior presented to the world, and wonder how firm
direction would ever emanate from such a figure. Often they
were right to ask such questions; Balfour's vitality ebbed and
flowed, occasionally in a thin trickle, sometimes in a full strong
flood. If engaged, his energies, intellectual and physical, were a
match for any man and his purpose as strong as that of the most
determined idealist, yet such periods of activity always came in
short intense bursts before an eventual relapse into calm inaction.
The reason for this was partly temperamental, also partly
physical. Balfour needed to conserve his strength. All his life he
was to be subject to periodic breakdowns in health and he knew
his constitution needed careful coaxing rather than hard driving.
This early discovery led to Balfour outliving almost all his contemporaries, most of whom started with constitutions far more
robust than his own. They expended their energy, perhaps
rashly; he conserved his, perhaps sometimes to the detriment of
his achievement.

Balfour's education was conducted by Lady Blanche and a
series of governesses and tutors. His mother read French novels
to her children, leaving out passages which she considered un-
suitable. A German governess supplied the rudiments of German
and tutors coped with the rest, Balfour later remembering one of
these who pulled the boy's ears during Latin lessons and constantly compared the Balfours unfavourably with the Percys who
had been his last pupils. Lady Blanche introduced her family to

English as well as French literature. She herself admired Mrs. Gaskell and Jane Austen, spurning Thackeray whom she had thought an unattractive snob when once sitting next to him at dinner.

The Grange, Hoddesdon, was Balfour's first school. The Reverend C. H. Chittenden, its headmaster, was the son-in-law of a former Rector of Hatfield and brother-in-law of Miss Emily Faithfull, Lady Blanche's devoted helper and companion. The Grange was an unusual establishment, remarkable among Victorian private schools for its tolerance and lack of bullying. Its small size allowed Mr. Chittenden to give personal attention to each of his pupils and he found young Balfour an interesting boy. Balfour's health was, as he himself writes, 'so delicate that the ordinary school routine had often to be seriously relaxed in my favour',[18] and this led to long walks in the open air with Chittenden during which the Headmaster expended his considerable knowledge and range of intellectual interests on the boy; these included music, science, the poetry of Tennyson and philosophy. During these walks, Chittenden listened to Balfour, drew him out, answered his questions, generally stirred his curiosity. Then, remarkably, when on the Doctor's advice Balfour took an afternoon rest, Chittenden would play the organ softly in the Hall below to soothe his pupil's nerves.

The picture is a strange one. Balfour clearly captivated Chittenden and the boy was fortunate to discover a Headmaster so removed from the fearful robustness of most Victorian private schools. Chittenden later told Blanche Dugdale that his pupil's conversation was 'much more like that of an intelligent boy of eighteen than that of a boy of twelve' and went on, perhaps aided by hindsight, to describe advanced powers of deduction and a philosophical liking for 'reducing chaos into order'. Yet his words should be noted when the Headmaster speaks of Balfour never being able to 'persuade himself, as boys generally do, that what he wished for would happen—he could never live in a fool's paradise'.[19]

Balfour's health forbade his participation in organized games at the Grange. At Eton, where he went in 1861, this was also true, yet his enthusiasm for sport, later to find fulfilment in golf and tennis, began to show itself. He wrote to his sisters of the

Eton cricket eleven's progress, although not participating
himself. The inability to succeed in team games handicapped his
Eton career, for this was the age of ferocious public school
athleticism. Balfour's memories of Eton were always to be
ambivalent. 'Whether looked at from the scholastic or athletic
point of view, I was quite uninteresting'[20] he wrote, and one
suspects he might have felt the same about the school itself. He
once told Ian Malcolm that Eton 'even if it taught one nothing,
prepared a boy to learn anything'[21] and probably the possibilities
of being left alone, greater at Eton than most public schools
because each boy had a room to himself, appealed to Balfour
more than anything else about the place.

His first housemaster was Mr. Birch, succeeded in 1864 by
Mr. Thackeray. From their letters to Lady Blanche, and from
Balfour himself, a picture of her son's Eton life emerges. In 1862,
Birch writes of 'a slow development—the more this boy is pressed
in the brusque mass of division of over forty, the less as yet he
shines', worries about the boy's excessive consumption of 'light
literature', yet notes 'I do not think he is an ordinary boy'. Later
in the year there is a note of panic. 'Arthur,' writes Birch, 'is just
now so very listless and purposeless, so late and unenergetic that
I think a few lines from you would help him.' But with Birch, as
with Chittenden, Balfour possessed that gift of magnetism which
inspires hopes of promise and attracts sympathy. In 1864 Birch
gave up his house and wrote to Balfour: 'If God spared your life I
know no one of the pupils I shall soon be sorrowfully leaving so
likely to do well intellectually as yourself.'[22]

The teaching at Eton brought few moments of intellectual excitement for Balfour; however, one came when the master,
William Cory Johnson, poet and translator of Heraclitis, set an
examination paper on matters outside the school curriculum and
placed him second among all the competitors. It is significant that
this paper had nothing to do with any appointed syllabus; Balfour
later recorded his dislike of the large Eton classes, the lack of
personal attention accorded to the boys by their teachers and his
inability to master Latin and Greek, which formed the backbone
of an Eton education, or any other foreign language under these
conditions. Yet in his spare time, he was reading Macaulay (particularly the essays), Milton and Dryden, also dabbling in

philosophy, theology and science, obtaining a general conception of the new theories of evolution in Lyell and Darwin. Much of this activity went unmarked by his masters who continued to be troubled by the languid exterior. The new housemaster, Thackeray, wrote to Lady Blanche in 1865 of her son's laziness, warning: 'I have seen instances of men throwing themselves away at College by giving way to languor, and I am therefore very anxious that your son should do something worthy of his undoubtedly fine powers.' But in July 1866, when Balfour left Eton, Thackeray too spoke of his pupil's personal qualities and charm of manner saying: 'His tastes are so refined and his conversation so much more intellectual than that of most lads of his age, that I shall miss him as a companion.'

Eton had not suited Balfour. Cambridge was different. In his brief autobiography, Balfour describes his university years as 'a period of almost unmixed satisfaction', and goes on to speak of the atmosphere of 'free interest both in things intellectual and things athletic, which I found infinitely attractive'.[23] During the summer of 1866 he had toured Italy with his sister, Nora; in October he came up to Trinity College to read Moral Sciences as a fellow-commoner, a privileged undergraduate who, in return for higher fees, wore different robes (blue and silver gowns), had the right to live in college and dine with the dons at High Table. It was the closeness to his teachers which appealed to Balfour and developed his intellectual interests and tastes, for two aspects of Cambridge transformed his life: the flowering of his philosophical investigations and his discovery of games and sport.

Philosophical speculation had an early fascination for Balfour. Later he told his niece that he had worked at philosophy since Eton and then qualified this by saying that it was really before Eton that 'I believe I began muddling about with those ideas'.[24] At Eton, he had read Lyell and Darwin, also Lecky's history of rationalism and some parts of formal logic, guided by Archbishop Whateley, Mr. Chittenden's favourite philosopher. No doubt, the walks and conversations with Chittenden encouraged Balfour in his first investigations, for on arrival at Cambridge he was already launched on the great Victorian quest which was to occupy him intellectually for the whole of his life: the reconciliation of religion with science, or the search beyond the prevailing positivist or naturalistic view of the universe for a spiritual justification of its existence as well.

Balfour turned to the dons rather than the undergraduates for elucidation in such matters. Henry Jackson (the professor of Greek), his tutors Percy Hodgson and 'Joey' Pryor, the young scientist John Strutt, later Lord Rayleigh: these widened his mental horizons, but it was Henry Sidgwick, the classicist and philosopher, who left the deepest mark. Sidgwick, who became one of Balfour's closest friends and also his brother-in-law, had turned to philosophy after winning early distinction in the field of classical scholarship. Some ten years older than his new pupil, the two of them immediately entered into the closest sympathy. 'I learned best,' Balfour noted, 'from books and conversations'[25] and Sidgwick's informal tutorials, conducted in a conversational manner in his private rooms with at the most one or two others present, appealed exactly to Balfour's spirit of gentle but thorough intellectual probing.

Sidgwick had been partly responsible for the founding of the school of Moral Sciences which, admitted as qualification for degrees in 1861, enabled undergraduates to study philosophy without, unlike the Oxford greats, having to be classical scholars as well. Like all philosophers of his generation, he had been influenced by Mill and the utilitarians, yet was repelled by Mill's agnosticism. Positivism was not, for Sidgwick as later for Balfour, the final answer and, however certain he was that a reformation of religion was necessary in the light of recent scientific discovery, he maintained an equivocal attitude towards Christianity. In 1869 he was to surrender his fellowship at Trinity, believing he could not, in good conscience, subscribe to the necessary religious test; however, in 1880, a letter to an old school friend reveals that, if no longer a conventional Christian, Sidgwick still held theistic beliefs even if he had to wrestle hard with himself to produce them. Two sentences of the letter are significant for they echo Balfour's own philosophical investigations. 'You will say,' Sidgwick tells his correspondent, 'perhaps the question is not whether we should like or find it convenient to believe in a God, but whether such a belief is true. To this I answer, What criterion have you of the truth of any of the fundamental beliefs of science, except that they are consistent, harmonious with other beliefs we find ourselves naturally compelled to hold.'[26]

Sidgwick, like Balfour, thought ethical morality as naturally essential as rational scientifically-proved truths. This was where he parted company with John Stuart Mill. He wanted to believe, and hoped he could believe, in theism, even Christianity, as a force for order and truth, a barrier against worldly chaos, yet he could not avoid this belief clashing with the cold rationality on which his whole spirit of philosophical enquiry was founded. 'I sometimes say to myself,' he wrote, 'I believe in God, while sometimes again I can say no more than I hope this belief is true, and I must and will act as if it was.'[27] Balfour was to answer the question with more confidence, but not necessarily more completely than his old tutor and to demonstrate, throughout his political and philosophical life, the same preoccupation with man's need for an ethical framework, the authority of metaphysical laws, as a protection against nihilistic barbarism.

Another fellow of Trinity with whom Balfour became acquainted was F. W. H. Myers, a classicist, poet and essayist. Sidgwick, Balfour and Myers later joined together in the Society for Psychical Research, founded in 1882 after several years of experiment and, although coming to fruition later, it was at Cambridge that the foundations of this were laid. The search for psychic phenomena, for evidence of an external world and an after-life was tied up with the wish to escape from the naturalistic concept of death as the ultimate extent of man's personality and his existence. The investigations were to prove the power of telepathy, the possibility of transferring and sharing thought processes but not, at least to Balfour's mind, wholly satisfactory scientific evidence of an after-life.

The intellectual awakening Balfour experienced at Cambridge set him on a course that was to last a lifetime. The delight in finding shared interests, suppositions and approaches among his tutors and fellow undergraduates invigorated him, physically as well as mentally. Mysteriously the poor health of his schooldays improved, and the provision of spectacles led to enjoyment of sport, especially tennis and golf. Inevitably, he participated in the lighter side of undergraduate life, canoeing on the Cam (described to his sister Eleanor as 'the golden mean between a ditch and sewer'),[28] falling in several times, once being fined for jokingly ringing a don's doorbell. His undergraduate friendships were wide, embracing George Darwin, later to become Professor of Astronomy, who introduced him to his father, Charles; and two Scotsmen, Arthur Kinnaird and Reginald McLeod, with whom, in the long vacation of 1867, he canoed from McLeod's home at Dunvegan on Skye sixteen miles across the sea to the Island of Rhum. Lady Blanche, questioned by a friend about the wisdom of this, is said to have answered, 'Would you have me spoil a character?'[29]

Her influence was still strong. At this stage, Balfour, perhaps partly because of Sidgwick, seriously considered devoting the rest of his life to philosophy. 'Do it if you like' his mother told him, 'but remember that if you do, you will find you have nothing to write about by the time you are forty.'[30] He took her advice; it was, as he later said, a turning point in his life. Cambridge, too, cleared the way to the future. Now Balfour knew his interests, the friends he wanted, the pleasures he wished to follow. His tripos result, a second class, disappointed him; perhaps it sprang from his inability to write fluently under examination conditions (Balfour's writings were always to go through many exacting drafts), perhaps also from his lack of interest, shared by Sidgwick, in the history of philosophy as opposed to contemporary speculation. Yet Balfour characteristically remembered 'it was in no sense a discouragement', for 'by this time [November 1869] I had my own views as to the philosophic work which lay immediately before me'.[31]

2

Love and Death

In later life, Balfour described his Cambridge days as 'on the whole I think the pleasantest I have ever passed'.[1] He had, on his departure from Trinity in 1869, equipped himself with friends and enthusiasm, gained immeasurably in physical and intellectual self-confidence. Yet he was still a young man, moved by the intense discoveries of youth. On leaving Eton he had written a poem, looking ahead to imagined cares, mourning the passing of boyhood:

> I may well grieve,
> O Eton, to desert thy shade,
> To speak to thee that parting word
> So often uttered and so sad.

> The man who in the well of life
> Has lost the ease no glory buys
> Of strife and empty honours tired
> Looks fondly back on life and sighs.[2]

Such youthful romanticism was echoed in a letter from Cambridge to his sister Nora about the great 'tide' scene in 'the Antiquary', with Balfour clearly fascinated by Walter Scott's likening of clouds forming in a darkening sky to massive indistinct forces that cause the rise and fall of great temporal empires. 'There is,' he wrote, 'something peculiarly grand in it which I cannot well explain and which I do not know whether you will feel with me.'[3]

Contrary to popular legend, throughout his life Arthur Balfour was to be profoundly moved by human tragedy, friendship, literature and music. Later impressions of coldness derived

27

from a perfect control, a composed exterior which originated from a fear of feeling, a fight against irrational capitulation to emotion as opposed to reason. His niece speaks of this fear, using it to banish any accusation of coldness, but this is too complete a solution. Balfour became colder than most humans because he managed, as time passed, largely to exorcize sentimentality from his dealings with colleagues and opponents, especially those whom he dealt with on an official level. For his close friends, like Alfred Lyttelton and George Wyndham, or relations, like his Cecil cousins, he possessed, as we shall see, feelings that were both emotional and sentimental; to others he was always genial but occasionally ruthless. It was this geniality which led them to expect favours and friendships which were often far from Balfour's mind or his intentions.

The hardening did not come until later. Yet the young Cambridge graduate contained the embryo of his future public self. Although the 'delicacy' had improved there still lingered an impression of preciosity and of languor. Despite his new found delight in games, Balfour was known to some of his university contemporaries as 'Pretty Fanny', and mocked for his habit of collecting blue china. The games he enjoyed were tennis and golf and his style in the former was strategic rather than energetic. Stalking at Strathconan was his only indulgence in blood sports; fishing did not interest him, he disliked game shooting (particularly the vast massacres predominant at that time) and once observed of fox hunting, 'I did not see why I should break my neck because a dog chooses to run after a nasty smell.'[4] Balfour still remained doubtful of his powers. In 1870 at the age of twenty-two, he told Oscar Browning, the Eton master, that doctors had assured him he could 'not possibly live to the age of thirty',[5] yet, as the canoe trip to Skye showed, the languor could suddenly vanish. This oscillation between physical weakness and unusual outbursts of energy lasted for the rest of his life.

In 1869, at the age of twenty-one, Balfour came into his inheritance. This made him master of Whittingehame and Strathconan, and one of the richest young men of the country. During the next few years, the pattern of his home life was changed by certain new family developments. The most important of these, in May 1872, was the death of his mother. Lady

Blanche had succumbed, at the age of forty-seven, to a fatal heart condition. For the last year, she had lived an invalid's existence, travelling to Germany to take the waters at Schwalbach, to Madeira and the South of France to avoid the East Lothian winters, accompanied by her younger children or one of the two devoted companions, Miss Rose Balfour of Balbirnie or Miss Emily Faithfull of Hatfield. She died in London, in her house in Eaton Terrace and was buried at Whittingehame in the old burial ground close to the tower. Her funeral instructions, written in December 1871, were characteristic: 'I wish that my body should not be consigned to the coffin till unequivocal marks of corruption have shown themselves; I wish to have no leaden coffin or leaden wrapping about the body, and nothing more expensive than a plain oak coffin. I wish to have no stone on my grave.' At the service, there was to be no unnecessary ostentation or expense; 'If Arthur wishes me to be buried at Whittingehame I have no objections, but remember, not in lead.'[6]

Two marriages added to the changes. They pleased Balfour by bringing two of his closest friends into the family circle. In 1871, John Strutt, later Lord Rayleigh, married Evelyn Balfour and in 1876, Henry Sidgwick married Eleanor. Both husbands had been introduced to their wives by Balfour from Cambridge. Strutt was a brilliant scientist, discoverer of the Argon gas, a future Nobel Prize winner, later President of the Royal Society and Chancellor of Cambridge University. He also inherited an estate at Terling in Essex and maintained a dual life as country squire and physicist. Balfour and he would discuss scientific matters together, Strutt keeping the politician abreast of the latest discoveries, encouraging Balfour's lifelong concern with government encouragement of research. The Strutts had four children. Evelyn, a woman of intelligence but few pretensions, followed her husband from Cambridge to Terling or London for meetings of the Royal Society where they would stay with Balfour at his house in Carlton Gardens.

The Sidgwick's marriage was less conventional. Henry Sidgwick was sexually impotent; his wife once announced regretfully that 'she doubted whether she had ever really felt excited in her life',[7] yet their union was a happy one. In the family circle at Whittingehame, Sidgwick, with his quickness of wit and gentle sense of humour, given extra point by a slight stammer, became a much loved figure. Together the Sidgwicks devoted themselves to furthering the cause of female education and Eleanor, despite lack of formal schooling, became Principal of Newnham College at Cambridge. Sidgwick died in 1900 but left his wife to carry on their campaign. Arthur Balfour was especially close to this most intellectual of his sisters. When seated among guests at a large dining table they would communicate by winking, smiling as the silent message struck home.

In 1870, Balfour bought a large London house at 4 Carlton Gardens. One of the reasons he had chosen this property was its close proximity to the Gladstone's residence at No. 11, thus demonstrating what was perhaps the strongest, most involved of all his youthful friendships: that with the Lyttelton family. Spencer Lyttelton, a Cambridge contemporary, had brought about the introduction. Lyttelton was a reserved boy, whose first shared enthusiasm with Arthur Balfour was music. Son of Lord Lyttelton, he had ten brothers and sisters and three half-sisters. Balfour was rapidly assimilated into boisterous informal life at Hagley, the Lyttelton home in Worcestershire. Lord Lyttelton was a strange man, guided partly by a strong religious faith, partly also by increasingly severe attacks of melancholia which eventually led to his suicide in 1876. A great games player and fine classical scholar, he enjoyed his family and would amuse his sons by having napkin fights with them after dinner. Lyttelton had married Gladstone's wife's sister and the Liberal leader appointed him Under-Secretary at the Colonial Office for a brief period which, largely because of his tactlessness, was not a success. Two of Lyttelton's sons, Spencer and Alfred, were to be lifelong friends of Balfour.

The Lytteltons of Hagley and the Gladstones of Hawarden were a united cousinhood. They stayed frequently with each other in Worcestershire or Cheshire, assiduous in their church-going, massing for great summer family picnics, sharing family secrets and confidences. It was music, for which he possessed a deep interest and enthusiasm, which brought Arthur Balfour into their lives. Balfour developed into a fine performer on the piano and, more lightheartedly, the concertina, of which there were two at Whittingehame, nicknamed 'the infernals'. Later he was to write of 'the unpictured beauties which music shows to her worshippers', expressing his enjoyment of this, 'the greatest of popular arts'.[8]

Balfour's favourite composer was Handel. He was to guarantee financially the performances of Handel oratorios in the Albert Hall and in 1887 contributed an article on Handel to the *Edinburgh Review*. In Handel he admired the soaring passages of religious inspiration erupting out of definite classical form, also the perfecting of an inherited style, the superb adherence to a set tradition. This admiration is characteristic, especially when he writes of 'the first heralds of a new order,' declaring: 'It is not for them that I feel disposed to reserve my enthusiasm,' but 'for those who have brought to the highest perfection a style, which, because perfected, must have been probably in the main inherited, – who have pressed out of it every possibility of excellence that it contained, – and who leave to their successors, if these must need attempt the same task, no alternative but to perform it worse.'[9] Of such, Balfour believed, was Handel. He went on to remark, with satisfaction, how, in the age of Voltaire and Hume, Handel produced profoundly religious music. This neglect of the enlightenment and adherence to ancient well-tried ideals delighted Balfour, whose distrust of radical reform was already deep.

'I danced three times with King Arthur',[10] Mary Gladstone, later Drew, the Prime Minister's daughter, wrote in her diary for 28 May 1870. Balfour was taking his place in London society, feted for his good looks and charm of manner, guaranteed a welcome by his connections and position. But he also contributed enthusiasm, lightheartedness, a propensity to rush headlong into friendships and situations. Such characteristics were to be tempered by time and circumstance, yet, for the moment, the young Balfour wished to please, even occasionally demonstrating a beguiling artlessness of manner and intention. In December 1870, he was asked to stay at Hawarden with the Gladstones and Mary recorded in her diary that at first it was 'rather shy work for him, I being the only person here that he knows'. Yet soon 'laughter was the order of the day. He has a grand sense of the ridiculous'. There was also his habitual vagueness. One night when Mary's uncle, Sir Stephen Glynne, blew out the candles on

the piano after evening prayers, Balfour vaguely walked round
the room 'puffing out every candle'. 'The room', Mrs Drew
remembers, 'was soon almost in total darkness. We did not like to
stop him, we were too shy, but all had to be lit again to his great
embarrassment.'[11]

Mary Gladstone was a little in love with Balfour. Music,
again, was what brought them together. One afternoon 'we got
rid of everybody and I played . . . Mr Balfour is an intoxicating
listener, and brought the very best out of one.' He gave Mary a
cheque for £70 for an orphanage of which she was a patron,
impulsively offering to adopt one of its inmates. 'Many and
various are our discussions,' she noted. 'He is mad on Zanoni
[Bulwer Lytton]. What does this signify? He thinks it is best
to sit hard on one's sympathies and will not look at a paper for
fear of seeing a tragedy. At present he is the most pitying
person in the world . . .' There was plenty of humour as well.
Balfour and Mary went for 'an immense tramp' with two other
guests; 'Quite two miles from home Mr Balfour collapsed and
laid down in the snow, utterly refusing to move. Weak with
laughter we had to drag him home as best we could.' When asked
how old his sisters were, he replied, 'Oh, just about the usual age
I think'.

The Gladstones, Lytteltons and Balfour were constantly
together in London. The Saturday concerts at the Crystal Palace,
the Monday Pop, the annual Handel Festival: all these 'almost
always found our mad little company in the gallery and indeed we
were all at that time perfectly insane on music'.[12] In addition the
social round made calls upon them. In July 1871 Balfour took a
carriage at the Eton-Harrow match and, when the cricket ended
unexpectedly early, announced that the real business of the day
had now begun and invited 'everyone he met' to be his guest.
'Spencer and I,' Mary noted, 'were jammed up with ten others,
numberless perched on wheels and steps and buzzing round and
scrambling over food. Our host in the maddest of spirits,
shouting Handel choruses hatless, hair flying all over the place,
in spite of a handkerchief wound round his head.'[13] 'In those
days,' she later wrote regretfully, 'there is no doubt, such epithets
as lovable, winning, would naturally be applied to his personality – almost a caress in certain tones of his voice, pretty nearly

irresistible. There was something fragile, delicate, in more than one sense that made it appeal to the mother instinct latent in nearly all of us'.[14]

Mr and Mrs Gladstone's relationship with the young Balfour was, for a brief time, almost parental. In 1889 Gladstone remarked to Margot Tennant, later Asquith, during Balfour's controversial time at the Irish Office, 'I think I loved him better than any young man I ever knew. But he is changed now'.[15] At Hawarden they had many conversations ranging over philosophy (where the young man found the ageing statesman's knowledge of recent developments sadly wanting), religion and politics; and Mrs Gladstone's unconventional ways and warmth delighted Balfour. The Gladstones visited Whittingehame and Strathconan; once, in 1872, being so slow in leaving the latter that the Prime Minister almost missed the train which was to take him back to London for a cabinet meeting. In August 1871, Mrs Gladstone wrote to Lady Blanche, then ill in London, of their days at Whittingehame, remarking of Arthur: 'I have never seen an older brother more anxious to do his duty and more charming with his brothers and sisters',[16] and from Hawarden in December relayed news of Gladstone being 'greatly struck' with him. Perhaps the Gladstones hoped for a romance between Balfour and Mary; if so, they were to be disappointed.

Mary herself gives away the name of her rival. 'During the years of 1871, 2, 3 and 74', she writes, 'the small group of intimate friends, which began at Hawarden in 1870, consisted mainly of four. Mary Lyttelton, always called May, Mary Gladstone, Spencer Lyttelton and Arthur Balfour.'[17] It was with May Lyttelton, sister of his friend, Spencer, that Balfour was to become romantically entangled, drawn to her by her intelligence and spirited manner, also her dark, serene good looks. May had been involved in one romance with Edward Denison, a man some ten years older than herself and already a Member of Parliament. At first it seemed as if marriage was a possibility, despite his rich uncle's mysterious opposition, but then Denison's chronic poor health manifested itself. He was sent on a long sea voyage to recover and died at Melbourne, leaving May to be comforted by her devoted family. In the family circle, her sister Lavinia, a priggish figure preoccupied with religion and high-minded good works, only some fifteen months older than May, was the one closest to her. Lavinia's diary note on May's twelfth birthday ('wish more feeling for religion, I should love her a great deal more')[18] reveals a refreshingly incomplete involvement in the sugary but stern Victorian christianity which dominated Lyttelton family life. May might write in June 1870 of the service of Ordination at Cuddesden, Oxford, as 'most wonderful and striking' and describe the principal of Cuddesden's preaching as 'most beautiful' going on to remark that 'the most beautiful application of text . . . the persuasive lovingness was what I shall never forget';[19] but she was also capable of noting 'Bliss not to go to Church'. She knew her own mind and was impatient with those who bored her. After visiting the House of Commons her diary castigated its poor performers, breaking into 'I long to be a man'.[20] It leaves no doubt as to her likes and dislikes, one woman being described as 'an ugly fat invalidish old maid'[21] and fellow guests at a dinner enumerated – 'quite the vulgarest man I ever met', 'a chirrupy little fat lady, uninteresting but with the loudest laugh I ever heard', 'duller than ditchwater'.[22]

At first she did not regard Balfour with any great enthusiasm. Indeed, on his visit to Hawarden in December 1870 (their first meeting with him) he was judged harshly by both May and Lavinia. The latter, who had recently married Edward Talbot, first Warden of Keble and later Bishop of Rochester, was disapproving, glumly noting the efforts to promote a liaison with Mary Gladstone. 'He is at bottom', she wrote from Hagley on 9 January 1871, 'I have no doubt very clever and good and starts in life with an attractive dreamy sometimes amusing manner . . . but he is a bit spoilt by a round of visits lasting four months, and is to my mind conscious of his impulsiveness and attractions, as well as of the fact that all the young ladies during his four months visit have been at his feet. You know we were quite agog over Mary G. and he, hoping something could or might happen one day.'[23] Neville, one of the younger Lytteltons, was heard to remark, 'I don't think much of Spencer's friend, he was always hanging round the girls.'[24]

Balfour by this stage probably was, as Lavinia Talbot noted, aware of his charm, yet his gaiety and lightness of touch were unlikely to have immediately appealed to one so imbued with

Victorian christian duty. May's view was, initially, more
enthusiastic. 'Mr Balfour', she noted, 'is certainly clever and very
much unlike other people which may be affectation and conceit.'
The tone of the new guest was light, his conversation 'flighty and
visionary' and the next day there was 'music and madness on the
part of Mr B.', whom May went on to describe as 'neither
affected nor conceited'.[25] Balfour left, only to return in January
1871, when 'much Handel' was played 'Mr B. being an enthusi-
ast about him'. May's admiration, however, was faltering. She
did not deny that Balfour was 'a suggestive and clever person' but
he was 'condemned as being affected by most of the others'. By
the last day she was echoing Lavinia, remarking that 'Mr Balfour
dangles about and does nothing to an extent which becomes
wrong', noting of his departure, 'Mr B. went at 8.30, rather glad
though I like him very much only I feel ten years older than
him'.[26]

May was aged twenty at this time and her brief involvement
with the older Denison may have made Balfour's young high
spirits seem jarring and obstructive to deeper friendship. Undoubtedly she was interested, yet the frivolity seemed a barrier.
May was intolerant of the dull or the foolish; at a Gladstone party
in March 1871 some of the guests were dismissed as 'a lot of
little men',[27] Balfour being included in their number. However,
four days later they met at the Gladstone's house in Carlton
Gardens and there was 'much talk as usual when Mr B. is present, he has lent me a pile of delightful music'. Next day Balfour
came to lunch and again led the exuberant conversation. 'How',
May noted, 'we have lived and died with him these few days,'
even though 'the poor man was exhausted . . . and Spencer and I
played and sang to refresh him'.[28]

Balfour and she met often during the early summer of 1871.
Then on 20 June while riding in Rotten Row with her friends,
Amy and Frances Graham, May was forced by a rainstorm to
take shelter in their house in Grosvenor Place. There she
encountered their brother, Rutherford, 'rather an attractive
youth'.[29] On 30 June she attended a ball at Montague House,
'deathly at first' but the party improved 'and I enjoyed it'. Among
the guests was Rutherford Graham 'of whom I saw a good deal,
an odd attractive youth whom one instinctively mistrusts, but

clever and interesting'. The diary entry for the day ends 'not home til a quarter to four, dreadful; rather an interesting talk with Mr Balfour', but 'supper with Mr Graham'.[30]

Graham, still an undergraduate at Balliol, completely usurped whatever position Balfour may have had at this time in May's favours. The romance progressed rapidly, to the despair of her family. Graham's father, an early patron of the pre-Raphaelites, was in trade, a self-made Glasgow merchant and, worst of all for the Lytteltons with their unshakable loyalty to the established church, a Presbyterian. Furthermore, Graham himself, despite his youth, already had a bad reputation and was reputed to have trifled with several young girls. May reluctantly refused his two proposals of marriage during the course of the next year, yet, typically, declined to banish him from her life. Her father forbade her to attend parties where they might meet, but again music came to the rescue and she often saw him at concerts and musical lectures. In the summer of 1872 it seemed as if Lyttelton might relent, stipulating only that they should wait another year; but in October Rutherford Graham died of diphtheria at Liverpool on his way to America.

May was distraught. Throughout the spring and summer of 1873 she lived in a deep depression, profiting from nothing, exasperated by old pleasures, uninterested in her friends. Balfour and she continued to meet in London and in August he came to Hagley where she writes, almost contemptuously, of a 'jabbering dinner'.[31] At last, on 1 September, there is an arousal of the old shared gaiety and enthusiastic talk. First, a great family picnic at the Wrekin, then a large and good-humoured company of cousins and friends combined to uplift her. The picnic was a 'very ideal hour',[32] Handel choruses and songs were sung, and two days later May was enchanted by the sight of Arthur Balfour having 'a grave historical discussion' with her ten-year-old niece, the little girl 'kneeling at his feet with dilating eyes and red cheeks, he with his usual nonchalant manner but not talking a bit less cleverly than he would to Lord Salisbury'.[33] Her interest in her brother's friend was rekindled and throughout the next year they were constantly meeting, following the old round of concerts and family gatherings in the country and London.

In December 1874, May, Spencer Lyttelton and Balfour

went to stay with Lord Chesham at Latimer in Buckinghamshire, and it was here that Balfour later claimed he had discussed marriage. In May's diary there is no reference to this, only descriptions of tennis in the frost ('something of a failure as neither he nor I could play') and a reference to her return to London with Lyttelton and Balfour as 'a funny journey'.[34] In London, Balfour stayed to tea and dinner and May played the piano 'a little, a great failure'. Later she told Lavinia Talbot, her sister, that at Latimer 'there were words on his part which made May have little doubt what they were intended to mean'[35] and Mrs Talbot believed the couple to have been unofficially engaged, yet there is no explicit statement to this effect in May's diary. Perhaps the subject was mentioned without Balfour seeking any conclusive response or perhaps May, used to his lighthearted approach, had misunderstood the extent of his affection. What is certain is that after her death, Balfour told several who were close to him that, had she lived, he would have married her.

This, however, was not to be. In January 1875, she contracted typhoid fever, staying at the Rectory at Hagley while the roof of the big house was being repaired. Here she lay in a state of delirium for ten weeks, nursed by her old nanny and watched over by her relations, dying on 21 March, Palm Sunday, with Mrs Gladstone at her bedside. Balfour, who was quickly written to by her brother Edward in order that he should not first hear of the death from the newspapers, was horrified. He answered Edward's letter, Lavinia Talbot later noted, 'in a state of passionate sorrow',[36] enclosing an emerald ring which had belonged to Lady Blanche, asking if it might be put into May's coffin. Edward Lyttelton was surprised, yet complied with his wishes.

On Maundy Thursday, Balfour came to Hagley for the funeral. Legend has it that he was too upset to go into the church, remaining outside leaning against a tree, weeping uncontrollably, but Lavinia Talbot remembers him kneeling beside her at the Holy Communion which preceded the burial service in an unforgettable 'agony of distress'. Later he regained his composure and 'with the control he could always be sure of'[37] discussed China with Gladstone over tea at the house. Then, walking away with Edward Lyttelton, Balfour said 'in greatest agitation, "I was to have made her my wife".'[38]

'Nothing,' Mary Gladstone wrote of May, 'is so hard to recapture as the charm and beauty of a young girl.'[39] Looking at photographs of May Lyttelton one sees a slender tall figure of ethereal good looks, the careful poses suggesting nothing of the vitality claimed for her by her friends or the spirited attitudes to people and events demonstrated in her diary. Balfour was clearly moved by May, perhaps came as near to falling in love with her as with any woman. Later Lady Elcho, his devoted confidante, was to write of May's effect on him, perceiving its shadow over their own friendship, telling her daughter that May Lyttelton had been the one great love of his life. Lavinia Talbot, to whom Balfour turned for comfort and who was so moved by his grief that she overcame her initial disapproval of him, believed 'the irreparable loss of the wife he had chosen' to have been 'the greatest of losses' as well as a 'lifelong sorrow'. For many years he celebrated the anniversary of May's death by spending Palm Sunday at Keble with the Talbots, re-reading her diaries, talking over her life. 'I realised', Lavinia wrote after the first visit, 'the length of time he had loved May and how all his deepest hopes were bound up with her. Night after night he took one of her journals to his room on going to bed and I had to explain many things and try to comfort'.[40]

In 1876, the Talbots visited Whittingehame and were shown the tentative plans for alterations Balfour had made to be put into practice after his marriage. The only request he would have refused May was a Church of England chapel, for in Scotland he always attended the Church of Scotland as the established church, and in England, always the Church of England. Balfour was grateful to the Talbots. He showed this by endowing an organ scholarship at Keble and settling £1000 on their daughter, also called May, to be paid to her after his death.

That May Lyttelton's death was a tragedy for Balfour cannot be doubted. In May 1875 he went to the Music Festival at Dusseldorf with Mary Gladstone, Spencer Lyttelton and two other friends. Lady Ponsonby, the wife of Queen Victoria's secretary, acted as chaperone and in her diary she recalls a new sardonic Balfour, although the old lightheartedness could break through. 'Mr Balfour,' she wrote, 'is I think the cleverest of our party, but he does not give himself the trouble to know one exists . . . the net result is that he is formidable, one is always afraid of boring him.' At the end of the journey Mary Gladstone declared, 'Mr Balfour is sometimes very mad . . . in every phrase interesting and delightful. He, of course, gave cachet to the party; the whole character of the thing would have been absolutely different had he been absent. In him culminated the interest, the charm, the mystery'.[41]

The interest, the charm, the mystery: this was surely a perceptive view. After 1875, the sudden impulses, the quick decisions stemming from the heart rather than the head, were to be curbed, almost driven underground. The young Balfour offered, quickly and hopelessly, to adopt an orphan, rapidly wrote a cheque for a deserving charity, blurted out his thoughts to an audience of Lytteltons and Gladstones without care for their consequences. Now he withdrew. The youthful spontaneity was replaced by a mysterious reserve, breaking often into sympathy, scarcely ever into the revelation of an innermost self. Was this new reticence caused by the realization, brought about by May's death, that the potential loss, the disappointment resulting from love, anger, compassion or any sensation uncurbable beyond a certain point by purely intellectual control, were burdens too great, too upsetting and debilitating to risk bearing again? What is certain is that a fear of emotion rather than an absence of feeling or coldness of spirit led to this withdrawal. Balfour was to have other deep friendships, to be moved again to tears, to possess fierce loyalties and convictions, but they were to be subjected to the iron control which gradually began to take over his life.

3

A Political Philosopher

In November 1871 Alice Balfour wrote to her mother, Lady Blanche, from Hawarden where Alice and Arthur were staying as guests of the Gladstones. 'Mr Gladstone,' she declared, 'talks a good deal with Arthur, whom he really likes'. The night before they had discussed banking and currency, the Prime Minister saying to Balfour, 'I am glad you have read Goschen's book on the exchange; I should think the men who are not in business, who have read that book might be counted on one's fingers' and later added, "It required a good deal of head to understand it."[1] Despite a lack of political involvement at Cambridge (he never spoke at the Union), Balfour's curiosity extended to public affairs and it was this that a powerful mentor persuaded him to develop in 1873.

Perhaps the greatest single influence in Arthur Balfour's early life, apart from his mother, was his uncle Lord Salisbury. Hatfield, the great Cecil house in Hertfordshire had been much visited by the Balfours throughout their childhood. These visits were awe-inspiring. There was a magnificence, a grandeur, to Hatfield which was lacking at Whittingehame; Evelyn Rayleigh later remembered her grandfather Salisbury wearing the Ribbon of the Garter at dinner every evening, even if there was only a small family party. After the death of old Lord Salisbury in 1868, his son, who had already made a mark as Secretary of State for India (from 1866 to 1867) and an obdurate opponent of the Tory Reform Act of 1867, succeeded to the title and the Cecil estates. Born Lord Robert Cecil, he had not expected to inherit from his father, although his older brother Cranborne had always suffered from poor health. Lord Robert's marriage, to Georgina Alderson, daughter of a distinguished judge, was violently opposed by his family on the grounds that Miss Alderson was neither socially nor financially equipped to enter the Cecil hierarchy. His father told him that he, as a younger son, would have little enough money anyway and that he was a fool to endanger his prospects by such a match. Lord Robert's answer was characteristic. 'The persons', he declared, 'who will cut me because I marry Miss Alderson are precisely the persons of whose society I am so anxious to be quit.'[2]

They married, despite parental objections, having tried a separation to satisfy the opposition. The marriage was remarkably happy. At Hatfield, her intellectual tastes and love of discussion were a fine antidote to Salisbury's bouts of melancholy and distaste for social intercourse. Their early life together was occasionally hard; although Lord Exeter, his cousin, had found Lord Robert a parliamentary seat at Stamford, near Burghley, money was always short and the young Cecil resorted to acerbic journalism to add to the meagre allowance given him by his father.

Balfour's uncle had always stood for the old, unchanging Tory principles. While at Eton, he wrote to his sister, denouncing the Maynooth grant, criticising Peel and defending Church establishment. His early articles were often fierce denunciations of Disraeli, whose opportunism and preoccupation with social reform he intensely distrusted. They were expressed in violent language and Salisbury's father, who served with Disraeli in Lord Derby's cabinet, remonstrated with his son, whose reply was that he had 'no trust whatever in Mr Disraeli', and 'I must write in the style that is most likely to attract and therefore sell.'[3] This style was a faithful reproduction of a side of its author. Salisbury was subject to deep brooding depressions, which he called 'nerve storms', and, perhaps partly because of these, often inclined towards profound, almost nihilistic pessimism. Yet he would fight with great tenacity for a cause he believed in, resigning from the cabinet in 1867 rather than support the Reform Bill which he thought would open the gates to mob rule.

In a letter from Cambridge in 1868 to his sister Nora, Arthur Balfour shared his uncle's disdain for Disraeli's measure. 'The first result', he declared, 'of the new Reform Bill has been to elect a stupider six hundred and fifty-odd gentlemen than have ever met in Westminster within the memory of man.'[4] Salisbury's influence had begun to assert itself several years earlier during Balfour's Eton days. Salisbury, then called Cranborne (his older brother having died in 1865), was aged about thirty-six. He conversed easily with his nephew, weighing up the latter's opinions, according them respect, speaking 'as a man speaks to a man, and not as a man speaks to a boy'. The talk covered a broad field, the older participant giving full rein to his knowledge, assuming total comprehension, opening up, for the younger, 'prospects full of interesting possibilities, and encouraged me if I could, to explore them'.[5]

In 1873 this encouragement took a practical form. The Hertford constituency, adjacent to Hatfield, was about to become vacant. Salisbury, possibly aware of the drifting nature of his nephew's life, possibly also feeling a sense of family responsibility after the death of Lady Blanche the previous year, suggested to Balfour over lunch at the Cecils' London house in Arlington Street that he might like to stand for Parliament. Balfour accepted. Later he remembered the uncertain nature of his politics at this time. Although his family traditions were Tory, his most 'enlightened' friends at Cambridge had all been Liberal and in the 1860s 'the line between moderate Liberal and moderate Conservative was more than usually blurred'. What finally decided him was his dislike of the basic principles behind radical domestic and foreign policies; also 'the speculative outlook of the philosophic radicals' filled him 'with contempt'. John Stuart Mill, whose philosophic stance Balfour condemned outright, had once called the Conservatives the 'stupid' party. 'If Mill really thought this', Balfour wrote in his autobiography, 'my own course was clear.'[6]

At first it seemed as if Balfour would be opposed, perhaps by two opponents. Salisbury was not the only territorial magnate in the constituency, the Whig interests being looked after by the Cowper family of Panshanger. In 1873 Salisbury gloomily cautioned his nephew that 'under the ballot all is uncertain';[7] but Lord Cowper's brother was already Member for the county division of Hertford, so perhaps thought a hopeless fight in Hertford Borough unnecessary. In 1874 Balfour stood for Parliament for the first time. The candidate's previous experience of public speaking had been confined to two occasions (the first at a tenant's dinner at Hatfield, the second at his own coming of age at Whittingehame) and he was alarmed as to what might be expected of him at Hertford. But there were few speeches and he was surprised at the facility with which he dealt with them. 'It was not', he noted, 'so much that I felt at ease, as that I had no leisure to feel anything but the absorbing effort to find the words which would least inadequately express the arguments I was struggling to enforce.'[8] Balfour's speaking was always to take this form of a dialogue with himself, searching for an exact word or phrase to communicate the contents of his mind without notes or a prepared text but with all the immediacy of a freshly conceived idea, expressed, occasionally haltingly, in this most personal of ways.

Balfour celebrated his entry into politics by remaining silent in the House of Commons for two years. Indeed in 1875, after the death of May Lyttelton and his visit to the Dusseldorf Festival, he set off round the world with Spencer Lyttelton. They toured America, Australia, New Zealand (where Balfour bought a ranch) and the Far East, Balfour being constantly tormented by appalling seasickness. In Australia he was forced to abandon Lyttelton and travel from Sydney to Melbourne overland while the other took the steamer. Balfour was an unenthusiastic sightseer, preferring people to scenery or buildings, yet he was moved by the spectacular landscapes of the American West and the Yosemite Valley. Lyttelton's quiet good nature made him an ideal travelling companion. Spencer enjoyed teasing his friend, who was still subject to bouts of fatigue and ennui, once observing during the Dusseldorf trip: 'Balfour, I don't know if it's the vulgarity of your manners, or the ugliness of your appearance which attracts public notice, but we are the centre of attraction for all observers.'[9] Spencer Lyttelton never married and, having been left an annuity by an uncle, never took a job, except for a brief period as Gladstone's unpaid private secretary. He died in 1913, leaving an impression of gentleness, refinement of taste, also a slight sense of nullity.

The young Balfour, left to his own devices, might have opted for the way chosen by his closest friend. One remembers the early desire to devote his life to philosophical study, the removal by inheritance of the need to work, his months of almost inconsequential drifting after coming down from Cambridge, from concert hall to house party through the London season where his good looks and appealing manner won prominence without trouble or effort. Fortunately, there were sufficient obstacles in the way of this progress: first, Lady Blanche with her determination that the life of a retiring contemplative was insufficient for her oldest son; then his uncle's encouragement and virtual offer of a Parliamentary seat; lastly, perhaps, the death of May Lyttelton leading to a new seriousness, a realization of the impermanence of even the deepest of human relationships, and the need for a lasting occupation which could give some impersonal purpose to his rather listless life. Yet his entry into politics showed the spur was still needed. On his return from his world tour, it was Lady Salisbury who 'made no secret of her opinion that my third session should not be allowed to close without overt signs of Parliamentary activity'.[10] Balfour was in no doubt that his uncle shared her view and 'so in my heart did I'. The result was a speech on Indian silver currency, a subject chosen for its incapacity to attract either interest or audience.

The 'sole interest' of the speech, as Balfour later admitted, 'is autobiographical'.[11] He did not speak again until the Committee stage of the Universities Bill in 1877, proposing several amendments, one advocating degrees for women. The Sidgwicks were proud of him, but the idea was fiercely opposed by, among others, his uncle Beresford Hope, one member (Lord Edmund Fitzmaurice) declaring that it was 'disgusting' to hear so much talk about women 'both inside the House and out of doors'.[12] In the spring of 1878, Balfour introduced his first piece of proposed legislation, a bill for the reform of the Burials Law. Salisbury, to whom he sent the draft, was lukewarm towards this and Beresford Hope, a high churchman, was opposed to what he saw as an unnecessary concession to the nonconformists. The bill was thus 'talked out',[13] Balfour having resigned himself to its failure.

Salisbury, however, had previously given his nephew an unusually privileged view of international diplomacy. The Eastern Question dominated the last years of the 1870s. In 1876

Salisbury had been sent by Disraeli to the conference of the great powers at Constantinople, and in 1878 he succeeded Derby at the Foreign Office, inviting his nephew to become his private secretary. In this role, Balfour accompanied his uncle to the Congress of Berlin in the summer of that year.

This was an extraordinary gathering, a vast exercise in the social excesses of old European diplomacy. The first evening there was a gigantic state dinner, but as the British party's luggage had been left behind at Brussels, Balfour had to go round the embassy staff 'begging, borrowing and stealing' the suitable diplomatic dress. None could be found to fit the tall young secretary who, with several others, was forced to attend in ordinary clothes ('I suppose they took us for Chaplains!').

Disraeli, now Earl of Beaconsfield, was in Berlin and Balfour told Alice on 15 June that 'he, Bismarck and Andrassy (the Hungarian Foreign Minister) are certainly three of the strangest-looking mortals ever got together in one room. Dizzy you know. Bismarck is a very tall and very fat man, with white hair. His face may be remarkable – but so far as I have watched him it is thrown into the shade by the enormous dimensions of his body. . . . As for Andrassy, he looks like a gypsy, who ought to mend pots by day and steal your chickens by night.'[14] Salisbury loathed the socializing which was supposed to leaven the conference business. At first, his more sociable nephew was intrigued by this but then he too became exasperated, praising to his sister the good company of Lord Odo Russell, the British Ambassador in Berlin, in contrast to 'the appalling diplomatic dinners and still more appalling diplomatic parties without which, it appears, the affairs of Europe cannot possibly be conducted'. At one of these, however, he was introduced to Bismarck, who asked him if he was a descendant of Scott's Balfour of Burghley from *Old Mortality*. On being told this was not the case the Chancellor observed, 'When we were young we all had to read Sir Walter. He was considered so very proper.'[15]

Balfour found Beaconsfield 'really very amusing'. Often he would have to take the Prime Minister's arm, supporting his tottering footsteps from an embassy to the delegation's hotel, and he reported that the old man's conversation had 'the peculiar literary flavour of his writing – epigram and extravagance which occasionally verged on nonsense but which never quite lost the consciousness of its own absurdity'.[16] Balfour was intrigued by the relationship between Beaconsfield and Salisbury. 'Never,' he later wrote, 'did two statesmen holding the same political creed, furthering the same foreign policy, faced day by day with the same difficulties, and in constant consultation, differ more sharply in temperament', but, despite Salisbury's earlier dislike and distrust of his master, 'the more they worked together the better became their relations'.[17] Salisbury might complain to his wife that Beaconsfield 'understands everything crossways, and imagines a perpetual conspiracy',[18] yet he grudgingly told Balfour that his speeches undoubtedly gave 'the foreigner a very favourable idea of our parliamentary eloquence'.[19]

'I cannot be said', Balfour told his sister on July 11, 'to be overworked here'. His labours consisted of 'ciphering and deciphering a few telegrams and seeing to other odd jobs'. His interest in the negotiations began to falter. 'I find', he wrote, 'to my disgust that the orthodox or stage idea of a diplomatist is thoroughly carried out by various important plenipotentiaries here: some of them indeed seem to overact their part, and are a little too unscrupulous to be artistically successful'. Altogether, the eventual signing of the treaty came as a relief. 'Thank goodness', Alice was told, 'we shall leave this beastly town and its detestable inhabitants, I trust, forever. My temper you see is not of the best.'[20]

Apart from his trip to Berlin, politics made few sustained calls upon Balfour's time in the late 1870s. He was free to pursue his interests in music and philosophy, also to involve himself in family life. Two of his sisters (Evelyn and Eleanor) married early, and in 1879 were followed by his brother Eustace, who married Lady Frances Campbell, daughter of the Duke of Argyll. Alice kept house for Arthur at Whittingehame and in London, and Gerald and Frank both achieved considerable academic success, the former taking a first in classics at Trinity, Cambridge, and being appointed a fellow of his college, and the latter becoming the first professor of animal morphology in the university.

'It would be difficult', Balfour's niece has written, 'to find a parallel among any group of relations, all under middle age, for the intellectual driving power assembled round the Whittingehame table at this date.'[21] She is correct. The Balfours alone produced a formidable array of intellectual interests and achievements and, when added to by Henry Sidgwick and Lord Rayleigh, the scientific and philosophical possibilities of discussion were indeed wide. Yet Mrs Dugdale neglects the darker side of Whittingehame life. The profligate Cecil Balfour was to die virtually bankrupt in Australia, Alice's shyness gradually led to unusual introversion and now Frances Campbell, who had married Eustace Balfour, provided a further source of difficulty. Eustace Balfour became an architect and territorial soldier, one of the founders of the London Scottish Regiment. An amiable man, lacking the intellectual power of his brothers, he was to prove no match for Lady Frances who was passionately interested in politics, the Scottish church and, later, votes for women. Arthur Balfour recognized her family loyalty, her wish to involve herself and to be informed of each stage of his political career because he provided that view, so lacking in Eustace, of momentous events with which (her father having served in Gladstone's cabinet) she had grown up and which she could not bear to be without; but he was aware of her trouble-making, of the damaging sharpness of her tongue, of her impatience with the docile or the commonplace.

Lady Frances was one of those Victorian women who, restricted by the subservient position of their sex, were in an almost permanent state of intellectual frustration. Unable to obtain indirect satisfaction through the public life of her husband, she thrashed about within the confines of the unemancipated role society had handed down to her. In her letters to Arthur Balfour she passes on titbits of political gossip, gives (at considerable length) her own unsolicited opinions on the current scene, seeking, in return, some intimate connection with the thinking of those who shaped it. Initially, Balfour was pleased, perhaps a little flattered, by this. The departure of his sister Eleanor for Cambridge and the death of Lady Blanche had left him without a regular relationship with a woman on more or less equal terms of intelligence. His new sister-in-law appeared capable of fulfilling this role.

Balfour relaxed easily in feminine society. He shared few of the conventional tastes of his aristocratic male contemporaries, such as cards, racing or blood sports, yet was fond of gossip, of enacting delicate social nuances, also of the subtle shafts of feminine malice. He appreciated feminine admiration, unbending in its warm glow, unembarrassed by gushing late-Victorian sentiment yet scarcely ever allowing this to wash away his own self-control. Lady Frances was not subtle, but she was admiring. Both she and Alice fixed their admiration on Balfour, and this led to trouble between them.

Balfour did not entirely abandon philosophy for politics. In 1877, he worked on a philosophical book and in 1878 instalments of this began to appear, first in *Mind* and then in *The Fortnightly Review*. The editor of *The Fortnightly Review* was John Morley, later a political adversary. Morley told Balfour at their first meeting that he could not understand a word of the book, called *A Defence of Philosophic Doubt* but was prepared to use extracts in his magazine. In 1878 Macmillans published a thousand copies of the finished work, at the author's risk.

The title had originally been *A Defence of Philosophic Scepticism* but Balfour's uncle Salisbury preferred *Doubt*, believing the other to be too suggestive of agnosticism. In fact the scepticism referred to science rather than to religion, Balfour's idea being to prove that scientific theory was as subject to uncertainty as religious argument and therefore scientific objections to religion which relied for proof on natural laws were by no means conclusive. The questions asked are: 'Has science any claim to be thus set up as the standard of belief? Is there any ground whatever for regarding conformity with scientific teaching as an essential condition of truth; and non-conformity with it as an unanswerable proof of error?'[22] To both of these, Balfour firmly answered in the negative. There is, he postulates, no law of universal causation, no uniformity of nature that can lead to absolute scientific certainty. 'Every cause', he remarked, 'is complex',[23] and it is this very complexity, or multiplicity of possible forces forming a particular phenomenon, which must rule out total reliance on scientific proof. 'In all cases of induction', Balfour writes, 'we can do no more than prove a certain law to be probable.'[24] He goes on to say that John Stuart Mill's method of proof by elimination of the improbable is inadequate, for this can only lead to a conclusion of extreme probability rather than of incontrovertible certainty.

What really concerns Balfour in *A Defence of Philosophic Doubt* are the uncertain ingredients of causality. 'It may be admitted', he writes, 'at once that, in the world which we assume to be governed by law, the invariable sequence of B on A is a proof that there is probably some causal link, direct or indirect, between them. In other words, it is very unlikely that this constant coincidence is the work of chance. . . . But it gives no probability at all in favour in A being the whole cause of B.'[25] There may be a host of other factors involved, whose arrangement and varying influences are unknown. Scientific knowledge of such phenomena as ether and atoms passes beyond the powers of ordinary human imagination or perception, as do the essential basic premises of theology. To Balfour science and religion were compatible. His complaint was that followers of science should demand from religion the definite proof which their own premises so manifestly lacked. For him the two were equally necessary and important and, if it is impossible to promote a perfect rational congruity between the two, an equality of scepticism can lead to an understanding of the intellectual impossibility of using one to eradicate the other.

Balfour's Christianity was practical. He believed that human beings need an ethical framework to protect them from anarchy and barbarism, also that the state should connect itself to, and thus support, this framework by maintaining links with an established church. When he was at home family prayers were conducted every Sunday evening at Whittingehame with Balfour presiding, and he was a constant communicant in the Churches of England and Scotland. He believed in an after-life and in both his long philosophic works there are passages of an almost mystical intensity concerning the impossibility of total intellectual comprehension or proof of the foundations of the Christian ethic. The most famous of these is the piece in *The Foundations of Belief* about the purposelessness he sees to be inherent in an earthly existence if a purely scientific explanation is given for the origin, history and future of the human race. Yet Balfour's early preoccupation with spiritualism shows that he was looking for more definite evidence of a life beyond the grave.

During his visit to Keble in 1875, shortly after May

Lyttelton's death, Balfour told Lavinia Talbot that, together with
Henry Sidgwick and other friends, he had held several séances at
Carlton Gardens but received 'no real result in any real line'.[26]
His connections, begun at Cambridge, with the Society for
Psychical Research, continued to be strong and he was its presi-
dent in 1894. However he never became wholly certain of the
success of efforts to make contact with the dead and the messages
that were supposedly transmitted through mediums. His brother
Gerald, after leaving politics in 1906, devoted the rest of his life
and his considerable intellectual powers to psychical research and
Sir Oliver Lodge, a convinced spiritualist, became a friend.

In spiritualism, Balfour sought to bring together his growing
interests and respect for science with his religious belief in the
soul's immortality. He had grown up a Christian, his Cambridge
studies and friendships (especially that with his brother-in-law
Rayleigh) opened up a scientific vista, and, later, in his uncle
Salisbury he found the two combined. Salisbury believed civilization was doomed without Christianity. He knew of the philosophical and scientific challenge to his faith, yet still possessed an
unyielding acceptance of its principles. Salisbury's Christianity
was less rational than his nephew's; he spurned any logical
analysis of its basic premises, once exclaiming when faced with
such an attempt 'as if that had anything to do with it!'[27] His
daughter has written that his belief rested upon 'a spiritual vision
which had an existence altogether apart from his intellectual processes',[28] but there were serious ethical considerations as well.
Salisbury was profoundly pessimistic in his view of the natural
state of man. He was distrustful of democracy, saw the dividing
line between civilization and anarchy as narrow, believed in the
necessity of hierarchies and codes to enforce structure on a potentially chaotic society.

'God is all powerful,' Salisbury once explained, 'and God is all
loving – and the world is what it is! How are you going to explain
that?'[29] This, he saw, as the limit of religious discussion, for such
matters were surely, by their nature, inexplicable in ordinary
human intellectual terms. At Hatfield, Salisbury had a laboratory
and maintained close knowledge of modern scientific developments but for him, as for Balfour, science and religion were not
incompatible; they were different, and one should be able to exist

alongside the other. Yet Salisbury would never have attempted to prove this from a philosophical standpoint. Unlike Balfour, he saw no reason to rationalize the grounds of his belief, but they shared a strong conception of Christianity as a force for order and stability in a changing world.

A Defence of Philosophic Doubt was, for a young man of thirty-one, a self-confident work. In its pages Balfour attacks Kant, John Stuart Mill, Herbert Spencer and other philosophical giants. The book attracted little attention at first, although as its author's career progressed the first limited edition gradually sold out and a new one was printed in 1920. Academics, however, took early note of this amateur philosopher. In *Mind* there was a respectful review by Professor Caird and Professor Vaihinger, a disciple of Kant, rose to the defence of his master. The book brought Balfour a friend in the form of Andrew Seth, later to change his name to Pringle Pattison, from Edinburgh University. Seth read *A Defence of Philosophic Doubt* and wrote to its author asking him to address a class of Edinburgh students. Friendship resulted and Balfour endowed a course of lectures at Edinburgh, two sets of which were delivered by Seth on Hegel and philosophers of the Scottish school.

The last years of the 1870s saw the resurgence of Gladstone. Balfour could now have no doubt as to his political allegiances, but the Liberal leader continued to have a friendly regard for him. There had been an early difficult experience in the House of Commons when, in May 1878, Balfour had had to reply to a Gladstonian tirade ('Supposed', his daughter noted, 'to be one of his greatest') and Mary Gladstone recorded, 'It was funny watching—much emphatic gesture, too much.'[30] Then, in March 1880, during the election, Gladstone sent Balfour a copy of one of his speeches. 'Awkward!' Balfour told Alice. 'I wrote to thank him, and added at the end of my letter that politics had not been favourable to private friendship in the immediate past and were still less likely to be so in the immediate future! A distant allusion to my intended appearance in Mid-Lothian'.[31]

The Conservatives, misled as to the extent of their support, called an election in the spring of 1880. Despite Salisbury and Beaconfield's triumphant return from Berlin in 1878, the government was not popular. An economic depression was leading to industrial closures and unemployment, cheap American grain and poor harvests were stifling agriculture and a bellicose imperial policy in the East and in Southern Africa failed to attract support. In addition, there was Gladstone's great Bulgarian atrocities campaign. In a series of vituperative speeches and pamphlets the Liberal leader thundered against the oppression of the christian minorities of the Turkish empire, leaving retirement to capture the public imagination with his new cause.

Balfour's part in the contest was small. This time he was opposed at Hertford by a Harrow schoolmaster and the fight was close, the Tories only winning with a majority of 164. Since the seat was one of the first declared, its candidates had time to campaign for others and he journeyed up to Mid-Lothian to support Lord Dalkeith in the contest against Gladstone. Here, however, matters were hopeless. Although Dalkeith's local connections (he was the son of the Duke of Buccleuch, a large lowland landowner) might under other circumstances have carried the day, Gladstone enjoyed a triumphal progress. Furthermore, Lord Rosebery, whose territorial influence was also substantial, was organizing the Liberal campaign. Gladstone was returned to parliament and to power. The Liberals had a majority of 137 over the Conservatives, with the Irish Nationalists winning sixty-five seats, not enough to hold the balance. The Tory leadership was shocked at the extent of their miscalculations. 'The hurricane', Salisbury told Balfour, 'that has swept us away is so strange and new a phenomenon that we shall not for some time understand its real meaning'.[32]

Politics had taken Balfour out of his old circle. He maintained contact with the Gladstones and the Lytteltons, but the death of May and his close association with Salisbury inevitably led to a drift away from the intimacies of the early 1870s. Music was still a great interest, joined by art when he was introduced to Burne-Jones by his mother's friend, Blanche, Lady Airlie. Balfour often visited Burne-Jones's studio in the North End Road, Hammersmith, commissioning from the artist a series of pictures to decorate the drawing room in Carlton Gardens. The Perseus legend was the subject, chosen by Burne-Jones, and other pictures by the same artist, including the great 'Wheel of Fortune', were bought by Balfour over the years. Although painting was never to occupy the exalted place of music in Balfour's enthusiasm, through Burne-Jones he came to know several prominent late Victorian artists. Indeed, it was in the studio of Sir Frederick Leighton that he first met Mrs. Percy Wyndham, her son George and her daughter Mary. This meeting, which probably took place around 1879, marks the beginning of two of the closest friendships of his life.

4

The Arts of Opposition

During the election of 1880 Lord Salisbury escaped to Biarritz. Peers were precluded from taking part in the campaign and Hatfield had been lent to Beaconsfield for use as his electoral headquarters. Here Balfour came, fresh from his Hertford victory, to be congratulated amidst the flood of bad news. 'I recall him', the young candidate later wrote of the Prime Minister, 'standing at the north door of the house looking down the avenue – a strange, almost a picturesque figure, dignified and calm, though not, I thought, unmoved.'[1] Some days later they met in Downing Street, Balfour acting as a representative of Salisbury. Beaconsfield favoured resignation rather than defeat in the Commons, eschewing the use of the Lords' majority to sustain the Conservatives in office. He believed his party would never be returned to power in his lifetime, stating that much must depend upon the Tory peers who should not be discouraged but restrained until there was a substantial reason for conflict.

'The Old Man', Balfour told his uncle, 'seemed very well, and extraordinarily communicative. There was nothing of the fallen statesman about him as he marched up and down his room in Downing Street.'[2] Salisbury was not so ebullient, gloomily informing his nephew that the defeat 'seems to me to be inspired by some definite desire for change: and means business. It may disappear as rapidly as it came, or it may be the beginning of a serious war of classes. Gladstone is doing all he can to give it the latter meaning.'[3] The 1880 election, the rougher campaign at Hertford and the increasing intimacy of his relationship with Salisbury combined to banish Balfour's dilettante approach to politics. If defeated he had made up his mind, despite his mother's early advice, to leave the House of Commons for philosophy, but by May 1880 he was discussing with Salisbury the advisability of writing, as propaganda, some account of the late government, 'especially in relation to the history of their foreign policy'.[4] Thus evolved the partnership of uncle and nephew that was to dominate the closing years of the nineteenth century.

The Conservative front bench in the lower house was ill-equipped to deal with Gladstone's new government. Beaconsfield, Cranbrook and Salisbury, the three most powerful Tory debaters, were in the House of Lords; in the Commons the party was led by the stately figure of Sir Stafford Northcote, assisted by two worthy but prosaic lieutenants, Richard Cross and W. H. Smith. Northcote, once Gladstone's private secretary, was no match for the Liberal leader and his deferential approach to his opponent coupled with a pompous platitudinous style did not please the Conservative rank and file. In July 1879, before the election, Balfour was warning his uncle of 'the already large amount of discontent which Northcote's method of conducting business had aroused', also prophetically remarking that 'since there is no possible outlet for this action, since there is neither an alternative leader nor an alternative policy on the larger questions of the day, which any Conservative is prepared to support, I suppose the discontent will end in words, and perhaps in a certain difficulty in getting men to support the Government'.[5]

When the government of 1879 was defeated, Balfour's prognostications were proved correct. To fill the vacuum the Fourth Party arose. This, a Conservative ginger group, had no particular policy or purpose other than to embarrass Gladstone. It consisted of four Tory backbenchers: Lord Randolph Churchill, John Gorst, Sir Henry Drummond Wolff and Arthur Balfour. Of these, Churchill was the youngest at thirty-one, with Balfour next at thirty-two, followed by Gorst and Wolff who were respectively forty-five and fifty.

They were an interesting quartet. John Gorst, a lawyer, had played a part in the Conservative party organization as principal agent and was a firm proponent of the need for the Tories to attract working class support. In 1877 he quarrelled with the Chief Whip, refused to have anything more to do with Tory central office and blamed the defeat of 1880 on its refusal to listen to his warnings. Gorst, although able, was not an easy colleague. His prickly and aggressive manner, aggravated by bitterness, was well suited to attack if not to persuasion. Appointed executive officer to a central committee set up under W. H. Smith to investigate the party machinery, he resigned from this in 1882 having already become a member of the Fourth Party.

Sir Henry Drummond Wolff, a descendant of Sir Robert Walpole, was less abrasive. The oldest of the group he had, before coming to politics, been a financier and a diplomat. Wolff was, in Balfour's words, 'a man of the world by temperament and training' whose conversation 'even when not strictly edifying, never failed to amuse'.[6] But the most prominent of the Fourth Party was its youngest member, Lord Randolph Churchill, younger son of the Duke of Marlborough. Balfour and he, only seven months apart in age, had been contemporaries at Eton yet had not known each other. They entered Parliament at the same time, each owing his seat to family influence, Lord Randolph standing for Woodstock, adjacent to Blenheim Palace. Each, too, did secretarial work for their mentors, Churchill when his father was Lord Lieutenant of Ireland and Balfour for Salisbury at the Foreign Office, these tasks keeping them occupied and largely silent in parliament from 1874 to 1880.

Here the similarities end. Lord Randolph, unlike Balfour, enjoyed the aristocratic pursuits of hunting and racing; music meant nothing to him, pictures very little, although he read deeply. Churchill was impetuous and foolhardy where Balfour was wary and restrained. In 1876, this impetuosity led him to take the field against the Prince of Wales in the Aylesford divorce scandal which he saw as a conspiracy against his brother, Lord Blandford, whom Lord Aylesford wished to cite as a co-respondent. Using a package of love letters from the Prince of Wales to Lady Aylesford, Churchill tried to blackmail the Prince into advising Aylesford to drop the divorce proceedings which would ruin the reputation of his wife and Lord Blandford.[7] There was no divorce, but Lord Randolph's behaviour resulted in social ostracism completed by his departure for Ireland with his father in December 1876. The Prince of Wales did not speak to the Churchills until March 1884. This treatment at the hands of society infuriated Lord Randolph, awakening the fierce passions of his political ambition.

'Our Parliamentary history', Balfour wrote of his colleague's career, 'shows indeed nothing like it.'[8] Churchill was equipped for opposition. He was a compelling orator with a brilliantly destructive turn of phrase and a superb verbal memory. At first he regarded Balfour with disdain, calling him Postlethwaite after the aesthete in Patience, and remarking, 'Go and take my wife to a concert while I stay and talk real business.'[9] Balfour's biographer Mrs. Dugdale claimed that he only chose to sit on the front bench below the gangway beside the three *frondeurs* because there was room for his long legs; but she added, significantly: 'So he drifted into their neighbourhood, just as throughout life he drifted so often, but so seldom into any position where he did not wish to be.'[10]

The Bradlaugh debates were the true genesis of the Fourth Party. Charles Bradlaugh was an atheist who refused to take the full parliamentary oath. Gladstone called for tolerance, respecting the demands of Bradlaugh's conscience, but the Fourth Party, in an unlikely alliance with Liberal nonconformists and a majority of the Irish party, pressed Bradlaugh's exclusion from the House. Balfour regarded Bradlaugh's religious views as his own affair and refused, as he later remarked, 'to entrust my theological views to that partnership',[11] in other words the Fourth Party. Churchill did not press for a speech from him, but Balfour told Salisbury on 14 May 1880 how poor an impression Northcote's equivocating manner had made during the controversy writing that 'the division on Tuesday was as much directed against him as it was against Bradlaugh'. Thynne, a Tory member, had declared that, 'it would teach Northcote not to be always jumping up and agreeing with the other side without first consulting his friends.'[12]

Balfour had tried to persuade Thynne that it was a bad idea to divide the House against the wishes of the party leadership and his letters to Salisbury demonstrate that his overriding allegiance was still to his uncle. Indeed, Winston Churchill suggests that one of the reasons Balfour became associated with Lord Randolph and his supporters was to embarrass Northcote, Salisbury's rival to succeed Beaconsfield as leader. Certainly he despaired of Sir Stafford and in August, at a party gathering in the Carlton Club, agreed to voice the party's back-bench grievances, 'in order to prevent worse happening (by which I mean an attack on North-cote in the House)'.[13] He claimed to dislike having to make such a speech, believing that this was a task better suited to an older man, protesting against the embarrassment of Northcote's presence at the meeting. By all accounts it was a subtle perform-ance, never mentioning names but leaving no doubt as to the object of discontent.

The Fourth Party's attitude towards Northcote at this time was one of extreme disrespect. They nicknamed him 'the Goat', because of his beard as opposed to his sexual appetites, and when, in September 1880, he proposed to Gorst that the group should disband and 'quietly take their place in the main body of the House', Gorst 'ignored the suggestion of dissolution altogether'. Gorst believed Northcote was angling for a possible coalition with the Liberal Whigs, noting how 'in some quarters this has been spoken of as the next political combination'.[14] This appease-ment had no attraction for the *frondeurs* who were enjoying the fray.

After the end of the session in September, Gorst and Wolff spoke with Beaconsfield. The old statesman counselled caution, stating that Northcote's respectability was of great value to the party although 'I wholly sympathize with you because I was never respectable myself'. Beaconsfield's advice was not, on any account, to break with Northcote. 'Whenever,' he said, 'it becomes too difficult, you can come to me and I will try to arrange matters.'[15] Some months later Beaconsfield was dead and the doubts about his successor out in the open at last.

Before this, in the last months of 1880, Balfour had been used by his colleagues as an emissary to his uncle. Churchill asked him to invite Salisbury to speak to the Woodstock Conservative Association in November. Salisbury accepted but wrote disapprovingly of the Fourth Party's blatant impudence to Northcote, remarking, 'I have no doubt Wolff's language gets round to his ears and he thinks it represents the feelings of all Wolff's friends.'[16] Wolff's attitude to Sir Stafford is perhaps best summarized in a letter to Balfour of the following year. 'I saw the Goat', he wrote, 'more goaty than ever. He is a loathsome creature, full of small spite and destitute of virility – a kind of earthworm.'[17] But, after Beaconsfield's death in April 1881, it was Northcote whom the Queen, for one, regarded as the leader of the Conservative party, despite the uneasy arrangement of a split leadership with Salisbury in the Lords and Sir Stafford in the Commons. Salisbury made no ostensible attempt to harness the discontent against Northcote for his own advantage and his speech at Woodstock to Lord Randolph's constituents took the form of a strong appeal for party unity.

In 1880, Arthur Balfour's promise as a parliamentary performer was already perceptible. 'The member for Hertford', wrote Henry Lucy of *Punch*, 'is one of the most interesting young men in the House. He is not a good speaker, but he is endowed with the rich gift of conveying the impression that presently he will be a successful parliamentary debater, and that in the meantime it is well that he should practise. He is a pleasing specimen of the highest form of culture and good breeding which stand to the credit of Cambridge University. He is not without desire to say hard things of the adversary opposite, and sometimes yields to the temptation. But it is ever done with such sweet and gentle grace, and is smoothed over with such earnest protestations of innocent intention, that the adversary rather likes it than otherwise.'[18] Ireland was now to give Balfour his first chance to demonstrate to the House of Commons the steel that lay beneath his geniality.

The condition of Ireland was once more at the forefront of British politics. The saga of Irish troubles and discontent goes back to Elizabethan times, but in the last half of the nineteenth century it was articulated with especial vigour. In 1875 Charles Stewart Parnell was elected to Parliament as member for Meath. In 1879 he became President of the Land League and in 1880 leader of the Irish parliamentary party, henceforth conducting a double campaign for home rule at Westminster and in the Irish countryside, aided by the severe agricultural depression of the late 1870s. Gladstone, after his first electoral victory of 1868, believed he had a mission to pacify Ireland. In 1869, he disestablished the Irish church and in 1870 passed a revolutionary Irish Land act, compensating evicted tenants and introducing state-financed loans to facilitate purchases of leased land from landlords.

The detestation of the often absentee and generally Protestant landlords was given further power by Gladstone's legislative recognition of it in 1870. Queen Victoria warned that his act would dignify the widespread agrarian disturbances by firmly identifying the landlords as oppressors. By 1880 Ireland was aflame, with rick burning, intimidation and murder prevalent in many districts. Gladstone, reluctant at first to resort to oppression, eventually decided he had no alternative and his Chief Secretary for Ireland, W. E. Forster, introduced a coercion bill which became law in March 1881.

Churchill wished to oppose coercion. He saw a chance of uniting the Tories, the Irish and the radicals in opposition to Gladstone's bill, but his three colleagues disagreed. Beaconsfield, to whom they appealed, sided with the majority, yet Lord Randolph would have pressed his amendment had it not been for the intervention of his father, the Duke of Marlborough. Eventually he desisted, relapsing into a silent sulk, separated from Gorst, whom he saw as the main destroyer of his plans, by Balfour on the bench below the gangway. In April, Gladstone introduced another land measure, guaranteeing tenants 'the three Fs': fair rent, fixity of tenure and free sale. This the Fourth Party set about amending in Committee. Balfour with his respect for the rights of property owners, disliked the legislation intensely.

Parnell refused to work with the new act's land courts and the League's agitation continued. Gladstone, in October 1881, took a drastic and impetuous decision. He arrested the Irish leader with two of his lieutenants and imprisoned them in Kilmainham jail. 'Captain Moonlight', Parnell prophesied, 'will take my place', and the Irish response was a terrifying escalation of agrarian violence. Finally, in May 1882, the secret treaty of Kilmainham was negotiated by Gladstone through intermediaries. Parnell was released and new measures taken by the government to deal with arrears of rent in return for an end to anarchy in the Irish countryside. The Chief Secretary for Ireland, W. E. Forster, and the Vicerory, Lord Cowper, neither of whom had been informed of the treaty beforehand, resigned in protest. On 6 May in Dublin, Forster's successor, Lord Frederick Cavendish and his under-secretary, Thomas Burke, were cut to death by assassins with surgical knives while walking in Phoenix Park.

The debates on the Kilmainham treaty moved Balfour for the first time to parliamentary passion. Gladstone denied the existence of a secret contract, but under pressure from all sides, including Forster from the Liberal back benches, the truth began to emerge. The treaty, Balfour said, 'stood alone in its infamy' and the government 'had negotiated in secret with treason'.[19] Gladstone, hurt by this assault, indignantly denied the charge. Later Balfour came to regret the tone of his attack but justified himself by remembering the impersonal sincerity of his indignation. 'I can', he later wrote to Gladstone, 'most earnestly and sincerely assure you that no merely political disagreement, however profound it may be, has, or can alter my feelings towards you and your family; these feelings do not arise from political agreement and, so far as I am concerned, are not likely to be attacked by political differences.'[20] To Warden Talbot of Keble, who protested that these attacks on Gladstone evinced 'feelings which it is the glory of a Christian heart to keep under, natural as they are',[21] Balfour patiently gave a similar reply. The speech of 1882 was another sign that the dilettante was making way for the young statesman.

For Balfour, politics in these years were offset by family tragedy. In 1881, Cecil Balfour, the nearest in age to Arthur of his brothers, was killed in Australia after falling from a horse. Cecil, always the weakest link in the family chain, is described by Lady Rayleigh as having 'neither Arthur's brains nor his charm'.[22] In fact his life was a series of disasters and humiliations, starting with a different education from his older brother (at Harrow and Magdalen at Oxford instead of Eton and Trinity, Cambridge) to prevent unfavourable comparisons, continuing with an unsatisfactory career with a firm of merchants and ending in hopeless indebtedness which he tried to settle with a cheque forged in Arthur's name. Lady Rayleigh notes, frostily, that Cecil had 'no special tastes'[23] and hired a yacht, for health reasons, to cruise in warm climates, finishing up in Australia. This death was followed, a year later, by another more tragic loss. In July 1882, Frank Balfour was killed in a climbing accident in the Swiss Alps.

Frank had, at first, evinced little of the great brilliance that led him to be regarded as one of the most promising scientists of his

day. He too was sent to Harrow to avoid unfair competition with
his cleverer brother, but later went to Trinity where his series of
academic triumphs began. His interest in biology had started as a
boy at Whittingehame through the dissection of shellfish picked
up on the seashore; he became a university lecturer, was offered a
professorship at Edinburgh but accepted a chair of animal
morphology specially created for him at Cambridge. Like Arthur
he possessed charm as well as intellect; and there seemed no limit
to the possibilities ahead.

His death was a terrible blow to his family. Before Frank's
departure, Arthur had joked 'Don't get killed – it would be such
a bore' and now, whilst staying at Wilton with Lord and Lady
Pembroke, he received the tragic news. As he entered Carlton
Gardens, where his grief-stricken relatives had gathered, Lady
Frances Balfour, his sister-in-law, remembers that 'one look at his
face was enough to tell how his very being had been struck
down'.[24] Characteristically, while travelling from London to
Wilton Balfour had made no mention of the tragedy to his companions; he still hoped that Frank might be found alive but some
days later Eustace and Gerald, who had left immediately for
Switzerland, returned home with the body. 'Science', Lord
Salisbury declared, offering mordant consolation to Lady Frances,
'like any other truth, never suffers from the loss of any individual.' These family losses gave additional strain to Balfour as
the oldest, a responsibility which he discharged with calm
strength. After Frank's funeral at Whittingehame, Lady Frances
noted 'my love and reverence for Arthur grows'.

In 1882, Balfour's relationship with the Fourth Party
changed as Lord Randolph Churchill's ambitions asserted
themselves. Tory democracy, the fight for the National Union
and Lord Randolph's own bid for the party leadership were, as a
recent historian of the Conservative Party has noted, separate
from the initial rather anarchic aims of the original four con-
spirators.[25] These were bound to find disfavour with Arthur
Balfour, if only on account of his intense loyalty to Lord
Salisbury.

In October, Lord Randolph Churchill opposed Gladstone's
closure proposal, introduced to prevent the Irish parliamentary
obstruction at which Parnell was a master, but Balfour spoke

against his colleague, supporting Northcote's scheme to amend the measure so as to permit closure only by consent of the two thirds majority. This was the first time Balfour had openly opposed Churchill in the House, but in April 1883 he was again angered by Lord Randolph's impetuosity. The Fourth Party had protested, in an anonymous letter to *The Times*, about the choice of Northcote to unveil the statue of Beaconsfield in Parliament Square and the relegation of Salisbury to proposing a vote of thanks. Then, on 2 April, Churchill wrote again to *The Times*, this time urging the immediate relegation of Sir Stafford and the succession of Lord Salisbury to the party leadership.

Lord Randolph had gone too far and there was a massive re-action. Two hundred Tory M.P.s including Balfour, Gorst and Wolff but excluding Churchill, signed a letter expressing confidence in Northcote who received an ovation in the House of Commons. The Conservative press echoed their disapproval and Balfour, perhaps seeing harm in this for his uncle's prospects, was furious with his friend. 'I never', wrote Lady Frances, 'saw Arthur so violently annoyed by anything as this question of Randolph and the leadership', and he shouted with irritation at his sister-in-law, 'If you sit there looking so meek I'll shake you.'[26] Yet no one could stop Lord Randolph. In an article in May in the *Fortnightly Review* he argued for a leader who was capable of returning the Conservative party to a Disraelian platform of 'imperial rule and social reform'. Few doubted that he was now thinking of himself.

Tory democracy was the catch phrase of Churchill's campaign yet, as he himself admitted, opportunism was its chief characteristic. Lord Randolph's approach was overwhelmingly aristocratic. He referred to Smith and Cross as 'Marshall and Snelgrove' or 'Lords of suburban villas, masters of pineries and vineries', and refused to countenance at all Gladstone's plans for the extension of the franchise. Balfour, after listening on an Edinburgh platform in December 1883 to Churchill on this subject, publicly contradicted his colleague, agreeing with his uncle that such a bill should be supported if there was also a re-distribution of constituencies. Eventually, Lord Randolph joined the rest of his party on this issue, claiming to have been converted by Balfour's Edinburgh arguments.

The leadership was the dominant question. Beaconsfield, by his ennoblement and death, had left a vacuum. He had declared that, had he known Gladstone was to come out of retirement, he would never have left the Commons, also that he hoped soon to abdicate his leadership in the Lords to Salisbury, thus preparing the way for the latter to succeed him as Party leader. But Beaconsfield died too soon to ensure this and now, with Lord Randolph's hat in the ring, a wrangle was inevitable. At first the Fourth Party was divided, with Balfour strongly for Salisbury, Churchill and Wolff somewhat ambiguous in their attitude, yet leaning away from Northcote, and Gorst inclining towards Sir Stafford, believing his ineffectiveness to be due to the interference of Smith and Cross. However, Gorst and Wolff threw in their lot with Churchill once he made his ambitions plain in the autumn of 1883. Lord Randolph's bid for power was conducted through the National Union, an amorphous, previously insignificant body whose duty was to keep the Conservative party in touch with constituency opinion. Churchill was elected its chairman and he demanded a say for the National Union in the running of the central committee, the party's organizing executive dominated by what he termed 'the old gang'.

Balfour kept his uncle informed about his contacts with Churchill. 'He is', Balfour wrote of Lord Randolph in January 1884, 'I think quite capable of denouncing in a public speech the existing organization. At least he told me so the other day when having asked me whether it was to be peace or war between us on this subject, I said that if peace meant yielding to his pretensions, it was war! We are excellent friends at the moment otherwise.'[27] With Wolff he was equally firm, causing his old colleague to write in April 1883, 'You said several things to me last night which were very wounding and unjust.'[28] However, Balfour advised against premature action. 'We should', he told Salisbury in January 1884, 'avoid . . . all "rows" until Randolph is put entirely and flagrantly in the wrong by some act of party disloyalty which everybody can understand and nobody can deny'.[29]

The battle for control of the Conservative party machinery was fought through the spring and summer of 1884. Churchill's national popularity was such that Salisbury could not afford to ignore his challenge, but Lord Randolph never reached a position from which he could dictate his own terms. In July Sir Michael Hicks-Beach acted as a mediator between the two sides, Wolff representing Lord Randolph and Balfour acting for Salisbury. Hicks-Beach became chairman of the National Union with Balfour a vice-chairman, this organization gradually returning to its old position as an advisory body. Salisbury disbanded the central committee, keeping the party direction very much in the hands of the party leadership to whose inner counsels Lord Randolph was to be admitted.

The eclipse of Sir Stafford was complete. Steadily Salisbury had asserted his authority: first by dominating the negotiations with Gladstone over the passing of the 1884 Reform Act and the constitutional crisis brought about by its initial rejection by the Lords; second through the creation, after the dispute over the central committee and the National Union, of a new Tory leadership consisting of himself, Lord Randolph Churchill and Sir Michael Hicks-Beach. Balfour's role as intermediary and confidant of his uncle had raised his prospects. The Gladstone administration, plagued by foreign setbacks in Egypt, the Sudan, Afghanistan and Africa, was in an unhappy state. Gordon's death at Khartoum in February 1885 caused universal horror, Queen Victoria publicly rebuking her Prime Minister. Once again Ireland was causing discord, the cabinet rejecting Joseph Chamberlain's scheme for Irish local government boards. Chamberlain, one of the government's most powerful members, resigned, accompanied by Sir Charles Dilke, and Lord Randolph Churchill, using his new influence, angled for Parnell's support by stating that the Conservatives would discontinue coercion.

In June 1885 Balfour entertained the old Fourth Party to lunch at Carlton Gardens. The other guests were Cecil Raikes and Sir Michael Hicks-Beach; together they discussed and drafted an amendment to the budget which Sir Michael later moved in the House. Gladstone was defeated by twelve votes and the Tories shouted in exultation, Lord Randolph Churchill leading the pack, standing on a bench, waving his handkerchief wildly in the frenzy of victory. 'Such', Balfour noted, 'was the last gesture of the Fourth Party made by its most brilliant member.'[30]

5

Apprenticeship

Balfour was now on the brink of power. He was also a prominent young bachelor in London's society, enlarging his circle of acquaintances. The Fourth Party had added a more raffish element to this; Lord Randolph Churchill's description of a meeting with Gorst and Wolff in a letter to their co-conspirator seems far removed from the Monday Pops or philosophical discussion at Hawarden. 'Wolff', wrote Lord Randolph, 'had to be suppressed several times and very strong language was used. The only unseemly incident was the entrance of a female in black, who was ushered in by the waiter. She apparently had an appointment with either Wolff or Gorst, but I was unable to discover which as they both pretended not to know her and we had some difficulty in persuading her to retire'.[1]

Balfour gravitated away from Churchill's traditional aristocratic pleasures, searching for some point at which his intellectual and social needs might meet. He enjoyed society and was a success within it; yet the stupidity of many of its members, their lack of curiosity, their contentment in pursuing the same crude course year after year, had little appeal for him. He knew that these people, with their territorial and financial power, were, in a sense, the backbone of his party and his class; he bore no ill will towards them and was prepared to articulate their prejudices, but their company offered no lasting satisfaction. Thus in the 1880s Balfour established around himself the beginnings of a small group which was to become in the next decade his social refuge and a meeting point for those with similar tastes, or at least pretensions towards them.

In 1881 Balfour met Margot Tennant for the first time. Miss

Tennant was aged seventeen; later she married Asquith but at this stage was a young girl loose in London, startling people with her originality and directness of approach. She invited Balfour to stay at the Tennant family house in Scotland, Glen near Peebles, and there introduced him to her sister Laura who later married his great friend, Alfred Lyttelton. The Tennants were daughters of Sir Charles Tennant, a rich businessman whose fortune originally came from a Glasgow chemical works. As a family, they were Liberal but this made no difference to Balfour in the easy political concourse of the 1880s and 1890s. Margot's interest was immediately aroused. Throughout Balfour's life they were to be friends, yet he was wary of her recklessness, impatient of her efforts to bulldoze him. At one time, before she married Asquith, there was a rumour in the newspapers that Margot and Balfour were engaged. 'I hear', a friend remarked to him, 'you are going to marry Margot Tennant'; to which he replied, 'No, that is not so. I rather think of having a career of my own.'[2]

It was in the early years of the 1880s that Balfour's friendship with Mary Wyndham, later Lady Elcho, began. Percy and Madeleine, her parents, must have introduced them. Percy Wyndham, younger brother of Lord Leconfield, was a Conservative member of Parliament from 1860 to 1885, resigning as a result of his disapproval of Gladstone's extension of the franchise. In 1860 he had married Madeleine Campbell, grand-daughter of Lord Edward Fitzgerald, the Irish revolutionary. Among their friends were William Morris, Burne-Jones, Watts and the architect Philip Webb, who built them a large country house called Clouds at East Knoyle, near Salisbury. Clouds, completed in 1885, decorated with Morris materials and designs, symbolized in its mixture of clear restrained architectural lines without and sudden outbursts of unexpected colour within, Mrs. Percy Wyndham's temperamental juxtaposition of Victorian sobriety with unrestrained sentiment, a combination inherited by at least two of her offspring.

The Wyndhams had five children (three girls and two boys) and it was with the eldest daughter (Mary) and the eldest son (George) that Arthur Balfour made two of the closest friendships of his life. Their first meeting was at the studio of Sir Frederick Leighton, and Balfour was invited to Madeleine Wyndham's musical parties at the Wyndham town house in Belgrave Square. In 1880, Mrs Wyndham and her daughter, Mary, visited Strathconan as his guests. At this date, Mary was seventeen and Balfour thirty-one; she later saw this Strathconan visit as the true beginning of their intimacy.

In London they continued to meet, attending theatres and concerts, always heavily chaperoned but watched with approval by Mrs Percy Wyndham. Twenty-three years later Mary remembered an expedition in 1882. Balfour and she, together with her mother and Lord Cowper, went to *Much Ado about Nothing* and 'sat in a box and when the audience tittered at the wrong parts you said savagely "I would gladly wring their necks".' Yet the evening led to a 'vague sense of dissatisfaction' and Mary Wyndham somewhat obscurely wondered 'had there been magnificent mischief makers – matchmaking plotters – in the case of one gentle girl and busy political "boy" or had she been as audacious as Margot or Laura or many a maid then might you have been after all "Benedict the married man" but she was too proud and shy and wanted as much luring as Beatrice and he was too busy and capricious and so the tale had another ending'.[3]

The Wyndhams invited Balfour to stay at Wilbury, the house they had rented in Wiltshire during the planning and construction of Clouds, but, strangely, he never came. By now Mrs Percy Wyndham's plans for her daughter's future definitely included him, although there was a rival suitor in the form of Lord Elcho, son of the Earl of Wemyss. Elcho was more determined in his pursuit, but Mary's mother, and Mary herself, seemed to prefer Arthur Balfour. 'Mama', she later remembered, 'wanted you to marry me. . . . You got some silly notion in your head because circumstances threw Hugo and me together and accidents kept us apart – you were the only man I wanted for my husband and it's a great compliment to you! (for many wanted me to wife!) but you wouldn't give me a chance of showing you nicely and you never came to Wilbury and you were afraid, afraid, afraid!!'[4]

Balfour's detachment, whether it sprang from fear or not, thwarted the Wyndhams' wishes. In 1883 Mary married Lord Elcho who, in the same year, became Conservative member of Parliament for Haddingtonshire.

The marriage was not to be altogether easy. Elcho, although

affable and lazily clever (St. John Brodrick writes of his 'genius for facile speech . . . universally recognized in the House of Commons')' was a gambler and a philanderer, turning their life into a series of domestic and financial crises, driving his wife towards Balfour for sympathy and encouragement. Inevitably, given their early attachment and his endlessly receptive manner, Mary Elcho's feelings for her sympathizer deepened. How much this process was reciprocal is more doubtful.

Mary Elcho inherited from her mother complete lack of self-consciousness, a warmth which encouraged confidences and broke down reserve. This easiness opened up for Balfour a more satisfactory world than the mannered stiffness of the great London hostesses like Lady Londonderry or the aggressive masculine philistinism of late-Victorian country life. Indeed the early influence of Mrs Percy Wyndham, exercised personally and through her children, sowed the seeds of a more relaxed social alternative set up by the Souls during the last ten years of the century, although this alternative was to become, in its way, as self-conscious and ritualistic as that which it sought to replace.

After Mary Elcho's marriage, Arthur Balfour and she still saw each other in London and the country. The Tennants and the Lytteltons were friends of Balfour and the Elchos, and when Alfred Lyttelton married Laura Tennant, there was rejoicing among their circle. Lyttelton, yet another of May's brothers, was some nine years younger than Balfour and, in the Lyttelton tradition, a great games player. The two became friends and later colleagues in cabinet. At this stage, Laura Tennant and Lyttelton, she beautiful and vital, he a hero at school and university for his remarkable feats of athleticism, symbolized to their contemporaries youthful grace and promise. The Victorians were apt to be sentimental; the young Lytteltons quickly became repositories for the vicarious hopes and wishes of many of their friends. Balfour was not excluded from this and when, in 1886, Laura Lyttelton died in childbirth, he was distraught. In the wretchedness of his grief, he accused Mary Elcho of not understanding the true nature of their loss. Her desperation at his displeasure illustrates the growing intensity of the feeling between them, at least on her side.

'It sickens me', she wrote, 'to think that I say things that you mind or in a way that you mind for I think of you always so much and write you many letters (in my head) and I do feel so sorry for you now. I would do anything for you. I long to be able to do anything that would in a little way lessen the awful blank that the loss of such a friend as Laura leaves: I feel and know I am dumb and awkward – not a friend though with all the will, but a miserable makeshift of a friend but if you could really know my thoughts "hard" would be the very last word you could apply . . . you must forgive me'.[6]

Laura Lyttelton's will showed the closeness of her friendships with Balfour and Mary Elcho. Mary was left a Chippendale cradle, a diamond and red enamel crescent and the wish that she should have 'such a blessed life, because I think her character is so full of blessed things and symbols'. To Balfour, 'Alfred's and my dear, deeply loved friend', went 'my Johnson' because 'he taught me to love that wisest of men' and 'my ugly little Shelley'. 'If', the will continues, 'he married I should like him to give his wife my little red enamel harp – I shall never see her if I die now, but I have so often created her in the islands of my imagination – and as a queen has she reigned there, so that I feel in the spirit we are in some measure related by some mystic tie.'[7]

Balfour's young manhood had been disfigured by death. First his mother, then May Lyttelton and his two brothers, Cecil and Frank, and now one of his closest and most valued friends. Inevitably, the losses left their scars. In 1889 Gerald became seriously ill; Balfour's letter to Lady Elcho shows how deeply he felt the possibility of another tragedy. 'I do not think', he wrote, 'so far as I can judge in the absence of actual experience, that I am at all afraid of dying. But I have a shrinking horror of separation caused by the death of those I love. I thought of Alfred and Laura: of Gerald and of others, of what had been and what might be, and went to bed a most miserable man. What horrible capacities for pain we have: if only our other gifts were in proportion!'[8] These are not the words of a cold man.

In November 1883 Sir Stafford Northcote wrote to Arthur Balfour about a meeting he had had with Conservative party workers from Manchester 'who are very anxious to secure you as a candidate for the general election'.[9] In the same year, Salisbury encouraged his nephew to move from Hertford, a seat later to be abolished in the re-drawing of constituency boundaries which accompanied Gladstone's Reform Act, and spurred him on to consider Manchester. 'I do not think', he said, 'there is anyone who could approach the contest with so great a chance of success', going on to advise that 'if you win Manchester your position as a public man will be very much stronger'. Salisbury believed Balfour's connection with him was 'a benefit – at all events mixed' and 'the fact that you sit for a seat reputed – quite falsely – to be mine, joined to our other ties makes many people take you too much as my double; and this detracts and may detract more, from the natural effect of your powers'.[10]

Salisbury was sure Balfour's standing in the party would be greatly increased 'if you spoke as a representative of a large working class constituency'. Happily the Lancashire party workers agreed, perhaps anxious to accommodate Lord Salisbury's nephew. 'The need', one wrote in January 1885, 'is for such a man as you to get well amongst the masses who have the power and give them a lofty idea – a noble aim to lift them out of narrow local conceptions of national life and progress . . . some of our friends have been watching with interest your growing popularity amongst the well-to-do citizens. I have been observing your growing touch and power amongst "the people". You have a great part to play – and you are singularly gifted with the necessary qualifications for playing it successfully."[11] Thus, in the 1885 general election, Balfour stood for the first time for East Manchester, a constituency he was to hold until 1906.

Balfour's association with the Fourth Party and his diplomacy in the controversy over the National Union had drawn attention to him. *The Spectator*, struck by his initial support of Lord Randolph's aristocratic rebelliousness, compared him to Lord John Manners in the days of the 'Young England' crusade. Praise also came from an unexpected quarter. In 1882, at a garden party, Captain Briscoe of the Merchant Navy met Gladstone and remarked that he supposed Lord Randolph Churchill must be the future leader of the Tory party. 'Never', the aghast Prime Minister replied: 'God forbid that any great English party should be led by a Churchill! There never was a Churchill from John

Duke of Marlborough down that had either morals or principles.'
Somewhat taken aback, Briscoe searched around for an alternative and eventually produced the name of Arthur Balfour. 'Quite
a different young man', declared Gladstone, saying that although
he sprawled all over the House of Commons and was laughed at
by some of its members 'as they often do when their judgement is
invariably wrong, Arthur Balfour is a young man of great ability
and character, a high and the best type of an English gentleman,
in my opinion the future leader of the Tory party'.[12]

Balfour was beginning to enjoy Westminster, telling his
friend, St. John Brodrick, in 1884 that the House of Commons
was the only real centre of political life and 'of all evening entertainment in London, the House of Commons, taking the year
round, was incomparably the best'.[13] Now, with the Conservatives coming into power in June 1885, he could expect to be
offered a post in the new government. The Tories had not wished
to be faced with office, but, when the hour came, Salisbury could
not resist the opportunity to restore Britain's international
prestige after the failures of Liberal foreign policy. Balfour was
used as an intermediary by his uncle to arrange a smooth transition with Gladstone; Salisbury's position, further strengthened
by Northcote's poor health, was secure as party leader and, on 12
June 1885, it was he whom the Queen summoned to Balmoral.
A five month interval was needed before an election to complete
the arrangements for an extension of a franchise caused by
Gladstone's Reform Act.

Salisbury agreed to try to form an administration. Lord Randolph Churchill negotiating from his new position of power,
demanded the exclusion of Cross, Northcote's old lieutenant, and
said he would not work with Northcote if the latter were
appointed leader of the House of Commons. Lord Randolph believed he had asked for too much and Salisbury would refuse him.
He was partly wrong; Northcote was created Earl of Iddesleigh
and installed in the House of Lords as First Lord of the Treasury,
although Cross accepted the Home Secretaryship. Thus Sir Stafford's honour was satisfied by Salisbury's acknowledgement of
him as second man in the new government and Churchill would
not have to serve under Northcote in the Commons. Lord
Randolph himself went to the India Office, also securing positions

for his old party colleagues, Gorst becoming Solicitor-General and Wolff a Privy Councillor.

Balfour had helped his uncle calm Lord Randolph over the question of appointments, and at first Salisbury believed he should keep his nephew close to him in order to facilitate such intimate tasks. An Under-Secretaryship at the Foreign Office was contemplated and Balfour seemed enthusiastic, writing that he 'would do anything that most conduced to the smooth working of your arrangements'.[14] In the event he was appointed President of the Local Government Board, without a seat in the cabinet.

Balfour had been given his own department, the first real test of his administrative and parliamentary talents. On the last score he fell down badly, demonstrating a slowness to realize the difference between government and opposition. His health, at any rate, was no problem. In 1882 Lady Frances Balfour wrote that 'unless he gets stronger, I really don't see how he could stand office work',[15] but a heavy workload strengthened Balfour's constitution, partly because his iron determination, if aroused, was generally capable of coping with any minor physical disability.

Joseph Chamberlain exposed the new minister's clumsiness when Balfour introduced into the House of Commons the Medical Relief Disqualification Bill, a measure designed to give votes to those receiving assistance from poor law funds. Jesse Collings, one of Chamberlain's closest associations, had already tried to pass a similar measure under the last government but had been rejected by the House of Lords; there should have been little difficulty in arranging its acceptance now. However, Balfour unwisely taunted Chamberlain who took revenge by heavily amending the measure in committee in addition to mocking the extraordinarily rapid conversion of the Tories to Collings' scheme. As a result of this Balfour wondered if he was really suited to ministerial office, but Salisbury was soon made to understand once more the usefulness of his nephew as a confidential intermediary.

Ireland was again the subject. The Conservatives had come to power on the understanding that they would move away from Gladstonian coercion; another land purchase act was passed, further encouraging transfer of land from landlord to tenant, and the Earl of Carnarvon became Viceroy of Ireland. Carnarvon was a moderate, conciliatory when dealing with the desire for colonial self-government as he had shown during his rule in South Africa and Canada. Parnell and he met secretly in an empty house in London, attempting to start some sort of dialogue between the government and the nationalists.

The Liberals were divided on Ireland. Chamberlain, personally embittered by the cabinet rejection of his scheme for Irish local government and Parnell's cold killing of his proposed Irish tour in June, reacted strongly against the nationalists' call for a separate Irish parliament. Lord Hartington, whose brother Lord Frederick Cavendish had been assassinated in Phoenix Park, also voiced strong opposition. Gladstone was silent. We know that he had already decided Home Rule was the only solution to the Irish question, but in his election address, issued on 17 September, the passage concerning Ireland was ambiguous, demanding only a large Liberal majority unreliant on nationalist support.

The election was set for the end of November. Salisbury had declared, in a speech at Newport, against Home Rule and had subjected Chamberlain's local government scheme to severe criticism; his words were not, however, harsh enough to discourage Parnell, Carnarvon or Churchill. The Newport speech, delivered on 7 October, also concentrated on English local government reform, with references to elected County Councils, a restructuring of the rating system and measures to make more land available for sale. These were the Conservative's answers to Gladstone's domestic proposals and Chamberlain's socialistic 'unauthorized programme'. If the Tories won, Balfour, at the Local Government Board, was clearly going to be among the more active ministers.

The result of the election was a small Liberal majority over the Conservatives, the Irish, with eighty-six seats, holding the balance of power. Salisbury continued in office with Irish support, and Gladstone still issued no pronouncement on the subject of Home Rule. Then in December Arthur Balfour, while staying at Eaton Hall, the Duke of Westminster's vast gothic pile in Cheshire, learned of the reason for this silence when Gladstone suddenly appeared one afternoon from Hawarden. It was Balfour he wanted, for he knew this was a safe way of communicating with Salisbury. In the conversation between the two of them which followed, the Liberal leader described the violence and outrage which must take place in England itself if the demands of Irish nationalism were not satisfied. He had, 'information of an authentic kind' that unless some concessions were immediately forthcoming a terrible campaign of terror would begin. 'In other words', said Balfour, 'we are to be blown up and stabbed if we do not grant home rule by the end of the next session.' 'I understand', answered Gladstone, 'that the time is shorter than that.'[16]

From this conversation, and the correspondence which followed, Gladstone's plan became apparent. He wished Home Rule to become an issue above party politics, to be dealt with by Salisbury's government. Balfour, in a letter to Salisbury of 23 December surveyed the present state of the Liberal party and believed Gladstone's manoeuvres were largely inspired by the wish to prevent a serious split among his own front bench. Hartington, Goschen, Chamberlain and Dilke were anti-Parnellites; Spencer, John Morley, Granville and Childers would probably support Home Rule, either from conviction or blind loyalty to their leader. 'We must, get out of office, and at once', counselled Balfour. 'Even if we have to return in consequence of no one being able to fill our places, it is all important that that fact should be driven well into the minds of the public.'[17]

Gladstone's initiative came at a time when Balfour's ministerial record was undistinguished. In December, he attended the cabinet for a discussion of the proposed local government bill; Lord Randolph Churchill passed him a note saying 'How d—d dull this is. I am getting sick',[18] and Balfour probably agreed. Soon he was relieved of these responsibilities. On 17 December, Herbert Gladstone's news of his father's conversion to Home Rule was made public in the press. Salisbury's government rejected the Liberal leader's plea for joint action on Ireland and the Conservatives moved back towards coercion. On 27 January 1886, the Irish joined the Liberals to vote the Tories out of office and Gladstone set about forming his third administration.

The Liberals, as Balfour had predicted, were in disarray. Hartington and several of the Whigs, or Liberal patricians, would have no part in the new government; Chamberlain, after taking office as President of the Local Government Board, resigned on 26 March, ten days after the Prime Minister first presented his

Home Rule Bill to the cabinet. Previously, on 22 March, Chamberlain and Balfour had met at dinner with Reginald Brett, later Lord Esher. Chamberlain, aware of Balfour's intimacy with Salisbury, spoke with 'engaging frankness' about future political possibilities, conscious, no doubt, that the Tory leader would almost certainly be later informed of his views. He saw an eventual alliance of Conservatives, radicals and Hartington's Whigs against Liberal Home Rulers and was at pains to emphasize, at the expense of the Whigs, his reliability. The Whigs, Chamberlain remarked, had killed his proposals for Irish local government reform; 'now we see them in the shape of Spencer and Granville, going in for Home Rule!' Balfour noted in his report to Salisbury that Chamberlain clearly wished to supersede Hartington as 'the man who is to throw out Gladstone's scheme' and that there were possibilities in his proposals. His uncle was more cautious, noting that Chamberlain was 'as touchy as a schoolgirl and as implacable as Juno' and that 'the personal element is very strong'. 'He will never make a strong leader,' Salisbury declared. 'He has not yet persuaded himself that he has any convictions; and therein lies Gladstone's infinite superiority.'[19]

The aristocratic Whigs had always appeared, in the event of a Liberal split, to be the Tories' natural allies. Balfour, after this conversation, was sufficiently impressed by Chamberlain's personality to judge otherwise. 'We shall find in him', he told Salisbury, 'as long as he agrees with us, a very different kind of ally from the lukewarm and slippery Whigs whom it is so difficult to differ from, and so impossible to act with.'[20] In June, after the defeat of Gladstone's Home Rule bill in which ninety-three Liberals had voted with the Conservatives for the preservation of the union, Chamberlain and Balfour met again, this time as guests of Ferdinand de Rothschild at Waddesdon. They discussed the possibility of the Liberal unionists joining a Tory administration, Chamberlain declaring that for him it was impossible 'and though I cannot of course speak for Hartington I doubt whether he would join me' but 'there ought to be no difficulty in obtaining sufficient unity of action by means of consultation behind the speaker's chair'.[21] These were the seeds of the Unionist alliance which successfully frustrated Gladstone's last years of office.

The election resulted in a House of Commons composed of four main parties; the Conservatives with 316 members, the Liberal Unionists with 78, the Gladstonian Liberals with 191 and the Irish Nationalists with 85. Balfour, having won East Manchester by a slightly reduced majority, retired to rest at the Abbey Hotel, Great Malvern, accompanied by his valet, Woods. Here he sought solitude, telling Lady Elcho that his time was entirely occupied in 'reading, writing and playing golf with the professional'. The only newspaper he saw was *The Field* in the golf clubhouse but a sign of his supposed influence was that 'one or two people in the simplicity of their hearts have written to me to get them office'.[22]

Balfour's disenchantment with the Local Government Board was taking the form of doubts about his future. Brooding alone at Great Malvern, he told his sister-in-law, Lady Frances, that 'I feel no natural vocation of being a great man's great man, still less for being thought to be so, therefore there are obvious motives for not leaving these solitudes; but of course they would not for a moment stand in the way of my coming up if I thought I could be of the slightest use to Uncle R.'[23] But if Balfour felt worried about thrusting himself upon a reluctant Salisbury, a chastening letter from his twenty-two year old cousin, Lord Robert Cecil, the Prime Minister's third son, must have been an encouragement. Cecil said he had seen Lady Frances Balfour ('your diplomatic agent') and 'tried to convince her that you are acting in a manner highly dangerous to those objects for which you profess to care. You say you are quite ready to come to town when anyone asks for you. You ought by this time to know your uncle well enough to be aware that when he asks for you, you will already be too late.'[24] Shortly after this Salisbury offered his nephew the position of Secretary of State for Scotland.

Balfour was surprised. Having heard previously from Salisbury's eldest son, Lord Cranborne, that his performance with the Local Government Board had not impressed the Prime Minister, he wrote to Cranborne for reassurance. His cousin replied that 'Papa knows quite well what he is doing'; Balfour must have a post from which accession to the cabinet was easy and 'it is a most important moment in your career'.[25] Cranborne was right; the Scottish office gave the first intimation of his real ability.

Balfour came to a new department and a difficult inheritance. The Scottish Office had been separated from the Home Office in 1885 by the Liberals, largely at the instigation of Lord Rosebery. Balfour had experience of Scottish affairs from the Local Government Board; in June 1886, he had spoken for the Conservatives on the Liberal Crofters Act and knew, from Strathconan, of the problems of Highland land ownership. There was, at this time, a land war in the Highlands similar to that in Ireland with the same array of disaffected tenants, absentee landlords, a land league, boycotting and agrarian violence. In the 1885 election, a crofters party consisting of four new members arrived at Westminster to represent, like the Irish nationalists, a challenge to the old system of land tenure. Violence in Skye in 1884 had been met by Harcourt, Gladstone's Home Secretary, with the arming of the police and the despatching of a gunboat and a troop ship with three hundred marines.[26]

The Liberals had been reluctant to use force. Balfour believed the Liberal Crofters Act of 1886, of which he was 'no fanatical admirer',[27] had, by granting security of tenure and setting up a Crofters Commission, removed all justification for unrest and when on 31 July 1886, marines landed on the Duke of Argyll's island of Tiree to assist the local police, he ignored protests which followed the ensuing arrests and heavy jail sentences. Argyll, father of Lady Frances Balfour, had resigned from Gladstone's cabinet in protest against the Irish land legislation; now he advised Balfour of the best methods of dealing with Scottish discontent.

On 21 August, the new Scottish secretary sent a combative memorandum to the cabinet, asking for greater powers for his office. 'While', he wrote, 'the condition of lawlessness . . . exceeds that of any part of Ireland, the machinery which necessity has given rise to in Ireland (in the shape of a strong central authority having direct control over practically unlimited forces of police, and having at its command constant and accurate information with respect to all parts of the country) does not exist even in its most rudimentary form in the Highlands.'[28]

Balfour wished the Scottish office to have the same powers over law and order as the Chief Secretary for Ireland, but the Home Secretary, with whom he at present shared those powers, and the Lord Advocate, disagreed. Their bureaucratic objections brought Balfour near to uttering veiled threats of resignation to Salisbury. 'I think you will find,' he wrote, 'more difficulty than you anticipate in overcoming the red tapism of your cabinet; – and if you fail it becomes rather an interesting question what I ought to do.'[29] Balfour had his way; the powers were granted to him and in September he was advocating more marine support for the police on Skye.

In October, seventy-five marines and forty policemen began operations on the island. From the start, Balfour was determined that writs for overdue rent and rates must be served at the same time. In this way landlord and tenant would be placed on the same footing and there could be no suspicion that the Tory government was merely an agent of the landowners. 'Everything', Salisbury wrote to his nephew on 22 October, 'seems to be going on charmingly on Skye. By deliberate pressure such as you have used . . . you will get them under surely enough'.[30] As a solution for the desperate Highland poverty, Balfour, as at Strathconan, recommended emigration and took steps to encourage this. Here, as in other ways, he was being well prepared for the Irish office.

Balfour had shown his strength. In November, Salisbury recognized this by appointing him to the cabinet, informing his nephew that 'the announcement was very cordially received'.[31] Balfour reacted with typical nonchalance, telling Lady Frances on 17 November 'I forgot to say what will probably interest you (though not me) – that I am in the cabinet – I like it, but am provoked with myself for not liking it more. Am just off to dine with Randolph.'[32]

To his uncle he was more sanguine. 'If I am able', Balfour wrote, 'to be any use in the House it can only be as a Cabinet Minister – no other can be asked without a slur on the Cabinet to take part in General Debate. And also, it may be, that I shall prove of some use as a counterpoise, even though a feeble one, to Randolph.'[33] Salisbury must have appreciated the reference to Churchill. Lord Randolph, now Chancellor of the Exchequer and leader in the Commons, was an erratic colleague, yet seemed indispensable to the government. In the election, his playing of the Ulster card had caught the popular imagination and many regarded him as the apostle of a new vigorous Conservatism. Churchill was only thirty-seven; on 22 December he suddenly resigned from the cabinet, protesting against the objection to his proposed cuts in defence expenditure.

On the same day, Balfour wrote to Salisbury to say that he had long considered Churchill's departure inevitable and had only 'hoped it would occur before we were committed to principles we disapproved of'.[34] W. H. Smith at the War Office told Balfour of Churchill's attempt to cajole him into revising his budget estimates downwards and the impossibility of working with Lord Randolph for 'he must be Chief Supreme' and 'cannot follow'.[35] The government was in grave danger. Chamberlain, an admirer of Churchill, began abortive discussions with Gladstone for a re-unification of the old Liberal party and there were ominous rumblings among the Conservative rank and file. Yet Salisbury survived, appointing the Liberal Unionist Goschen to the Exchequer and W. H. Smith to the leadership in the Commons.

Balfour continued at the Scottish office. The land war was in a temporary lull. 'I must confess', Sheriff Ivory, the senior Inverness law officer, wrote from Skye on 30 December, 'that I did not expect that the agitation would collapse as soon', and went on to attribute the present calm 'entirely to your sagacity in discerning the true remedy, to your exertions in providing all necessary means of applying it and above all the courage and firmness with which you carried it out'. Already rumours were circulating of Balfour's possible advancement. 'I hope', declared Ivory, 'you are not going to leave us for a higher sphere of usefulness either in Ireland or elsewhere. But wherever you go I shall take the greatest interest in watching the career of a Scotsman in whom we may all be proud.'[36] The agrarian troubles in Scotland were, in fact, far from over, but Balfour was to have no more part in them. In March 1887, he was appointed Chief Secretary for Ireland, possibly the most demanding post in the government.

6

'Bloody Balfour'

In December 1886, after Churchill's departure, Balfour was not expecting the government to last long and told Salisbury that, even if it did, he thought Sir Michael Hicks-Beach could not 'be spared from Ireland'.[1] This was strange thinking; Hicks-Beach had not been a success at the Irish Office, partly because he could never wholly suppress a grudging sympathy with Irish grievances, shared by his Under-Secretary, General Sir Redvers Buller. Their policy was necessarily, if reluctantly, harsh. The Tories, after Gladstone's conversion to Home Rule, swung away from conciliation, and the Irish Office prepared a new coercion bill. The ambivalence of its authors was shown when Buller told the Cowper Commission, set up to inquire into the land question, that bad landlords ought to be coerced as firmly as bad tenants.

In the winter of 1886 fresh agitation began in Ireland, sparked off by a new wave of brutal evictions on the notorious Clanricarde estates in Galway. Parnell, his attention increasingly occupied with Mrs. O'Shea, wife of one of his parliamentary colleagues, stayed aloof, fearing a popular reaction against Home Rule. The leaders now were two other members of the Irish Party, John Dillon and William O'Brien. The plan was to offer a supposedly reasonable reduction in the full rent to the landlord. If this was refused the money was paid to the Irish National league, successor to Parnell's old Land League. In October 1886 details of this Plan of Campaign (as it became known) were published in the nationalist newspaper *United Ireland* and the situation in the countryside rapidly deteriorated. 'I honestly think', Buller wrote to Hicks-Beach, 'that matters are getting serious. If Paddy once

gets regularly to no rent you will require to kill a good many
before you get him back again.'[2]

Buller advised simultaneous severity and conciliation. Salisbury disagreed. 'I agree with Buller', the Prime Minister told
Beach, 'as you cannot govern the Irish, or anybody else, by
severity alone; but I think he's fundamentally wrong in believing
that conciliation and severity must go together. The severity
must come first. They must "take a licking" before conciliation
will do them any good.'[3] Beach was unable personally to put this
to the test. In March his doctors warned him that on account of
general exhaustion and cataracts in his eyes he must give up the
Irish Office. Of the Cabinet, Smith, Goschen and Cranbrook
agreed to Balfour's appointment before Salisbury even consulted
his nephew.

Beach was doubtful. He warned Salisbury that 'physique is, in
this office, quite as important as ability'[4] and wondered if Balfour
was strong enough for the post. Balfour, who himself shared these
doubts, therefore underwent a full medical check-up. He was told
by Sir William Jenner, his doctor, that 'you are a sound man –
one whose life, in insurance office language, is a first class life'.[5]
There was another precautionary task to be performed. In the
course of the past year Balfour's relationship with Mary Elcho had
gradually deepened, leading, in the first months of 1887, to what
she later remembered as 'a small very private and personal incident
(gear changing!)' in 'your downstairs room at 4 Carlton Gardens
(you were reading Rider Haggard's *She*—me 25, you 31)'.[6]
Whatever that incident may have been, by March Balfour was
writing to Lady Frances, his sister-in-law, with instructions about
what to do with a leather pouch which accompanied his letter.

'My dear Frances,[7]

Accidents have occurred to a Chief Secretary for Ireland and
(although I think it improbable) they may occur again. If the worst
(as people euphemistically say!) should happen, cut open with
your penknife the accompanying pouch and read the scrawl inside.
It relates to a matter with which only you can deal – but leaves
unsaid through want of time all the things I would have said to you
and all the other dear ones whom (in the highly improbable event
above alluded to) I should leave behind.
I do not at all feel in the situation of a soldier going on a forlorn
hope: but one cannot be sure in this weary world of *anything* – not
even the competence of the police force.'

The pouch contained the following note:

'My dear Frances,

I write this in a great hurry: but as you will only have to read it in the event of my death you will forgive my handwriting. I think you and all whom I love will be sorry that I am not any longer with you. But you will be able to talk it freely over with each other and all whom such an event may concern. There is however one who will not be in this position. I want you to give her as from yourself this little brooch which you will find herewith: and to tell her that, at the end, if I was able to think at all, I thought of her. If I was the means of introducing any unhappiness into her life I hope God will forgive me. I know she will.

I think I have made arrangements by which all letters will be burnt which ought to be: but I am in such a hurry that omissions may have occurred.

Warn anyone who looks over my correspondence.

God bless you.'

In April 1930, after Balfour's death, Frances Balfour brought the letter and pouch to Mary Elcho, now Countess of Wemyss. Together they opened the pouch and found the note, with a small diamond brooch: communications from another world.

Balfour's appointment was greeted with delight by the Nationalists, who knew only his effete appearance and lackadaisical manner. The Scottish Office had given him little chance to make a parliamentary reputation and, at this stage, the mask was known better than the man. 'On the whole,' wrote T. P. O'Connor, a member of the Irish Parliamentary Party, 'the impression he would give to a stranger, who saw him for the first time and did not know him, would be that he was a more than usually mild member of the mild race of curates';[8] and another Parnellite remarked, 'We have killed Forster, blinded Beach and smashed up Trevelyan; what shall we not do with this weakling?'[9] The Irish were particularly pleased to have broken Hicks-Beach, regarded as one of the most combative and forceful front bench Tories. Balfour, however, did not count himself amongst Sir Michael's admirers, observing in connection with Beach's celebrated temper that he had 'the manners of a pirate and the courage of a governess'.[10] Over Ireland, the new Chief Secretary believed his predecessor had been too indecisive, too reliant on his permanent officials, or 'always he would and he wouldn't'.[11]

At first it looked as if Salisbury had made an appalling mistake. On 29 March, introducing the Crimes Bill into the House of Commons, Balfour fumbled badly and was constantly barracked by the Irish. He had been up until three the night before, called back to the House early the next morning and then, later in the day, had to deal with a tremendous barrage of interruptions in his introductory speech. Fatigue, coupled with too deferential treatment of the heckling, caused the failure; but Balfour was not downcast. 'I got my cases a little mixed,' he told his sister Lady Rayleigh, 'and the effect of my speech was spoilt by the howls of the Irish, and they [the Conservatives] begin to call out "our man has failed!" '[12] Lord Randolph Churchill told Beach that his successor had 'made a terrible fiasco . . . want of knowledge, the most elementary want of tact and judgment coupled with an excited manner and a raised voice. Of course the Irish interrupted brutally and he was quite unable to cope with them.'[13]

The Crimes Bill did not become law until July. In the course of its stormy passage through the House of Commons Balfour made his parliamentary reputation. His skill at fending off Irish taunts at Question Time delighted his party, soon eradicating the memory of that first failure. The new Chief Secretary developed an artfully nonchalant style; his exaggerated use of a pince-nez, his sprawling etiolated figure draped seemingly inattentively over the front bench during Irish tirades, infuriated his opponents and amused his friends. 'He has one qualification for being Irish Secretary,' Salisbury told Lady Rayleigh, 'which is absolutely unique – his perfect indifference to what is said of him.'[14] Now, met with their gravest challenge yet, Balfour's formidable powers came into their own.

Balfour, of course, did not work alone. At the Irish Office, and in Ireland at Dublin Castle, he had a team of permanent officials and temporary advisers. Supreme among these was his technical superior, the Vicerory Lord Londonderry, once his fag at Eton. Londonderry was a rich landowner, dutiful but unintelligent, given to outbursts of pomposity. In February 1887, with the Plan of Campaign causing widespread disorder, his contribution was to inform Salisbury of the gratifying increase in society attendance at the Viceroy's levees. Balfour had little respect for Londonderry, forgetting to inform him of his proposed land legislation which was to accompany the Crimes Bill so that the Viceroy's first knowledge of this came from the Irish newspapers. The Chief Secretary's senior civil servant, or Under Secretary, was very different. General Sir Redvers Buller was a distinguished soldier, on loan from the Army to the Irish Office, who well understood the complexities of Irish government yet was associated with the failures of the past and doubted the wisdom of unbridled coercion. However he came to admire Balfour and was delighted when, after a first visit to Dublin at the beginning of March, the Chief Secretary backed the decision of Captain Plunkett, Divisional Magistrate for Cork District, to tell the police to fire on a rioting crowd in Youghal. 'You have', Buller wrote on 16 March, 'earned the gratitude of every Irishman I have spoken to by your reply about Plunkett; it is that sort of support Irish officials have so long needed.'[15]

Balfour further angered the Nationalists by appointing Colonel King-Harman, a rich landowner and former member of Isaac Butt's Home Rule party, as his Parliamentary Under-Secretary. Buller, who had known King-Harman at Eton, intensely disliked the Colonel, calling him 'bullying' and 'domineering', informing Balfour in April that King-Harman was 'quite impossible for me to work cordially with'.[16] They were not to have to endure each other for long. In August Buller was replaced and in June 1888 King-Harman suddenly broke down and resigned, dying soon after: another casualty of Irish government.

None of these officials were on close personal terms with Balfour; but when he asked George Wyndham, twenty-four-year-old younger brother of Mary Elcho, to act as his Private Secretary, the personal and the professional were united. Balfour, through his friendship with the Wyndhams, knew George well and was aware of his political ambitions. Yet politics were not Wyndham's only interest. He had served in the Coldstream Guards in Egypt and wrote verse, representing with his flamboyant good looks, love of sport and devotion to literature a conjunction of the physical and the poetic which particularly appealed to late Victorian sentiment. Wyndham, unlike Balfour, was sentimental. His romantic obsession with feeling and tradition, his inability to distinguish between the general and the particular, eventually ruined his career. In 1887, however, he was young, eager to do anything that might please his new master: a congenial companion amid the chores of office.

The 1887 session was a hard one for Balfour. The Irish legislation was opposed at every step, but he seemed almost to enjoy the fray. 'I had the luck', he later told Mrs Dugdale, 'to do it all myself. There was literally no one to help me. Night after night I had to stand up in the House and defend myself to that raging lot opposite, and no one had a word to say for me. Old W. H. Smith would put in some generalities occasionally, but nobody knew the facts but me'.[17] By 15 September, when Parliament was at last prorogued, the Crimes Act and further land legislation, after use of the parliamentary guillotine, were at last on the Statute Book, and the National League was declared a 'proclaimed' or illegal organization. 'I congratulate you heartily on the close of the session,' wrote Salisbury, 'which must have been tiring enough but in which you have enormously added to your reputation.'[18]

The Crimes Act was a strong measure. Courts of summary jurisdiction were to be used for the prosecution of certain offences, among them boycotting, conspiracy to withhold rent, illegal gatherings and intimidation. Cases involving trial by jury could now be moved from one district to another to avoid prejudiced verdicts; the Lord Lieutenant was given the power to 'proclaim' those parts of the country which were to be governed under the terms of the act, and certain assemblies were declared unlawful. The first real challenge to the act came in the early autumn when, on 9 September, the National League called a meeting at Mitchelstown in County Tipperary to protest against the trial of William O'Brien, the Irish Nationalist M.P., which was taking place in the town. O'Brien was charged with inciting resistance to the proposed evictions on Lady Kingston's estate at Mitchelstown; Dillon and Henry Labouchere, the English radical, came, together with several other members of parliament, to protest against this. A riot erupted in which the vastly outnumbered police opened fire on the crowd, killing three men and wounding more. Liberals and Nationalists united to condemn the killings.

In Parliament there was an outcry. Balfour would not give an inch. Labouchere, supported by the Liberal front bench, launched an impassioned attack on the Chief Secretary although the opposition moved no vote of censure against the government. Balfour instituted an inquiry into the débâcle but quashed the verdict of wilful murder passed against the police by the local coroner's jury. He knew the affair had been badly mishandled by the authorities and that the police had panicked, yet officially he admitted no error. Carson, who was at this time embarking on his career as a young government prosecutor in Ireland, later told Mrs Dugdale: 'It was Mitchelstown that made us certain we had a man at last.'[19]

The Crimes Act alone was not enough. Balfour realized that he must invigorate his permanent staff, demoralized by the equivocations of the past, into determined application of its principles. 'You have', Salisbury told his nephew in October, 'the stupidest lot of lawyers in Ireland any government was ever cursed with.'[20] The Chief Secretary rectified this by appointing Peter O'Brien, later known as 'Peter the Packer' for his ability to 'pack' juries for the government, as Irish Attorney-General in the place of the ineffective Gibson and using Carson, whose skill he immediately appreciated, as one of the Crown's most ubiquitous prosecutors. 'I made Carson', Balfour told his niece, 'and Carson made me.'[21] In October Sir Redvers Buller departed for the War Office, to be succeeded by Sir Joseph West Ridgeway, a competent Indian civil servant committed to coercion. 'Buller', Salisbury told Balfour, 'had reached that pitch of eminence at which men become indocile.'[22] By November Ridgeway was writing: 'I do not like to be too sanguine but I really believe that we are steadily winning.'[23]

George Wyndham played his part in all this. One of his jobs was to answer criticisms in the Press; another less onerous task was conversing with the Chief Secretary, taking the latter's mind off affairs of state. 'Arthur and I', Wyndham told his wife in January 1888, 'have had an interesting talk about Shakespeare, Shelley, the story of Hero and Leander, the difference of accent, quantity and numbering of syllables in the English, Latin and

French poetry; politics, principles, warfare, etc.'[24] Wyndham usually travelled with Balfour and was almost always within sight of his master. The Irish officials in Dublin were denied this privilege. Through most of the summer of 1887 Balfour was kept in London by the parliamentary session and in September, when it ended, chose to go to Whittingehame to rest rather than to Ireland. Finally, in early October, he left for Dublin after criticism of his prolonged absence, Lady Frances, for one, believing he should have gone earlier, telling her brother-in-law Gerald Balfour: 'I am just a trifle afraid that his great success hitherto is putting him a little off his guard.'[25]

In Ireland the major part of the south and west were now under the jurisdiction of the Crimes Act and prosecutions were proceeding apace. Balfour had the immense benefit of knowing he had the full support of the cabinet and Prime Minister. Where support was not forthcoming, however, was from the one class who perhaps stood to gain most from the return to law and order: the Irish landlords. Balfour became furious at their vacillation and incompetence. He also had no doubt of the frequent justness of tenant discontent and brought in land legislation at the same time as the Crimes Act, giving tenants right of appeal to County Court judges in the case of eviction and a loosening of landlords' security. Lord Salisbury once observed 'how Arthur hates the Irish landlords'.[26]

Balfour objected to both the landlords' immoderate attitude in demanding evictions and their inability to combine in any coherent way against the plan of campaign. In Cork Sir Arthur Smith-Barry formed a local landlord defence organization against the Nationalist boycotting and intimidation. His success demonstrated what might be achieved on a larger scale but Irish landowners were too disparate and ill-organized to make such a combination easy. The most difficult for the government to deal with was the Marquis of Clanricarde, an eccentric who lived in Albany, never visiting his vast properties in Galway, demanding reductions in rent from his London landlord while instructing his agents to pursue a policy of brutal eviction and rack renting. His estates at Woodford and Portumna were in a state of permanent uproar and his representatives in constant fear for their lives, the assassination of one leading the Marquess to send the message to his tenants: 'If you think you can intimidate me by shooting my agent, you are mistaken.'[27]

This chaos provided a perfect hunting ground for English Home Rule sympathizers, and it was to Woodford in October that Wilfrid Scawen Blunt, the poet and political activist, came to agitate on behalf of the Nationalists. After addressing a 'proclaimed' meeting, he was arrested and imprisoned in Galway Jail. Blunt, a cousin of the Wyndhams, knew Balfour who described him to Lady Elcho in October as 'a goodish poet, a goodish lawn tennis player and a goodish fellow'.[28] He was determined to make some gesture on behalf of his cause and by quoting from a conversation he had had with Balfour at the Wyndham's home at Clouds in September hoped to embarrass the Chief Secretary.

Blunt's report of the Clouds gathering shows Arthur Balfour at his least sympathetic. Just as he had mastered a pose in the House of Commons to infuriate and quell his Irish opponents, so Balfour came to develop a social manner of exaggerated cynical languor, encouraged perhaps by the fawning delight with which his heartless quips were often received. At dinner at Clouds, John Dillon, whom Blunt knew, was discussed and Balfour observed, in connection with Dillon's poor health: 'I am sorry for Dillon as if he gets into prison it is likely to kill him. He will have hard labour, and it will be a different thing from Forster's ridiculous imprisonments at Kilmainham. There is something almost interesting about Dillon; but it is a pity he lies so.'[29] During the course of his visit Balfour remarked that there was no more vain or foolish feeling than remorse. Now, by announcing to the Press that as a result of the conversations at Clouds he believed that it was the Chief Secretary's intention that Irish agitators should die in jail, Blunt tried to demonstrate the cruelty of the Conservative Irish government, even declaring that he himself felt unsafe 'in Mr Balfour's hands'.[30]

George Wyndham was embarrassed by his cousin's activities. 'It must be admitted', Balfour told Lady Elcho, 'that there is a certain awkwardness in George's position',[31] but the charges, which the Chief Secretary immediately denied, made little impression on the public. There was something theatrical about Blunt and often more than a touch of personal vanity in his flamboyant Byronic espousal of political causes. From prison he stood as a Liberal candidate in the Deptford by-election in January 1888 and lost. Balfour bore no grudges against his would-be tormentor. In 1889 the two of them were brought together again at dinner by George Wyndham, and Blunt, who had once petitioned the Chief Secretary from Galway Jail for permission to wear his own overcoat, was charmed when Balfour, at the end of the evening, borrowed a similar garment from his old prisoner as protection against the cold night air.

The Crimes Act steadily tightened its grip on Ireland. By August 1888 some twenty-one Irish Nationalist members of parliament had been given prison sentences although, as Ridgeway informed Balfour in February 1888, during the five and a half months succeeding the passing of Gladstone's Coercion Act of 1882 1114 people had been prosecuted under its provisions, as against 659 in the corresponding period following the present legislation. The Chief Secretary was amused by the abuse which was constantly heaped upon his head. 'Greetings,' he wrote to Lady Elcho on Christmas Eve 1887, 'from Bloody Balfour' and in encouraging her to come across to Dublin warned 'there is absolutely nothing to do for those who are not occupied in torturing innocent persons in prison'.[32] William O'Brien called Balfour 'a perfumed Captain Moonlight' and Gladstone, when speaking of Irish matters often cryptically observed 'Remember Mitchelstown'. Balfour, however, pushed forward, taking Salisbury's advice of October that 'the only course is to go on "pegging away". You will soon by experience learn the precise limit of your powers, and then within those limits you will be able without ever, or often, incurring a defeat, to inflict an intolerable amount of annoyance.'[33]

Salisbury cautioned Balfour at the end of 1887 about the inadvisability of prosecuting newspapers and, more particularly, newsvendors, who published details of proclaimed meetings. The Prime Minister doubted if English public opinion would stand this but one weapon the government were not afraid to make use of was religion. In 1887 a Roman Catholic mission went to Rome under the Duke of Norfolk and, as a consequence of this, after sending his personal emissary to Ireland, Pope Leo XIII issued a Papal rescript condemning boycotting and the plan of campaign. The effects of this were limited; most of the Irish bishops, led by the Nationalist Archbishop Walsh of Dublin, ignored it and Parnell, a Protestant, dismissed the rescript as 'a document from a distant country'.

Parnell had taken little part in the Irish debates of the summer of 1887. His health was poor and the fatal involvement with Mrs O'Shea seemed to take up more and more of his time. In the spring of 1888 he emerged at last from the shadows to demand a select committee to examine the evidence produced by *The Times* in 1887 linking his name with the Phoenix Park murders.

The story of Parnell's tumultuous last years is almost too celebrated to need retelling. The Irish leader's demand came as a result of a libel action brought against *The Times* by F. H. O'Donnell, a former supporter, which O'Donnell had lost after the newspaper had produced a further batch of letters incriminating Parnell. Salisbury refused a select committee but agreed to a special commission of three judges to carry out a more general investigation into the links between the Irish Parliamentary Party and Irish crime. The Nationalists and Home Rulers saw this as a poor alternative; certain Liberal Unionists, among them Hartington, warned the government of the dangers inherent in such a broad public inquiry and Lord Randolph Churchill told W. H. Smith that 'prudent politicians would hesitate to go out of their way to play such high stakes as these'.[34] In September preliminary hearings for the great investigation began.

Balfour was doubtful from the start, realizing the immense damage that could be done if *The Times*'s case collapsed. The government, however, was now inextricably linked to the fortunes of the newspaper; Sir Richard Webster, the Attorney-General, who had acted as counsel for *The Times* against O'Donnell, was forced, against his will, by Salisbury to represent the paper again. The Irish Office gave help to *The Times*, Ridgeway telling Balfour in November after a visit to Dublin by the newspaper's solicitor, that 'the result is to make *The Times*'s case quite safe in the coming action, and . . . to break Parnell's reputation. . . . Altogether the case looks very promising.'[35] Then, in December, the Under Secretary discovered that the letters on which *The Times*'s case was founded had been sold to the newspaper by Richard Pigott, a hack journalist, blackmailer and pornographer, who was known to have an all-consuming hatred of Parnell and his party.

Ridgeway told Balfour that Parnell's counsel should have little difficulty in showing these letters to be forgeries. Balfour informed the cabinet, but the proceedings dragged on, culminating, in February 1889, in Pigott's collapse in the witness box under the relentless cross-examination of Parnell's counsel, Sir Charles Russell. The forger fled to Madrid where he committed suicide in a hotel. *The Times*'s case folded, Parnell became a national hero, entering the House of Commons on March 1 to a standing ovation from the opposition benches, receiving the Freedom of Edinburgh and paying a well-publicised visit to Gladstone at Hawarden. Years later Balfour defended the special commission to Mrs Dugdale on the grounds that it had revealed 'the whole truth about Ireland'[36] and Irish crime, yet the Pigott revelations were the part which caught the popular imagination. The government were defeated in by-elections and a drift of public opinion towards Home Rule began to manifest itself. Then in December 1889 Captain O'Shea wrote to Balfour to announce that he had filed a petition for divorce against his wife, naming Parnell as the co-respondent.

Balfour refused to become involved in Parnell's private life. He wrote a cool answer to O'Shea, yet clearly realized the immense political implications for the Unionists. Henceforth the fall was inevitable. On 17 November 1890 a divorce was granted to the Captain who had known for years of his wife's adultery but, hopeful of a legacy from Mrs O'Shea's rich aunt and political advancement, had previously accepted it. Now, with the legacy out of reach (the aunt had left her fortune to Mrs O'Shea alone) and possibly with the encouragement of Joseph Chamberlain, O'Shea saw no advantage in persisting with the old arrangements. Indeed a divorce, with himself as the innocent party, might assist his attempts to contest the aunt's will.

The rest of the story is well known. Gladstone's disowning of Parnell after non-conformist pressure; the condemnation of Parnell by the Irish bishops; his candidate's defeat in the Kilkenny by-election following the Irish Party's jettisoning of him as their leader; the emergence of Dillon and O'Brien as anti-

Parnellites and further by-election humiliations, followed in September 1891 by the collapse of his health after addressing outdoor meetings in the rain and his eventual death in October after returning to Brighton to be with Mrs O'Shea whom he had married in June. His burial, at Glasnevin Cemetery in Dublin, was shunned by the priests, yet special trains from all over Ireland brought over one hundred thousand people to participate in the funeral procession. 'I had expected', Ridgeway told Balfour, 'nothing so dignified or genuine.'[37]

After the fall of Parnell, the Irish Party degenerated into factionalism. Balfour had fuelled the flames of the feud by persuading Unionists either to abstain from voting in by-elections or support a candidate whose victory would, 'do least benefit to the party of separation'.[38] Meanwhile the constructive side of his Irish policy had been gaining force. The Chief Secretary had always believed that coercion alone was not enough. In January 1890 the Crimes Act was lifted from much of Ireland, Balfour having informed Salisbury in November 1899 that 'crime was lower, I believe, during October than in any month since 1879. May it last!'[39]

Several of the proposed remedial measures were to be doomed, including the plan for a Roman Catholic university and legislation to coerce the landlords into reasonableness; others were successful. In 1890 the potato crop failed after a disastrously wet summer and Balfour instituted a programme of public works and relief grants, also buying up large quantities of seed potatoes for distribution to the afflicted areas. In 1889 bills were introduced to provide funds for the drainage of rivers and a light railway to the impoverished west. In 1890 the Congested Districts Board was created to assist agriculture and development in the same region and in 1891 a land act to encourage land purchase made £33,000,000 available as a guarantee for the required loans to tenants. Balfour was proud of the Unionist record in Ireland. 'What was the Ireland the Free State took over?' he asked his niece in 1928. 'It was the Ireland that we made.'[40]

The even tenor of Balfour's life had been changed by his Irish appointment. First, there were the detectives who constantly followed him and the loaded revolver he carried in case of attack.

In fact the only incident involving the bodyguards was when their jaunting car in which they were shadowing the Chief Secretary ran into the back of his brougham in Dublin; the revolver was never needed. Then there were the social functions in Dublin. 'Consider', he wrote to Lady Elcho in 1889, 'the horror of driving three miles out to Phoenix Park [the Chief Secretary's lodge] to dress for dinner; then three miles back again to dine with the Attorney General; to sit at dinner from 8.15 to 11.25; sit for that period between Princess Edward of Saxe-Weimar who is intolerable when sober and still more intolerable when drunk; and Lady Ashbourne who is only saved from a similar condemnation by her excessive and almost preternatural ill-nature; and then to drive three miles back again to bed! This is what in Dublin we call pleasure!'[41]

For relaxation there was golf and tennis, played usually with either George Wyndham or Hayes Fisher, the successor to Colonel King-Harman. Balfour still cared for his health, telling Lady Frances from Dublin in 1888 'I am taking much care of myself, golf or real tennis 12 to 2, the Castle 2 to 7. The work that does not get done in the five hours remains undone: for I positively decline to take anything home.'[42] One of the difficulties of the job was the two centres of operation, Dublin Castle and the Irish Office in Queen Street in London, and Balfour was often forced to travel between these, his congenital seasickness making the crossing a special burden. Occasionally, there were Nationalist Members of Parliament on the boat and the Chief Secretary might find himself cheek by jowl with Dillon or O'Brien.

In October 1890, Balfour decided to venture further into his territory, breaking all precedents by undertaking a tour of the impoverished districts of the west, taking his sister Alice, Ridgeway and George Wyndham along with him. At first he had been reluctant to make such a trip, believing it would only encourage the thought that 'public money was to be squandered like water on every kind of jobbery', but Hartington told Salisbury the journey was necessary for 'if anything should go wrong there will be a terrible outcry about his absence'.[43] They visited Mayo, Galway, Connemara and other distressed areas and were greeted with enthusiasm, even the nationalist priests joining in the welcome. The detectives had been left behind and the only moments of embarrassment came when Balfour caught his thumb in the window of one of the inns where they stayed and 'Pongo' NcNeill, Nationalist M.P. for Donegal, attacked him in that county for his policy of coercion. McNeill called Balfour a 'spiteful tyrant' yet, as Wyndham wrote to his sister, 'the spiteful tyrant – held a crowded meeting in the schoolhouse, spoke for twenty minutes amid loud and prolonged cheers which fairly blew the roof off when he announced the railway was given for nothing'.[44]

The Irish Office made Balfour's reputation. A transformation had taken place, perhaps attributable first to his knowledge that he had, as Chief Secretary, the unstinting and absolute support of the Prime Minister; his extraordinary intimacy with Salisbury, their close family ties and the easy access to his uncle at all times made this certain. Here, of course, he was remarkably lucky. Few public figures have enjoyed such a relationship with their superiors, few been given such a series of chances to prove themselves. Initial failure would have proved fatal for others, but Salisbury's faith in his nephew, gained through their early close association, survived.

Once installed at the Irish Office, the task immediately appealed to him. He knew the Prime Minister's wishes and could proceed, unencumbered by remorse or doubt, with coercion, aware that the cabinet's course was certain. In addition, his own beliefs were exactly suited to the fight against Irish chaos. Always fearful of anarchy, conscious of the thin line of authority which he believed divided civilization from barbarism, Balfour undertook what he saw as a civilizing mission in Ireland. 'To allow the latter to win', he wrote of the Parnellites in 1888, 'is simply to give up civilization'.[45] Here again Salisbury and he were at one. In 1888 Balfour told Lady Rayleigh that his life was 'A very happy one',[46] indeed that he knew of few people happier. At the Irish Office, as the defender of authority and what he believed to be reason, Arthur Balfour felt sure of both himself and his purpose. In fact the partial return to order proved temporary and the Unionist ideal of simultaneous application of coercion and conciliation failed utterly to take into account the emotive appeal of Irish nationalism. Economic improvement and firm law enforcement were not enough for Ireland; Balfour's connection with the country that had hastened his political advancement was not ended by his appointment to the leadership of the House in succession to W. H. Smith in October 1891.

7

The New Leader

From Dublin, in October 1891, Balfour told his colleague Goschen that he did not like leaving Ireland for 'there have grown up ties with the grim old castle, and this beastly town, which it is painful to sever'. There were other reasons for regret which have a contemporary ring. 'I have never before,' he continued, 'so clearly understood how much more important in the eyes of ordinary men are nominal differences than real ones; how indifferent they are to substantial agreement if only the catchwords are not identical.'[1]

His accession to the leadership of the House of Commons had been the subject of speculation for some months. W. H. Smith suffered from poor health and as early as November 1888, Balfour, ill with a severe cold, drafted a letter to Salisbury about Smith's possible successor. He mentioned two names, his own and Goschen's, then immediately ruled himself out because Goschen (Chancellor of the Exchequer and a Liberal Unionist) would probably not consent to serve under someone who was not even in parliament when he was first a cabinet minister. Yet Goschen hardly seemed a satisfactory choice either; he still did not call himself a Conservative, had not joined the Carlton and possessed irritating mannerisms which 'have driven Smith mad'.

Balfour went on to propose the idea of coalition with the Liberal Unionists, introducing Lord Hartington as a possible leader of the Commons and Sir Henry James as Home Secretary. The objections, as Balfour noticed, were obvious; possible losses in two pending northern by-elections; appointments given to other Liberal Unionists; two new members of the cabinet, one of whom 'always recommends standing still, and the other of whom

always recommends running away'; the probable return of
Chamberlain and his supporters to radicalism if deserted by
Hartington and others; the likelihood of Hartington's father's
(the Duke of Devonshire) death, and Hartington's elevation to
the Lords; and finally 'a Cavendish leading the Conservatives!'[2]
These could be weighed against such possible advantages as the
gaining of Liberal Unionist votes, a leader as respected in the
country as Hartington undoubtedly was, and help in obtaining
easier majorities in the House of Commons.

The letter was never sent, yet is important. At its end, the
reader is left thinking that the least complicated course for
Salisbury to follow would be to appoint his nephew leader. It was
written in November 1888, during the exhilaration of his first
two years in the Irish Office. Balfour had already shown himself
to be a resourceful and effective parliamentarian. In addition he
was the member of the cabinet with whom his chief felt most at
ease, whose intellectual approach he could share and appreciate,
whose assumptions, humour and sympathies Salisbury most
easily comprehended.

With Ireland, Salisbury saw with delight his nephew prove
his full worth to an enthusiastic public. 'I always knew', he told
Lady Rayleigh, 'that he had the qualification for an Irish
Secretary if only he could be got to take enough interest in the
work to do it thoroughly. We first tried him at the Local Government Board but he was so hopelessly bored that it was no use
thinking of that again. Then we tried the Secretaryship for
Scotland where he was a little less bored, but he has never been
really interested till now.'[3] Lady Frances Balfour, at Hatfield during the winter of 1887, observed her brother-in-law arriving late
at dinner to the cheers of his cousins. She also caught sight of 'the
Prime Minister's face, and its immobility was lighted as it rarely
was, by a look of radiant pride and complete confidence'.[4] It is
scarcely surprising that, amidst such an atmosphere, Balfour was
tempted to offer confident thoughts on the leadership in 1888.

"You will be truthful', a friend said to Lady Frances Balfour,
'and say that Arthur was the most ambitious of men.' Lady
Frances denied this, declaring that 'Arthur's opportunities were
all made for him', yet admitted that he 'liked to excel'.[5] Balfour
was often to be accused of ambition. Equally he himself propa-

gated the notion that he did not really care about politics, never read the newspapers and was bewilderingly ignorant about the press's opinion of himself and his party. In September 1893, he asked his sister, Lady Rayleigh, what the papers had said about a parliamentary debate of the night before. She replied, 'I can't tell you for you have none in your house'. He then admitted 'that he had not looked at a paper for weeks, never read them, knew he ought to, Buckle of *The Times* often scolded him for it'.

On the same day, they discussed his life as a politician and 'how it afforded him little time for philosophy. 'He remarked', Lady Rayleigh recorded, 'that his mind did not naturally run to politics, he never thought about them in bed which was the test. He regarded them with calm interest, but as for getting excited over them as some people did, he could not do it,' although Goschen and Chamberlain, he knew, 'thought of nothing else'.[6] Such detachment was to be both a strength and a weakness in the future; in any case this is not the whole story, for when Balfour's interest was aroused, as over defence, the trans-Atlantic alliance and Ireland, he worked tenaciously to achieve his desired result. Mary Gladstone believed his dislike of newspapers sprang from his fear of reading tragedy in their pages; his secretaries, however, had instructions to keep him in touch with press opinion. To John Morley he once observed: 'When I am in politics I long to be in literature and vice versa.'[7] The truth was that he needed both and the contrast offered by each perfectly suited the two sides of his temperament, the active and the contemplative.

Balfour's ambition never took the fierce, dynamic, self-advertising form of Joseph Chamberlain or, later, Winston Churchill. Lady Frances Balfour is correct in saying that all his early opportunities were made for him; however, these led to the discovery of certain courses open to humanity and his country, and his own power to influence, even determine, which of these courses were followed. Balfour was no rash idealist, yet, like Lord Salisbury, he possessed a certain vision of the State. This was a conservative vision, less pessimistic than that of his uncle, but also concerned with authority, hierarchy and the imminent danger of anarchic barbarism. His ambition, such as it was, stemmed less from a personal delight in power or acclaim, more

from a reasoned idea of power's possibilities and his own undoubted ability to utilize these for his own ideals. Allied to this
was the aristocratic notion of public duty, once used by the
Salisburys to persuade him to cease the aimless existence of his
early twenties and enter politics.

By 1891, Salisbury's faith had been fully justified. Balfour's
early allies, beside whom at one time he had seemed tentative and
cautious, had been left behind. In 1891, before Smith's death,
Hartington had come to Balfour to say that obviously the present
leader of the House could, for health reasons, not last much
longer; might Lord Salisbury consider promoting Lord Randolph
Churchill who 'evidently both desired and expected it?' Balfour
replied that his uncle had no intentions in this direction, remarking that the Tories could not serve under Churchill or Hicks-
Beach, and 'all we could do was to pray for a continuation of the
present regime'.[8] In 1891, Beach forestalled any difficulties by
making it known that he was not to be considered for the position
which he had held before. Leaving Smith's funeral with Lord
George Hamilton, he remarked: 'There is, under existing conditions, only one candidate for poor Smith's post; the party will
have no one but Balfour.'[9] Churchill had distanced himself from
Salisbury's government, attacking ministers over Irish coercion
and the Parnell commission; in any case, it was inconceivable
that Salisbury should again become involved with so unpredictable an ally.

'So Arthur Balfour is leader', Lord Randolph wrote in 1891,
'and Tory Democracy, the genuine article, at an end.'[10] The old
camaraderie of the Fourth Party days was over. In November
1891 Churchill wrote to his old friend, asking to be made
Ambassador in Paris, announcing he 'would obey all instructions' for it was 'the one thing I have longed for for years'.[11] The
embassy went to Lord Dufferin. In January 1895 Churchill died,
a victim of the terrible disease which had made his last ap-
pearances in the House of Commons embarrassing disasters. Of
the other Fourth Party members, Wolff had returned to
diplomacy, writing to Balfour, regretting his absence from
England and declaring 'What a fool I was ever to go to Egypt' but
'the wheel goes on and must crush somebody', remarking how 'at
the best times you never wrote'.[12]

Sir John Gorst, now a member of the government, could not suppress his rebellious nature. In 1891, he openly criticized certain aspects of the government's Irish policy, in particular the proposed Roman Catholic university, and Balfour exploded with anger. 'We should get rid of him', he told Salisbury, for Gorst 'is not bound by the ordinary rules of honour which regulate the relations between colleagues' and 'is irreclaimably treacherous both by temper and calculation'.[13] Salisbury chided his nephew for overestimating the importance of the affair, refusing to dismiss Gorst as 'resolute government is only possible in Ireland'.[14] The incident shows an unusual break in Balfour's studied imperturbability.

'I am at my wits' end to know what emollients to apply to Goschen,'[15] Salisbury wrote to Balfour on 14 October 1891 about the leadership of the House of Commons. Balfour agreed that 'Goschen is most unjustly treated and has good cause of complaint', but suggested Salisbury use the excuse that the Chancellor of the Exchequer was not, as yet, a formal member of the Conservative Party. 'I think', he added soothingly, 'there must be exaggeration in the estimate I have heard of his unpopularity.'[16] Next, the leader of the Liberal Unionists had to be consulted. Here there was a moment of delay, Salisbury noting dryly that 'Hartington is at Newmarket and all political arrangements have to be hung up till some quadruped has run faster than some other quadruped'.[17]

By now, the decision was in no doubt. 'All the information', Salisbury told his nephew on 16 October, 'that reaches me from every quarter shows clearly that the party and the Liberal Unionists expect you to take Smith's place. I do not think it wholly for your comfort or advantage. It will make you the target for very zealous and exacting criticism. But I do not think you can avoid it or refuse it as matters stand.'[18] Akers-Douglas, the Chief Whip, had reported the opinion of the party to Salisbury and the Irish Secretary, perhaps the most obvious parliamentary and administrative success of the government ministers, was the favourite choice. The Irish Office was taken over by W. L. Jackson, previously Financial Secretary to the Treasury, whom Balfour had, patronizingly, described to Salisbury as 'that rara avis, a successful manufacturer who is fit for something besides manufacturing'.[19]

Thus Arthur Balfour left Ireland. 'We have not heard', Ridgeway wrote on 11 November, 'when Mr Jackson comes over. I cannot yet realize that you have ceased to be my immediate chief. I regard the last three or four years as the pleasantest of the thirty years of my official life and am truly sorry that they have come to an end'. The Irish attitude was probably more mixed, but in Dublin, at a Home Rule meeting addressed by John Redmond, Balfour's name was cheered heartily and Gladstone's jeered. 'They are', Ridgeway consequently remarked to his master, 'a queer people!'[20]

'Arthur Balfour', Sir Henry Ponsonby, Queen Victoria's private secretary wrote from Balmoral to his wife on 1 September 1890, '. . . did very well here. He has an opinion of various questions and gives it – but not roughly or over-decidedly as if everyone else must be wrong but himself. Still his opinion is good and he sticks to it.'[21] As a member of the cabinet, Balfour was drawn into contact with Queen Victoria; as a successful Irish Secretary he excited her special interest, for she was a dedicated preserver of the Union.

The Queen could be intimidating to her Ministers. 'I remember', she once said to Sir Henry Campbell-Bannerman, 'Lord Melbourne using the same argument many years ago, but it was not true then and it is not true now.'[22] Bannerman afterwards remarked that he felt like a little boy talking to his grandmother. Balfour was not frightened of the Queen, simply stating his view with balance and logic, never indulging in Disraelian courtliness, maintaining his reserve. 'I think', Sir Henry Ponsonby wrote in 1891, 'the Queen likes him but is a little afraid of him',[23] and his son, Sir Frederick, her assistant private secretary, noted that Balfour 'was a great success with the Queen, although to me he never seems to treat her seriously'.[24] By 1896, she like so many others was captivated. 'I am much struck, as is everyone,' she wrote, 'by Mr Balfour's extreme fairness, impartiality, and large mindedness. He sees all sides of the question, is wonderfully generous in his feelings towards others, and very gentle and sweet tempered.'[25]

In August 1890, while staying at Balmoral, Balfour's impartiality was challenged by a royal romance. The Duke of Clarence, eldest son of the Prince of Wales and eventual heir to the throne, had fallen in love with Princess Hélène, daughter of the Comte de Paris, Pretender to the throne of France. There were obvious political objections to the proposed match; she was a Roman Catholic, and her father's status in his own country and Europe was diplomatically difficult from England's point of view.

The Duke of Clarence was, in the words of a recent royal biographer, 'dissipated and unstable'.[26] His previous romantic excursions had not met with success; Princess Alix of Hesse (later to marry the last Tsar of Russia) had refused him and he himself rejected Princess Margaret of Prussia. The young lovers told Queen Victoria that she was the first to know of the projected marriage but as Balfour reported to Salisbury 'that the Princess of Wales knows exactly what is going on I have not the least doubt'.[27] The Duke of Clarence's parents were pleased. They saw prospects of a settled domestic life for their wayward son, were fond of Hélène and, in the case of the Danish Princess of Wales, keen to avoid a German daughter-in-law. Clarence's mother had been at Mar Lodge, staying with the Duke of Fife, at the same time as the young couple earlier in August when they were first contemplating marriage; she had then driven with them to Balmoral where they were to make their appeal.

The Queen, despite Salisbury's rapidly telegraphed warnings, was moved by Clarence and Hélène's predicament. 'She insisted strongly', Balfour told his uncle on 30 August, 'on the fact that he ought to marry and that there was no one else whom he should be asked to marry or whom he would consent to marry, if asked. According to her there are but three marriageable princesses at the moment in Europe, besides the Teck girl and the Hesse girl. The Teck girl they won't have because they hate Teck and because the vision of Princess Mary haunting Marlborough House makes the Prince of Wales ill. The Hesse girl won't have him. There remain a Mecklenburgh and two Anhalt princesses (I am not sure if I have the names right). According to Her Majesty they are all three ugly, unhealthy and idiotic: – and if that be not enough they are also penniless and narrow minded! – or as she puts it German of the German! – they might do perhaps (as she said) for a younger son. . . .'[28]

The Princess of Wales pressed the matter, writing to her

mother-in-law of the 'astounding but delightful news', and the
Comtesse de Paris, a pipe-smoking devotee of field sports, cordially supported the match, seeing no objection to her daughter
giving up her religion to become the future Queen of England.
'Nothing more', Balfour told his uncle, 'in my opinion can now
be done until the Comte de Paris has been consulted.' Balfour
saw the obvious difficulties: the harshness of having to 'interrupt
the course of true love and destroy the solitary opportunity
which, for the present, the heir apparent has of marrying somebody who is not ugly, unhealthy, and stupid!; also the possibility
of a united Royal family pressing the marriage against the government's wishes'.[29] Salisbury's reservations were strong. He
believed a French girl who appeared anxious to give up her
religion for the English throne would be unpopular and the
sincerity of her conversion to Anglicanism doubted. In addition,
her parentage and nationality would cause offence in Europe with
both France and Germany. Balfour, however, thought that a long
courtship should provide adequate evidence of her feelings for
him to calm popular opinion.

Clarence, perhaps urged on by his mother, scorned the politicians' opposition, writing to the Queen, 'Forgive me, Grand-
mama, for saying that I believe in this case it is quite sufficient to
have the Sovereign's consent and that the Prime Minister need
only be told of her decision'; but noting of the Comte de Paris 'I
fear he will be very difficult to move'.[30] Here, the Duke of
Clarence was correct. Balfour told Salisbury that 'the Prince of
Wales anticipated much more serious difficulty from the father
than from us'.[31] The Comte de Paris, despite his formidable wife's
support for the young lovers, would not hear of his daughter giving up her religion and the Pope, visited by Princess Hélène in
November, was shocked by the 'iniquity'[32] of any proposed conversion. The Prince of Wales suggested that she might be able to
marry the Duke of Clarence and remain a Catholic, provided that
any children were brought up as Anglicans. This Salisbury firmly
opposed on the grounds that it would lead to popular distrust and
the consequent unpopularity of the royal family.

Eventually, the proposed match was abandoned. In December
1891, the Duke of Clarence became engaged to Princess Mary of
Teck. In January 1892, he died of pneumonia. The Princess later

married his brother, Prince George, and after the death of Edward VII became Queen Mary.

In October 1891, Lady Emily Lytton, seventeen-year-old sister of Lady Betty Balfour (Gerald Balfour's wife), and daughter of the Earl of Lytton, arrived to stay at Whittingehame. At lunch on the first day she had her initial encounter with Arthur Balfour and described to a friend her own reactions and those of the family circle. 'I saw Betty', she wrote, 'and Frances (Lady Frances Balfour) look at me, expecting I should sink into the ground with shyness. He is certainly very pleasant and not at all alarming in himself, except that he never tried to talk to people who do not talk to him. I am shy of him chiefly because I know I am expected to be.'[33]

Whittingehame was not lonely for the bachelor head of the house. In the late eighties and nineties his brothers and sisters made it their home as much as his. Eustace Balfour and his wife Lady Frances and Gerald and his wife, Lady Betty, came to Whittingehame with their growing families for six months of most years; Alice, Balfour's unmarried sister, presided over the domestic arrangements there and at Carlton Gardens; Strathconan being sold in 1891 to a Mr Coombes for a hundred thousand pounds. At Whittingehame, Balfour reigned as 'a sun', in the words of Lady Elcho, 'with those worshipping female planets – those sisters of yours'.[34]

Balfour's routine at his Scottish house has been dutifully chronicled by Mrs Dugdale. He breakfasted in bed, remaining upstairs dictating letters or concluding business until lunch when the family, competing for the favour of his attention 'vied with each other to tell him what was in the newspapers'. In the afternoons he might bicycle, or later drive in a motor car, around the locality, perhaps to play golf or take exercise; then there was tea after which he retired to read until dinner. Dinner might be followed by 'a rubber of pretty bad bridge' or some music. At eleven o'clock the party would break up and Balfour retired to bed, reading for an hour or two before going to sleep.[35]

Visitors to Whittingehame often remarked on 'the veiled

idolatry' of the household towards its head, also the competitive
ardour of some of the worshippers. 'Meals at Whittingehame',
Lady Cynthia Asquith wrote, 'were at times atmospheric. If Miss
Alice Balfour and her brilliant, not seldom fiery sister-in-law,
Lady Frances Balfour agreed in nothing else, they were at one in
their opinion that no one else should ever speak with any object
other than to lead up to "Arthur . . ." '; but she noted that he appeared 'to be sublimely unconscious'[36] of this adoration. Balfour
must have noticed the acute tension that existed between his
sister Alice and his sister-in-law, Lady Frances Balfour. In any
case in November 1899, after staying at Whittingehame, Mary
Drew, formerly Gladstone, told him that Alice 'requires a little
protection from Frances', urging Balfour 'to sometimes give her a
word of loving kindness and appreciation' although 'I know that
sort of thrilling look gets on your nerves'.[37]

Balfour, in common with many others, could be exasperated
by unthinking admiration. Alice Balfour was devoted to him,
vulnerable to his every word; this irrational devotion was
irritating. Once she came down to lunch in an ugly new fur
jacket, only to have her 'look of satisfaction' rapidly dispersed
by her brother's cold scrutiny and remark: 'Alice, you look
vulgar.'[38] Later he spoke to Lady Elcho of a family exodus from
Whitting hame and how he would also have to leave because of
'the impossibility of living with Alice alone'.[39] Once Lady Elcho
thought of asking the two of them to Stanway together but
changed her mind for 'I believe you are really happier when she is
not with you'.[40]

Alice was the least gregarious Balfour. Her enthusiasms were
gardening and collecting butterflies, although in her youth she
had travelled through South Africa in a waggon, publishing in
1892 an account of this experience. To outsiders she seemed
to have few opportunities to escape the humdrum chores of
domestic organization. 'Alice's life', Mrs Drew told Arthur
Balfour, 'is a grind, and her adoring love for you is not enough in
itself to give her the amount of happiness to which her goodness
and unselfishness entitled her.' The palliative Mrs Drew advised
was 'a little extra kiss, or touch, or word, or gift, showing that
you think of her' for 'you never write to her except on business,
and your time is too full to think much of her'.[41]

Lady Emily Lytton observed the feeling between Alice and Frances Balfour during her visit to Whittingehame. One evening Alice remarked to Arthur that she was thinking of changing the name of one of the bedrooms to suit its new wallpaper, whereupon Lady Frances thundered 'Can you believe that anyone except a perfect fool would change the name of a room because they changed the paper? I for one shall call it by its old name as long as I live.'[42] An additional source of conflict was the drinking habits of Lady Frances's husband, Eustace. Alice was a careful housekeeper and invariably there was not enough wine at dinner to cope with Eustace's capacity. More would be demanded, then refused by Alice and a further explosion inevitably resulted. In March 1897 Lady Frances, in a ferocious letter, took her sister-in-law to task for supposedly gossiping about Eustace's condition. 'Nothing more serious', she fulminated, 'can happen to Eustace than that his family should say these things of him. It does not magnify Arthur to run down Eustace, and though I cannot say I am surprised at the lack of breeding, I am surprised at the total absence of all family feeling and loyalty.'[43]

Balfour generally contrived to stay above such disputes. 'I always have a weakness', Lady Frances told him, 'for your approval and I should like to think my actions were on the lines you thought good. Consequently, you are the one person who causes exhibitions of which the recollection makes me hot, so like life! Nevertheless, my chief, go on bestowing on the vassal that feeling that in that *odd* mind of yours you docket "affection" and I will endeavour to live up to it.'[44] He skilfully kept his sister-in-law at a distance, once coldly writing: 'You are as necessary as you ever were: but how necessary is that? How necessary are any of us to any of us? It is enough that we should get on much worse without each other, and that surely may satisfy us unless we are very egotistical – or jealous.'[45] Occasionally a firmer hand was needed. In 1896, Lady Frances, a Liberal, wrote critical letters to her friends about the Balfour brothers' policies in Ireland (Gerald was the Chief Secretary at the time), and Arthur administered a magisterial rebuke, threatening to ban her completely from Whittingehame.

Such jealousies and petty quarrels did not succeed in disrupting the Balfour family. Whittingehame, with its communal

gathering of brothers and sisters and nephews and nieces, provided Arthur Balfour with a substitute for domestic married life,
even substitute children. The young Balfours loved their visits to
East Lothian; in their later lives the pony rides, trips to the sea
and vast family picnics all merged into a matchless idyll against
the background of the great house, presided over by the endlessly
benevolent Uncle Arthur, their heroic example and understanding friend. This arrangement suited Balfour, producing the unity
and relaxation of a contented family with few of its immediate
cares or unavoidable responsibilities. Never a father or a husband, to him two of the chief preoccupations of the human race
could mean little or nothing, merely supplying further evidence
of a life lived apart from common concerns.

Contemporaries remarked upon this, also upon the Balfourian reserve, the impossibility of penetrating the elaborate
courtesies and refinement of manner. Some wondered if anyone
ever succeeded in entering the innermost sanctuary of Balfour's
feelings, that plane on which ultimately all is laid bare in the
brilliant glare of sunlit perception. Generally it is in a man's
friendships and his loves that such a vision is revealed. Here at
least Balfour's bewildering concealment was apt occasionally to
break down.

8

'Playful Little Arthur'

In the spring of 1891, Wilfrid Scawen Blunt returned from Egypt to London, anxious to enjoy the social pleasures he had missed in the desert. He found himself drawn into the 'Souls', ' a group of men and women bent on pleasure, but pleasure of a superior kind, eschewing the vulgarities of racing and card-playing indulged in by the majority of the rich and noble, and looking for their excitement in romance and sentiment'.[1] Of this group, the acknowledged idol was Arthur Balfour. To Margot Asquith Balfour seemed 'the most distinguished of the Souls and idolized by every set in society',[2] although his approach to life and human relationships was very different to that of most of his disciples. They were romantics, seekers after romance and feeling; he was a realist, proud of his powers of balanced appraisal, reluctant to commit himself to personal intimacy.

This clique had been given its name by Lord Charles Beresford, the Admiral and friend of the Prince of Wales, at a dinner held by Lady Brownlow in 1887, because its members always seemed to be talking about their souls. The guest list for another dinner, given by George Curzon in July 1889, provides perhaps the best record of the chief members of the group; these included Balfour, the Dukes of Sutherland and Rutland and their wives, Lord and Lady Pembroke, Lord and Lady Elcho, Lord and Lady Ribblesdale, Mr and Mrs Willie Grenfell (later Lord and Lady Desborough), Harry Cust and Margot Tennant (later to marry Asquith). George Wyndham was absent; if he is added the occasion reveals the kernel of the Souls. The predominant tone was aristocratic; most members were rich, invariably by inheritance, and professed, unlike others of their class, to admire intelligence and artistic sensibility. In July 1889 Curzon wrote a poem of welcome for his guests, mentioning each by name. Balfour's verse ran:

> There was seen at that feast
> Of this band, the High Priest,
> The heart that to all hearts is nearest;
> Him may nobody steal
> From the true common weal
> Tho' to each is dear Arthur the dearest.[3]

The Souls began as a reaction against the aggressive philistinism of aristocratic society of the time. The Prince of Wales personified this. Under his sway the upper classes would move between Newmarket, Ascot, the great country houses and London, indulging primarily in sport, good living and amorous intrigue, oblivious to art, literature and aesthetic beauty. Arthur Balfour did not despise this life; he knew that the majority of his most powerful political supporters enjoyed it, yet its empty ritual and proudly uncultured character bored him. Margot Asquith claimed that the Souls grew out of a group of friends who, while in mourning for her sister Laura, were forced to rely largely upon each other's company. Balfour was one of these, but through his earlier friendship with the Wyndhams of Clouds he must already have experienced the course the Souls wished to follow.

Mrs Percy Wyndham created at Clouds an atmosphere different to that of most large country houses of the period. The company was not exclusively sporting or aristocratic. Burne-Jones, Philip Webb, Morris and Sir Oliver Lodge were frequent guests; good conversation was valued, in a rather self-conscious way. Such self-consciousness was probably inevitable, given the strength of philistine opposition. The Souls, in fact, were mild rebels, although most of them had no wish for material change, at least not in their own circumstances.

Mrs Percy Wyndham had five children, three of whom perpetuated the spirit of Clouds. These three were George Wyndham, Balfour's protegé and later Chief Secretary for Ireland; Lady Glenconner, who after the death of her first husband married Lord Grey, the Liberal Foreign Secretary; and Lady Elcho who became, on the death of her father-in-law in 1914, the

Countess of Wemyss. Lady Glenconner played little part in Balfour's life, although they met on social occasions and she felt strongly that he betrayed her brother in 1905 at the time of George's Irish debacle. The other two Wyndhams were to be inextricably tied to his public and private worlds.

George Wyndham was mesmerized by Balfour. Wyndham seemed, at the beginning of his career, to possess more promise than is perhaps good for any man. His notable looks, supposed literary skill, inherited connections and undoubted intelligence made up a formidable catalogue of advantages. With these came a strong sporting instinct, the notion of the healthy mind in a healthy body so dear to the heart of the Victorian public school, which led him to hunt, ride and exercise ferociously. 'Come out and join me,' he shouted to his niece, Lady Cynthia Asquith, who observed him running round the garden at Clouds in the early morning, 'and then help me write an Aubade before breakfast.'[4] Once, while staying with Wilfrid Blunt at Crabbet Park, he completed a long poem, in complicated metre, while resting for an hour between sets of tennis.

The poetry now seems dull, full of jangling rhymes and neo-Keatsian exaggeration; with Wyndham the style or method of production was always more impressive than the content. He was so eager to learn and please, so reluctant ever to offend or be definite. Arthur Balfour knew this. 'George is here', he wrote to Lady Elcho from Dublin, '– very keen as usual about all literature, all science, all philosophy and all politics.'[5] There was an extraordinary closeness between them which led Balfour, after Wyndham's death in 1913, to tell the House of Commons that he had thought of him almost as a son. But the contrasts were wide: the eager young romantic and the cynical realist; the reckless optimist and the cautious pessimist; one wantonly scattering energy and enthusiasm, the other husbanding his health and intellectual resources with care.

Wyndham knew Balfour was different. 'The truth', he told a friend, 'about Arthur Balfour is this; he knows there's been one ice-age; and he thinks there's going to be another'.[6] However, Wyndham's devotion to his master, at the Irish Office in the early days and in government, was slavish; later he tried to go his own way and the results were disastrous. For Wyndham there was

always the formidable appeal of Balfour's charm, which generally
enslaved all who worked closely with him; also the fascination
of opposites, the chastening and remarkable effect of coldly
deliberate reason on wild fancy. To Balfour George Wyndham
must have represented a world that to him was closed but nevertheless strangely intriguing; an instinctual world of vigour and
blind sentiment, moved by irrational feeling, unfettered by intellectual restraint. All this was ultimately hopeless, even foolish.
But the potentialities of power fascinated Balfour; Wyndham undoubtedly possessed a force, a vitality, which was different from that
of his master, yet equally formidable in its natural strength. The
trouble was that this force was essentially unsuited to the static
world of political drudgery.

Wyndham was, by inheritance and inclination, a Soul.
Balfour and Margot Asquith deny that there was any common
denominator linking the Souls. This may have been true of the
larger group of people they liked to consider as being within the
circle, which included such disparate figures as H. G. Wells and
Oscar Wilde, but the nucleus at its centre was predominately
aristocratic. Wells and Wilde were occasional guests in Soul
houses such as Taplow and Stanway, but did not share in Soul
romances or agree with Soul politics which generally were
soundly Conservative. John Morley, on leaving a Soul house
party with St. John Brodrick, remarked: 'My dear Brodrick,
these last two days have been delightful, but most blighting to
one's democracy.'[7] The ideal meeting place was a large country
house, preferably fairly near London so people could easily escape
from political or social cares. These entertainments depended
upon the presence of a large retinue of servants and were generally carried out against a background at least the equal in luxury
to that of the despised Prince of Wales set. This was not deemed
luxurious by the Souls; it was life, not even a necessity but an unquestioned part of their existence, and when the challenge to
their property and, indirectly, their existences came, they rallied
fiercely.

The emotional excesses of the Souls are partly explained by
this background. There was no reality of domestic difficulty, no
contact with the firm basics of life, to tie them down to earth.
With the women this was particularly true; most of the men

followed careers but their wives and mistresses had all the time in the world to weave fantasies and wallow in sentiment. This emotional self-indulgence and almost desperate search for feeling was not shared by Balfour; but another unifying feature of the clique was its extraordinary idolization of him.

Harry Cust, like Wyndham, was emotionally far apart from Balfour. Their lives took vastly different courses, yet Margot Asquith noted Cust's 'passionate admiration for Arthur Balfour'.[8] Cust, a son of Lord Brownlow, had the same facile brilliance as George Wyndham, displayed in a more spectacular, less responsible way. A scholar at Cambridge, he became editor of the *Pall Mall Gazette* in the nineties and a Conservative Member of Parliament. He and Wyndham were both members of Wilfrid Scawen Blunt's Crabbet Club which met in masculine exclusivity at Blunt's house in Sussex, passing the night in writing poetry and making speeches, adjourning at dawn to swim in the lake and play tennis naked. Balfour, once Blunt's gaoler, never came to these gatherings; they exemplified the more rumbustuous, earthier side of the Souls.

Cust's weakness was women. Here he inspired both devotion and mistrust. One of his many mistresses wrote to Lady Elcho during one of his election campaigns: 'Pray for him Mary',[9] but Lady Desborough later told Balfour: 'I don't like Harry Cust – I cannot bear people who finger one's sleeve and hold one's bread at dinner – and he's so dreadfully uneasy and ingratiating.'[10] Lord Salisbury objected so much to Cust's behaviour with the opposite sex that he refused to have him at Hatfield; Cust obtained revenge by giving breakfast parties in London to watch Salisbury tricycling down the Mall and Birdcage Walk for exercise. On more than one occasion Balfour's aid was invoked to assist his friend out of some disaster brought about by his obsessive philandering. Once there was trouble about a child produced by a married woman who had been involved with Cust, then attempts by a spurned former mistress to discredit him in his constituency. The latter involved George Wyndham who had obliged Cust by speaking in his favour to the constituency committee without having been told the whole truth by the seducer. The situation was further complicated by the fact that Wyndham's sister Pamela was at this time under Cust's spell and later had a minor nervous breakdown when he left her to marry another.

Balfour was amused by Cust's amorous exploits. 'H.C.' he wrote to Lady Elcho after staying in a country house with him, 'seemed to me to rather neglect his harem — those who were there.'[11] Their conduct was markedly different. H. G. Wells, a contributor to the *Pall Mall Gazette*, remembers Harry Cust sobbing in the office over some instance of unrequited, or more likely over-requited, love, and when Cust declared to George Wyndham's wife that 'I must write my soul out to you or I shall suffocate'[12] his words would not have been read with much personal understanding, as opposed to objective sympathy, by Arthur Balfour. Yet Cust's daring juggling with his private life, his cynical handling of intimate relationships, never shocked his friend; and his imperturbable way of surmounting any crisis resembled Balfour's own deep philosophic calm. In 1902 Cust gave a dinner; among the guests, all men, were Winston Churchill, Alfred Lyttelton, F. E. Smith, H. G. Wells and Arthur Balfour. Half way through the meal a servant announced that the house was on fire, to which Cust replied: 'We have not finished dinner. Bring in the next course, and ring up the fire brigade.'[13] The party continued, amid the flames of the burning house and douches of water from the firemen's hoses, later being used by Wells as the basis for a scene in his political novel *The New Machiavelli*.

Mrs Sidney Webb saw Balfour in London society in 1887, in the early days of the Souls. She described him as 'a charming person. Tall, good-looking and intellectual', but could not approve of the general tone of the party. Mrs Webb later remarked that the only excuse for a dinner was that it should end in a committee; here she dismissively wrote: 'The conversation was easy and pleasant, but it was all froth. No one said what they thought, and every one said what they thought to be clever.' Balfour himself 'says cynical and clever things, which are meant to be cleverer than they turn out to be'.[14] Mrs Webb disapproved of frivolity; Balfour did not. Once he said to Lady Rayleigh that he liked 'either to be with people who will be serious and full of new ideas, or who are thoroughly frivolous and understand the art of doing nothing. The half and half houses are intolerable.'[15]

On the surface a gathering of Souls might seem to be exactly

such a 'half and half house'. There were usually the amateurs, in
the form of aristocratic dilettantes such as Cust, and the professionals, such as Wells, Wilde and Professor Walter Raleigh;
but, as outsiders, the professionals invariably, and with great
gusto, entered into the country house spirit of relaxed conversation and graceful intellectual frivolity. After-dinner word-games,
humorous displays of verbal felicity, long aimless walks, bicycle
rides, uncompetitive tennis and mild flirtations: these were the
chief ingredients of a visit, or 'Saturday to Monday', to the Elchos
at Stanway or the Grenfells at Taplow, two Soul houses. Occasionally the rowdier spirit of Crabbet asserted itself, as when once
at Stanway, George Wyndham, Cust, the *litterateur* Charles
Whibley and Professor Walter Raleigh talked fiercely until midnight, then 'relaxed and wrote composite sonnets' before
Wyndham lay down on the floor and turned somersaults while
spouting Virgil, eventually departing to serenade Arthur Balfour
who had retired to bed, with 'The Lark now leaves his watery
nest'. Balfour, Lady Cynthia Asquith remembers, 'took it extraordinarily well, appearing at his window, his face one large
benevolent beam, playfully shaking his fist and tapping his
temple'.[16]

Like most cliques, the Souls had certain conventions and
rituals. In January 1895, staying in the desert with Wilfrid
Blunt, Mary Elcho explained some of these to her host. 'Nearly
all of the group', she said, of its female members, 'were married
women with husbands whom they loved and by whom they had
children, but each had her friend who was a friend only.'[17] Harry
Chaplin, the bluff country gentleman Tory politician, once
observed that the Soul creed was: 'Each woman shall have her
man, but no man shall have his woman.'[18] Lady Elcho's friend
among the group was Arthur Balfour. She was not alone in seeking his favour.

'I wish', Margot Tennant (later Asquith) wrote to him in
1886, 'you were here. When I feel lowest you give me a sort of
confidence.'[19] Margot was only one of the women who, fruit-
lessly, tried for years to reach some sort of depth in her shallow
knowledge of Balfour, to feel the warmth of obviously reciprocated affection. He would not allow such closeness. 'If Mary
[Elcho, later Wemyss], Etty [Grenfell, later Desborough] and I

died', she exclaimed bitterly to him, 'you would not miss us. I know you are devoted to Mary Wemyss, but for us others, you don't care two hoots! You have a taste for us as you might have in clocks and furniture'; to which Balfour replied: 'I should mind if you all died on the same day.'[20] Lady Desborough succeeded in getting closer. In his correspondence with Lady Elcho she is constantly mentioned, under the name of Delilah, as a competitor and source of jealousy. Mary Elcho was always the undoubted favourite and his choice, perhaps because its objectivity was undistorted by love, is revelatory.

Etty Desborough entertained constantly at her husband's large Victorian home at Taplow, beside the river Thames in Buckinghamshire. Her husband was a distinguished athlete and politician who had started life as a Liberal, joining the Tories because of his opposition to Home Rule. Of massive size and strength, his chief political enthusiasm was bi-metallism, an interest shared with Balfour. Desborough did not have his wife's social acumen and was often abroad on hunting trips or serving on international sporting bodies. There were jokes among the Taplow regulars about being trapped after dinner by their host's lengthy expositions of the advantages of bi-metallism, for his slow manner belied the fact that he had been a scholar at Balliol.

Lady Desborough took great care to be well-informed. She also liked to use her influence, gained through a wide and powerful set of friends. 'Could not', she wrote to Balfour in 1904, on behalf of Edmund Gosse, 'the House of Lords library possibly be got for Gossekins? How happy he'd be and how well he'd do it!'[21] During Balfour's premiership it was rumoured that Lord Desborough was to be made Governor-General of Canada, and his wife was said to be working hard to promote the idea. Others revealed their jealousy of the châtelaine of Taplow; Lady Elcho telling Balfour that 'she may wish for it as a convenient "break" at the right moment – to turn from amorous philandering to ambitious devotion to a public cause! And Margot's most anxious to know whether she will drop her lovers or take them with her!'[22] Lord Desborough was not offered the post.

Etty Desborough's relationship with her 'lovers' bears out Chaplin's dictum on the amorous adventures of the Souls. She seems to have engaged a number of men, including George

Wyndham, in a series of intense romantic friendships which rarely, if ever, developed into sexual liaisons. There was generally an exchange of letters ringing with flamboyant declarations of devotion and extravagant praise, the man often adopting an abjectly suppliant position of courtly love. Wyndham, for example, addressed Etty as 'Dear April', writing 'for so I must be allowed to call you – April you have been and must ever be! An April of sunshine and no rain: of laughter and no tears: all radiant and dazzling blossoms from May. Please remember always to be April, and to refuse anything but flowers.'[23]

There was a ritual to such relationships which ensured that words, in certain circumstances, were merely inconsequential froth, existing apart from the real world of lasting attachments and authentic passion. Balfour was never involved in this ritual; as a philosopher who understood the vital link between language and truth, particularly in the area of human feeling, he avoided such casual and self-deluding charades. To May Lyttelton he had written love poetry; to Lady Desborough he wrote factual, informative and affectionate letters, refusing to be subjugated like Wyndham and others. Her letters to him have a puzzled tone, anxious to please, rather stiff as if afraid to relax lest she make a fool of herself.

Etty Desborough was a self-conscious woman, aware of how she wanted others to see her; Mary Elcho was supremely natural, with a spontaneity rare among the polished Souls. Balfour and she would laugh together at Etty's behaviour. 'There were', he wrote to Mary Elcho in 1892 about walking with Lady Desborough in London to see a picture, 'two routes by which we could have walked from St. James's Square to the Studio; one, the shortest and most agreeable by Green Park; the other by Piccadilly (you recollect "the straight and important looking strut"?) No one would have chosen the latter at 1 p.m. unless they had wished to be seen of all men – and women! She did choose it.'[24] In 1895 he discussed *The Foundations of Belief* at Taplow and confided in Mary Elcho that his hostess 'had got stuck in some very unexpected places'.[25]

Mary Elcho was often perplexed by Lady Desborough's motives. 'Ambition', she wrote of Etty to Balfour, 'is a vague word – but her social keenness is beyond doubt and she works very hard. Margot says vanity – that is a thing which may grow incidentally and flourish on feeding but it is not enough as a spur! What is her object?'[26] Her object probably was to act as a social impresario, a catalyst at Taplow for those whom she liked and admired, a hostess fulfilling her natural gregariousness and fascination with the famous in the most natural way open, in those days, to one of her sex and class. Mrs Sidney Webb once observed that in another age she might have made an admirable head of a great administrative department. Balfour was perhaps her most prized guest. He always obliged with his customary charm and ease of manner, but never allowed any serious deepening of their ultimately frivolous relationship.

One of Etty's admirers once fell out with her and told Mary Elcho of the consequence. 'He said', Lady Elcho told Balfour, 'she was as hard as steel with her eyes flaming with fury – he was apparently amazed and horrified at her hardness.' Lady Elcho was not hard. In the same letter she describes her reaction to Wagner's *Das Rheingold*. 'I thought of you', she told Balfour, 'all the time. . . . Sometimes – rarely – you have said "I should like to die now happy" – The thing I am most grateful for is that you do not humbug me or tell sham things to flatter me. We do treat each other more sensibly than that. . . . You know, I never want to know anything for the sake of knowing or to gratify a shallow vanity – but it is different and it's the most exquisite pleasure that I can have – that if you are worried, about money, politics, enemies, friends or – loves! I never want you to say anything you are not in the mood to say and I always respect you! Above all I should deplore anything that might spoil our relations which have worn for more than a dozen years.'[27]

In 1895, in the desert with Wilfrid Blunt, Lady Elcho spoke of her relationship with Balfour. Blunt had remarked on their closeness during the ill-fated Clouds week-end in September 1887, noting in his diary that Balfour 'has been hardened by politics and is now a cynic I fancy also in the affairs of the heart. He has a *grande-passion* for Mary – that is quite clear – and it is equally clear that she has a tenderness for him. But what their exact relations may be I cannot determine. Perhaps it is better not to be too wise and as all the house accepts the position as the most natural in the world there let us leave it!'[28] At Sheykh

Obeyd Mary Elcho made the situation clear. She and her husband, although living affectionately together, had agreed that 'he goes his way; she has her "friend" '. Lord Elcho was far from faithful to his wife; she sought solace with Balfour and to him, Blunt noted, 'she is pledged far more than to Hugo'. Their's, however, was not a passionate liaison; 'she loves, honours and respects him, and he is constant to her, and she has been always constant to him, and she is bound to him by a thousand promises never to give herself to another. On this understanding he has been content that their love should be within certain limits – a little more than friendship, a little less than love.'[29]

Later, in England, Blunt asked Lady Elcho if she thought Balfour was jealous of their Egyptian journey. 'Arthur is not jealous', she replied, 'you know he is not like other men.'[30] In the desert Blunt, an accomplished seducer, and Mary Elcho had a brief affair, yet so strong were her links to Arthur Balfour that on her return she was soon back in the unchanged conventions of their old friendship, terrified lest he discover her deviation. These conventions were clear; certain bounds of intimacy were never crossed and they were not lovers in the full sense, yet there was room for the preliminaries of a sexual liaison. For her, undoubtedly the more involved of the two, this restraint was often exasperating. 'There is', she told Balfour angrily in 1890, 'something peculiarly irritating in the cold philosopher talking about "unreasonable woman" as if he had ever had any intimate acquaintance with the article!'[31] In 1889 she wrote: 'Do you know I have once or twice been asked by people if Arthur Balfour was a relation. I said "oh no (only) a great friend!" But I have thought what a good idea it would be if the world would look upon you as my brother! – would regard us as brother and sister or brother-in-law – even first cousins would be better than only friendship!'[32]

Mary Elcho's domestic life was not easy. Her husband gambled on the stock exchange, taking terrible risks, and Balfour, as a trustee of the Stanway estate, was involved in the family financial crises. The Elchos were never poor, but she lived in a state of constant financial uncertainty and this, in addition to Hugo's philandering, led to worry, even hysteria. Balfour became her confidant, an emotional prop amid the chaos; hence the

fulsome tone of her letters, the extravagant use of terms which today would denote a full-blooded tempestuous romance. She wrote
in the language of the Souls freely mixed with the rhetoric of
desperation; he answered in cool sentences of balanced comfort,
often referring affectionately to Hugo.

Balfour teased Lady Elcho out of jealousy. She would occasionally accuse him of paying too much attention to other
women such as Mary Curzon, Lady Desborough, even Mrs
Joseph Chamberlain. 'You needn't worry', he wrote in 1887,
'about Mrs Eddie Bourke. If she is still with you when I come I
will promise to make the most violent love to her!'[33] Once he
conjured up a picture of a romantic walk with a companion along
the moonlit sea shore near Whittingehame, reassuring her at the
letter's end that this companion had been his private secretary.
Yet their friendship, falling somewhere between the romantically
platonic and the satisfactorily sexual, was not without its own
inner tensions. 'I also think', she declared in 1903, 'that the sex
question and a vexed conscience accounts for things I feel with
you and show and I think I understand it more now.'[34]

May Lyttelton, perceiving the depth of Balfour's emotional
reticence, had tried playfully to shock him. A fellow-guest
remembered her at Chatsworth 'sitting on a billiard table swing-
ing her legs – a trifle outré for those days – and saying to Mr
Balfour "I see you're shocked". And he said something showing
he was.'[35] Balfour was not prim, but the stern morality of his
Presbyterian upbringing never left him. 'In the graver matters of
conduct', John Buchan noted, 'people were surprised to find that
this urbane man of the world had a stiff knuckle of puritanism,
the stiffer because it was so completely intelligent.'[36] Here may
have lain the origins of the strange agreement with Lady Elcho
whereby adultery was foresworn in favour of friendship; but even
this friendship sometimes came near to breaking out of its
boundaries. 'I should have liked', she wrote to him in 1894,
'some fun with you in the morning. I was in great spirits and full
of mischief when you rushed in . . . then came the long walk and
one hour in your room seemed very little in all the day . . . and it
was wasted in talking business. Two hours is what I like: one for
boring things and one for putting you in your place.'[37]

It would be foolish to conjecture what form the 'fun' took. In

Lady Elcho's letters there are mentions of discipline, once a Valentine message containing a drawing of a birch rod; a teasing remark at Whittingehame draws her to admit that 'I was rather angry but was unable at the moment to give you the retort you deserved, a sound smack, so I held my peace but have only postponed retaliation'.[38] What is in no doubt is their lasting attachment, a solid monument constructed out of the shifting affections of the Souls. In her Balfour found freedom from the world of emotional make-believe inhabited by so many of those who idolized him. He and Lady Elcho were plain with each other, made a bargain at the beginning and kept to it, and if there was little romance in such a contractual arrangement, that was the way he, with his temperament and needs, preferred.

Amongst Lady Elcho's papers is a rhyme given to her by a friend:

> Playful little Arthur, he
> Plays with things so prettily
> To him everything's a game
> Win or lose it's all the same –
> Plays at politics or war
> Trivial little games they are –
> Plays with souls and plays at golf –
> This must never be put off.
> Plays with deep philosophies,
> Faiths and minor things like these,
> Plays with praise and plays with blame
> Everything is but a game
> Win or lose, it's all the same.
> Playful little Arthur, he
> Cannot take things seriously.[39]

Such was the Balfour of the Souls. This image, with which he came to be associated, did him harm. It was of course incomplete, but became the image the public knew best, the caricature people grasped. However life with the Souls was only a part of Balfour's existence. Lord Salisbury was the antithesis of this clique, scorning its much-vaunted concern for literature and art. 'Hatfield', he told Violet Maxse, recently engaged to his son Lord Edward Cecil, 'is Gaza, the capital of Philistia';[40] of George Wyndham he once cryptically observed: 'I don't like poets.'[41] Then there was philosophy. Here some Souls tried to keep up, with mixed success. 'It is really hard', Lord Esher wrote of the publication of Balfour's *The Foundations of Belief* in 1895, 'when you are the apostle of a charming sect, to trouble their minds with abstract speculations. . . . However, Mrs Grenfell and the others will no doubt feel that no one is likely to tackle them about details – so they can pretend to know all about it.'[42]

Balfour went elsewhere for his philosophical discussion. He was a member of the Metaphysical Society, founded in 1869 by Tennyson and others supposedly to check the growth of agnosticism. The Metaphysical had included among its members Henry Sidgwick, T. H. Huxley, Leslie Stephen, John Morley, Frederic Harrison, Mark Pattison, Froude and Ruskin: a veritable roll call of Victorian intellect. Balfour was elected in 1879 but had a brief membership, for the society folded in 1880. The Metaphysical Society seemed to some an extension of the Cambridge Apostles, a secret and exclusive discussion group of graduates and undergraduates which had apparently not included Balfour. However, if brought together purportedly to provide a link between religion and science, the room for agreement among so many diverse thinkers appeared small. The result was, surprisingly, evenings of polite, careful discussion. Huxley later observed: 'The Metaphysical died of too much love', W. G. Ward, another member, remarking, 'friendliness became the order of the day and debate grew less useful'.[43]

In April 1895 Wilfrid Ward, son of W. G. Ward, wrote a review of Arthur Balfour's *The Foundations of Belief*. Later they met at the house of Lord Edmund Talbot and agreed to found a society for the discussion of questions such as those raised in the book. The membership was not as varied as that of the old Metaphysical: it included Roman Catholics like Baron Von Hugel, Ward and Father Tyrrell; high Anglicans such as Lord Hugh Cecil; the orientalist Sir Alfred Lyall, Myers from the Society for Psychical Research, Sidgwick and Haldane, a Hegelian philosopher and Liberal politician. From the House of Commons came Balfour, Alfred Lyttelton and George Wyndham. The Synthetic Society, for so it was called, was too late for the great Darwinian debates of the sixties and seventies. By 1895, although the old controversies lingered, the society's tone was mild, partly because it lacked the inspired unbelief of pioneers like Huxley; indeed the membership seems tame compared to the lions of the Metaphysical. One is not surprised that the waiters at the Westminster Palace Hotel, where the Synthetic met, thought the group was called The Sympathetic Society.

George Wyndham and Wilfrid Ward were joint secretaries of the Synthetic Society; Balfour, a friend of both, was one of its guiding spirits. An acquaintance told Ward of her surprise that he and Balfour should be close 'for you know he does so hate your church'.[44] Balfour occasionally voiced his prejudice against Roman Catholicism, a feeling shared by many of his party and class partly on account of the role of Irish priests and Bishops in Home Rule agitation. 'We talked', Lady Rayleigh noted in her diary in 1899, 'about Roman Catholics and the way they had taken the part of forgery and injustice in the Dreyfus case. A. expressed his loathing of all their ways – and declared he was getting bigoted in his old age. They had always been unscrupulous controversialists, using lies and every unfair weapon.'[45] Later he complained of 'their sacerdotalism'.

In *The Foundations of Belief* he develops his attempted reconciliation of religion with science, begun in *A Defence of Philosophic Doubt*. The main controversy of the book is with the 'Naturalists' or believers in the absolute power of scientific proof. Huxley told Ward he objected to the term, saying: 'No human being holds the opinions he speaks of as "naturalism". He is a good debater. He knows the value of a word. The word "naturalism" has a bad sound and unpleasant associations. It would tell against us in the House of Commons, and so it will tell with his readers.'[46]

Balfour's pessimism is evident in *The Foundations of Belief*. His view of humanity in a state of nature is almost Hobbesian in its contempt. 'Man', he writes, 'comes into the world richly endowed with the inheritance of self-regarding instincts and appetites required by his animal progenitors, but poor indeed in any inbred inclination to the unselfishness necessary to the well-being of the society in which he lives. . . .'[47] Balfour's riposte to the potentially anarchic condition of man is the importance of authority and morality, also the acceptance of authority as a legitimate reason for belief. For Balfour the great difference of opinion is not between what is right and what is wrong but why certain standards of moral behaviour exist; he therefore uses the almost universal acceptance of a crude ethical code as an example of a legitimate use of authority (in this case the authority of custom), as opposed to scientific proof, as grounds for a belief.

From this he moves to a justification of the rationally imperfect reasoning behind religion, restating his opposition to scientific standards being used as 'the sole test of truth, and scientific methods the sole instruments of discovery';[48] for him they share this imperfection of proof. All this is a repetition of the arguments of *A Defence of Philosophic Doubt*. Where *The Foundations of Belief* differs is in its new, almost authoritarian paternalistic approach to mankind, a reinforcing of the old notion that humanity, poised on the brink of chaos, depends vitally upon a strong moral structure of authority for support. A part of this structure is religion; for Balfour this was Christianity and its acceptance of life after death. In a long passage, too famous to quote, he supplies his own appalling vision of a purely scientific view of existence, with no hope of knowledge or understanding outside the narrow boundaries of human comprehension, no room for a conclusion that does not include death, disease and destruction.

These paragraphs, of mystical intensity, show his own conception of life's essential aridity without the possibility of a continued existence beyond the grave. In this aridity perhaps one may discern the flickering of his own nature and its need to escape from its confines. Balfour's career, in 1895, was brilliantly successful; yet at the root of his private friendships lay a half-formed intimacy, probably physically satisfactory to neither participant and potentially harmful to both. Of this, however, he directly revealed nothing.

9

The Heir Apparent

Despite the profuse congratulations heaped upon the head of 'Prince Arthur' as he was sometimes termed, his leadership of the House of Commons started badly. W. H. Smith had been remarkable for his industry and availability, never leaving the palace of Westminster while the Commons was sitting; therefore a considerable stir was caused when Balfour first sauntered into the chamber in evening dress after the dinner hour. Three weeks after the opening of the session, in February 1892, Henry Lucy, the *Punch* parliamentary reporter, remarked upon the lukewarm attitude of the Conservatives to their new leader.

There was not time for much legislative progress before the election of 1892, but here again Balfour fumbled. An Irish Local Government bill was introduced, yet failed to progress beyond its second reading, satisfying neither Unionists nor opposition. This measure was partly intended to please Joseph Chamberlain, whose scheme of limited devolution for Ireland had been previously turned down in 1885. In February 1892 Balfour found himself further involved with the Chamberlains when he managed to dissuade the Conservatives of East Worcestershire from putting up a candidate against Austen Chamberlain, Joseph Chamberlain's son, who was standing as a Liberal Unionist in favour of church disestablishment. Arthur Balfour and Joseph Chamberlain were vastly different in character and style. The patrician Balfour never found the self-made Birmingham manufacturer socially sympathetic. In March 1892, he gave a dinner to bring Salisbury and Chamberlain together; the latter was stricken with an attack of lumbago and therefore could not come. Balfour believed his absence improved the evening's entertainment 'for Joe, though we all love him, somehow does not absolutely and completely mix, does not form a chemical combination with us'.[1] In work it was different. 'A,' Lady Rayleigh wrote in 1894, 'finds Joe very easy to get on with, straightforward and open and loyal – "and you always know what he is driving at".'[2]

Events of 1892 brought them closer together. On 30 January the Queen wrote in her journal: 'Had some conversation with Mr Balfour about the elections, about which he is not very sanguine.'[3] These took place in July, with Home Rule as the dominant issue. Balfour, still standing for East Manchester, although he had been offered the Cambridge University seat in 1887, was one of the chief opposition targets and crowds waited in Fleet Street on the night of the Manchester declaration to learn of his result. His majority was reduced, to 398 as opposed to 644 in 1886, largely because of his objections to an eight-hour day for coalminers and enforced absence from the constituency. Overall the figures in the country resulted in a Gladstonian victory, depending upon Irish support. Lord Salisbury waited to be defeated in parliament before resigning.

On 24 July, after the elections, Balfour told Salisbury of another conversation he had had with Chamberlain who was very bitter against the vacillating Hartington, supposedly leader of the Liberal Unionists. Chamberlain saw Hartington as the chief destroyer of his 'Unauthorised Programme' of 1885, believing that Gladstone had taken up Home Rule because 'he felt his position impossible between Hartington and me. He agreed with Hartington about the Unauthorised Programme but he felt the radical party was with me. Rather than be dragged into a policy he did not love by a man he disliked, he endeavoured to dish us all, Whigs and radicals, by starting a Home Rule programme.'

Chamberlain declared: 'I have nothing to complain of the Conservatives', and showed himself anxious to work with them in return for a programme of social legislation, even advising Balfour to disestablish the Welsh church, an idea deeply repugnant to most Tories. His chief message was 'that he would rather like if he saw his way to unite with us under the common denomination of a national party'. Chamberlain asked for a privy counsellorship for Jesse Collings and a baronetcy for a prominent

Birmingham supporter. 'You know already', Balfour told Salisbury, 'that generally speaking I am not in disagreement with Joe's view of the situation. I hope you will give him his baronetcy.'[4]

Salisbury was cautious. Chamberlain wanted social measures included in the Queen's speech, which was to be little more than a routine ritual before the inevitable Unionist defeat in the Commons by the new Gladstonian majority. 'I fear', Salisbury wrote to Balfour, 'these social questions are destined to break up our party – but why incur the danger before the necessity has arrived: and while the party may still be useful to avert Home Rule?'[5]

Home Rule was averted. There was a non-committal Queen's speech followed by the Gladstonian defeat of the Unionists on 11 August. Parliament did not meet again until 31 January 1893, to do battle over Gladstone's second Home Rule bill. Faced with this great obstacle, Balfour's leadership and his extraordinary capacity for mastering parliamentary detail came into their own. He directed the opposition with consummate skill, marshalling his forces through division after division; the criticism now was stilled. In March he visited Ulster, in Lord Salisbury's place, and was met by hysterical enthusiasm. On 8 September 1893, the House of Commons having passed Home Rule with a majority of thirty-eight, the House of Lords killed the bill with a massive vote of 419 to 41. Gladstone wanted to take the issue of this display of undemocratic power to the country, but his ministers feared lack of public support. On 3 March 1894, he retired and an era in British politics came to an end.

Lord Rosebery became Prime Minister. Gladstone had never entirely forgotten his affection for the young Balfour despite their later political differences, continuing to send him philosophical works and, in 1896, welcoming Balfour to Hawarden, shocked that the First Lord of the Treasury should ride up from the station on a bicycle. Balfour respected Gladstone's remarkable powers, although in private conversation the old statesman could be 'the prosiest bore'.[6] After Gladstone's death in 1898, Balfour refused, on political grounds, the Duke of Westminster's request that he should contribute towards a memorial, yet his tribute in the House of Commons to 'the greatest member of the greatest deliberative assembly that the world has seen'[7] was eloquent and moving.

Rosebery did not attract Balfour's admiration. 'He said', Lady Rayleigh recorded, 'he had yet to show that he possessed extraordinary powers. . . . It was difficult to see why he had attained his position, he had a genius for advertising himself.' Balfour also remarked disdainfully that 'a curious trait of Rosebery's character was his taste for the society of his intellectual inferiors'.[8] The dislike was reciprocated, Rosebery calling Balfour 'an ungenerous foe, and neither considerate nor thoughtful'.[9] Rosebery's government, hopelessly split, lasted only fifteen months, long enough for Harcourt, the Chancellor of the Exchequer, to introduce graduated death duties. In June 1895, St. John Brodrick moved a motion criticizing the War Office for an alleged shortage of cordite reserves; ministers were caught unawares and defeat followed. The Liberals resigned and in the July election the Unionists were returned with a majority of 133. Arthur Balfour was back at 10 Downing Street as First Lord of the Treasury and leader of the House of Commons.

Before the election, Salisbury and Balfour met Joseph Chamberlain and the Duke of Devonshire to discuss the composition of the new government, in which the Liberal Unionists were to serve with Conservatives. Devonshire became Lord President of the Council, Lansdowne Secretary for War, Lord James of Hereford Chancellor of the Duchy of Lancaster and Chamberlain (having refused the Exchequer) took the Colonial Office, previously regarded as an unimportant post. There were potential difficulties in this new alliance, not least because of the powerful character and national renown of the Colonial Secretary, and Balfour's diplomatic handling of his colleague did much to preserve the balance of the cabinet. Earlier, in December 1895, Salisbury had written to his nephew about a suggestion from Chamberlain that America should be brought in to help solve the crisis in Turkey. 'I read it', he declared, 'with perfect dismay. Randolph at his wildest could not have made a madder suggestion. I am afraid Mrs. J. [who was an American] is trying her hand at programme making.'[10] Balfour replied soothingly, acknowledging the impracticality of the scheme, denying that there was cause for alarm.

These three – Salisbury, Balfour and Chamberlain – were the triumvirate who governed from 1895 until Salisbury's resignation in 1902; and although Balfour was still his uncle's deputy an extraordinary amount of detailed direction was expected from him. One reason for this was that Salisbury, in the Lords, could not hope to be in touch with day-to-day management of the more recalcitrant lower House; another lay in his age and vagueness. The Prime Minister was a strange mixture of prescience and occasionally wilful neglect. He was supposed to recognize nobody nor remember any name and his behaviour could lead Balfour to despair. In May 1899 a Bill prescribing the provision of seats for shop girls reached the House of Lords, having been shepherded through the Commons by Colonel Denny, a businessman and, in Balfour's words 'one of our best young men', with the assistance of the Home Office. Denny brought the Provost of his borough to see what he imagined would be an easy passage through the Lords, but Salisbury 'never having heard of it, snuffed it out with a jibe about our not having yet got to deciding by law for people whether they should sit or stand!' It fell to Balfour to comfort the unfortunate Denny, who was 'almost in tears', and to declare that 'really he thought there was no excuse for Lord S.'[11]

Salisbury still kept in close touch with the party organization. Often on his way back from the House of Lords he called on Captain Middleton, the formidable head of Conservative Central Office, and Middleton, known as 'the Skipper', would show the Prime Minister 'the reports from the constituencies – the evidence of party prospects, the suitability of candidates, the atti-tude of the country towards legislative projects'.[12] Salisbury had a better grasp of national mood, a greater understanding of popular thinking, than Balfour, partly through these meetings, partly also because, despite a privileged background, he had that instinctive aptitude for popular leadership which his nephew lacked. Salisbury, almost in spite of himself, was an effective platform speaker; his slow exposition of his theme was once compared to the steady strokes of a great sounding bell. He achieved for himself a position in the electorate's mind almost above politics, that of a rock rising out of international chaos, steadfast amid the storm. Balfour never managed this; his speeches, suited to the in-timacy of parliamentary debate, were too subtle, too indefinite and rhetorically evasive to inspire a mass audience.

But in parliamentary tactics and management Balfour was

supreme. 'More was devolved upon A.J.B.', J. S. Sandars, his secretary, wrote, 'between 1895 and 1902 than I suppose ever fell to the lot of the second in command.' Although parliament during these years was not overburdened with new legislation, it was Arthur Balfour who guided each Bill through, assuming in the House of Commons 'responsibilities which were never attempted by his predecessors'.[13]

Balfour became fascinated by parliamentary procedure. His knowledge of this grew largely out of his desire, during the parliament of 1895, to change the system of voting supply, or finance. Previously this crucial vote had been allowed to drag on until the end of the session, thus giving the opposition, who still had this instrument in their hands, a time-consuming advantage over the government in its last stages of legislation. Balfour put discussion of supply at the beginning of each session, also carrying through other changes in the rule regulating the sittings of the House. His grasp of the technical minutiae involved was astonishingly quick and he made the best of them. 'I remember well', Sandars noted, 'the night he expounded the theory of his new arrangement, and how Palgrave, then Clerk of the House, came to me to express his profound admiration of the ability which the explanatory speech had shown, not only in respect of detail, but also the interest with which he had clothed an unattractive subject.'[14]

The subjects for domestic legislation Balfour dealt with in these seven years included workmen's compensation, London's government, education and, inevitably, Ireland. As at the Irish Office he assembled an effective and devoted staff. In 1897 Sydney Parry, a professional civil servant from the Treasury, became Balfour's private secretary for departmental business. Parry left an engaging account of five years with the First Lord. 'Courtesy and consideration', he wrote, 'was bred in his bones'; and 'I never heard him make a cruel or venomous remark'.[15] The latter observation could not have been applied to Balfour's dealings with his social companions or political opponents; but to his servants he was invariably the model of well-bred good manners. Parry's interview for the job in 10 Downing Street set the tone of his later admiration. He remembered 'a long and somewhat languid figure uncoiling itself from an armchair beside the fireplace – a figure so well dressed that one noticed nothing except possibly a pair of very white spats: a gentle, rather tired voice; an extraordinarily pleasant manner'. To Parry Balfour talked 'with a kindliness tempered by fun as if I had been another First Lord, and I came away knowing that I was about to serve a very great gentleman'.[16]

Balfour could be firm with his underlings. In 1894, he told Lady Elcho that he had turned his shorthand writer, Baker 'out of the House at half an hour's notice. His hopeless carelessness had reached a climax – and on top of it all I found that he was leading the kind of life with the kind of associates (public houses and Irish M.P.s) which are not what I desire.'[17] Baker was replaced with Wilfrid Short, the son of a schoolteacher and 'a sound Conservative' who had been previously with the Royal Commission on Labour. Short's loyalty became so great that he seemed to have no life outside his work for Balfour which lasted until after the First War. Once in 1917 he met Lady Salisbury in the street and told her he had 'such good news';[18] she immediately hoped for some great victory, but was breathlessly informed that Mr Balfour could dine with her that evening after all.

Balfour's most powerful assistant during these years was his political secretary, J. S. Sandars. Some five years younger than his master, Jack Sandars, educated at Repton and Oxford University, had married an heiress and was a sociable if rather mysterious figure. He began life as a barrister, practised until 1886, when he became a private secretary to Sir Matthew White Ridley, the Home Secretary. In 1892 he contested mid-Derbyshire unsuccessfully for the Conservatives and in that year joined Arthur Balfour. Sandars remained with Balfour until 1915. His interests were racing and golf; Balfour and he had a close working relationship but outside the office Sandars moved primarily among those who shared his enthusiasm for the turf.

Sandars came, partly through his master's negligence, to have great power in certain closely defined areas. A pungent writer of persuasive memoranda, he had the ability to summarize a situation with the concise clarity that Balfour, with his heavy workload and necessity for relaxation, desperately needed. He also supplied that contact with the knowledge of the party which Balfour ought to have maintained himself. 'He was bored', Lord George Hamilton wrote of the new First Lord, 'to extinction with party details'.[19] Sandars became the eyes and ears of his 'Chief', as he called Balfour, in party and press matters, also advising on patronage. Salisbury, disgusted by this subject, had handed it on to his nephew who, equally uninterested, came to rely on his secretary. Sandars's power and standing grew steadily. When Prime Minister, Balfour would send him to see King Edward VII when he thought he could avoid going himself. Sandars came to control almost all access of party members to their leader. This was to lead to discontent when Tory fortunes were low.

Bernard Mallet, a professional civil servant and husband of one of Queen Victoria's maids of honour, preceded Parry as Balfour's departmental private secretary, leaving in 1897 to become a Commissioner of the Inland Revenue. Mallet kept a diary and towards the end of 1896 wrote: 'Politically a damaging session – Education Bill and Mr Balfour's leadership much attacked and very unjustly, the attack led by the *Times*.'[20] Wilfrid Blunt echoed this with an observation that his rival's political affairs were 'going to rack and ruin' with 'mistake after mistake'.[21] In the session of 1896, Balfour met with and was blamed for a major legislative failure. Measures were passed concerning agricultural de-rating and reform of parliamentary procedure. An Irish Land act, prepared by his brother Gerald who was now Chief Secretary, was put on the statute book despite Unionist landlord opposition in the House of Lords. But it was with his Education bill that Balfour was thought to have failed.

In 1870, W. E. Forster, Gladstone's Vice-President of the Board of Education, had introduced an act setting up board schools, paid for and administered by ratepayers, to supplement the existing 'voluntary schools' provided by the churches with the assistance of certain state grants. By 1896, the board school system flourished in urban areas with rural communities still mostly served by voluntary schools. It was clear that voluntary schools were in financial difficulties due to the effects of an agricultural depression on the rural economy and a vastly increased demand for places after the introduction of compulsory school attendance in 1880; in January 1895, a Committee appointed by the Archbishop of Canterbury urged an immediate increase in state aid to church schools. In August 1895, a Royal Commission, set up by the Liberals but reporting after Lord

Salisbury had taken office, advocated local authorities taking over secondary education from the elected school boards, thus imposing more centralization on a desperate and often chaotic system.

The difficulty lay in religion. In 1870 Glastone had accepted an amendment from Mr Cowper-Temple, a Liberal, that excluded anything but the most elementary kind of religious instruction in schools supported by the rates. Thus the possibilities of close connection between board and voluntary schools had not existed and it was this which caused Balfour and Salisbury so much trouble with their measure of 1896. In January 1895, in a speech in Manchester, Balfour had made clear his view that voluntary schools should be given support; now, in 1896, a bill had been formulated to supply rate aid to these and a drastic replacement of the old school boards with the local education authorities created out of county and county borough councils.

This bill was largely the brainchild of the Vice-President of the Board of Education, Sir John Gorst, Balfour's old Fourth Party ally. Gorst, who had protested against Irish coercion, was not given a seat in Salisbury's cabinet; here the Duke of Devonshire, as Lord President of the Council, had responsibility for education, but Sir John, with the help of Michael Sadler and Robert Morant, two brilliant civil servants from his department, drafted these new proposals. The cabinet was uneasy; Salisbury instinctively disliked radical change, some Liberal Unionists feared nonconformist opposition and Balfour doubted Gorst's ability to carry the measure through Parliament, but the Vice-president had his way. The bill was introduced by Sir John on 3 March 1896, the day the Commons rose for its Easter recess.

In May the debate on the second reading showed that the most controversial part of the measure was religious instruction in elementary schools. A clause stated that this should be provided according to the wishes of a 'reasonable' number of parents, thus repealing the old Cowper-Temple amendment. The Nonconformists and Liberals opposed this. Certain Tories disliked the new burden on rural ratepayers, there was controversy over the exclusion of non-county boroughs, London Conservatives were loath to surrender education control to the progressive London County Council and Joseph Chamberlain was known to have

grave doubts as to the wisdom of the whole measure which soon
came to be decorated with over a thousand amendments. It
became obvious that the situation was hopeless. On 11 June
Balfour, in Gorst's absence, attempted an amendment to extend
local education authorities to non-County boroughs of over
20,000 people. Gorst had already rejected this proposal which
made any coherent formulation of a central education policy
impossible. On 22 June the bill was withdrawn and the government humiliated. In 1897 a measure granting further aid to
voluntary schools was passed, but no attempt was made to tamper
with religious instruction.

1895 had been an *annus mirabilis* for the Balfour family. The
Conservatives were returned to power, Balfour became First Lord
of the Treasury and published *The Foundations of Belief*, Alice
Balfour's account of her South Africa travels was serialized in the
press and Lord Rayleigh's discovery of the gas Argon was made
public. The failure of the Education bill of 1896 partially restored
the balance, but could not wholly interrupt Arthur Balfour's apparently effortless ascent. One of the reasons for this was the poor
state of the Liberal opposition. Between 1893 and 1899 the
Liberal party changed leader three times: from Gladstone to
Rosebery, from Rosebery to Harcourt and from Harcourt to Sir
Henry Campbell-Bannerman. Its internal divisions, exacerbated
by electoral failure, were widening. Halevy has remarked upon
the dullness of parliamentary debates during these years, partly
due to the lack of a unified opposition.

In 1898, Harcourt resigned in protest against Liberal factionalism, taking John Morley with him. The two chief aspirants
for his post were Asquith and Sir Henry Campbell-Bannerman.
Asquith had in 1894 married Balfour's old friend, Margot
Tennant. Balfour and he met at social functions; they knew each
other well, yet there were from the beginning reservations in
their relationship, mostly on Arthur Balfour's side. Asquith's
formidable forensic skill, his debating powers and intellectual
brilliance, were undeniable. What Balfour questioned were his
imagination and character. 'But for the split in the Liberal party',
he told Lady Rayleigh, 'he [Asquith] would have never been more
than a fairly successful lawyer, earning his three thousand
pounds and ending perhaps as a Judge.'[22] He also observed, and

perhaps despised, Asquith's increasing affection for the trappings of a society into which he was enthusiastically led by Margot; later too there came the problem of drink. Balfour, himself subject to iron self-control, was not often understanding of the personal weaknesses of others. Margot was correct when she said that her husband 'was probably fonder of you than you were of him'.[23]

Nevertheless, in December 1898, Balfour, at Margot's request, tried to help his political adversary. Supporters of Asquith had urged him to run for the Liberal leadership but he had refused, declaring that he could not afford to give up his practice at the bar. Margot, whose extravagance was partly to blame, persuaded Balfour to write to her father, Sir Charles Tennant, to ask him to provide enough money to make Asquith independent.[24] Sir Charles, a supporter of Campbell-Bannerman, refused and on 6 February 1899, Sir Henry was elected leader of the Liberals, with Asquith's support. A shrewd Scot, without Asquith's intellect, of unprepossessing appearance and manner, Campbell-Bannerman was consistently under-rated both by his opponents and supporters. In the House of Commons he was often a poor performer, usually outclassed by Balfour's ingenious dialectic, yet there was a curious solidity to him which could devastate with its apparent simplicity and proud lack of artifice. C.B. disliked Balfour and was always impervious to his charm. Balfour was not fooled by his opponent's unsophisticated exterior; when W. T. Stead remarked on the likeness of Campbell-Bannerman to W. H. Smith he agreed but added that he was 'much cleverer'[25] than the former Tory leader.

In December 1895, President Cleveland of the United States intervened in the dispute between Venezuela and British Guyana over boundary claims, using the Monroe doctrine as his reason and taking the side of Venezuela. For a few months there was talk of war. Balfour in January made a bravely conciliatory speech in Manchester declaring that 'the idea of war with the United States carried with it some of the unnatural horrors of a Civil war'. He expressed a wish that 'the time will come' when 'some statesman of authority more fortunate even than President Monroe, will lay down the doctrine that between English-speaking peoples, war is impossible'.[26] A journalist, W. T. Stead, wrote to him: 'Why should not you or your uncle have been the statesman to whom you referred?'[27]

In the event, Salisbury secured a satisfactory arbitration. He had no romantic notion of a trans-Atlantic alliance. On this Balfour and Chamberlain were as one. In 1898 Balfour wrote of 'a firm perpetual alliance between these two branches of one family', declaring that 'if I can contribute even in the smallest degree towards it, I shall feel that I have done something worth doing'.[28] During the First War he was to help make these vague words a concrete reality.

Salisbury's last administration was faced with a shifting international scene. On the European continent, France was allied with Russia in potential conflict with the triple alliance of Germany, Austria-Hungary and Italy; in the wider world the United States and Japan were emerging as great powers. The race for imperial possessions provided a further course of tension. Britain was still following a policy of splendid isolation whose fragility became apparent in 1896 after the disastrous Jameson raid. Doctor Jameson had led an ill-conceived attack on the President Paul Kruger's Transvaal where the rights of *Uitlanders* were an explosive issue. These *Uitlanders*, or foreigners, lived mostly in Johannesburg where they worked, and vastly profited from the gold and diamond mines. The Transvaal government denied them political rights, although they paid taxes. Jameson's expedition, connived at by Cecil Rhodes and probably Joseph Chamberlain, failed miserably. The expected *Uitlander* rising in support never took place and Kruger's troops captured the raiders. On 3 January, the German emperor sent a telegram to the Transvaal President, congratulating him on his country's escape from this foreign threat.

Balfour had met the Kaiser at Hatfield in 1891, and remarked upon his 'extraordinary energy, self-confidence and interest in detail', also his belief in a 'mission from Heaven, though this will very possibly send him and his country ultimately to Hell'. On this occasion, discussing English parliamentary government, Wilhelm II declared 'Thank God I am a tyrant!'[29] Balfour laughed and later observed: 'He is the only royalty I ever met who was the least interesting to talk to. He talks like we all do'.[30] The Kruger telegram emphasized Britain's isolation; there was international delight at her misfortunes. Jameson was shipped home and tried at Bow Street amid popular expressions of jingoistic support. The government agreed to an enquiry, despite the efforts of Stead and other friends of Rhodes to stop it. In July Jameson was sentenced to fifteen months in prison. The enquiry, in the form of a Select Committee of the House of Commons, began on February 1897. Unaccountably, the Liberals failed to press the issue; Rhodes was censured, with Sir Graham Bower, the Imperial Secretary at the Cape, but Joseph Chamberlain who, surprisingly, was allowed to serve on the Committee, and the High Commissioner in Capetown, Sir Hercules Robinson, were cleared. Now their complicity in the plot is generally accepted.

Although an imperialist, Arthur Balfour was no jingo. He did not join Chamberlain's brash crusade but admitted, in private, an admiration for Dr. Jameson whose 'character was the only attractive feature in the matter, tho' he ought to be hung all the same'.[31] In public, at Manchester in January 1896, he spoke in pacific tones of Kruger's Transvaal while advising that concessions should be given to the *Uitlanders.* Yet the foundations for conflict had been laid. Britain, by the Convention of 1881, could maintain that she possessed suzerainty, which included control of foreign policy, over the Transvaal, even though the British had been forced to grant independence as a consequence of the crushing defeat at Majuba Hill in that same year. The London convention of 1884 modified these terms, making no mention of the word suzerainty yet preserving control over foreign treaties except those with the Orange Free State. Thus the basic principles of British control were arguable. In addition the Boers were wary and self-confident; they had humiliated the British twice in the last fifteen years and saw no reason why, if threatened, they should not do so again.

In 1898 Salisbury twice handed over the Foreign Office to his nephew and took leave to recover his health. These periods tested Balfour's aptitude for diplomacy. First, there was the problem of China. China's defeat by Japan in the War of 1895 had been followed by a rush by the West for Chinese outlets. In January 1898, Balfour emphasized Britain's policy of maintaining Chinese independence, declaring 'Our interests in China are not territorial; they are commercial';[32] but it was difficult in this age of imperial expansion to stand back. In November 1897 the Kaiser had seized the port of Kiaochow for Germany. The British attempted to come to an understanding with Russia over Chinese territorial acquisitions but failed. Salisbury did not wish to be the first to follow the Kaiser. In February 1898, when the Chinese offered Britain the lease of Wei-hai-Wei, he refused and went to France to recover from a sharp attack of bronchitis, leaving Balfour in charge.

The Russians, meanwhile negotiated with China the lease of Port Arthur, an ice-free port, and Talienwan. Britain's earlier refusal of Wei-hai-Wei was reconsidered. First Balfour followed his uncle's advice that 'the only thing to be done is to object to the military occupation of Port Arthur in a language sufficiently measured to allow Russia to find a way out'.[33] This failed and eventually on 25 March the cabinet agreed to demand from China the lease of Wei-hai-Wei. Throughout these events, Joseph Chamberlain had favoured a much harsher attitude towards Russia including the possible formation of an alliance against her. Now he dissented from the government decision to accept the occupation of Port Arthur. In Parliament, the Liberals revelled in Balfour's discomfort as he explained that a strong British stand might have led to war with Russia, 'a risk not worth taking'.[34] *The Times* was also critical but of Salisbury rather than Balfour, declaring that Russia's triumph was "attributable at least in some degree to the attempt of Lord Salisbury to discharge the double duties of Prime Minister and of Foreign Secretary'.[35]

One of Chamberlain's possible allies was Germany. Count Hatzfeldt, the German ambassador, had already opened discussions on colonial policy and on 25 March 1898 he saw Balfour at Alfred Rothschild's London house. Their talk progressed well and Hatzfeldt was encouraged to set up further meetings with Chamberlain who, to the surprise of the ambassador, proposed an Anglo-German alliance, brushing aside German colonial complaints as being merely 'in the nature of a skirmish'.[36] Hatzfeldt tried to make the best of the proposal but Bülow, the Kaiser's Chancellor, turned it down. Balfour disliked Chamberlain's methods; the cabinet had not been consulted and the Colonial Secretary was assuming extraordinary powers. Yet he mocked rather than scolded. 'Although I am inclined,' he told

Salisbury in April, 'to favour an Anglo-German agreement, it must, if possible, be made at the worst on equal terms. On this loving couple I should wish to be the one that lent the cheek not that imprinted the kiss. This I take it is not the German view; and they prefer, I imagine, reserving their offers until they are sure of being well paid for them.'[37]

Meanwhile there was still the Anglo-German colonial dispute. Here Balfour and his uncle held different opinions, Salisbury favouring intransigence and his nephew, together with Chamberlain and the majority of the cabinet, taking a softer line. The problem was brought to a head by the offer made by a bankrupt Portugal to Britain of temporary occupation of the port of Delagoa Bay in Portuguese East Africa in return for a loan. With an explosive situation in the Transvaal, Delagoa Bay was strategically important, but the Germans wished for a share of any break-up of the Portuguese empire. Salisbury would have refused them this, but on 30 August 1898, Balfour signed an agreement which provided for an Anglo-German loan to Portugal with her empire as security, a secret clause dividing this empire into separate spheres of interest. Balfour claimed thus to have obtained British control of Delagoa Bay and German neutrality in any dispute that might arise in the Transvaal. He presented the agreement to Salisbury as a *fait accompli* and the Prime Minister acquiesced. It was to lead to international charges of dishonest diplomacy and eventual recriminations between Britain and Germany.

In April 1898 Balfour was in charge of the Foreign Office during the difficult crisis of the Spanish-American-Cuban War. The Cubans had rebelled against their Spanish masters in 1868; since then a guerilla war had been in progress with the United States supporting the rebels against the corrupt and inefficient Spanish regime. In 1898 President McKinley, who had made forceful demands on behalf of the Cubans, sent the American battleship *Maine* to Havana where she was sunk, with great loss of life, by an explosion whose cause was disputed. An American commission, appointed by the President, assessed that the cause was external and the American press and popular opinion quickly assumed Spanish guilt. The Spaniards had given way to almost all of McKinley's initial demands and the President did not want war, but in the United States feeling was overwhelmingly bellicose. On 21 April America went to war with Spain.

There was no doubt that, as far as Britain was concerned, friendship with the United States was of greater importance than good relations with a bankrupt and largely powerless Spain. Balfour held this view, but both he and Salisbury wished to keep out of the conflict. More than his uncle, Balfour believed in great power co-operation, hoping for an understanding in the Far East between Germany, Britain and America; therefore he received Spanish officials asking for support with non-committal courtesy and instructed Sir Julian Pauncefote in Washington not to offend American sensibilities by joining with other European ambassadors in protesting against possible hostilities before they had broken out. The war resulted in an American victory. In Britain the public had been overwhelmingly sympathetic to the American cause and there were demonstrations of support at the Lord Mayor's show. On 13 May Chamberlain spoke in Birmingham of Anglo-Saxon solidarity.

The Spanish government was infuriated by Britain's attitude. In August it erected fortifications along Gibraltar bay and Balfour, again at the Foreign Office, considered sending a stern ultimatum. Salisbury favoured delay, but his nephew was determined to extract from Spain an agreement to British rights in Gibraltar. The Spaniards gave way and the guns were withdrawn. The Cuban war had wrecked Anglo-Spanish relations, but furthered Anglo-American goodwill and understanding.

In 1897 reinforcements had been sent out to South Africa, at the instigation of Joseph Chamberlain. Yet there were divisions in the cabinet. Balfour and Hicks-Beach were worried about Chamberlain's aggressive stance; Salisbury seemed to waver between supporting it and alarm at its possible consequences. Chamberlain himself was, by temperament, against war, looking for some chance of an understanding with the Boers, but his High Commissioner in South Africa, Sir Alfred Milner, saw no solution outside military subjugation. Milner, certain of his aims, dominated the situation. In the Colonial Office, Chamberlain and his permanent officials inclined towards caution but the High Commissioner, aided in London by the Colonial Under-Secretary,

Lord Selborne, forced the pace.

Balfour understood the Boer predicament. 'Were I a Boer', he wrote in May 1899, 'brought up on Boer tradition, nothing but necessity would induce me to adopt a constitution which would turn my country into an English republic, or a system of education which would reduce my language to a *patois* of a small and helpless minority'. Under normal circumstances, he believed 'there does not seem to me to be anything like a *casus belli* established', but he admitted that the position of the *Uitlanders*, whom he found unattractive as a class, did justify 'exceptional measures'.[38] He hoped for a peaceful settlement with Kruger, telling Lady Elcho on 27 August 'I somehow think that war will be avoided'[39] and later on 10 September 'I still hope for a peaceful solution of the South African difficulty. We are sending more troops there.'[40] On 27 September the Orange Free State joined the Transvaal, negotiations having broken down between Milner and Kruger despite last minute attempts at conciliation by Chamberlain.

Once the war had started, Balfour's support for Chamberlain and Milner was absolute. There is no need to relate here the dispiriting details of the early British humiliations in South Africa. On 15 December, after the disaster at Colenso, General Sir Redvers Buller seemed to have proved himself unfit to retain command of the British expeditionary force. The preceding week had seen a catalogue of disasters; Balfour dining with St. Loe Strachey to meet the South African Sir Percy Fitzpatrick, was apprised of the latest blow. After dinner he saw Lord Lansdowne, Secretary of State for War, and they agreed that Lord Roberts should take the place of Buller. Next morning Balfour talked to Salisbury. The Prime Minister, worried about Roberts's age, insisted that Kitchener should accompany him as Chief of Staff. Balfour saw Roberts at the War Office and was moved by the old soldier's calm acceptance of his new task. There had, however, been one grave omission. The Queen had not been informed of the new appointment and Balfour had to hurry to Windsor where he exercised his diplomacy on her ruffled feelings.

'His courage never failed', Sandars wrote of his master, 'even when the news was the worst from South Africa'.[41] Balfour tried to keep a balanced view. 'If you compare our losses', he wrote to a correspondent on 1 January 1900, 'up to the present moment with what we have sustained in previous wars, I doubt whether anything has occurred of a very exceptional character.'[42] On January 8 and 9 he spoke in East Manchester, attempting to minimize the disasters. The speeches struck exactly the wrong note with the public, most of whom were waiting for at least a partial admission of failure. Instead he seemed to be blaming the British people and parliament for lack of military preparedness, stating that government could only reflect their state of mind. His words were resented and he was accused of flippancy, which surprised and angered him. 'I know', he wrote petulantly on January 24, 'this war has never been out of my thoughts for one moment for the last two months, that I sacrificed my whole holiday to assisting to the best of my ability those colleagues in whose special departments the conduct of the war rests, and that the time of anxiety I have been going through is far greater than anything of which I have had experience, even the worst periods of our Irish troubles.'

At Manchester, Balfour had refused to satisfy the public's search for a scapegoat, defending Lansdowne and the War Office up to the hilt. He privately acknowledged there had been blunders, attributing them for the most part to 'our generals in the field', but 'I cannot give my full opinions without blaming gallant men whom I do not wish to blame – but I entirely decline to make a scapegoat of people whom I do not think deserve any such fate. Far rather would I leave public life forever.'[43] Yet the Manchester speeches demonstrated a serious inability to comprehend the national mood. Bernard Mallet noted in his diary of the government: 'I shall be surprised if they survive the spring unless victories speedily come. *Morning Post* most violent against Mr. B. and *The Times* far from friendly.'[44] St. John Brodrick, now a junior minister at the Foreign Office, offered Balfour some encouragement, writing 'You have a genius for managing the House of Commons – which will pull you through'. Brodrick however also observed: 'The feeling is by no means confined to the Press that we have blundered terribly and that Great Britain could not be in its present position if we had shown reasonable foresight. They want to pull down someone.'[45]

In the House of Commons, Balfour was fortunate. The

Liberal party was divided between pro-Boers, such as Lloyd George and Morley, and Liberal imperialists like Asquith, Edward Grey and Lord Rosebery. In South Africa throughout the spring and summer Roberts was gaining ground, but Balfour could not entirely escape parliamentary retribution. In July, Campbell-Bannerman succeeded in riling him on the question of medical arrangements for the war and in August, on the same issue, Balfour uncharacteristically lost his temper. This caused considerable comment, Akers-Douglas, the Tory Whip, remarking the next day that his leader 'was completely unhinged last night'. Queen Victoria said 'It really is most extraordinary' and Marie Mallet noted, 'I can see she is very much disappointed with A.J.B'.[46]

In September the government decided to capitalize on the Boer defeats by dissolving parliament. In December 1899 Balfour had prophesied a Conservative defeat, 'probably not by a very large majority, and that the next administration will be a short-lived one'.[47] The Khaki election of 1900 resulted in a Unionist victory, but the surprise was, given the jingoistic nature of the campaign and Tory attempts to identify the opposition with the Boers, that more than two million people voted Liberal. The government was returned, with only a small increase in its majority, although Balfour won by a large amount in East Manchester.

The first priority was a cabinet re-shuffle. St. John Brodrick replaced Lord Lansdowne, who had previously threatened twice to resign, at the War Office. Sandars was worried about this appointment, reporting that 'both in the House of Commons and in the country it would be very difficult to maintain the position that in sending St. John to the W.O. we have designated our best man for the post, the most onerous and important (for the moment) in the Administration'.[48] Brodrick's great fault was lack of tact. Sandars would have preferred Lord Balfour of Burghley or George Wyndham, who had served as Lansdowne's Under-Secretary, for the post, but Balfour believed this 'too rapid a jump'.[49] Wyndham, elected to the Commons in 1889, had made good progress, although in 1898 Lansdowne told Balfour 'I have heard doubts expressed with regard to his popularity with members of the House',[50] some of whom tended to distrust his flamboyance and in-

tellectual tastes. Now Salisbury and Balfour made him Chief
Secretary for Ireland, without a seat in the cabinet.

Hicks-Beach was more difficult to accommodate. He was an
effective but obstructive Chancellor of the Exchequer and Balfour
had thought of moving him to the Home Office or the Admiralty.
At first Beach seemed interested in the latter post, then abruptly
changed his mind. 'I am sorry', Balfour told Salisbury, 'for he will
certainly go on dropping little grains of sand into the wheels of
every department in turn. If, as I fear, we have to spend large
sums of money on Army re-organization and Naval construction
I suppose he will describe our policy as "Jingo" and resign!'[51]

Salisbury himself provided a problem. His family thought he
should, on health grounds, give up the Foreign Office, but he was
reluctant to do so, telling Bigge, the Queen's secretary, that he
would stay on if she so wished. 'The Queen', Akers-Douglas
wrote to Balfour from Balmoral, 'thinks the responsibility of asking Lord S. to give up the F.O. will rest on her, and she shrinks
from having to ask him to go.' The Queen, encouraged by Lord
James of Hereford, at first thought his departure would cause
consternation abroad but eventually agreed that Salisbury 'cannot without injury to his health undertake again the double
office'. Lansdowne, to whom she had "no objection", took his
place, although Akers-Douglas noted 'she had rather thought of
Pauncefote'. Anyway 'the profound change is rendered more attractive to her by the thought of Cranborne as Under-
Secretary'.[52]

Lord Cranborne was Salisbury's son, and Salisbury and
Balfour seemed to some to be sacrificing ability for nepotism.
Cranborne, of whom Balfour had remarked in 1898 'he has not
always shown tact in public speeches and though I think his
judgement good this is very far from being the common view'[53]
was, moreover, not the only relative to be promoted. Lord
Selborne, married to Salisbury's daughter, took Goschen's place
at the Admiralty and although Balfour called the appointment
"admirable" he told his uncle, who had thought it imprudent to
move Gerald Balfour to the Home Office, 'the only doubt I have
is that whether the arguments which weighed with you (and not
less with me) as to the difficulty of making your nephew Gerald a
Secretary of State had not at least equal weight in the case of your

son-in-law'.[54] In the event, Gerald Balfour left the Irish Office to become President of the Board of Trade.

In December the issue of nepotism was raised in the House of Commons by a disgruntled Conservative. Salisbury took a robust line. 'Please note', he told Balfour, 'that exactly the same number of "relations" (minus Jim) were in the government in July 1895 as are there now. The arrangement has therefore been before the country during two general elections without provoking an adverse comment. Herbert Gladstone may pair off with Jim. No doubt one or two have been promoted. But they cannot be treated as a class apart who can be employed but not promoted, like second division clerks.'[55] Balfour vigorously defended the new cabinet, but the Hotel Cecil was a charge which lived on in the popular imagination.

The Boer guerilla campaign dragged on. In January 1901 it became clear that the only way to satisfy discontent as to the general management of the war was to appoint a commission of enquiry. The Queen, urged on by Bigge, who was a close friend of the discredited Buller, was opposed, but Salisbury and Balfour persuaded her that there was no alternative. Her agreement was one of her last official acts. On 22 January she died. Balfour's valedictory speech in the House of Commons demonstrated his genuine sadness at her passing. In 1898 a dinner guest at Whittingehame noted down his host's opinion of Queen Victoria. 'Of course', Balfour had stated, 'there have been many things in her life which could have been laughed at such as John Brown and the *Diaries in the Highlands*, and if we had been a nation like the French, we would have made some epigram on such things and turned them into ridicule, but this nation has always felt that there was something in the Queen's personal character to be greatly admired.' The guest remembered that 'again and again Mr Balfour repeated that the great power of her character was from the combination of great simplicity and modesty with dignity required by her position in the world'.[56]

As leader of the House, Balfour had come into close contact with the Queen, writing her reports of parliamentary business, trying (largely unsuccessfully) to put her chaotic household finances in order, noting, with great admiration, her defiant courage in the darkest days of the war. A year later, in June

1902, the peace of Vereeniging was signed, bringing hostilities in South Africa to a close, and he regretted she had not lived to see it. King Edward VII was now his sovereign. On 10 July 1902 their relationship became closer when Lord Salisbury retired and Balfour, at the age of fifty-three, succeeded his uncle as the King's chief minister.

10

Prime Minister: The Statesman

Balfour was Salisbury's natural successor. His only possible rival was Joseph Chamberlain, and Chamberlain saw that so potentially divisive a figure as himself could not lead the Unionist Party, at least for the moment. Chamberlain's devoted supporters thought otherwise; in 1902 articles in *The National Review* and *The Nineteenth Century* advocated his accession to the leadership. But Balfour called on the Colonial Secretary, who was recovering from a cab accident, before kissing hands and Chamberlain, who had cause to be grateful for his new leader's unstinting support during the South African war, expressed absolute loyalty.

'I suppose you know', Lady Elcho wrote to the new Prime Minister, 'that you won't have a happy or peaceful life with me until brother George is in the Cabinet!'[1] A reshuffle was needed. Wyndham, as Chief Secretary for Ireland, was brought into the cabinet to replace Lord Cadogan, the departing Lord Lieutenant, as its principal Irish representative. The most important loss was Sir Michael Hicks-Beach, the Chancellor of the Exchequer, whose relations with Balfour had never been ideal. 'The real reason he is going', Sir Edward Hamilton, a senior civil servant at the Treasury and Gladstone's former Secretary, noted, 'is that he can get no support in the Cabinet',[2] and Beach told Harcourt that 'Arthur never backed him up, and gave him the impression the sooner he was gone the better'.[3] Hamilton thought that 'the worst of it is there is not a soul to succeed him'[4] although he stated his own preference for Austen Chamberlain or Lord George Hamilton. In Sandar's list of possible ministerial combinations, Joseph Chamberlain is suggested as one candidate (Lord

Selborne taking over the Colonial Office) and St. John Brodrick as another.[5] 'I trust', Hamilton wrote to Balfour, 'we may be spared from having to serve a man like Hanbury or even Ritchie. The two essential qualifications for the post are common sense and to be a gentleman'.[6]

Balfour tried to persuade Beach to stay until August, but he refused. The Prime Minister then moved C. T. Ritchie from the Home Office to the Treasury, ignoring Hamilton's advice. Ritchie, a reforming Unionist who had piloted through a bill introducing elected county councils while President of the Local Government Board, had an unattractive demeanour but was hard working and conscientious. Akers-Douglas, a former Chief Whip, went to the Home Office. Outside the cabinet Lord Dudley became Lord Lieutenant of Ireland and Sandars remained as private secretary, continuing to bear out Sydney Parry's earlier observation that he 'lived solely and wholly for our chief'[7] until Hamilton noted in 1904 that he was 'almost more powerful than any private secretary I remember'.[8] There was still criticism of the government's supposed nepotism. Gerald Balfour stayed at the Board of Trade despite Hamilton's opinion that he was 'the real man who ought to go'[9] for he 'was no good and thought little of'.[10] Austen Chamberlain entered the cabinet as Postmaster General, Balfour telling Joseph Chamberlain that his son and George Wyndham were both 'quite first rate'.[11]

Balfour's relations with King Edward VII were not easy, the bluff pleasure-loving King having no comprehension of his Prime Minister's intellectual subtlety or sympathy for his outward vagueness of manner. Balfour believed King Edward's advice and opinions to be usually worthless. 'Now so far as I remember', he wrote to Lansdowne in 1915, 'during the years during which you and I were his ministers he never made an important suggestion of any sort on large questions of policy.'[12] Edward VII and he began badly, with a complaint from Sir Francis Knollys, the King's private secretary, to Sandars about the inadequacy of the new Prime Minister's reports of cabinet proceedings. At first Edward did not care for Sandars either, declaring 'one has heard of the "New Woman", but he is the "New Man" ',[13] but soon Knollys was telling Sir Edward Hamilton that 'he does not know what would happen to Arthur Balfour if there was no Sandars who is indispensable. A.B. wants to be perpetually kept up to the mark – to be "ridden".[14]

In the late summer of 1902 and spring of 1903, there were two disputes which demonstrated that the King had to be treated with care. The first concerned the offer of the Garter to the Shah of Persia, which Edward VII declared he had never approved. The Foreign Office had advocated this, to lure Persia away from Russia, and Lord Lansdowne was determined not to have to retreat from his promise to the Shah. Balfour supported Lansdowne, Sandars believing the King was encouraged to resist by Lord Rosebery. In November Edward gave way 'but', as Knollys told Balfour, 'is much depressed about it all'.[15] In April 1903, the King obtained partial revenge by forcing the government to retract their opposition to a visit by him to Pope Leo XIII in Rome, although the meeting was ostensibly at the Pope's invitation, as opposed to the King's request, as a gesture to militant protestant subjects.

At the end of July a by-election in Leeds resulted in a large Tory loss. This was partly attributable to the long battle over the Education Bill which had been continuing, in one form or another since 1896. The story is complicated but important. After Gorst's failure in 1896, the cabinet decided that Balfour should take over the management of a new bill. Balfour wanted a short bill, but there was cabinet disagreement over the problem of paying for voluntary schools out of rates. In 1897 Balfour carried through measures of relief for these voluntary schools, increasing grants for board schools in need. In 1898, teachers were given pensions and in 1899 the school leaving age was raised to twelve. The Boer war delayed further reform but in 1899 the Cockerton decision forbade school boards to use the rates to provide funds for higher, as opposed to elementary, education. Sir John Gorst introduced another unsatisfactory bill which Balfour, as in 1896, was again forced to withdraw. Eventually, in December 1901 a cabinet committee was set up, including Balfour and the Duke of Devonshire but excluding Gorst. This committee decided to take the courageous step of introducing a comprehensive bill which effectively gave state aid to voluntary schools, regardless of the Cowper-Temple amendment, and brought them under the control of local education authorities.

Balfour, guided by the brilliant Morant, soon saw that the only option open was to give rate aid to voluntary schools, including those under control of the Church. Both Salisbury and Chamberlain disagreed; Salisbury because he shied away from such comprehensive reform and feared over-burdening the ratepayer, Chamberlain because he knew the strength of nonconformist opposition to rate aid for denominational schools. Reluctantly they acquiesced and on 24 March 1902 the Education Bill was introduced into the House of Commons.

At first Balfour was not sanguine about the possibilities of success. He told Lady Rayleigh in January 1902 that the cabinet had insisted that he should conduct the measure through the House for 'they would not have Gorst at any price and the worst of it was he [Balfour] did not believe in education, and whatever line he took the Bill would be torn to pieces'.[16] For someone who professed not to believe in his cause, Balfour put up an astonishing exhibition of determination and dexterity. He had undoubtedly been inspired by Morant although for his sister to note that he had 'apparently no decided views of his own'[17] cannot have been correct.

Eventually, as with his Irish policy, Balfour came to tolerate no deviation from his objective. In July 1902 he re-organized the Education Department. In 1899 a Board of Education had been established, with Devonshire as its first President and Gorst his Parliamentary Private Secretary. Balfour replaced Devonshire with Lord Londonderry, scarcely an inspired choice, and Gorst with Sir William Anson. Gorst's disappointment led him later to join the Liberal party, even flirt with Labour; Sandars categorized him as 'a traitor' and had no doubt as to who was responsible for the 1902 measure. 'All the official help', he wrote, 'that the Prime Minister could obtain was from Morant. Morant was excellent and his industry phenomenal. Thring, the draughtsman, did good work. The Act as we know it was a product of these three brains, while the carriage of it through the House of Commons was the sole work of A.J.B.'[18]

Joseph Chamberlain's worst misgivings seemed to be borne out by the strength of the opposition. The Liberals, previously divided over the Boer War, came together over the Education Bill, and a great nonconformist campaign was launched against it in the country. The Leeds by-election upset was followed in August by a near victory by a Liberal Baptist in the Tory stronghold of Sevenoaks, and in November Orkney and Shetland was captured by the Liberals. In October Balfour spoke at Manchester, attempting in an hour and a half to simplify the bill's tortuous clauses. 'I tell you', he said, 'there are at stake issues greater than the fortune of any political party; there is at stake the education of your children for a generation.' If 'this great reform' was not passed, 'we shall receive the contempt of the parents and the children living and to be born, and that contempt we shall most justly earn'.[19]

Parliament re-assembled in October after the summer recess. Many Unionists, dismayed by the strength of feeling in their constituencies, believed that some concession should be made to the nonconformists. Colonel Kenyon-Slaney introduced an amendment which made the managers of a school responsible for religious instruction, thereby avoiding control by the parish clergymen. This, unopposed by Balfour, was carried on a free vote, leading to an uprising by those who saw themselves as protectors of the Church of England. Among the church party were Balfour's Cecil cousins, particularly Salisbury's youngest son, Lord Hugh Cecil, Member of Parliament for Greenwich. Lord Salisbury himself expressed his displeasure. 'He said', Lady Frances Balfour wrote from Hatfield to her brother-in-law, 'if you had given the least indication that you meant to take power from the clergyman, he would have put off his resignation a year to prevent it.'[20] Later the friction between Balfour and his cousins was to become sharper; now Lord Hugh contented himself with vociferous protest, admitting that the bill should not be lost.

On 18 December there was more controversy when Balfour issued a superlatively skilful reply to a pamphlet circulated by Doctor Clifford, a leader of the nonconformist campaign. Sandars drew Balfour's attention to Clifford's work which had been widely read and the Prime Minister wrote, as his secretary remembers, 'for the most part on his knees in the House of Commons during the concluding debates, one of the most brilliant rejoinders in political controversy that I know'.[21] Even today some of its telling phrases are worthy of quotation.

On the same day, parliament was prorogued. 'Arthur

Balfour', Sir Edward Hamilton noted, 'has come out of the
session very well. He has certainly improved his position.'[22] Yet
there were murmurings from an unexpected quarter. Harry Cust,
hoping for some sort of office in the new government, had been
disappointed. On 27 December, Herbert Maxwell, a back
bencher, wrote to Balfour to say that 'Harry Cust sounded me
out last week about my willingness to join a movement to upset
the present administration in favour of one with Rosebery at the
head'. Cust declared that 'the country is sick of the present
people. There is no man in the cabinet except Arthur Balfour and
Joe Chamberlain and we want something else;' he also admitted,
as Maxwell told Balfour, 'that the great obstacle to his project
was the affection our people had for you'.[23] Sandars estimated this
movement to be only half a dozen strong; probably it manifested
little more than Cust's disappointment and curious definition of
friendship.

The new Education Act did not start to operate until April
1903, the delay deliberately designed to allow nonconformists'
anger to cool. There was, however, formidable 'passive resistance' in the form of refusal to pay the education rate; by the start
of 1904 7324 summonses had been issued against resisters and
329 distraint sales of resisters' goods had taken place. For all this,
the opposition in England was fragmented and comparatively ineffective. In Wales, however, Lloyd George, conscious of his role
as a spokesman for nonconformism, led a campaign in which
county councils themselves were the resisters. The government
deliberately did not enforce the act in Wales until February
1904, and by this time only two county councils were refusing
to follow Lloyd George. Morant believed that it was impossible to
coerce the Welsh, but Balfour refused to be deflected, although
Lloyd George was privately hoping for some compromise. In
1904 a Default act was passed and when the government resigned in 1905 three counties and two municipalities in Wales
had been penalized under this legislation. The education
problem was to follow Balfour into opposition but the courage
of his 1902 legislation can hardly be doubted now.

One of the remarkable features of Balfour's premiership, indeed
of his official career, is the constructive interest he showed in

defence. To understand this, it is necessary to go back to the beginning of the previous decade. The Hartington commission, set up under the chairmanship of Lord Hartington (later the Duke of Devonshire) to enquire into 'the civil and professional administration of the Naval and Military Department', had remarked upon the serious lack of co-operation between the services. To remedy this it had suggested the establishment of a defence council, composed of the War and Admiralty Ministers together with their professional advisers under the chairmanship of the Prime Minister. This council should be given extensive powers of co-ordination and policy-making and minutes kept of its meetings.

Little at first was done to put these ideas into practice, although since 1885 a Colonial Defence Committee, under the direction of the Colonial Secretary, had been supposed to operate between departments to oversee the defence of the empire. In 1891 the War Office set up the joint naval and military committee, used in 1892 by General Sir Redvers Buller in his attempt to bring the Colonial Defence Committee more firmly under the War Office control. Buller's tactics were not entirely successful, but he was able to precipitate the departure of Sir George Clarke, the Colonial Defence Committee's Secretary.

In 1892 the Liberals returned to power and in 1895 a Cabinet Defence Committee was set up consisting of Campbell-Bannerman (then Secretary of State for War), Rosebery, Spencer and Lord Ripon. This idea had long had the support of Arthur Balfour who pressed it on Asquith. At the end of 1893, Sir Charles Dilke, an advocate of an imperial defence policy, wrote to Balfour suggesting all party pressure should point to 'the creation of a Defence Ministry, of which the War Office and Admiralty would be branches, or to a more active control of the Secretary of State for War and the First Lord of the Admiralty by the Prime Minister personally'.[24] Balfour, some thirty years later, was to emphasize his opposition to a united Ministry of Defence for 'What a Ministry of Defence professes to do is to co-ordinate the fighting services' whereas an overall co-ordination of 'every department of the government, and, in time of war, every national activity which can be enlisted in support of a common cause'[25] was needed; the fulfilment of this need, Balfour believed, was one of the greatest services of the Committee of Imperial Defence, created by his own government in 1903.

In 1894 this was still some way distant, but in a debate on the Army estimates in March of that year Balfour spoke in support of a cabinet committee with records and minutes kept of its deliberations. The Liberal Cabinet Defence Committee, begun in 1895, kept no minutes and neither did its succeeding body set up by Salisbury when the Unionists returned to power. Indeed Salisbury's committee did not even number the Foreign or Colonial Secretaries among its members and was under the dilatory chairmanship of the Duke of Devonshire, of whom Balfour was to write in 1901 'poor Devonshire is, with the best intention, the worst chairman of the committee I have ever known – not excepting the Prime Minister'.[26]

The Boer War showed the inadequacy of defence planning and also the need for War Office reform. In 1900 Salisbury replaced Lansdowne as Secretary of State for War with St. John Brodrick. 'Let me utter a word about the Defence committee', Balfour wrote to Brodrick after his appointment. 'For purposes of re-organisation I believe it to be utterly useless. It can criticise, but it is quite incapable of construction.'[27] Brodrick had previously served as Lansdowne's Under-Secretary at the War Office from 1895 to 1898 and could claim experience of military matters, yet this was not an entirely satisfactory appointment. His awkward, tactless manner made him unpopular with his party and in the House of Commons. 'Why', Lord Hugh Cecil wrote to Balfour in July 1900, 'is St. John's manner in answering questions so insufferable? Hectoring pomposity stiffened with pipe clay.'[28] In November 1901 the War Minister was publicly hooted in the streets.

Brodrick produced a scheme of reform which reorganized the Army into six corps of which one (stationed at Aldershot) was to consist entirely of regular soldiers, two of irregulars, and three of a mixture of regulars, militia and volunteers. This, given the state of recruitment, was too ambitious, especially as it included the ability to send abroad a force of 120,000 men at a time. Brodrick was unpopular with the soldiers who thought him interfering, and in February 1903 his name was blackened with society as well when the aristocratic Grenadier Guards were visited by a scandal which caused a temporary sensation in the press. An unofficial subaltern's court-martial was uncovered at which young officers had been 'tried' by their colleagues for minor breaches of regimental etiquette and then whipped, one supposedly collapsing from pain and loss of blood. It was alleged that their commanding officer, Lieutenant-Colonel David Kinloch, knew and approved of such goings-on. An enquiry took place, presided over by a Major-General, and Kinloch was suspended on half pay, his punishment confirmed by the Commander-in-Chief, Lord Roberts.

Balfour had seen, in 1897, the power of Tory sentiment towards the Brigade of Guards when there was an outcry about sending a detachment overseas to Malta and Gibraltar. 'Society', Lady Rayleigh noted, 'is up in arms about it, there is an agitation against it in the clubs and Pall Mall.'[29] Now, in 1903, there was strong feeling that Kinloch had been misused and his father, a Scottish neighbour of the Balfours, wrote to the Prime Minister in support of his son. Balfour answered that he could do nothing; military discipline was a matter for the military authorities but, characteristically, he hoped his own relations with the Kinloch family would not be affected by this unfortunate incident.[30] Brodrick and the War Office were blamed by Kinloch's supporters. In February, Balfour wrote to Lady Elcho that 'many of us think the feeling against St. John so violent that we shall never get through our army estimates without a fall! He is naturally depressed, poor old boy. . . .'[31]

St. John Brodrick managed to up-date the army's equipment, ordering weapons some of which were still in use at the start of the First World War. He also, in November 1902, together with Lord Selborne, First Lord of the Admiralty, submitted a memorandum to the cabinet which provided the bare essentials for the Committee of the Imperial Defence. In November 1900 the Duke of Devonshire, chairman of the Cabinet Defence Committee, had tentatively proposed that this should be placed on a more regular and official footing, but Goschen, then First Lord of the Admiralty, and Sir Michael Hicks-Beach, Chancellor of the Exchequer, had disagreed. Selborne reversed the Admiralty's earlier opposition because he believed that such a committee

would assist his hopes for larger naval estimates. Brodrick and
Selborne congratulated themselves on this document, Brodrick
telling his old colleague years later that 'you and I devised the
Defence Committee and had to force A.J.B.'s hand',[32] also
remarking 'we shall soon have A.J.B.'s biographers declaring
that he established the Defence Committee!'[33] Yet, Arnold-
Forster, then Selborne's Under-Secretary, had little doubt that
the paper circulated to the cabinet had originated in a memorandum submitted by him to the First Lord of the Admiralty. 'On
this paper', Arnold-Forster wrote, 'Selborne and St. John were
asked to write their remarks, which they did, but I do not think
these remarks add anything at all to my proposals'.

Arnold-Forster was sure of his claim. 'Eventually', he
declared, 'nearly everything I had suggested was carried out,
down to the selection of the very man I proposed as secretary to
the committee . . . there is no truth in the statement that either
Selborne or Brodrick originated the Committee of Defence'.[34] But
Lord Hankey, who served as the Committee's secretary from
1912 to 1938, had no doubt as to whom the major part of the
credit was due. 'No one', he wrote in his memoirs, 'has ever
seriously contested that Balfour was the founder of the
Committee of Imperial Defence. Others made valuable contributions and suggestions, but it was Balfour, then Prime Minister,
who in 1904 took the initiative and responsibility, in the teeth of
much opposition, of bringing the Committee into existence.'[35]

The idea behind increasing the powers and effectiveness of
the old Cabinet Defence Committee was to improve co-ordination
between the services and to formulate a coherent defence policy.
In 1902 pressure from the service ministers and the investigations of Lord Elgin's commission into the South African War,
facilitated such a reform. At first Devonshire continued as chairman, but the Prime Minister attended meetings and assumed the
chairmanship when the Duke left the cabinet in September 1903.
The service ministers were both members, together with their
senior military and naval advisers, and the old joint naval and
military committee on defence and the Colonial Defence Committee became sub-committees of the new organization.
Meetings were held more often and records kept of the proceedings. In March 1903 Balfour introduced the new scheme to

the House of Commons, declaring that 'there is one point on which there ought to be no discontinuity, and that is the military and naval policy of the Empire'.[36]

Besides its permanent members, the Committee of Imperial Defence was able to summon other officials, such as the Chancellor of the Exchequer, or, for Colonial or Dominion questions, the Secretary of State for India and other representatives of the Imperial and Dominion governments. The fact that the Chancellor was not a permanent member ensured that defence policy was not entirely subordinated to financial considerations. In 1904, as a result of the recommendations of Lord Esher's committee on the reform of the War Office, the body was further strengthened; the Prime Minister was henceforth to act as its permanent chairman and a civilian secretary, together with a secretariat, was appointed. The appointment of a permanent secretary at first worried Balfour and he told Esher 'I am a little afraid of it'.[37] But in August 1904 the Prime Minister, having been won round, asked the House of Commons for £2,960 a year for a secretary, two assistants and other expenses.

The first secretary of the Committee of Imperial Defence was Sir George Clarke, former secretary of the Colonial Defence Committee, which he had left in 1890 to become Governor of Victoria. Clarke, the son of a Lincolnshire vicar and previously an officer in the Royal Engineers, regarded imperialism as 'almost a religion'.[38] He was also ambitious, maintaining extensive contacts with the press and in the War Office. Balfour, in reporting to the King the Cabinet's decision to appoint Clarke, wrote in April 1904: 'Mr Balfour is in favour (though not without some little misgiving) of appointing Sir George as secretary. And though a certain number of the Cabinet feared that Sir George's well known connection with the press was a serious objection to the appointment, they agreed to Mr Balfour's proposal. Mr Balfour promised to make it perfectly clear to Sir George that all communications with the press – direct or indirect – must henceforth cease'.[39] The professionals were jubilant. In November 1903 Admiral Sir John Fisher had written to Sandars that 'One place in the whole wide world he is specially born for is permanent secretary of the Cabinet Defence Committee'[40] and Esher, on whose committee Clarke served in 1904, praised him highly.

Between the Committee of Imperial Defence's inception in 1902 and the end of Balfour's government in December 1905, it met eighty-two times. In 1903 its imperial nature was emphasized by the attendance of Frederick Borden, Canadian Minister of Defence and Militia, during his visits to Britain. The Committee's discussion covered a wide range of problems, including the defence of India's north-west frontier, the possibilities of invasion and the advantages of a Channel tunnel. It survived the change of government in 1905 and Balfour's association with it was to last, with short intervals, for the rest of his active life.

The Prime Minister was not so successful in his attempts at War Office reform. In the cabinet re-shuffle of October 1903, St. John Brodrick was moved to the India Office and replaced by Hugh Oakeley Arnold-Forster, adopted son of Gladstone's minister W. E. Forster and previously Selborne's subordinate at the Admiralty. Brodrick's removal had clearly become a necessity, but his successor presented difficulties. The King and Balfour tried several candidates, among them Akers-Douglas, Selborne, Lord Esher and George Wyndham, but all either refused or could not be spared from their posts. King Edward and the court were opposed to Arnold-Forster, partly because, as Knollys informed Balfour, he was 'not a gentleman'.[41] Sandars told Selborne: 'The worst of it is that – I fear – the King wants someone whom he thinks that he will find obliging and complacent.'[42]

Balfour was firm. He informed the King on 4 October that 'He fully appreciates your Majesty's objections to the appointment of Mr A-Forster, but he does not deny that manner may prove a real and serious obstacle to success. But all other combinations have proved impossible, he feels no other policy is possible – .'[43] The King reluctantly accepted and on 12 October Knollys told Sandars, 'the King had some conversation with Arnold-Forster this afternoon and was pleased with him on the whole. Mr Balfour may like to know this.'[44] Relations between Minister and monarch were never to be ideal, but in October 1904, Knollys provided a curious vignette when he reported to Balfour on the War Minister's visit to Balmoral. Arnold-Forster, he wrote, 'got on very well with the King, and somewhat to H.M.'s amusement, he expatiated at length at a picnic luncheon on ladies' dresses, and how they should be cut etcetera. I think that the more one knows him the better one likes him but he reminds me of a French Minister more than an English Cabinet Minister.'[45]

Arnold-Forster's appointment was popular with the press. He was regarded as an expert in defence matters and it was thought that at least there was a reasonable chance of War Office reform. Arnold-Forster took office with a scheme already in his mind. He proposed the formation of two armies, one for general service, the other for home service, and the integration of the militia into the home service army. These proposals rapidly ran into serious opposition.

One of Arnold-Forster's problems was that at the same time that he was trying to implement his ideas, the Esher Committee for the re-construction of the War Office was also at work. The trouble was not so much that the two were incompatible but that Esher's committee and influence, both at court and with Balfour, made him a formidable power with which to contend. Esher's position was difficult to define, but his power was immense. He had doubts about the practicality of Arnold-Forster's proposals and voiced these constantly to the King and the Prime Minister. In April 1905 the new Lord Salisbury, Balfour's first cousin, on the *Britannia* in the Mediterranean as minister in attendance, relayed to Balfour more complaints about Arnold-Forster from the King, whose source was Esher. 'I suspect', Salisbury wrote, 'A-F has again made a mess of it, but I think Esher's relations with the King are in the highest degree unsatisfactory. He ought either to be a responsible minister and defend his views in Parliament or (at the very most) he should confine himself to intensely confidential communications with yourself.'[46]

Esher had refused to be War Minister because he had no wish to surrender the role of which Salisbury was so critical. 'I am purely selfish in the matter,' he declared, 'and I really do not think that I can bring myself to sacrifice all independence, all liberty of action, all my *intime* life, for a position which adds nothing to that which I now occupy.'[47] However his committee's report, published in February and March 1904, revolutionized the army. An Army Council was set up, modelled on the Board of Admiralty; a general staff came into existence, the office of Commander-in-Chief being abolished in favour of a Chief of

General Staff; the post of Inspector-General was created to super-
vise training and to implement the direction of the Army
Council, and the War Office administration was drastically
reconstituted. The government accepted its recommendations,
although it seemed as if Arnold-Forster was being circumvented
by the ubiquitous Esher. 'How Esher can be allowed to have so
much power in the War Office, I don't know', wrote Sir Edward
Hamilton. 'As Prime Minister Arthur Balfour ought not to allow
it. But one of his weaknesses is his want of self-assertion.'[48] As if
to emphasize Esher's links with the Crown, the Duke of Connaught, a serving soldier and Edward VII's brother, was appointed the first Inspector-General, Lord Roberts having refused
the post.

    Arnold-Forster's scheme ran into fierce opposition from the
military and the cabinet. The abolition of the militia was viewed
with grave disfavour by both Sir George Clarke of the Defence
Committee and such part-time soldiers as Lords Salisbury and
Selborne. Within the new Army Council the Chief of General
Staff, Sir Neville Lyttelton, openly attempted to frustrate the
minister. Lyttelton, brother of Alfred and Balfour's favourite,
May, was scarcely remarkable for his intelligence but, as Sandars
wrote, he was 'the brother of a Cabinet Minister and a great
friend of many more'.[49] The Duke of Connaught complained to
Knollys that the War Office 'was worse now than in Brodrick's
time'[50] and the Army Council was against the Secretary of State.
In June 1905 Arnold-Forster tried to force a decision, demanding Lyttelton's resignation. Balfour attempted to promote a
compromise scheme of his own, but by December, when the
government left office, there was still deadlock.

    Arnold-Forster, already in poor health, came to believe he
was the victim of a conspiracy. Balfour, he thought, was loyal
only to 'the family' or 'ring' of friends and relations who could ex-
ert pressure on the Prime Minister by virtue of their personal
ties. Arnold-Forster's work was an obsession with him and the
strain of promoting his scheme within a tight budget imposed by
the government almost resulted in a breakdown. 'To tell the
truth', Balfour said in November 1905 of its economies, 'I never
believed you would be able to reduce.' Later, the War Minister
recorded his desperation in his diary. 'Now what', he wrote, 'is

one to say of a leader like this? Here have I for the two years past been groaning and sweating to carry out strict injunctions in which the necessity for a reduction came first and foremost. I was to improve the volunteers, but I was to spend no more money. Time after time I have brought the matter before the Cabinet: day after day I have fought weary battles in the House of Commons, and all this time the Prime Minister presumably has been amusing himself with his bad joke. Why in the name of all that is wonderful he could not have told me eighteen months ago what he now says he has been thinking all the time passes my comprehension. Of course the whole difficulty could have been got over a twelve month ago. But he really is a maddening man in many ways."[51]

The vexed question of Army reform demonstrated the Prime Minister's strengths and weaknesses. On the one hand he had sensibly adopted the proposal of the Esher Committee for War Office re-organization, yet on the other had failed to extricate some sort of reasonable scheme from the tribulations of Arnold-Forster. It is difficult not to sympathize with the War Minister, pitted against so many formidable opponents who seemed, like Esher, Lyttelton and the Duke of Connaught, to work largely through influence and by stealth. King Edward took the side of the objectors; in June 1905 Knollys told Balfour that 'the King is strongly of the opinion that what the Army, especially the officers throughout the Army, requires at the present time, is a period free from disturbance and constant change'.[52] By December the tone was fiercer and the court was hoping that Esher would re-consider his decision of 1903. 'I am very sorry', Knollys wrote to the Prime Minister, 'to hear that your plan for the removal of Arnold-Forster has made no progress. Precious moments are surely being wasted and if the matter is not settled until say the middle or end of October, I think Esher would be most unwise to accept the post of S. of S. for War only three months before the meeting of Parliament.'[53]

Arnold-Forster did not depart and Balfour failed to promote a compromise plan of his own. Critics condemned his lack of force on this issue, Hamilton writing that 'he does not play the part of Prime Minister. He is "Arthur" to all his colleagues who don't look up to him enough and treat him as *Primus inter pares*. It is no doubt a very weak government."[54] After 1903 there were so many attempted compromises under way, primarily in the field of tariff reform, that perhaps Balfour's greatest achievement was in not allowing the War Office to destroy itself during the conflict between its minister and his advisers. The Liberal government of 1906 was left to salvage the situation; today we may be surprised that it was not worse.

With the Navy, the Balfour government was more fortunate. This was largely due to the remarkable activities of Admiral Sir John Fisher, the foremost naval strategist of the age. Lord Selborne, First Lord of the Admiralty, had brought Fisher back from the Mediterranean fleet to the Board of the Admiralty in 1901 and from there the Admiral had, with Selborne's support, changed the shape of the British Navy. On Christmas Day 1902, the so-called Selborne scheme was issued, putting forward drastic reforms in officer training. In October 1904 Fisher became First Sea Lord and modernized the fleet, striking 150 out-dated ships off its strength. In 1905 the first Dreadnought, a revolutionary warship powered by turbine engines and equipped with increased fire power, was laid down, the submarine introduced and the scheme of dockyard reorganization instituted. By these changes Fisher succeeded in increasing naval efficiency and effecting economies, albeit at an initial cost. Throughout, Balfour, Selborne, and Selborne's successor, Lord Cawdor encouraged him and in October 1903 Fisher told Balfour 'It is not for me to refuse the Prime Minister more especially as I worship the ground he treads on!'[55] Later, during the First War, they were to quarrel; but now Fisher was fervently grateful to Selborne and Balfour for giving him his chance.

Arthur Balfour's Foreign Secretary was Lord Lansdowne, a great territorial magnate who could claim, through his maternal grandfather, the Comte de Flahaut, to be Talleyrand's great grandson. Lansdowne and Balfour began their relationship early, for the Prime Minister had been his Foreign Minister's fag at Eton. Lansdowne, partly because of the power of his name, had served as Governor-General of Canada and Viceroy of India, but as War Minister in the South African War displayed little verve or imagination. Balfour was very fond of him, although he told Mrs Dugdale that his old friend was 'not very clever' but 'better than competent'. For someone of such patrician ancestry, in a party where this was treated with deference, Lansdowne surprisingly often failed to assert himself and Balfour viewed him as 'very diffident'. Yet he was suited to the correct, almost fussy, world of old European diplomacy, for to the Prime Minister 'he wasn't quite an Englishman – I always felt a sort of continental quality of mind in Lansdowne'.[56]

Lansdowne had been doubtful about accepting the Foreign Office in 1900; after the abuse that had been directed against him as War Minister he wondered if he was worthy of the post. Such diffidence needed overcoming and Sandars remembered that 'Lansdowne liked to be fortified by his leader's judgement in nearly every step of importance he took in that department. I can say that no despatch of any real importance was ever sent without the draft being submitted to the Prime Minister, and that submission was no idle form, for A.J.B. would not hesitate to handle drastically the draft from top to bottom, not confining himself to mere matters of drafting.'[57] Lansdowne was to be susceptible to influence, from his permanent officials as well as his political colleagues. At the Foreign Office, Sir William Sanderson, the Permanent Under-Secretary, was unlikely to force his views on the minister, having served under Lord Salisbury who had always scorned 'the professionals'; but Sir Francis Bertie, the Assistant Under-Secretary, had a deep distrust of German intentions and from the autumn of 1901 worked against an Anglo-German alliance in favour of one with Japan.

German intentions, particularly under the mercurial Kaiser, were difficult to fathom. In November 1899, during the Boer War, the Kaiser had visited England, having long conversations with Balfour. Much of these were taken up with condescending remarks about British strategy in South Africa, yet he also spoke with great favour of the Anglo-German agreement of 1898 and remarked that 'all countries of Latin race, not excluding France, were in his opinion (as Lord Salisbury had said) "decaying nationalities" '.[58] Balfour himself did not disagree, writing to his old associate Sir Joseph Ridgeway in January 1899 'France remains the incalculable quantity and the most obvious danger to European peace'.[59] In January 1901 the Kaiser came to the bedside of the dying Queen Victoria, causing an outflow of national gratitude by his dignified conduct. However, the rise of German industrial and naval power and her growing colonial ambitions could not be ignored. Britain, her isolation apparent after the chastening experience in South Africa, seemed to face a potentially hostile world alone.

In December 1901 Lansdowne was in the process of concluding an alliance with Japan. A rapprochement with Germany had been attempted, but the terms appeared too high, the intransigence and the unpredictability of the Kaiser and his officials too great. For Lansdowne the Japanese alliance was, as far as his country's interests in the East were concerned, less useful but he believed there was no longer any chance of the German alternative. Balfour was even more doubtful, particularly in the light of the combination between Russia and France. Britain's intentions in the Far East were merely to maintain the present situation, whereas Japan's were essentially aggressive. 'It is', he wrote to Lansdowne on 12 December, 'a matter of supreme moment to us that Italy should not be crushed, that Austria should not be dismembered, and, as I think, that Germany should not be squeezed to death between the hammer of Russia and the anvil of France. If, therefore, we had to fight for the Central European powers, we should be fighting for our own interests, and for those of civilization, to an extent which cannot be alleged with regard to Japan.'[60] He also believed that, in the case of a Russian attack on the Indian frontier, one of the Empire's most vulnerable points, a Japanese alliance would be useless whereas an agreement with the Triple Alliance would probably prevent France from supporting Russia.

Lansdowne replied that he could not justify the entanglements involved in negotiations with Germany. The Japanese alliance seemed to leave Britain fairly free of these. Despite cabinet doubts, it was concluded and British isolation came to an end. In November 1902 the Kaiser came on another visit; there were comparatively friendly talks with Balfour and Lansdowne, but public opinion, in the form of violent newspaper articles, spoke loudly of the German threat. In December, the government were criticized for co-operating with Germany in an attempt to protect British and German interests in Venezuela from the Dictator, Cipriano Castro. The German navy opened fire on the Venezuelan fleet and it seemed as if the United States, under President Theodore Roosevelt, having previously turned a blind eye, might have to enforce the Monroe doctrine. The Balfour government withdrew British warships from the area and the claims were settled by arbitration in Washington. Early in 1903 German anger was added to by Britain's disassociation from the German plans for the Berlin/Baghdad railway. Fisher's naval modernization programme and the new naval base at Rosyth further demonstrated concern at the possibility of foreign aggression.

In February 1904, war broke out between Russia and Japan. Britain was under no treaty obligation to aid her new ally unless France joined Russia. Balfour opposed the granting of a twenty million pound loan to the Japanese and saw advantages in the conflict, particularly the inevitable weakening of Russia. The war, and Balfour's determination to stay out of it, accelerated negotiations with France which Lansdowne had begun the year before. In August 1902 the French had proposed a settlement of certain colonial differences; at first the government had rejected this, but increasing tension and public alarm with Germany led to a change of mind. Negotiations conducted chiefly by Lansdowne and Delcassé, his French opposite number, resulted in a declaration of the *Entente Cordiale* in April 1904, which defined possible areas of international tension between the two countries and concluded almost universal settlement of them. Edward VII paid a popular and successful visit to Paris in May but, in later years, Balfour was always quick to deny his supposedly important role in the negotiations as a 'foolish piece of gossip'.[61]

Britain was now involved in the tergiversations of European power politics. Before the end of Balfour's administration in December 1905, covert talks had begun between the staffs of Britain and France, although these were not brought to the full attention of the government until 1912. Balfour told a friend in that same year of his 'shock of surprise – I am far from saying of disapproval – when I found out how rapidly after I left office the *Entente* had, under the German menace, developed into something resembling a defensive Alliance'.[62] "The German menace" seemed to grow during Balfour's premiership. In the

summer of 1905 the government took an aggressive line against
German interference in Morocco, although the French acceded
to the Kaiser's demand for an international conference on the
question, Delcassé having been forced to resign. Balfour was
alarmed by this display of French weakness, but the issue
emphasized the threat posed by the unpredictable Kaiser.

The Russo-Japanese war provided one extraordinary moment
of diplomatic unease for Britain which did not involve Germany.
On 21 October 1904 the Russian Baltic fleet, on its way to the
Far East to assist its country's hard-pressed forces, ran into some
British fishing trawlers near the Dogger Bank. Imagining the
fishermen were Japanese torpedo boats, the warships fired on the
trawlers and sank one, killing two men and wounding several
others. There was a national outcry, fanned by the press; the
British government immediately demanded an international
enquiry and adequate compensation. The Russians delayed and
then on 28 October, the day Balfour was due to speak at
Southampton on the subject, acceded to the British requests.
Balfour received the telegram announcing the Russian agreement
at the moment of his arrival at Southampton; the meeting was
told that war had been averted. On 5 September 1905 the Treaty
of Portsmouth ended hostilities between Japan and Russia. In
August 1905, Britain's alliance with Japan was renewed, one of
the last acts of Balfour's ailing government.

11

Prime Minister:
The Approaching Smash

In 1906, after the great Unionist defeat, Lord George Hamilton, Arthur Balfour's Secretary for India, told Beatrice Webb that when Lord Salisbury had been Prime Minister 'we were all addressed by our official designation – the Secretary for Colonies, etc.,' but 'When Balfour took his place, cabinets degenerated into cliquey conversations between "Arthur" and "Bob" and "George" – sometimes almost unintelligible in their intimate allusions, to the outer circle of the Cabinet'.[1] Balfour's ways could seem informal. 'He must be', Sir Edward Hamilton wrote, 'the first Prime Minister who in accordance with modern ways is called by his Christian name by the bulk of his colleagues.'[2] Many of these had been associated with Balfour for several years; as Prime Minister, he was to find his loyalty to some severely tested.

Sometimes he had little choice. The Financial Secretary to the Treasury, W. Hayes-Fisher, had previously served as Balfour's private secretary at the Irish Office. In 1903 a company of which he was a director was involved in a court case, Hayes-Fisher initially believing this did not merit resignation. In April the cabinet discussed the matter and Edward Hamilton noted 'Arthur Balfour did not like to take all the responsibility himself'.[3] Fisher resigned, encouraged by Balfour, but the cabinet discussion, rather than instant prime ministerial dismissal, bears out Lord George Hamilton's observation that his chief 'had an innate antipathy to unpleasant interviews with colleagues and subordinates'.[4] Later, in 1911, Balfour obtained a Privy Counsellorship for Hayes-Fisher, arousing charges of misplaced loyalty.

More difficult were the problems of India and its government. George Curzon had been appointed Viceroy of India in 1898 by Lord Salisbury and given the title Lord Curzon of Kedleston in the peerage of Ireland. Curzon and Balfour had an equivocal relationship. They met frequently at social functions and in country houses. Curzon, as an ambitious young Tory politician, admired Balfour's parliamentary skills and was a Soul, an accomplished participant in the romantic and intellectual activities of Taplow and Stanway; but here the similarities ended. Curzon did not share Balfour's fastidiousness. He was at ease in the Crabbet Club's exclusive masculinity, playing tennis naked with Wilfrid Scawen Blunt and George Wyndham, pursuing women with an earthy vitality bordering upon coarseness, and in conversation preferred the trumpeting monologue to Balfour's almost diffident interrogatory probing.

Curzon was intellectually well-equipped for India. At Eton and Oxford he had been the outstanding pupil of his generation, winning a string of academic honours and prizes, including a Fellowship of All Souls. At first he seemed to be one of Lord Salisbury's more imaginative appointments. Fanatically industrious and incapable of delegation, often in severe pain from a serious spinal defect, Curzon drove himself hard, despising those who lacked his local knowledge. 'It was eminently characteristic', he wrote in July 1900 to Lord George Hamilton, then Secretary of State for India, of Balfour's speech on the Indian budget, 'of the cultured ignorance of Arthur Balfour to talk of Sindhia as "the Sindhia" throughout his speech.'[5]

When Balfour became Prime Minister, Curzon declared his loyalty. 'You will rest assured', the Viceroy wrote on 16 July 1902, 'that you have not a more faithful or devoted henchman anywhere than myself: and that I am as proud to be your first Viceroy as to have been Lord Salisbury's last'.[6] Soon the communications became less effusive. First Curzon demanded that the Treasury, as opposed to the Indian government, pay for the expenses of the Indian representatives at King Edward VII's coronation, using as a justification India's support and loyalty in the Boxer rebellion in China and the Boer War. Balfour agreed but refused the Viceroy's request that he should announce certain tax reductions at the Delhi Coronation Durbar in January

1903. The Prime Minister was angered by Curzon's attempt to appeal direct to the King for permission to do this. The Viceroy was allowed only to make a general promise rather than specific concessions.

Curzon showed his anger by writing combatively to the Prime Minister. Balfour, understanding the Viceroy's extraordinary need for praise and reassurance, sent a gentle reply, mixing flattery with firmness. 'You seem', he wrote, 'to think that you are injured whenever you do not get exactly your own way! But which one of us gets exactly his own way? Certainly not the Prime Minister; certainly not any of his Cabinet colleagues. We all suffer the common lot of those who having to work with others, are sometimes overruled by them – but do not let any of us forget that there cannot be a greater mistake committed by a British statesman than to interpret any difference of opinion as a personal slight, or as indicating any want of confidences among colleagues.' The admiration surely was genuine. 'Dear George', Balfour declared, 'I do assure you that no one has marked with greater pride or greater pleasure your triumphant progress and the admirable courage, energy, and sagacity with which you have grappled with the immense difficulties of your task, than your old friend and colleague.'[7]

Curzon's response, sent on 29 December 1902, evinced reproachful disappointment, also self-pity. 'It was', he wrote, 'the greatest pleasure to me to see your handwriting again. I think that one of the things that have weighed upon me most in my long four years of exile was that I have never had one line from you, now my chief, and always, as I hope, my friend.'[8] Balfour by February 1903, was worried about the Viceroy. 'Our friends', he told Lady Elcho, 'are now beginning to return from the Durbar. They seem unanimous on two things. 1) the show was the best show ever shown, 2) that George was the most unpopular Viceroy ever seen. Whether this is because his reforms are too good or his manners too bad seems doubtful.'[9] If Curzon was unpopular, it was often through his merits rather than faults, for his phenomenal energy reached almost every aspect of Indian government, whether agricultural, military or educational. He vigorously punished racial intolerance and brutality, particularly among the military. Although his ways with subordinates were

often bullying, his zeal was felt throughout the great sub-
continent.

At the beginning of 1903 Curzon intimated to the British
government that he would like six months leave, followed by an
extension of his term of office. Balfour was doubtful about both
the length of the leave and the extension. This led to another
epistolary irruption. 'I received last week', Curzon wrote to the
Prime Minister, 'your answer to my letter of 5 February. In it
you speak more than once of "my plan" and "my suggestion" as
though I had asked you to keep me on in India. If this was your
interpretation of my words, I wish to repudiate it. I only offered,
in what I perceived to be the public interest, to stay on, should
the government desire me to do so.'[10] Curzon was further incensed by Balfour's offer of a leave of between six weeks and two
months, a period, the Prime Minister wrote, suggested by the
King.

In April the Viceroy complained bitterly to his friend St.
John Brodrick, the Secretary of State for War, and his letter
shows unmistakable strain and hysteria. 'I have been greatly
hurt', he wrote, 'by the grudging tone of Arthur's letters to me.
He has written to me twice since I have been in India, and each
letter has contained a scarcely veiled reproach. He seems to think
that I want and have asked to stay and to treat me as though I
were the recipient of a great favour. Above all when Cromer
returns every year for his three months and Milner has already
been home twice and is I believe coming a third time in six years,
he offers me six or eight weeks after five and a half years. Can't
you every one of you realise that if I stay, I am staying at a
positive risk both to my reputation and my health and that it is
only the strongest feeling of duty to India that leads me to contemplate it? Fancy haggling over a few weeks with the only
Governor General who will have been re-appointed for nearly a
hundred years. I was almost thunderstruck at the proposal.'[11]
Brodrick passed this communication on to the Prime Minister.
Curzon also wrote to the King asking for leave of at least three or
four months.

In June Balfour tried again to calm the Viceroy. He refused to
deny that the extension of office had been Curzon's suggestion,
although admitting that it was a good idea, and remarked that the

tariff reform crisis made the survival of his own government doubtful so any extension might prove worthless. He gave Curzon another dose of praise, once more tempered with a personal rebuke. 'Now', Balfour wrote, 'I am going to utter a very humble protest against your epistolary style! You and I are old friends; why should you adopt towards me the tone of your last communication? – You often reproach my slackness as a correspondent and I plead guilty to the charge. I admit I always take up my pen with the utmost reluctance and lay it down with a sigh of satisfaction. But I sometimes think that the weakness has a good side. You do not share it; but are you not sometimes tempted to use your extraordinary readiness of composition in a way which does not facilitate the co-operation of those who would find it especially easy to work together since they are not only colleagues but life-long friends?' The Prime Minister closed his letter with the words: 'My dear George, take care of your health'.[12]

'In spite', as Balfour told Knollys, 'of Curzon's extraordinary behaviour and still more extraordinary letters',[13] the Viceroy obtained what he wanted. His period of office was extended for a second term and he was allowed six months leave. On 30 April 1904 he left India for England, where he remained from May until November. During this time he was created Lord Warden of the Cinque Ports, but his frustrations outweighed any such honour. Lady Curzon became desperately ill and the government proved intractable.

In the cabinet re-shuffle in 1903, Balfour moved St. John Brodrick, a contemporary of the Viceroy, to the India Office. During his golden youth in the salons of the Souls Curzon had rather despised the prosaic Brodrick, and now the Viceroy, as Brodrick wrote, 'hoped that from our intimacy I should be able to carry for him points of policy of which he had utterly failed to convince my predecessor, George Hamilton, or the Cabinet. He did not and could not realise that matters involving peace or war, as in Tibet and Afghanistan, would be the concern of the whole Cabinet and that, in regard to these, once a decision was given, the affair was *chose jugée*.'[14]

Curzon misunderstood his relationship with the Secretary of State for India who, however splendid the Viceregal pomp and however able the Viceroy, was his constitutional superior. In 1904 this misunderstanding surfaced: first with Tibet and Afghanistan, second with the problem of Kitchener and the military member.

In 1903 Curzon had despatched Colonel Younghusband with a military mission to Tibet, which was under Chinese control. The mission's supposed purpose was commercial but Curzon and the Indian government were also concerned with age-old British fears of Russia on India's northern frontiers. Tibet and Afghanistan, Curzon believed, should be secured against the Russian threat. With this in view, Younghusband exceeded instructions from London by using force to enter the Tibetan capital of Lhasa and impose a treaty which gave Britain effective control over the country for seventy-five years, directly contrary to pledges Balfour had given both Russia and the House of Commons. The treaty's terms were repudiated by the cabinet against Curzon's strongest objections. The Prime Minister defended Younghusband in the House of Commons but was angry. 'Younghusband', Balfour told Lansdowne, 'doubtless with the most excellent intention, has not merely been disobedient, but by his disobedience has touched the honour of his country.'[15]

'His dissent', Brodrick wrote of Curzon's role in this affair, 'was so forceful and the effect on him was so deep seated that strong representations were made to the Prime Minister in view of this and other differences of opinion, that it would be unwise for Curzon to be re-appointed to the government of India after his leave expired.'[16] The disappointment was increased by the government's signing, over Curzon's strong objections, a treaty with Afghanistan in March 1905. Curzon wished to withdraw the original military mission from Kabul unless the Emir modified his father's agreement to make it more favourable to Britain. Balfour and the cabinet refused such drastic action and the old treaty was renewed, maintaining the previous position. But Curzon's greatest cause for discontent was his extraordinary quarrel with the Commander in Chief in India, the legendary Kitchener of Khartoum.

Kitchener went out to India in 1902, Curzon having been determined to obtain his services, believing that one of the most celebrated soldiers of the day could only add lustre to his

Viceroyalty. Brodrick, then at the War Office, claimed to have foreseen trouble between two such imperious and forceful men, and the clash came over the military member of the Viceroy's council who possessed independent control over army administration although he was junior in rank to the Commander-in-Chief. 'Curzon', Kitchener wrote in January 1903, 'is all that one could wish and as kind as possible; but the system by which a member of the council is made responsible for the administration of the army, independent of the Commander-in-Chief, while the latter has only executive functions, is extraordinary.'[17] Curzon rigidly supported such a system, believing it ensured civilian, or Viceregal control. The lines of battle were drawn up, Kitchener preserving, through his friendship and correspondence with Lady Cranborne (later Salisbury) an invaluable link to the Establishment and Tory society at home.

In June 1904, during Curzon's leave, the matter was discussed by the cabinet, which favoured reform. Curzon would not hear of this. Kitchener offered his resignation to Lord Ampthill, who was acting as Viceroy but was persuaded to stay on. In November, Curzon returned to India in a state of near breakdown brought on by his wife's illness and his quarrels with the government. Balfour made it clear that Brodrick and he agreed with Kitchener. 'We should', he wrote to the Viceroy, 'in this respect be found very representative of our countryman.'[18] A cabinet committee recommended that the military member's power should be drastically curbed. In July Curzon spoke against the cabinet and Balfour, referring to a report of the speech in *The Times*, told the King 'it is deplorable in taste and temper; and that no such public exhibition of disloyalty to the Home Government has ever yet been made by an Indian Viceroy'.[19] Curzon retaliated by appointing Sir Edmund Barrow, notoriously opposed to Kitchener, to the post of military member and Barrow's appointment was refused by the government.

The Prime Minister remarked of the Viceroy and Kitchener that 'neither of these eminent men can be said to emerge from the controversy with any credit whatever',[20] but he saw the former as the main offender, also realizing the seriousness of Curzon's personal condition. 'The way', Balfour told the King on 8 August 1905, 'in which Lord Curzon has used Lord

Kitchener's name, his extreme sensitiveness to even the gentlest comment and the violence of his language towards those who differ from him can only be due in Mr Balfour's opinion to the combined effect of overwork, climate and ill health.'[21] On 5 August, the Viceroy telegraphed his resignation to the cabinet and on 21 August Balfour formally accepted it. Any alternative was now clearly impossible; communications between Brodrick and Curzon had hopelessly broken down, the loss of the Viceroy would be, so far as the public were concerned, less serious than the departure of the more prestigious Kitchener, and it was obvious they could never work together. Balfour tried, in a private letter, to allay Curzon's more ridiculous charges, such as the notion that Brodrick had secretly wished to drive him out of India – also to soothe yet again by praise. 'Of one thing only', he declared, 'shall I be mindful – that for nearly seven years, in sickness and in health, you have devoted with untiring energy your splendid abilities to the service of India and of the Empire. And this is enough.'[22]

In September the King wanted to make the Viceroy an Earl, as a recognition both of his services and the grandeur of his office. Balfour advised strongly against this, seeing such a reward as an affront to the cabinet with whom, it was known, Curzon had quarrelled. The controversial partitioning of Bengal, in addition to the dispute with Kitchener, ensured that he left India amid anger and discontent; in Britain, his friends awaited his arrival in December with apprehension. Balfour, staying at Stanway, attempted with the rest of the party to send a telegram of greeting, but the demands of tact and truth made the phrasing difficult, Lord Elcho laughingly suggesting 'Glad your back's worse'.[23] On his return the Viceroy refused to speak to Brodrick and cut Balfour at the entrance to the Carlton Club. Only royal intervention persuaded him from airing the whole controversy in public.

For Balfour the affair had been a misery. Always confident of his powers of persuasion, he had hoped during Curzon's leave of 1904 to settle the trouble by personal mediation. Curzon's mental state, however, was not amenable to either conciliation or compromise. An extraordinary hysteria had entered into his behaviour and this, combined with ill health and self-pity, resulted in self-delusion, a condition which Balfour feared and despised. Faced with the unrestrained emotionalism of the Viceroy, he had found reason a useless weapon. Balfour had seen Curzon at his most hectoring and irrational and this he would never forget.

With George Wyndham, Arthur Balfour seemed to have chosen well. In November 1900 Wyndham was appointed Chief Secretary for Ireland and, after Balfour's accession to the premiership in 1902 entered the cabinet. At the Irish Office he had acquired as his Under-Secretary, or senior civil servant, Sir Antony MacDonnell, a former Lieutenant-Governor of the Indian North West Provinces. MacDonnell agreed to be transferred to the Irish Office on the condition that he was given a freer hand than that usually enjoyed by the Under-Secretary. Balfour was worried. Sir Antony was a Roman Catholic and was rumoured to have Home Rule sympathies, openly declaring that he favoured some form of Irish convention for the transaction of purely local business. However, Lord Lansdowne, whom the Prime Minister consulted, saw MacDonnell and approved the appointment.

Wyndham believed he had a chance of success in Ireland and, in 1902, refused Balfour's tentative offer of a transfer to the War Office. At first there had been the usual Irish chaos, with the revival of the land war, nationalist agitation and a return to coercion. Then in the autumn of 1902 came a remarkable offer from a group of enlightened landlords, led by Captain Shawe-Taylor and the Earl of Dunraven, proposing a conference of owners and tenants to discuss the land issue. The conference met in Dublin in December 1902, despite opposition from reactionary landowners. John Redmond, leader of the Irish Nationalists, and William O'Brien represented the tenants; in January 1903, a report was issued advocating peasant proprietorship in place of the existing system of dual ownership. Wyndham had encouraged this and in March 1903 introduced a new land bill which provided government finance for the scheme at rates attractive enough to encourage landlords to sell and tenants to buy.

The Land Bill of 1903, the climax of the Unionist attempt to kill Home Rule by kindness, gave the Prime Minister reason to be pleased with his protegé. 'Arthur Balfour', Sir Edward Hamilton noted in his diary in March 1903, whilst staying with

the Rothschilds, 'with whom I drove from the station this evening had a very high opinion of his Irish secretary. He regards him
as the ablest man in the Cabinet bar Chamberlain.'[24] Wyndham's
introductory speech added to his reputation and Sandars later
remembered how, afterwards; 'there was a kind of levée of his
admirers of both sexes in my room at the House of Commons
where incense rose in volumes. At that moment, the ball was at
his feet.'[25] The bill became law in August, King Edward VII having paid a state visit to Ireland in July, receiving a tremendous
welcome with Wyndham at his side.

Yet one instance presaged a darker future. In the cabinet,
Joseph Chamberlain, recently returned from South Africa,
opposed the bill on the morning of the day Wyndham was due to
introduce it. His opposition reflected the Colonial Secretary's
defiant mood on the brink of that great campaign which was destined to break up his party.

On 21 October 1902, at a cabinet meeting, Chamberlain had
proposed a policy of imperial preference by the exemption for
colonial wheat from the corn duty imposed by Sir Michael Hicks-
Beach to raise money for the Boer War. The idea was accepted in
principle a month later, although Ritchie, the Chancellor of the
Exchequer, avoided a final commitment to include it in his next
budget. Chamberlain left for South Africa content, believing he
had won the day.

He was wrong. The battle had hardly begun. On the one side
was the Colonial Secretary, convinced that it was his messianic
task to unite the empire by tariff reform and thus provide a basis
for an imperial federation through which Britain could triumph
over her industrial competitors such as Germany and the United
States. On the other side stood Ritchie, under the influence of his
permanent officials, Sir Francis Mowatt and Sir Edward
Hamilton (both Gladstonian apostles of free trade). At first, the
Treasury set the pace. During Chamberlain's absence in South
Africa, Ritchie threatened to resign unless Hicks-Beach's corn
duty was completely dropped, let alone decorated with
Chamberlain's alterations. The Chancellor saw no alternative to
such tactics; in November Sir Edward Hamilton had recorded of
Ritchie 'he says he has clearly a majority against him in the
cabinet. Arthur Balfour, according to him, is "rotten" on the

subject and so are most other members of the cabinet who are over-persuaded by Chamberlain.'[26]

Captain Middleton, in charge of the Conservative organization, reported to Sir Alexander Acland-Hood, the Chief Whip, that the grain duty 'is made use of on every Radical platform' and 'does the Farmers no good; the Brewers dislike it; the Labourers are dead against it; and it furnishes our opponents with a most damaging political cry'.[27] Sandars passed on this report to the Prime Minister. Ritchie had his way, for Balfour could not lose his Chancellor when the budget was due in a matter of weeks. On 23 April the corn tax was removed and Chamberlain, only partially calmed by Balfour's diplomacy, humiliated. He did not lie low for long.

Ritchie's budget was merely the latest of Chamberlain's frustrations. The Boer War had not increased his reputation; the Colonial Conference of 1902 revealed uncertainties among the self-governing colonies about the benefits of closer imperial fiscal co-operation; the Education Act had badly damaged his political standing with Liberal Unionist nonconformists; Brodrick's proposed army reforms virtually ignored his wishes to increase the garrison in South Africa; and the Colonial Secretary had serious doubts about the practicality of Wyndham's Irish legislation. In Lord Salisbury's cabinet, Chamberlain's power had been fully recognized; under Balfour he seemed in danger of losing that power through a series of partial defeats.

On 12 May Balfour told the King that the cabinet had been 'almost entirely occupied with the discussion on the present position of the corn tax. The difficulties attending the remission of the tax seems almost as great as those attending its imposition! But there can be no doubt that in spite of the agitation against the repeal, the weight of general opinion is in favour of it.'[28] On 15 May, Joseph Chamberlain spoke in Birmingham Town Hall, publicly declaring against repeal, advocating Colonial Preference. His supporters, adherents of vigorous imperialism, were delighted, Leo Amery comparing the speech to 'the theses which Luther nailed to the church door at Wittenberg'.[29] Campbell-Bannerman, for the Liberals, quickly saw that 'this reckless criminal escapade of Joe's is the great event of our time'.[30]

On the same day, at the Foreign Office, Balfour received a

protectionist delegation, led by Henry Chaplin, Conservative Member of Parliament and spokesman for Tory agricultural interests. He and his friends protested against Ritchie's action. Balfour tried to steer a middle course, emphasizing the difficulties of forming an imperial fiscal union, stating that 'if it were possible I would look forward to such consummation with unfeigned pleasure' but the support for such an idea 'must come from the heart and the conscience and the intellect of the great body and mass of people'.[31] In other words, there must be evidence of public support before such economic unheaval could be imposed upon the country. Chamberlain's speech swept away such tentative probing. The cause was made public, the message clear. Asquith, realizing the implications both nationally and within the Unionist party, wrote: 'It is only a question of time when we shall sweep this country.'[32]

In the House of Commons Chamberlain further alarmed free traders of his own party. 'If', he retorted to Lloyd George's taunts, 'you are to give a preference to the colonies – you must put a tax on food, I make hon: gentlemen opposite a present of that.'[33] Within the cabinet, Ritchie, Lord George Hamilton, the Duke of Devonshire and the Scottish Secretary, Lord Balfour of Burleigh, believed that any tax on food would be an electoral disaster and of dubious economic advantage; outside, the young Winston Churchill (elected in 1900), Sir Michael Hicks-Beach, Lord Goschen (both former Chancellors) and Lord Hugh Cecil were fervent 'Free Fooders'. Throughout the summer Balfour battled to keep his government together. In June he contrived to produce a compromise whereby the tariff question should remain undecided, having been submitted to an enquiry supervised by the Prime Minister; meanwhile ministers refrained from making divisive speeches. Yet the two camps were gathering supporters. Chamberlain launched the Tariff Reform League in July and in the same month the Unionist Free Food League came into existence with Hicks-Beach and Goschen at its head.

For Balfour the most painful part of the dispute was to be the rift in his own family. Lord Salisbury had five sons, three of whom were already politically active. These had been brought up in an atmosphere where cabinet politics and European diplomacy were commonplaces of conversation; each served for a brief period as his father's secretary and they were encouraged to voice their views. Lord Hugh Cecil as a small boy had rushed from Hatfield Post Office in the middle of the night to bring the news of the defeat of the first Home Rule Bill and once, on meeting Gladstone at Hatfield, had warned him of his inevitable assassination for political misdeeds.

Salisbury's sons inherited the strong Anglican religious beliefs of their parents, also their mother's outspokenness. In 1899, during an ecclesiastical dispute which had also troubled Balfour when he was leader of the House of Commons, Lady Salisbury wrote: 'we still have almost daily great family arguments on ritualism – Linky [Lord Hugh Cecil] in his usual character of grand Inquisitor, Jem [Lord Cranborne] trying to agree with everyone but finding it impossible owing to his unfortunate love of the truth – his Lordship humble and silent as he always is among his sons.'[34] For the boys such a united family and affectionate upbringing led to self-confidence and, encouraged by Lady Salisbury, a wish to take what seemed to be their rightful place in the councils of the nation. Cranborne, the oldest son, joined the government in 1900 as Under-Secretary at the Foreign Office, but for Balfour Lord Hugh Cecil claimed the most attention at first.

Lord Hugh, who entered the House of Commons in 1895, had already crossed his cousin over the Education Bill. Formidably articulate and intellectually gifted, he was never afraid to use extreme language, or tactics, in controversy. As a fervent free trader he went into battle after Chamberlain's declaration and, from Hatfield in June 1903, Lady Frances Balfour reported the views of Lord Hugh and his father. 'Salisbury', she wrote, 'is very strong against it all and says it means the loss of our colonies, because the country is asking what good are they to us. In his own manner he says our mistake is having an empire! He looks forward eagerly to Beach's attack, and hears Goschen is longing to let his big cannon off. Linky is absorbed and wild on the subject.'[35]

At the end of August there was a lull in the storm. Balfour received news that his uncle was critically ill. Uncertain as to whether he would be welcome at Hatfield or not, he sent a telegram to his cousin Cranborne and Cranborne's reply brought him to

Salisbury's bedside where his uncle, barely conscious, recognized him. This was to be their last encounter. Next day Balfour had to attend a cousin's funeral and while he was away Lord Salisbury died. All his children, apart from Lord Edward Cecil, who was in Egypt, and, as Balfour told Lady Elcho 'myself whom he had ever treated as one of his children',[36] were there. The funeral was postponed to allow for Lord Edward's return and the death of the great statesman drew those around him momentarily together, Balfour's natural sympathy moving his cousins to forget political divisions. 'Thank you', Lord Robert Cecil wrote, 'for all you did for us at Hatfield. We shall none of us ever forget it'.[37]

The tariff controversy continued. Balfour had compiled, after consulting economists, civil servants and other experts, a document entitled 'Economic notes on Insular Free Trade'. This proposed a policy of retaliation, or the imposition of tariffs on another country's goods in order to retaliate against a tariff wall erected by that country; thus the principle of free trade was abandoned but full scale tariff reform, involving food taxes and imperial preference, avoided, although the document was merely consultative, providing no authoritative lead. The cabinet seemed increasingly to lack firm direction, and on 13 August Balfour exacerbated this by putting before his ministers not only his own document but a Treasury paper attempting to set out the content and advantages of Chamberlain's scheme as well. No agreement was reached at this meeting which had been supposed to produce a conclusion to a promised fiscal enquiry. A final decision was postponed until 14 December.

Balfour, in an 1888 review of John Morley's biography of Richard Cobden, had earlier demonstrated his distrust of dogmatic free trade. Also Ritchie's crude tactics and his officials' obvious subjugation of him irritated the Prime Minister. 'He was really the villain of the piece', Balfour later observed of his Chancellor, 'in the tariff reform affair. Joe was really very hardly used over that.'[38] Yet Balfour had doubts about the popular and economic consequences of imperial preference, although he was nearer to Chamberlain than to Ritchie. On 9 September the Prime Minister's hand was forced. Joseph Chamberlain sent in his resignation, declaring his loyalty but stating that he believed his campaign could be better continued outside the government. On 14 September, an hour before the cabinet were due to meet, Balfour and Chamberlain constructed an agreement whereby Chamberlain, having resigned, would attempt to educate the country to tariff reform and, if this was successful, Balfour would pledge the Unionist Party to this course.

The following cabinet was confused. Chamberlain spoke of his resignation; other ministers, used to such threats, saw this as a mere gesture and Balfour attempted no elucidation. The Prime Minister then turned to the question of a free trade memorandum submitted by Ritchie and Lord Balfour of Burleigh, and fiercely attacked the document and its authors, leaving them no alternative but to resign. On 15 September Lord George Hamilton followed; the purge, Balfour hoped, was complete. The free traders were later astonished when Chamberlain's resignation was published on 18 September, claiming that this had never been revealed in cabinet on 14 September and they had therefore left under false pretences. Balfour had resorted to obfuscation to preserve party unity.

'The resignation of Chamberlain', Lord George Hamilton wrote to the Prime Minister on 19 September, 'and the abandonment, as a practical policy, for the time being by all members of the Government of any idea of a preferential tariff, was a sudden and unexpected revelation to me.' Hamilton declared 'I must add that I do not think I have been treated, in this matter, with the candour an old colleague was entitled to'.[39] Balfour believed the departures would enable him to maintain a united government, but there was still one great imponderable: the Duke of Devonshire.

Devonshire was Balfour's Lord President of the Council. As Lord Hartington he had led the Liberal Unionists out of Gladstone's government in 1886 and, in the course of a long political career, refused the premiership three times. Devonshire was ponderous, often dull as a speaker, but possessed extraordinary power in the country and in parliament, partly through the authority of his inherited position, also because he seemed to stand for plain, honest thinking as opposed to evasive intellect or verbal dexterity. Sir Almeric Fitzroy records how during the second reading in the Lords of the bill creating the Board of

Education, Devonshire was asked what advantages a Board would bring in the constitution of the new department. 'The Duke of Devonshire', Fitzroy wrote, 'characteristically replied that the point had been carefully considered by the Government, but for the life of him he could not remember the reasons which had weighed with them in adopting a Board, but he could assure their Lordships that they were sufficient. There is not another man in either House of Parliament who could have said this without making himself look foolish. . . .'[40]

Devonshire was regarded as sound, by both his colleagues and the electorate. His great passion was horse racing. In his youth he had been rather raffish, marrying late and keeping the courtesan 'Skittles' (Catherine Walters) as a mistress for several years. Balfour told Sandars the Duke 'was the greatest pleasure lover he knew'.[41] Devonshire felt he had not been treated properly at the time of Salisbury's departure. 'I cannot say', he wrote to Lord Lansdowne, 'that I am quite pleased at not having been consulted at all in the matter'.[42] He remained in the cabinet and, during the tariff controversy, the Prime Minister, realizing his importance, made every effort to offer reassurance. Devonshire, however, joined the meeting of Ritchie and free trade dissidents after the cabinet on 14 September and resigned with them. Balfour saw him the next day, partially revealed Chamberlain's resignation and begged the Duke to stay. The Duke, realizing 'there was really some prospect of Chamberlain retiring'[43] wavered. On 16 September Balfour and he had another meeting and Devonshire agreed to remain.

On 17 September, after Balfour had gone to Scotland, the Duke saw Sandars, remarking 'what a mistake he had made throughout the recent controversy allying himself with Ritchie, George Hamilton and Balfour of Burleigh'.[44] Earlier John Dunville, Devonshire's private secretary, had told Sandars, 'the Duke was struck with positive admiration for the courage displayed by the Prime Minister in calmly sanctioning the resignation of four colleagues; and, if that were not enough, being quite prepared to part even with him, the Duke of Devonshire. He said that in all his political experience he had never known a Minister face a situation of such unexampled difficulty with such calmness and courage.'[45]

The resigning free traders realized that, without the Duke, their resignations lacked weight. Ritchie, before leaving the cabinet, had spoken of the possibility of a coalition government being formed under Devonshire, with Rosebery, Grey and Asquith from the Liberals. This reached Balfour who was furious.[46] Devonshire was subjected to heavy pressure, not only from Ritchie and his old colleagues but from the Duchess (who saw her husband as Prime Minister), his private secretary and Lord James of Hereford (an old Liberal Unionist associate, dismissed by Balfour in 1902) as well. Balfour was to speak at Sheffield on 1 October, at the National Union of Conservative Associations; before this the Duke yielded to the implications of dishonourable contact and desertion of his friends. He wrote his letter of resignation but hesitated, not despatching it until after the speech, later using Balfour's Sheffield declaration as his reason. Lord Stanley, married to Devonshire's step-daughter, told Sandars, who reported to Balfour, 'of a long and impassioned interview he had had with the Duke on Thursday at Newmarket before your speech was made! The resignation was then written, but Eddie [Stanley] persuaded him to hold it back. This was unfortunate as it enabled him to get his material from your speech recorded the next morning. Eddie said the old boy could not sleep for thinking of the grip Ritchie and Co. had on his throat. They had been threatening him and he could not bear it'.[47]

Even after the letter was sent, Stanley informed Sandars 'the Duke was miserable, and that he was sure that he would have reversed his decision that day with the slightest possible pressure from the Prime Minister'.[48] But Balfour, his cabinet devastated, was not in a diplomatic mood. Infuriated by Devonshire's indecision, he despatched a stinging public letter to the Duke, accepting his resignation. 'The Duke of Devonshire's conduct', he told the King on 4 October, 'has been pitiable. Nor is it possible to excuse, or even to understand, his vacillations without remembering that he without doubt put himself somehow in the power of Mr Ritchie and his friends. He is forced to behave badly to me lest he should be publicly taxed for behaving badly to them. – His loss administratively is nothing. He led the House of Lords well, and possessed weight in the country. Mr Balfour's confidence that he can successfully carry on the government is in no way shaken by the Duke's defection.'[49]

Balfour later told Lady Rayleigh that he had tolerated Ritchie and the militant free traders until September because it was essential to secure the passage of Wyndham's Irish Land Bill through parliament.[50] On 14 August this had received the Royal assent and he believed he could now dispense with them, risking a serious cabinet split. In addition, Acland-Hood had produced another report, submitted on 10 August, from Conservative Central Office and local Tory agents which, while advising that there was still 'a strong feeling against taxing bread and wheat', remarked upon the 'indifference to preferential tariffs' and 'a general feeling to have fair play for our native industries as against the foreigner'. This encouraged Balfour in his belief in fiscal 'retaliation' without emphasis on food taxes. Acland-Hood further stated that 'in the towns every man is a protectionist of his own industry, a feeling which has been growing for years'. Sandars later wrote on the top of this document: 'It was this report that practically decided the Prime Minister's attitude at the cabinet on 14 September 1903.'[51]

The next task was that of cabinet reconstruction. The King telegraphed from Balmoral on 17 September: 'I cannot approve the resignations announced until I have thoroughly discussed the matter with you on Saturday and also the question of filling up the places. This great haste is to be deprecated and appears to be unnecessary and moreover it would not look well in the eyes of the public, that matters of such importance should be settled without my having seen the Prime Minister.'[52] The King was relieved to hear, however, that the Duke of Devonshire seemed to be staying on. As we have seen, he was not pleased with the replacement by Arnold-Forster of Brodrick, who had now moved from the War Office to the India Office. Balfour, anxious to obtain a prestigious successor to Joseph Chamberlain, offered the Colonial Office to Milner, still High Commissioner in South Africa; Milner refused, believing his work in South Africa to be unfinished, but recommended the Prime Minister's old friend, Alfred Lyttelton to the post. 'With regard to Mr Alfred Lyttelton', the King told Balfour on 1 October, 'taking the place which Mr Balfour recommends, it certainly did not occur to the King that' he would be named. He might fulfill his duties admirably, but what real experience has he? and will he give strength to the government?"[53] Edward VII was right to ask such questions. Lyttelton, largely under the domination of the powerful Milner, proved a failure at the Colonial Office, unequipped to deal with the explosive issue of Chinese labour.

The other changes were carefully designed to satisfy the factions. Austen Chamberlain was promoted to be Chancellor of the Exchequer, serving as his father's representative in the cabinet; Victor Cavendish, Devonshire's heir, became Financial Secretary to the Treasury; and Lord Stanley, married to the Duke's stepdaughter, Postmaster General. George Wyndham was given the chance to move but, as Lady Elcho told Balfour, 'he likes staying on in Ireland and he thought he could help you'. Wyndham wished to see the Land Act fully working, although his sister noted 'the heart's desire of his life is to be Chancellor of the Exchequer — he also said he was all for Austen's having it'.[54]

One surprising problem presented itself. In August, 'Jim' (or Jem) Salisbury succeeded his father. Previously, as Lord Cranborne, he had served as Under-Secretary at the Foreign Office, where his diffident manner and halting delivery had caused difficulties in the House of Commons. Balfour at first proposed to the King that the new Lord Salisbury should take Devonshire's place as Lord President of the Council. The King vigorously disagreed, and Balfour had to admit that the objections were 'well founded. It would no doubt (though most unjustly) have raised again the absurd cry of the "Hotel Cecil", and have thereby increased the difficulties of the Government at a difficult moment."[55]

Lord Londonderry, a free trader, was therefore appointed to the Lord Presidency, which he combined with the Education Office. Lady Elcho warned on 18 September 'you know what an awful fuss was made about family appointments'[56] but Balfour persevered with his first cousin, proposing to make Salisbury Lord Privy Seal in Londonderry's place. 'The King', Knollys wrote to the Prime Minister on 12 October, 'feels sure it is a misunderstanding, but he was certainly under the impression that Lord Salisbury was not to be created Lord Privy Seal at present, and he was surprised therefore when he saw the announcement in today's papers."[57] Balfour answered that, if the appointment were made at the same time as the others, it would come under the general discussion of the cabinet re-shuffle; if deferred it might be 'an isolated mark for attack'. He wrote, 'I may have been mistaken but I certainly was under the impression that the King quite agreed to the force of this reasoning.'[58]

Balfour had formed a new cabinet which was obviously weaker than its predecessor. Austen Chamberlain was no replacement for his father and the notion of inexperienced relatives substituting for their fathers or uncles, and cousins and close friends adding to an already incestuous arrangement, contributed to this impression. At the end of October, the Duke of Devonshire became president of the Unionist Free Food League, set up to combat Joseph Chamberlain's campaign, and the factionalism continued.

Balfour was caught in the middle, to the irritation of both sides. 'I don't know', Lord Hugh Cecil wrote to his brother Salisbury on 17 October, 'whether you will have any opportunity of reasoning with Arthur but if so I hope you will try and persuade him to declare openly either for or against protection. If he is against it he will have to fight hard as Joe has gone far to capture the party. I hear on all sides that the local wire-pullers are Chamberlainites, and there is a growing conviction among free fooders that they must either make terms with the opposition or prepare to lose their seats.'[59] The Sheffield speech had dwelt on the new policy of fiscal retaliation, but the two factions were still far apart. Lord Hugh Cecil and his younger brother, Lord Robert, Conservative candidate for East Marylebone, were bellicose and Lady Gwendolen, their formidable sister, told Salisbury that he must extract from Balfour a promise that there would be no surrender to tariff reform for 'the Cabinet are now almost wholly Chamberlain'.[60] In December, in reply to Salisbury's complaints about Chamberlainite activities in the constituencies, Balfour refused to move further towards free trade. 'The irresistible conclusion,' the Prime Minister told his cousin, 'at which I have arrived is that the party would be absolutely smashed, if I were to weaken in my advocacy of Fiscal Reform on the lines on which I myself believe. This does not mean, of course, that you are wrong in thinking that on these lines any near triumph for Unionism is impossible; but I am quite confident that the only chance of keeping together the one party organization which can save us from socialistic radicalism is to adhere unwaveringly and with emphasis to Fiscal Reform.'[61]

To the Cecils, Chamberlain's great campaign, by its divisive nature and call for food taxes, courted electoral disaster, placing at risk those causes that their father had fought for and in which they passionately believed. The established church, the union of Britain and Ireland and, ultimately, the power of the governing class itself: all these seemed threatened both by Joseph Chamberlain's style of politics, which they saw as a mixture of demagoguery and ruthless caucus organization, and the possibility of a massive radical victory. Balfour, who owed his position to their father's patronage, seemed about to sell the pass. It was as if they were to be betrayed from within, their cousin the chief agent of destruction. Henceforth, a personal note of family disappointment aggravated the political scene.

In November, Balfour suggested to the King that Joseph Chamberlain should succeed Curzon as Lord Warden of the Cinque ports; the King refused, believing the appointment would be too controversial. In December the Unionist Free Food League encouraged its supporters to work against protectionist candidates at by-elections. Chamberlainites spread the rumour that old Lord Salisbury, before his death, had favoured their cause; in January 1904 Lord Robert Cecil, at the instigation of Winston Churchill and other free fooders, denied this in a letter to *The Times*. Aristocratic landowners were often enthusiastic for tariff reform, encouraged by the support they hoped agriculture would receive from protection. The Unionist press was largely in favour, also many of the great 'Captains of Industry'. At the end of 1903, Sir Edward Hamilton had little doubt who was making the running. 'It is', this dedicated free trader wrote on 31 December, 'a marvellous testimony to the power of one man that he should have brought protection to life again; and that he, the man of hair about his heels, should have carried with him all the bulk of the aristocracy and upper classes! No other public man has improved his position. Indeed the Prime Minister has done very much the reverse'.[62]

In January 1904, Balfour stayed at Chatsworth with the Duke of Devonshire. He addressed a large meeting in Man-

chester, still emphasizing retaliation. His rancorous exchanges
with the Duke seemed forgotten and the visit was clearly supposed to pacify the more militant free fooders. In February, the
Prime Minister was briefly absent from the House of Commons
due to an attack of influenza and, according to Edward Hamilton,
'his absence brought home to one how absolutely dependent on
one man the Government is',[63] and on 18 February, Sir William
Harcourt told Hamilton that 'what he, as an old Parliamentarian
felt most was the degradation of the Treasury Bench, on which
he expected to see men of mark seated, instead of which they
were almost entirely mediocrities. Indeed it was the weakest
bench he had ever seen.'[64] This weakness was emphasized by the
question of Chinese labour on the Rand.

The Liberals had come together over the fiscal question and
Asquith followed Chamberlain around the country, denouncing
tariff reform. Now Lord Milner, High Commissioner in South
Africa, gave them a more emotive cause. In the autumn of 1903
Milner came to England to press his request for indentured
Chinese coolies to be introduced as workers into the mines on the
Transvaal, to rectify the shortage of unskilled labour. Joseph
Chamberlain, when Colonial Secretary, had refused to comply
with this, recognizing its political hazards. Alfred Lyttelton, in
awe of the formidable Milner, acceded to it; and the King on 28
November 1903 sent a telegram to Balfour expressing his full
support of the plan. Milner thought that he had also secured
Asquith, Grey and Haldane – the three leading Liberal Imperialists – but was proved wrong. In February 1904 the storm broke.
A Chinese labour ordinance was passed on 10 February by the
Transvaal Council and agreed to by the Colonial Office. At
Westminster, there was trouble: radicals saw Chinese labour as a
threat to British workers and the quick way to profits for mine
owners; the nonconformists and other churchmen expressed
shock at the living conditions and terms of employment given to
the Chinese, and Asquith joined in the clamour, protesting that
the House of Commons had not been made aware of the regu-
lations under which the scheme was being run. Henceforth, this
subject was to be constantly used to taunt the government, flar-
ing up in 1905 into a great national uproar. Alfred Lyttelton, as
Colonial Secretary, performed to the best of his ability, but was

often no match for his tormentors.

Balfour, throughout 1904 and 1905, performed an extraordinary tightrope act. 'In the evening', Arnold-Forster wrote on 9 March 'fiscal debate with a most animated speech from Balfour to a very large house. Our party was greatly refreshed and pulled together. The Prime Minister is a wonderful man. He had been suffering from a very bad toothache, slept thirteen hours under opium, had already spoken in the afternoon, now spoke again for a full hour in his very best form.'[65] Arnold-Forster, who sympathized with Chamberlain, wrote on 18 May, showing party discord: 'the rabid Free Fooders seem to be losing all manners and sense of decency, and to become openly offensive and intentionally insulting. I think Hugh Cecil and Jack Seely bear off the palm.'[66] On 31 March Winston Churchill crossed the floor of the house to join the Liberals. In August, Austen Chamberlain, confident of the success of his father's campaign, tried to persuade Balfour to announce more definite fiscal proposals and then put them to the country with a united party behind him. The Prime Minister refused; on 3 October at Edinburgh he presented his 'doubt election plan' whereby the party would enter an election pledged to no specific tariff policy and after a Unionist victory the Colonial Conference should be consulted on preferential tariffs, then another election held with the Unionists advocating the fiscal result of this consultation. Meanwhile Balfour still spoke of 'retaliation'.

Neither Joseph Chamberlain nor the free fooders were content with the Edinburgh pronouncement. Chamberlain, addressing huge audiences, was sure that the country supported him. Within the Unionist party, there was increasing turmoil. Local Tariff Reform League branches were threatening to dominate the constituencies, fighting against free trade candidates, and Chamberlain began to agitate for a representative at Conservative Central Office. By the end of the year the Liberal Unionist organization had been captured by Chamberlain. Among government ministers, Austen Chamberlain, Alfred Lyttelton and Lord Selborne spoke on tariff reform platforms. On 4 October, Acland-Hood, the Chief Whip, informed Sandars of the state of party opinion. 'The most discontented', he wrote of Unionist activists, 'say, "Who is our leader? If it is Balfour why doesn't he lead?"

The better disposed wish he would come forward now. A few openly display a preference for Chamberlain, or ask for a definite policy on tariff reform, though of those I have met, whole hoggers and Balfourites are about equally divided.'

Acland-Hood believed 'the chief is losing ground in the party' and expressed a view that Balfour 'will be squeezed out of the leadership and the party turn in despair to Joe or some very inferior leader'. He noted also the presence of a new threat, one which was to be more personal and painful to the Prime Minister than that offered by Joseph Chamberlain, telling Sandars that 'the MacDonnell affair is doing the Chief and through him the party enormous harm'.[67]

On 26 September, the Irish Reform Association, under the chairmanship of Lord Dunraven, published a scheme of devolution for Ireland. Inevitably this excited Unionist opposition, but *The Times* on 27 September pointed to a more serious implication when it remarked in an editorial that 'this insidious project' had its origins in 'an influential clique in Dublin Castle of which Sir Antony MacDonnell is regarded by numbers of Irish Unionists as the head'.[68] MacDonnell, of course, was George Wyndham's Under-Secretary at the Irish office. His involvement in the Dunraven scheme had grown out of a terrible misunderstanding. In August, Wyndham, suffering from nervous exhaustion, had left for a holiday in Germany, leaving MacDonnell, whose terms of appointment gave him greater powers than were normally accorded to an Under-Secretary, in charge. During Wyndham's absence Dunraven approached MacDonnell and Sir Antony wrote, on 10 September to Wyndham to say that he was helping with the proposed scheme of devolution. Receiving no answer, he pressed ahead. Dunraven was later to note that his general impression was that Wyndham had 'approved of the draft scheme agreed upon by Antony MacDonnell . . . and myself'.[69] It was this which was published on 26 September.

Wyndham, just back from Germany, immediately responded to *The Times* by denying that he had known about the project. At first, it seemed that this denial would be enough, but the more extreme Irish Unionists did not accept it. Within the government, Carson and Lord Londonderry were angry and a "measured censure" was passed on MacDonnell which con-

demned his action but exonerated him of disloyalty. At first Mac-
Donnell bore the brunt of the criticism. On 8 November Sir
Edward Hamilton noted in his diary: 'if anything happened to
Arthur Balfour, the man clearly destined to be his successor is
George Wyndham'.[70] But four days later Lord Stanley ominously
told Hamilton 'he was much too unpopular ever to be a leader.
He was moreover too fond of the glass'.[71]

Wyndham could not evade responsibility. The Irish Office
had exhausted him, playing havoc with his nerves. Alcohol, the
fatal crutch, was resorted to, and exhaustion, coupled with the
failure of concentration, was the terrible result. In 1903 after
the passing of the Land Act, he had the chance to return Mac-
Donnell to India, but had refused, asking the King to influence
Sir Antony to continue what seemed to be a fruitful partnership.
The Under-Secretary had Home Rule sympathies; in India he had
been known as 'the Fenian'[72] and the Irish Nationalists once
offered him a seat in parliament. MacDonnell, after the cabinet
criticism, was determined to clear his name and the main planks
of his defence were passages in letters he had written to
Wyndham on 10 September and earlier informing the Chief
Secretary of his dealings with Dunraven. The trouble was that
Wyndham had no recollections of ever receiving or reading these
passages.

Parliament was to meet again in February 1905. Wyndham's
nervous condition worsened, confronted with the inevitable
parliamentary storm, his difficulties with MacDonnell and his
suspicion that doubts had been cast upon his honour. 'I am
seriously alarmed', Balfour wrote to Wyndham's wife on 23
January, 'about George's state. His nerves seem to me – nay
are – (for the moment) utterly ruined.'[73] In the House of Commons the Chief Secretary could not expect a sympathetic hearing;
he had never been especially popular with his party, the stolid
Tories suspecting his literary tastes and friendships with such
figures as Belloc and Charles Gatty, a litterateur who had once
stood for parliament as a Liberal and been smeared by the Conservative press for supposed homosexual tendencies. Nor was his
florid style of oratory impressive to the back benches; as Sandars
later wrote 'he puzzled them and to mystify followers is to lose
them'.[74]

In February the parliamentary encounter was a disaster. Redmond, moving his usual motion of disapproval of Irish government, was supported by Unionist hardliners. Wyndham, attempting an explanation, was unconvincing, almost incomprehensible. He had already conceded to MacDonnell that Sir Antony had not erred by helping Dunraven; it had also emerged that Lord Dudley, the Lord Lieutenant, had known of the Under-Secretary's action, imagining that Wyndham fully approved. Balfour gave his friend whatever support he could. 'I think', Lady Elcho wrote of her brother on 24 February, 'he got into A.M.'s clutches somehow morally (you have never been influenced that way) – he had a hold on him, but it's very serious, it's breaking him so, but I think he will rebound alright.'[75] But the Unionist revolt, led by the Ulstermen, would not subside and Wyndham's nervous condition grew worse. On 4 March Sandars was despatched to Clouds where the Irish Secretary had gone to recuperate, to obtain his resignation in the interests of the party and his own health. 'I shall never forget', Sandars wrote, 'that painful embassy or the unhappiness or the depression of the adoring family circle.'[76] The previous day Balfour had spoken to Lady Elcho about the crisis. 'I felt', she wrote to him on 4 March, 'all the time yesterday that although you said you were in a state of wretchedness and indecision that deep down it was really decided that George must go.'[77]

Balfour told Lady Elcho that a mere change of post for Wyndham 'might not satisfy the wolves'.[78] On 6 March, the Prime Minister announced the resignation of his Irish Secretary. In May Wyndham discovered one of MacDonnell's letters; another was not found until 1912, and in both there were passages concerning Dunraven's devolution scheme which their recipient had, in his mental state, failed to absorb. The resignation did not end the affair; in May it was raised again in the House of Commons and St. John Brodrick told Selborne that 'unluckily George Wyndham's mistakes come out more and more. I think he must have lost his head altogether in the last two years.'[79] Selborne replied: 'I can only thank providence on behalf of yourself and myself that we have no share of the artistic temperament.'[80]

The implications of the Wyndham/MacDonnell imbroglio

The Third Marquess of Salisbury

Lady Blanche Balfour,
Arthur Balfour's mother

Whittingehame House in the snow

The Honble Mary Lyttelton.   1875.

May Lyttelton

Arthur Balfour in a House of Commons pose, around the time of his debating triumphs as Chief Secretary for Ireland

Lord Hugh Cecil, Balfour's cousin
and an ardent Free Trader

Harry Cust, whose amorous exploits
amused Balfour

George Nathaniel Curzon

The young George Wyndham

Lady Desborough
dressed for a fancy dress ball

Below:
Lady Elcho, later
the Countess of Wemyss

Below, right:
Gerald Balfour,
Arthur Balfour's brother,
who left politics in 1906 and
devoted the rest of his life
to psychic research

C.T. Ritchie, Chancellor of the
Exchequer in Balfour's government

R.B. Haldane, the politician and philosopher

Arthur Balfour and Joseph Chamberlain together in the House of Commons,
painted in 1903 by S.P. Hall

A Max Beerbohm caricature
demonstrating Balfour's vagueness.
Balfour points to the Houses of
Parliament and asks 'Can you tell
me what that large building is?'

Leo Maxse, editor of the *National Review*
and scourge of Balfour's leadership

The conference at Philip Sassoon's home at Lympne, Kent, in August 1920. Lloyd
George is next to the French Prime Minister, Alexandre Millerand, in the front row.
Immediately behind Lloyd George is Balfour, with Lady Desborough beside him.
Curzon is behind Millerand, to the left. Maurice Hankey looks out from the back
row, between Lady Desborough and the uniformed Admiral Beatty. Foch stands in
the front row, with the dog at his feet.

Balfour and the Earl of Wemyss on the tennis court. Wemyss, formerly
Lord Elcho, was married to Mary Elcho

were far-reaching. The diehard Unionists believed there was a plot, in which the Prime Minister was involved, to bring in Home Rule by stealth. Walter Long, a leader of the Tory squirearchy, and Carson led the opposition within the party. Long, despite a simple bucolic exterior, had high political ambitions. Balfour appointed him to take Wyndham's place at the Irish office where there was now a swing away from conciliation, although MacDonnell stayed on as Under-Secretary. Long was to raise the incident again in 1906.

Wyndham probably was sympathetic towards devolution, although he denied this; Sir Shane Leslie remembers him earlier enthusiastically discussing the idea.[81] Balfour later firmly stated he had known nothing of the Dunraven scheme, nor could he have ever supported it. Wyndham's immediate reaction to his fall was one of gratitude to the Prime Minister; 'tell him', he told his wife on 5 March, 'I love him' and she wrote: 'I want too to send you my love dear Mr Balfour for I have a great deal to thank you for.'[82] 'I wish', Wyndham wrote to Gerald Balfour, 'I had not failed Arthur by breaking down at a critical moment!'[83] Later, however, brooding led to anger, not only against Unionist extremists but his own master as well. 'I wish', Lady Elcho wrote, 'George would realise how much you have weathered and with what unbitter serenity.'[84]

Balfour had no alternative but to jettison his old friend, on grounds of health alone. He also realized that the critics would have to be placated if his party, already split by the fiscal controversy, was not to be devastated, and that Wyndham could never achieve this. 'Blunt simplicity' the Prime Minister later told Wilfrid Ward, 'was demanded by the situation; and George, even in the best of health and spirits, was rarely simple and never blunt.'[85] Yet Wyndham's departure, and his leader's apparently calm acceptance of it, added to the legend of Balfour's cold ruthlessness. 'He smiles upon his friends', declared A. G. Gardiner, the Liberal journalist, 'and leaves them to the wolves. No man ever had a more chivalrous follower than he had in George Wyndham, but when the Ulster pack were hot upon the scent, he sacrificed him without a word – sacrificed George Wyndham to Sir Edward Carson!'[86] But Balfour had not deserted his Irish Secretary. To the Prime Minister the incident, like the

Curzon debacle, had given great pain. Later, he was to say that the two greatest mistakes of his premiership were letting Curzon return to India and Wyndham continue in Ireland.

Balfour's government tottered on until December. The fiscal controversy continued, with Joseph Chamberlain trying to force the Prime Minister nearer to full-blooded tariff reform. In January, Balfour had responded to John Morley's demand for a summary of his views on 'a sheet of note paper'; the result was an evasive statement which could satisfy neither the Chamberlainites nor the free fooders. In May, it seemed as if Balfour might be prepared to drop his double election plan in favour of more definite support of Chamberlain's programme; Joseph Chamberlain, on the basis of this, offered to return to the cabinet as a minister without portfolio, but the Prime Minister, faced with a revolt of free food Unionists, retreated to his original policy, offering only vague statements to placate his old colleague. By the autumn, Chamberlain had captured the National Union and tariff reform was strong in the constituencies. An appeal for party unity by Balfour at Newcastle in November at the annual conference of the National Union had little effect. A week later at Bristol, Joseph Chamberlain called for an election and a strong policy of tariff reform. Finally on 4 December Balfour handed in his resignation to the King, and the Liberals set about forming a new government.

12

Fighting Back

On 15 December 1904, Evan Charteris, Lord Elcho's younger brother and close friend of Arthur Balfour, told Sir Edward Hamilton that the Prime Minister's greatest villains in political history were Sir Robert Peel and Mr Gladstone 'because both of them broke up their parties'. Balfour, Charteris declared, refused to express himself more decidedly on the fiscal question for 'by these balancing feats he still hopes to prevent the split. He believes that in doing this he is serving the best interests of his country, because he regards the break-up of the Unionist party as the greatest misfortune that could befall it. Evan Charteris says Arthur B. regards the strength of the Labour party as the most serious consideration of the future.'[1]

There will always be controversy over Balfour's handling of tariff reform. Letters from Acland-Hood quoting reports from the Unionist organization point out that the party, almost evenly split in October 1903 between Balfourites and Chamberlain supporters, was desperate for a lead. One may argue that if the Prime Minister, with his immense reputation and authority, had spoken out more clearly he could have carried his party with him. The trouble was that his speeches were so full of praise for Chamberlain on the one hand and protestations of anxiety about food taxes on the other that voters looked in vain for an unequivocal declaration of policy.

Arthur Balfour was not a demagogue. He had not Chamberlain's gift for popularizing, for filing down complicated issues into easily identifiable causes. Neither wholehearted tariff nor free trade dogmatism moved him. He saw grave difficulties in the former, especially in the growing independence of the

Dominions, and found the latter too inflexible, too rooted in the past. What he did believe in was the preservation of the Union and the threat of radical, even revolutionary, politics, already a force in Europe. Only a united Unionist party could stand against this; therefore he strove to preserve this unity. Like the Cecils he cherished those beliefs he and his uncle had fought for but, unlike his cousins, he would not risk their destruction by forcing Joseph Chamberlain and the Unionist imperialists into the wilderness. Despite factionalism, a tenuous unity was preserved; but after 1906 the Labour party became a force in British politics and the electoral debacle of that year ensured an immense Liberal majority. It is difficult not to wonder if the result could have been any worse had Balfour pledged himself to one side or the other in the fiscal argument.

The last year of the Balfour government showed his priorities. He would not resign earlier because of these, and first among them was defence. In May he made a brilliant speech in the House of Commons revealing the innermost deliberations of the Committee of Imperial Defence, concluding that an invasion of this country was impracticable. Balfour was still, on his day, a superb House of Commons performer. Lady Rayleigh wrote that 'the absorbed interest of the House was a sight such as I have never seen. It was fairly full and faces were turned towards him from all parts with an expression of eager interest. Party spirit seemed forgotten';[2] and Edward Hamilton approvingly noted 'He had put his back into it. In fact the Committee of Defence seems to interest him more than anything else.'[3]

Balfour was determined to secure the development of the 18-pounder gun to a stage where it was safe from an incoming radical government, also to conclude the second Anglo-Japanese treaty. On 20 July the government was defeated in the House of Commons on the Irish estimates. Sir Michael Hicks-Beach, a free trader and influential elder statesman, and Alfred Lyttelton were among those who, according to Sandars, favoured resignation. Balfour refused and secured unanimous support from his cabinet, later dining with Joseph Chamberlain who had wanted an election earlier in the year but now thought an August poll in the holiday season inadvisable. King Edward VII saw Sandars and 'insisted every effort should be made by Mr Balfour to maintain himself in office',[4] primarily because of unresolved diplomatic issues, particularly the Japanese treaty. In August the treaty was signed.

Then there was Ireland. Walter Long, fearful of losing his seat at Bristol, urged the Prime Minister to give him time to heal Unionist wounds inflicted by the devolution crisis. On 21 September Balfour wrote to Lord Selborne, who had succeeded Milner in South Africa, 'I think there is now no chance of an autumn dissolution. Walter Long, from the point of view of Ireland, is as vehement against it as you are from the point of view of South Africa.' In the same letter he revealed an impending storm, 'the quite inexplicable illegality of which Milner seems to have been guilty in permitting, before he left, overseers in the mines to inflict corporal punishment. I am anxiously waiting to see what excuse, if any, he can produce for this amazing blunder, which seems to violate every canon of international morality, of law, and of policy.'[5] During the election of 1906 the Liberals were to use this with great effect. In February 1906, in the House of Lords, Milner admitted his responsibility, also that he had been wrong. Selborne and Lyttelton stopped the floggings, but the damage was done.

On 22 November 1905 Sandars sent his master a memorandum urging that the opposition should be placed in power 'at the earliest possible moment' for 'nothing is more calculated to restore harmony to our ranks than the presence in office of a government whose whole career will promise to be the very opposite of that which will command the approval of our party'.[6] Yet the electoral prospects were bad. Throughout 1904 and 1905 the Unionist record in by-elections had been poor. Brodrick, in November, told Selborne of Balfour's weak position, declaring 'he has lost terribly in the country, and M.P.s, newspaper editors, constituents and others all come to one saying – Let him raise his own standard, and let those who dislike it recede from it: otherwise seat after seat must go'.[7]

After Balfour's resignation in December the bad omens continued. 'I am sorry to say', Acland-Hood wrote to Sandars on 16 December, 'money for the election is coming in very badly. Charles Hamilton cannot get one shilling from Lancashire from those who used to subscribe. "Hard times, inconvenient time of year, dislike of Chamberlain, don't understand Balfour" – these are the excuses.'[8] The Unionist organization, already weakened by the resignation of the formidable Captain Middleton in 1903, was suffering from the party split. In addition, Balfour's hopes that Sir Henry Campbell-Bannerman would be unable to form a united government came to nothing. The radical and imperialist wings of the Liberal party were brought together to win the greatest electoral victory of this century.

For Balfour the defeat was doubly painful; he lost his own seat at East Manchester, one of the first results to be declared and almost certainly the precipitant of further Unionist disasters. St. John Brodrick, Alfred Lyttelton, Gerald Balfour, Walter Long, Lord Hugh Cecil, Bonar Law: all these were ousted. On 14 January, in the midst of the bad news, Arthur Balfour came to Lyme in Cheshire, to stay with the Newtons. 'This was,' Lord Newton wrote, 'the first occasion on which I had ever seen him seriously upset. He asked for a book which I, fortunately, possessed, and he retired with it to bed, reappearing at luncheon quite restored and cheerful. In the afternoon we played golf and he thoroughly enjoyed himself, having apparently forgotten Manchester like a bad dream.'[9]

'Now poor Lovelace is at this moment pretty well played out', wrote Lady Elcho on 16 January 1906, remembering Samuel Richardson's *Clarissa*, 'after four meetings a day and a severe beating which he certainly deserved not on account of his public life but of his infamous private conduct.'[10] Her relationship with Balfour took on a more skittish tone as they grew older. She grew accustomed to her circumstances and could laugh at them, writing of one of Lord Elcho's friends: 'She, he tells me, is now the favourite lady – Lady Colebrook is another – they run in all degrees of friendship, wholly platonic, semi platonic or non platonic!!'[11] She came to enjoy teasing Balfour. 'Your visits in London', she wrote in 1895, 'were delightful and you were quite like a lover';[12] and in 1897 she complained in mock exasperation of his 'icicle ego', remarking 'I really must get me a fresh lover'.[13] In 1905, while in Paris, Lady Elcho was obliged to sit through a concert given by a brass band from Manchester, sent to France under the patronage of Balfour and others. 'Do you think', she told the Prime Minister, 'I felt artistic and pious . . . as I sat in the huge box at Trocadero – *not at all*, I felt a mass of impertinence and just longed to smack your "bottie".[14]

In 1907 the Webbs visited Stanway and Beatrice wrote admiringly of 'the beautiful-natured Mary Elcho – neglected wife, devoted and tenderly-loved mother, and adored friend – a beautiful soul in a delicately refined form'. Mrs Webb's judgement here is surely sound. 'In his courtly devotion to Lady Elcho', she declared of Balfour, 'in the intimate and sincere talk about men and thought that seems to be natural to him in her presence, Prince Arthur is at his best. It is clearly an old and persistent sentiment – good sound friendship, with just that touch of romantic regret that it could not have been more, that deepens sex feeling and makes such a relation akin to religious renunciation. One can believe that the relation between these two has always been at the same high level of affectionate friendship, without taint of intrigue."[15]

This romantic friendship was to be Balfour's closest and most lasting involvement with the opposite sex. The young flirtation with May Lyttelton had been brief, perhaps also more passionate in recollection than reality. Now there could be little possibility of a wife. Balfour once cryptically observed to his sister Mrs Sidgwick, when discussing a possible marriage for the sake of the family inheritance: 'But she must understand that I have no heart to offer her – nothing but ashes."[16] Whether this refers to the desolation of past disappointments, the years of iron control or simply the onset of age is impossible to tell. Yet it might also denote the extinction of feelings which had never been strong, never vital or important, never enough to disturb a bachelor's independence and devoted family circle.

His admirers, aware of the comfortable view people liked to have of their politicians' domesticity, wanted him to be different. 'But, ye gods! if he only knew', a fellow civil servant said to Sydney Parry, 'he might be the most popular Prime Minister on record. Give him a wife and half a dozen kiddies. Then let him walk to church every Sunday morning with his wife on his arm, a big prayer book in his hands and the kiddies two and two behind, and let him stop at intervals and pat a girl on the head. Talk of old Gladstone reading the lesson! He wouldn't be in it with your Chief."[17]

This was not to be; but there were consolations. At Whittingehame the congregation of worshippers was enlarged by maturing nieces and nephews. In 1902 Blanche, daughter of Eustace and Lady Frances Balfour, left to marry Edgar Dugdale and had an interview with her uncle Arthur (now generally known to the family as 'Nunkie') at which she broke down in tears at the prospect of leaving him. The domestic bliss remained unbroken, causing Lady Elcho to write chidingly in 1909 of 'other people's children (nieces and nephews), other people's dogs – all the beer and skittles and halfpence and none of the kicks (of domestic life) – this is a sudden attack on you for being a dastardly coward'.[18]

To those who only knew him slightly and observed the adoration of the Souls, the family devotion, the competitive attentiveness of society hostesses surrounding a charming but elevated figure, the impression was fascinating but elusive. The gentle conversational manner, the ease with which great philosophic and political issues were discussed and dismissed, the endless curiosity: then, at the centre, an impenetrable chasm, a man seemingly devoid of quick passion, love, attachments, the ordinary vital preoccupations of humanity. Occasionally there might appear an interlude of warmth, evidence of affection, perhaps a more than clinical interest in a cause or belief; then the darkness would descend, the cloak of amiability return. H. G. Wells, a visitor to Stanway, sketched his idea of Balfour, as Evesham in *The New Machiavelli* and Cecil Burleigh in *Men like Gods*. Both characters are charming nihilists, intellectually beguiling but practically unproductive. Burleigh is 'one of those people who seem to understand everything and feel nothing', believing 'in very little but the life of a cultivated wealthy gentleman who holds a position of modest distinction in the Councils of a largely fictitious empire'. Even John Buchan, an admirer, made Lord Appin, who in the imperialist novel *A Lodge in the Wilderness* is supposed to be a mixture of Rosebery and Balfour, absurdly raised above the common ruck of men.

To Wells and other intellectuals, Arthur Balfour's appearance of philosophic detachment was intriguing, if unsuited to practical politics. To others it merely distanced him from the rest of the world. 'He would be a better leader', Lady Gwendolen

Cecil wrote of her cousin, 'if he could get rid of the idea that logic has an effect on the judgement of the ordinary man';[19] and Arnold-Forster once declared 'It is evidently easy to be much too clever'.[20] This 'cleverness' seemed often to be used to delay, to complicate rather than to solve, and his first book – *A Defence of Philosophic Doubt* – was, wrongly, much quoted as evidence of Balfour's inability to make up his mind. These images coalesced to produce a decorative but politically unsatisfactory portrait; a procrastinatory, cold philosopher surrounded by society sentimentalists, discoursing in abstractions while his country faced the imposing challenge of the new century. In a brilliant short story – 'Below the Mill Dam' – Rudyard Kipling, an apostle of Joseph Chamberlain, satirized what he saw as Arthur Balfour's kind of Conservatism, able only to concern itself with the preservation of old aristocratic elitist life and pleasures, oblivious to scientific and technological change.

Kipling was probably correct in his assessment of the thinking of various Souls, but Balfour was different and it was his political misfortune that he came to be so closely associated with them. His interest in science was profound; Lord Rayleigh, a Nobel prize winner, once declared that he was severely tested in scientific conversation with his brother-in-law. Machinery and technology had always fascinated Balfour. He was one of the first public figures to own a motor car and fly in an aeroplane. He took great trouble to keep abreast of scientific development, delighting in the details of new weaponry which came before the Committee of Imperial Defence, and until the end of his life was an enthusiastic promoter of government aid for research. And once engaged, Balfour was quick, persuasive and determined. Perhaps his period at the Irish Office was the only time the public had an opportunity to appreciate his true strength, for here the issues were obvious enough for universal interest. The civil servants and ministers associated closely with him invariably came away full of admiration; to others he presented a mask of courtesy and indifference, preserving the traditional dislike of his class for the mixing of work and pleasure, the revelatory danger of intense discussion. Mrs Webb once asked him, after a dinner party, 'Have you ever wished to bring about another state of affairs to what at present exists?' Balfour's reply, given the direction of her

interests, must have exasperated his questioner. 'I am a Conservative', he rejoined quietly, 'I wish to maintain existing insti-
tutions.' Then . . . he added: 'There are some things about which
I have been keen; take for instance the clause in the Scotch Free
Church Bill enabling the established Church of England to
change its formulae – freeing it from the dead hand – I worked
very hard to secure that.'[21]

At the beginning of the twentieth century, reports and
statistics emphasized the terrible condition of the poor. Great
works of documentation by Booth and Rowntree shocked their
readers; but the Balfour government, preoccupied with tariff
reform and the desperate struggle for party unity, had a poor
record of social and domestic legislation. Balfour and his uncle
Lord Salisbury had, in 1899, made tentative steps towards the introduction of old age pensions and poor law reform, but the South
African War intervened, setting back the scheme. Balfour's
Licensing Act of 1902 introduced compensation for public house
licencees who lost their licences through decisions by local
magistrates or pressure from temperance groups; this offended
the temperance lobby and displeased the nonconformists. In the
same year aid was given to the unemployed in the form of
employment exchanges in London boroughs, followed in 1905
by the setting up of local employment committees in distressed
areas. But in 1901 the Taff Vale decision made union funds
liable for any damages done by trades union officials in the form
of industrial disputes or strikes. Balfour told Edward VII that the
judgement, by the House of Lords Court of Appeal, was 'In
substance right, and that the singular freedom of the country
from unnecessary trade disputes is largely owing to it'. He
remarked also, correctly, that it was 'very distasteful to the
Trades Unions'.[22]

However the Webbs, pioneers in social investigation, had
hopes of the Unionist leader. Balfour appointed Sidney Webb a
member of the Royal Commission set up to study the Trades
Unions in 1903, but organized labour, incensed by the Taff Vale
decision, was far removed in tone and temper from the genteel
socialist imperialism of the Webbs. Chamberlain and the tariff
reformers made social reform a part of their platform; Balfour, his
fiscal compromise difficult to understand and his record on social

questions poor, seemed ill-equipped to understand a restive, anxious working class.

Ian Malcolm, who entered the House of Commons in 1895, later remembered his first glimpse of Arthur Balfour at the dispatch box. 'Did I say thousands?' the leader of the House said in answer to a question. 'Oh, I meant millions, but it makes no difference to my argument.'[23] Such nonchalance was attractive in success, but in failure merely irritating. As happens often in politics, the caricature came to eclipse the man and if the caricature was inaccurate this did not lessen its effect. Some Unionists, tolerant, even proud, of Balfour's idiosyncrasies in the past, started to have doubts which, given the party's rural stolidity and customary distrust of ostentatious intellect, were scarcely surprising. Lord Winterton, a traditional Tory of the squirearchy, wrote that the public 'did not know exactly what the Souls were, but vaguely disapproved of them. Thus one's supporters would say to one, "We want a man like good old Joe Chamberlain as leader, not a 'Soul' like Balfour". If you asked them to define a "Soul" they were silent. It was just something they didn't understand and, in consequence, disliked, and that was that!'[24] At the start of the new parliament, Willie Bridgeman, a newly elected Unionist, was summoned to a meeting with his leader. He noted that the only person who was listened to was Lord Robert Cecil and 'the room was full of very excellent Burne Jones pictures, whose anaemic and unmanly forms seemed to give the meeting a nerveless and flabby character, and were to me painfully symbolic of their owner'.[25]

If Bridgeman and Winterton give the harsh criticisms of defeat, Balfour's political adversaries, particularly those who had experienced his sharpness in parliamentary debate, thought otherwise. In 1905 Lady Elcho dined with the Asquiths and told Arthur Balfour 'they all said you were the most alarming or formidable person they knew'.[26] Winston Churchill also understood the power beneath the urbanity. Churchill stirred Balfour's anger 'only on a few occasions, which I prefer to forget'.[27] But the public were largely unaware of such effective displays. Mrs Wilfrid Ward, showing him at his most socially difficult, gives evidence of a polished, unsympathetic hardness, declaring 'that when she talked to Mr Balfour he used to say "how interesting" in a voice which announced an extremity of boredom. She felt that if she had read the right book and expressed the right opinion, she was "marked up one", if not she was "sent down to the bottom of the class." [28]

Balfour's tastes were different from most of his followers. His reading ranged from philosophy and scientific theory, down through the great novels (Walter Scott, Jane Austen and Stevenson were his favourites), contemporary literature (Kipling and Shaw) to detective stories and light French fiction which he devoured at great speed. Later he conceived a passion for the works of P. G. Wodehouse. With poetry he remained essentially Victorian, a selective admirer of Tennyson, Swinburne and William Morris. In modern art he believed Burne-Jones to be supreme and in music maintained his enthusiasm for Handel and Bach, adding Wagner to these in the late 1890s when he visited Bayreuth with Ian Malcolm, meeting Cosima Wagner at the Villa Wahnfried. He once remarked that he found the later works 'too advanced' and had a positive dislike of 'that tiresome old gossip Wotan'. [29]

The range is conventional but wider than most of his party or class, a fact further emphasized by his association with a group who flaunted their intellectual predilections. Grandees like Devonshire, Rosebery and, later, Derby were popular in the country because there was an earthy quality about their lives and pleasures. Horse racing was a sport of the masses and it was possible for all to share, financially and otherwise, in an owner's successes. Balfour's diversions seemed too exclusive: too distant from the great uneducated, or ignorant, world: evidence of the passionless, single, carefully-calculated existence of someone who, in Lloyd George's words, could seem 'not a man but a mannerism'. [30]

Yet, in the midst of the 1906 defeat, as if to disprove this caricature, a meeting took place which marks the beginning of one of Balfour's greatest and most far-reaching enthusiasms. At the Queen's Hotel in Manchester, his election headquarters, he saw Dr Chaim Weizmann, a lecturer in organic chemistry at Manchester's Victoria University. Mr Dreyfus, the Jewish chairman of Balfour's constituency association, arranged the meeting after Balfour had evinced interest in the Zionist cause. In 1902

the Zionists had spurned Joseph Chamberlain's offer of a settlement in East Africa; this refusal to consider anything less than a
return to Palestine had aroused Balfour's curiosity and admiration.

In common with others of his time and class, Balfour could
make scathing references to Jewish influence and character, and
in 1905 had spoken, during the introduction of an aliens bill to
curb the influx of immigrants, mainly from eastern Europe, of
'the undoubted evils that had fallen upon the country from an im-
migration that was largely Jewish'.[31] But he had no connection
with the anti-semitic feeling rife in Edwardian Britain, exemplified by the polemics of Chesterton and Belloc. This was encouraged by the involvement of Jewish financiers in the Boer
War and disapproval of Edward VII's taste for plutocratic company. To Lady Desborough and others Balfour might joke about
'the Hebrews', but was equally capable of denouncing their
persecution. The rootlessness of the Jewish race, its influence on
the Christian tradition, its strongly individualistic culture: these
had long fascinated him, and Mrs Dugdale writes 'I remember in
childhood imbibing from him the idea that Christian religion and
civilization owes to Judaism an immeasurable debt, shamefully ill
repaid'.[32]

Weizmann, a Russian Jew, was supposed to stay with Balfour
for a quarter of an hour in January 1906. The interview lasted an
hour and a quarter, leading to an extraordinary sympathy
between the two men. Weizmann, recently arrived from Eastern
Europe, had a poor command of English, but his visionary
sincerity came through. Although they did not meet again until
1914, the Zionist was delighted. As for Balfour, he told his niece
some twenty years later: 'It was from that talk with Weizmann
that I saw that the Jewish form of patriotism was unique.'[33]

Willie Bridgeman, a newly elected Conservative member of
parliament, catches the uncertainty after the 1906 election defeat
in his description of his arrival in London in February. He found
the Carlton Club 'a hotbed of intrigue: tariff reformers and free
traders in small groups and all talking in excited and highly important tones. The free fooders were much alarmed at a supposed
plot to elect Chamberlain and depose Balfour; the tariff reformers

on the other hand accusing Balfour of wishing to throw over
Tariff Reform or to damp it down . . . it then was rumoured that
Chamberlain was going to scud from the Unionist party, refuse
their whips and act entirely independently, taking with him all
who would follow.'[34] The electoral debacle was complete. The
new House of Commons consisted of 377 Liberals, 132 Conservatives, eighty-three Irish Nationalists, fifty-three Labour
members and twenty-five Liberal Unionists. Of the block of
Liberal Unionists and Conservatives, 102 were estimated to be
supporters of Joseph Chamberlain, thirty-six allied to Balfour's
fiscal compromise and sixteen free fooders; three were still
undecided.

Balfour's position seemed weak, but he nevertheless determined to carry on, concentrating on the socialist challenge, telling Sir Francis Knollys that previously he might have considered
leaving politics, but 'I am so profoundly interested in what is
now going on that I should return a very different answer today'.
He saw the fiscal issue as merely 'squabbles' in front of the tide
of socialism for 'unless I am mistaken, the election of 1905
inaugurates a new era'.[35] Knollys told Sandars that the King
was alarmed that Balfour might not be back in the House of
Commons in time for the debate on the King's speech and
'H.M. thinks that this would be a very great pity as he presumes
in that case that Mr Chamberlain would practically lead the
opposition!!'[36]

A new seat was obviously vital; Balfour toyed with the idea of
one of the Scottish universities or Cambridge but then told
Sandars on 20 January that 'the most desirable seat of all, from
my point of view, is the City'.[37] The member for the City of London was Alban Gibbs, son of Lord Aldenham. It was decided by
Lord Salisbury and others that Gibbs should be persuaded to
make way for Balfour, as his father was over eighty and he could
soon expect to enter the House of Lords; also Salisbury noted that
'Alban is useless in the House and I should imagine takes little
interest in parliament'.[38] The trouble was that Gibbs did not wish
to retire, but the pressure, from his own constituency association
and friends, became too great and Balfour was adopted, easily
winning a by-election against a free trade opponent on 27
February.

There was also the painful family dissension. The Cecils were deeply disappointed at the election result and angry at Balfour's refusal to send a letter of support to Lord Hugh Cecil at Greenwich where a tariff reform candidate, endorsed by Joseph Chamberlain, had run and Lord Hugh had been defeated. Balfour had given his own view to Lord Lansdowne on 6 January. 'As for Joe and Linky', he declared, 'I think they are a well-matched pair. I am bound to say that I think Linky was the original aggressor and, so far as the House of Commons is concerned, the Free Fooders have given us more trouble than the extreme Tariff Reformers. But I confess I think that Joe might well have shown a little more generosity to his younger colleague.'[39] To the Cecils, the politics of the Chamberlain school were still strange and wrong. 'It appears to me', Lord Robert Cecil wrote to Balfour about the new face of Unionism, 'to be utterly sordid and materialistic, not yet corrupt, but on the high road to corruption. Take even this Chinese labour question. The Liberal lies on the question are scandalous and disgusting but I am sometimes almost as much repelled by certain types of Unionist defence. Almost my only hope in the party is yourself.'[40]

Balfour's cousins flinched at a compromise, despite the poor results of the free fooders. 'I am a bit sick of the Cecil family', Acland-Hood wrote to Sandars on 23 January. 'Whenever there is a crisis they take the opportunity to embarrass the Chief. They don't realise the one thing that has damaged him in the country as much as anything is his loyalty in sticking to Gerald and Jem Salisbury.'[41] Salisbury had been made President of the Board of Trade by Balfour in 1905 partly because, as he was a peer and already in the cabinet, a by-election could be avoided (newly appointed cabinet ministers had to seek re-election until 1926). This appointment, at a time when Britain's trade was in fierce competition with the United States, Germany and other industrialized nations, was criticized as inappropriate. Gerald Balfour, a lack-lustre performer, had also come in for criticism and both he and Salisbury were quoted as examples of Balfour's penchant for family preferment.

Family problems apart, there remained the necessity of some accord with Chamberlain. From Whittingehame, after the election, Arthur Balfour told Sandars on 26 January that: 'Balcarres,

who is here, thinks the vast majority of the party prefer me to Joe
as leader, but that they would decide, though by a much smaller
majority, where the question left an "open" one, to go for Joe's
fiscal scheme rather than for mine – I confess to feeling some
reluctance in remaining leader of a party who, on a matter so important (though doubtless not pressing) take a different view to
mine.'[42] Joseph Chamberlain, however, saw that only Balfour
could gather the fragments of the Unionist party into some
semblance of unity. 'The worst of our position', Chamberlain told
his supporter Leo Maxse, owner and editor of *The National
Review* on 30 January, 'is that while you say that many of our
people are confident that we cannot win under Balfour's leadership, it is equally certain to me and to others that we cannot win
without him. If we could secure a thorough change in the
organization and especially in its control, we might manage, and
perhaps this is the best policy to go for now'.[43]

On 2 February Balfour dined with Joseph and Austen
Chamberlain in Joseph Chamberlain's house in Princes Gardens.
Chamberlain called for a party meeting to decide between the two
fiscal programmes. If Chamberlain's programme was defeated, he
would leave the party to carry on his campaign on his own, supported by his adherents; if it was accepted, the free fooders should
be expelled from the party's ranks. Chamberlain suggested that,
in the event of a tariff reform victory, Balfour could not continue
as leader and a suitable compromise candidate, possibly Walter
Long, might succeed him. St. John Brodrick, to whom Balfour
repeated the conversation, told Selborne that Chamberlain had
said that 'he (J.C.) not being a Churchman or in sympathy with
Land would never begin leading the Conservatives at 70.'[44] Joseph
Chamberlain's position was far from invincible, as the journalist
J. L. Garvin, another supporter, told Leo Maxse on 4 February.
'A united party will not follow Joe', Garvin wrote, 'and he never
was wiser than in refusing to lead. I am perfectly certain that at
least a score of nominal tariff reformers (according to the recent
lists) will rat to Balfour if there is a split – if Long is the man he
ought to be the game is our own, but the sentimental reaction
prematurely created in Balfour's favour is dangerous'.[45]

Balfour realized his strength. He agreed to a party meeting,
but obtained a concession from Chamberlain that the terms of the

motion would be kept vague and that its result need not pledge the party to any policy. In addition Joseph Chamberlain conceded that the free fooders need not be expelled if the vote went against them; he also went back on his call for Balfour's resignation. Then, having been informed by Balfour that the fiscal question and the leadership were too interwoven to allow their separation and that if tariff reform carried the day at the party meeting, Chamberlain could not refuse to take over from him, Joseph Chamberlain, knowing the impossibility of his acceptance by a united party, drew up a document which could serve as an agreement between them. There were further discussions with the Chamberlains involving Lansdowne, Gerald Balfour, Akers-Douglas, Acland-Hood and Sandars. A compromise was arrived at, eventually announced in the form of two letters, known as the Valentine Letters, which were published on 14 February. Balfour wrote to Chamberlain acknowledging that 'fiscal reform is, and must remain the first constructive work of the Unionist party', yet his acceptance of 'a moderate general tariff for manufactured goods', also 'the imposition of a small duty on foreign corn' was lukewarm, described as merely 'not in principle objectionable'.[46] Chamberlain answered that he was satisfied.

The party meeting took place on 15 February at Lansdowne House. The free traders remained in the party and Arthur Balfour was given a unanimous vote of confidence. To the Cecils it seemed a terrible surrender. 'Poor Jem', Lady Gwendolen wrote of her brother, 'I've never seen him more utterly disgusted – Bob and Linky have at least the pleasure of saying they always thought as much';[47] and Lord Salisbury told Lord Lansdowne 'the more I think of today's performance the more sick I am. I am afraid it has been a capitulation'.[48] St. Loe Strachey, the Unionist free trade editor of the *Spectator* congratulated Leo Maxse, declaring on 16 February that 'the Balfour climb-down is a great triumph for the *Nat*. In another way it is also a triumph for the *Spec*. for, as you know, we have always declared that Balfour was in reality a Chamberlainite and that he had not the courage of his opinions. Thank Heaven we shall have no more tedious Balfourian psychology in the newspapers.'[49]

For the moment, Arthur Balfour seemed to have succeeded

in establishing a semblance of unity. The next task was to rally
his followers in parliament, but first he found himself stricken
with one of his periodic bouts of sickness. His doctors advised
three months rest after the election; the negotiations with
Chamberlain precluded this. Towards the end of February, he
contracted serious influenza and could not take his seat in the
new House of Commons until 12 March. On 1 March, Mrs
Sidney Webb asked Balfour if he considered taking a holiday,
and he answered firmly that this was impossible, if only for the
party's sake. 'It is exactly now', he said, 'that they are beaten
and demoralised that they need me: I shall be with them as
continuously as if I was Prime Minister.'[50] But, on the occasions of his return, his subtle attempts at evading Liberal
criticism of the Unionist fiscal policy by moving an adjournment
led to Campbell-Bannerman's celebrated retort, supposedly
representative of a new parliamentary era. The Prime Minister
decried Balfour's questions as 'utterly futile, nonsensical and
misleading. They are invented by the right honourable gentleman for the purpose of occupying time in this debate. I say,
enough of this foolery . . . move your amendments and let us get
to business.'[51]

Sir Henry's sally was met with tumultuous applause by the
new Liberal majority. Within a few days Balfour was laid low
again with influenza, retiring to bed for three weeks in Carlton
Gardens with a nurse to look after him. His state of mind cannot
have been improved by the renewal of activity by Joseph
Chamberlain. During April and May, on a committee set up by
the National Union to enquire into party organization and the
relations between the National Union and Central Office, Henry
Chaplin, a supporter of Chamberlain, fought hard for the adop-
tion of Chamberlainite proposals. In the Unionist press, especially
the *Morning Post*, the *Outlook* and the *National Review*, articles
attacked Balfour and the Central Office from an extreme tariff
reform point of view and in the Commons and the Lords the campaign continued to put Central Office under the control of the
National Union, already susceptible to Chamberlain's domination. But in July there was intervention from another source.
Chamberlain, after celebrating his seventieth birthday in Birmingham amid a massive display of civic enthusiasm, had a stroke.

Henceforth he was effectively out of politics, capable only of sending rallying messages to his disciples, reliant upon their efforts to
perpetuate his vision and his name.

Balfour, for the moment, was unchallengeable. No other
Unionist possessed the power or the reputation necessary to
unseat him. Steadily he had set about restoring his own and his
party's parliamentary fortunes. Much has been made of Campbell-
Bannerman's devastating taunt of 12 March, but it should also
be said that Balfour's ingenuity in adversity was formidable. The
Unionists were rallied. For Balfour, faced with radicalism and
socialism, it was axiomatic that, as he had told his supporters on
15 January, 'the great Unionist party should still control,
whether in power or opposition, the destinies of this great
Empire'. Unionist power in the House of Commons was now
minimal so it was to the House of Lords, with its huge inbuilt
Tory majority, that the party turned.

Lansdowne, Unionist leader in the Lords, was unsure of the
peers' new role and on 13 April Balfour wrote to encourage him.
'I do not think', he declared, 'the House of Lords will be able to
escape the duty of making serious modifications in important
government measures; but, if this can be done with caution and
tact, I do not believe that they will do themselves any harm. On
the contrary, as the rejection of the Home Rule bill doubtless
strengthened their position, I think it quite possible that your
House may come out of the ordeal strengthened, rather than
weakened, by the inevitable difficulties of the next few years.'[52]
Thus was 'the revolutionary tide' to be turned back.

The Lords were selective. Much of the Liberal social legislation was allowed through, including a bill reversing the Taff
Vale decision; but an Education bill of 1906 (designed as a
palliative for the nonconformists), the Plural Voting bill of the
same year and the Licensing bill of 1908 were destroyed. Balfour
led the fight against the Education bill, brushing aside
Lansdowne's reluctance. His pugnacity was welcomed by his supporters. 'Arthur', Lady Gwendolen Cecil told Lady Selborne in
August, 'has been working like a slave with the Education bill
and is believed to have largely retrieved popularity in the party';[53]
and Augustine Birrell, Campbell-Bannerman's President of the
Board of Education, later wrote of this measure, 'its chief ex-

ecutioner was Mr Balfour, who had by a marvellous exhibition of intellectual supremacy recovered in a House from which scores of his old supporters had disappeared at the polls, a position almost as powerful as the one from which a few months before he had been almost contemptuously hurled – he blocked all roads that might have led to a settlement'.[54]

Yet there were murmurs of discontent, at this stage still muted. In September 1906, Walter Long, now member of parliament for Dublin County after his defeat at Bristol, again raised George Wyndham's relations with Sir Antony MacDonnell and the suspicion of Unionist involvement in a scheme of devolution. In a speech in Ireland he demanded publication of all the correspondence connected with MacDonnell's appointment; but Balfour refused. Long seemed to some to be too interested in furthering his own cause, St. John Brodrick noting that 'this talk of him in the papers as a possible leader has upset his equilibrium'.[55] Balfour declared that 'Walter Long is perfectly straight' but was forced to admit that there was 'a press conspiracy'[56] against his leadership. Leo Maxse and others were pressing their case. On 9 January 1907 Acland-Hood told Sandars that 'there is undoubtedly a press culmination against him [Balfour] and I get the echo of it from every shooting party and every smoking room in the country. The main cry is "want of backbone" and "vacillating policy".'

Hood enumerated the causes of Balfour's unpopularity: '1) He does not mix enough with the party, never goes near the Carlton. 2) His friendship with George Wyndham, and the latter's intrigues over devolution, have seriously impaired his position. 3) You are supposed to have a bad influence over him, and to prevent people from seeing him. 4) I am d—d unpopular with the Chamberlainite section and supposed to "boycott" Tariff Reformers.' Sandars and Acland-Hood were also concerned about Austen Chamberlain, Hood observing; 'I agree about Austen. He is going to give trouble. He has all his father's impulsiveness, with less than half his brain or the capacity for leading.'[57] But Chamberlain, although concerned about Balfour's evasive treatment of Long's resuscitation of the devolution issue, had told Gerald Balfour in October 1906, 'Arthur is our only possible leader', and 'I am doing all I can to steady Walter Long'.[58]

Akers-Douglas, writing to Sandars in January 1907, expressed Balfour's difficulties succinctly. 'He is alright in the House of Commons, and he is understood there, except by certain disloyal colleagues and M.P.s who after all you can count on your fingers and whose position nothing will alter. But he is not understood (and therefore looked on suspiciously) in the country. His intellect is far greater than that of his party and even than that of the bulk of his colleagues – and his thoughts and language are sometimes not understood by them. He is often over the heads of his audience – outside the H. of C. – and for this reason . . . they honestly don't know what his quality is – and therefore sincerely think he is vacillating. If he could consider that the major portion of his party were . . . stupid and uneducated and get himself down to their level he would be better understood and appreciated.'[59]

Balfour's response to his critics was disdainful. 'I am certainly not going to condescend', he told Lord Dalkeith in July, 'to go about the country explaining that I am "honest and industrious", like a second coachman out of place! and if people cannot find it out for themselves, they must, so far as I can see, remain in ignorance.'[60] Within the party there was another cause of criticism. Sir Edward Clarke, senior member of parliament for the City of London and a previous supporter of Balfour's candidature there, had, in 1906, been forced to resign his seat as the result of a disagreement with his constituency committee. Clarke later complained that throughout his troubles, Balfour had made no attempt to come to his assistance, not even troubling to give proper acknowledgement to his letter of resignation. In February 1907 Clarke refused an invitation from Lord Salisbury 'to meet Mr Balfour' and Salisbury wrote chidingly to his cousin 'I expect I should have done all in my power to stand by him'.[61] Lord Salisbury's reproof brought forth one of those periodic outbursts of petulance to which Balfour, under pressure, was prone. 'The whole world', he declared, 'seems in a conspiracy *first* to get into trouble by ignoring my advice, and *then* to abuse me for the result. Joe – G. Curzon – Clarke etc., etc. But, after all, it does not I suppose matter.'[62] The incident furnished critics with another example of Balfour's supposedly doubtful loyalty. 'He saw', A. G. Gardiner later wrote, 'honest Sir Edward Clarke hounded from the City, and remained darkly silent'.[63]

In 1907, the House of Lords continued its assault on the government's legislation. Of four Land bills introduced, two referring to Scotland were vetoed and the other two, concerning smallholdings in England and evicted tenants in Ireland, emasculated. A resolution introduced by Sir Henry Campbell-Bannerman for a curtailment of the Lords' power was also thrown out by the peers, having been passed in June by the House of Commons by 432 votes to 147. The Unionists, however, still lacked a potent rallying point. 'The government', St. John Brodrick wrote to Lord Selborne in August, 'are losing ground fast, but we are not gaining it. I hardly see how we are to do so while tariff reformers and free fooders continue to do battle over Arthur Balfour's body. The former are doing their best to see who they can find of their own to replace him, but it is all a sham fight'.[64]

One replacement, at any rate, was now impossible to contemplate. In November, Balfour, speaking in Birmingham, visited Joseph Chamberlain at Highbury. There with Mrs Chamberlain, Austen and Neville, he saw his old colleague but a speech impediment, brought on by the stroke, made communication difficult although 'his eyes seem bright and keen as ever, and the mind quite as clear'. Balfour, despite their old rivalry and its continuing effects, was moved by the encounter. 'I am rather afraid', he told Sandars, 'that he is getting worse: and in any case, one cannot hope that anything like complete recovery is possible.'[65]

Tariffs were not Balfour's only preoccupation during these years. In 1906 and 1907 Balfour criticized the Liberals for failing to end the system of Chinese labour, of which they had previously been so critical; in March 1907 he also pointed out the inconsistency of allowing indentured labour to work in the New Hebrides, where control was divided between the British and the French. 'If indentured labour', Balfour declared in the House of Commons on 11 March in a fine example of his bantering parliamentary style, 'is provided by a Unionist government, if the people who benefit are owners of goldfields, and the people indentured are Chinese – this is slavery [cheers]; yes, but if indentured labour is arranged by a radical government, if the indentured labourers are not Chinese, but people far less capable of protecting their own interests and if those who benefit by the indentured labour are people less important than the great industry on which the whole prosperity of the Transvaal depends, then that indentured form of labour is not slavery – it is social reform.'[66] Not until 1910 did the last of the indentured Chinese coolies leave South Africa.

Balfour's views on race were unprogressive. He saw no hope of equality in Britain's colonial empire, as there was an 'unbridgeable abyss' between the black and white races. In 1906 Sir Henry Campbell-Bannerman's government decided to extend self-government to the Transvaal and Orange River colony in South Africa. Balfour strongly opposed this, not only because these provinces had been the centre of Boer strength during the South African War, but also out of a fear that the giving of universal manhood suffrage to the whites might eventually give the blacks a claim to vote. Balfour was far-sighted enough to realize that the relationship between the two races was to be South Africa's greatest future problem, yet his only answer was restriction for 'the white and black races . . . are born with different capacities which education cannot and will not change'.[67] However, in 1909, after Boer leaders like Botha and Smuts had proved their capacity to work within the empire, he supported the creation of the Union of South Africa, thus at least bringing the white tribes together. In India he was similarly doubtful of the India Secretary Lord Morley's tentative moves to include Indians in government, concerned that this must only make British administration more difficult.

In April 1908, Sir Henry Campbell-Bannerman died and the premiership passed to Asquith. Campbell-Bannerman was one of the few people to be utterly impervious to Balfour's celebrated charm and there was little sadness among the entourage at Carlton Gardens at his passing. 'Asquith's [speech] was frightfully overdone', Sandars wrote to Wilfrid Short, describing the tribute on 28 April. 'In fact the death of this poor old mediocrity has been the occasion for the most unreasoning gush, and most people are only anxious to return to a proper atmosphere.'[68] Balfour and Asquith shared many friends, sometimes leaving dinner parties in the same hansom for the House of Commons to lambast one another in a late debate. During Asquith's premier-ship Balfour attained in certain matters concerning defence and foreign affairs, a position almost above party politics. In the first years of the Liberal government informants such as Lord Esher and Admiral Sir John Fisher had kept the Unionist leader up to date with new developments in this field; Haldane, the Secretary for War and an old friend with a shared interest in philosophy, had also been open. Then in 1908 Asquith invited Balfour to participate in a Sub-Committee of the Committee of Imperial Defence considering the possibility of invasion.

Balfour had long been intrigued by this subject and his expert performance in the House of Commons in 1906 had supposedly supplied evidence that it needed no more attention. In May 1908 he was also persuasive. 'The reason AJB was not cross-examined is very simple', Esher told Sandars on 30 May. 'His auditors were dumb-founded by his performance. You cannot conceive any-thing more perfectly done. The admiration and respect of the Committee very naturally held them spellbound. Nor, may I add, was there anything to be said. AJB's speech could be adopted as a report on the Defence Committee, without amendment.'[69] Balfour's views on defence were not always bi-partisan. In 1908 and early 1909, the Unionists, led by him, embarked upon a campaign for a stronger navy to compete with Germany's grow-ing fleet. As a consequence of this, Lloyd George framed his budget in 1909 and the stage was set for the great constitutional crisis which was to dominate the last years of Balfour's leader-ship.

13

The Constitutional Crisis

1908 seemed to presage a revival of Unionist fortunes. A trade depression led to economic uncertainty and unemployment; tariff reform was winning by-elections throughout the country. Balfour's Cecil cousins, however, were still obdurate. 'It really is a most deplorable situation', he wrote to Lord Selborne on 6 March 1908, 'and I cannot tell you how deeply I feel it, or how much pain it has given me. I care comparatively little about the members of the late cabinet who broke away in 1903; at all events, the bitterness of separation had long passed away. But this difference of opinion within the family has been the cause of untold vexation, and has more than once gone near to inducing me to leave the leadership to men unhampered by the memories and affections of which I cannot get rid. Unfortunately no one seems at this moment prepared to assume the burden – so I suppose I must go on.'[1]

The repetition of this theme – the elevation of family sentiment above almost all else – shows the strength of Balfour's feeling for the Hatfield connection, one of the chief reasons for his despondency and resignation in 1911. Selborne advised a personal approach. 'Go as near to outward warmth as your Cecilian blood will allow',[2] he wrote in April. But the Chamberlains were pressing their case. At the beginning of 1909, a secret society of tariff reformers called the Confederates launched a campaign in various constituencies against free trade Unionists. In East Hertfordshire, a free trade candidate backed by Lord Salisbury was challenged by a constituency rebellion. Lord Robert Cecil, member for East Marylebone, was forced out, eventually standing for Blackburn where he was defeated in the election of

January 1910. Lord Hugh Cecil, ousted from Greenwich in 1906, was adopted by Oxford University, having tried in vain for other constituencies. When out of parliament he continued to bombard Balfour with protests which even his own family sometimes found disconcerting. 'I must say Linky's attitude to Arthur enrages me', Selborne wrote to his wife, Lord Hugh's sister in June 1907. 'Can you wonder that Unionists don't jump at him as a candidate? What a contrast between your father's reserve and silence and Linky's hysterical rushing into print.'³

The spectre of Germany had the advantage of being removed from fiscal politics. British opinion grew increasingly disturbed by reports of the Kaiser's ambitions and his vast armaments programme, especially when the Royal Navy, bastion of Britain's defences, appeared threatened by the expanding German fleet. Balfour, in a statement to the Sub-Committee on Invasion of the Committee of Imperial Defence in May 1908, proclaimed his concern that, even if she did not challenge his country in war, Germany was in a position to profit greatly by any British upset. At the start of 1909 there was a split in the Liberal cabinet over the demands of the First Lord of the Admiralty, Reginald McKenna, for six new Dreadnoughts. Lloyd George at the Treasury and Churchill, now President of the Board of Trade, believed that only four were necessary and the expenditure on six would seriously weaken their social programme. Asquith compromised by laying down four at once, promising another four for next year. The Unionists rallied to the cry, originated by George Wyndham, of 'We want eight and we won't wait'. In the House of Commons on 29 March, Balfour denied Sir Edward Grey's claim that he had taken up the issue simply to provide his party with a good cause. To find the money for naval expenditure and the deficit caused by the introduction of old age pensions, the government turned to Lloyd George and his April budget.

Spring by-elections had continued to justify Unionist optimism, but the budget gave a new complexion to the political scene. Lloyd George added to income tax, estate and stamp duty and taxes on tobacco and spirits; he also produced innovatory measures which particularly hit the rich. These included super-tax, a 20% tax on unearned increment of land values, an annual payment of a half penny in the pound on the value of undeveloped land and a 10% duty payable by lessors when leases were terminated. Motor vehicle taxes, taxes on petrol and liquor licences were also introduced; and the new land taxes were to be coupled with a land valuation. The Unionist party, with roots still sunk in the old land-owning classes, was bound to baulk at this.

Asquith, in a speech delivered at the National Liberal Club on 11 December 1908, had shown his party's frustration at the blocking tactics of the House of Lords, describing this as 'the dominant issue in politics'. In the country, Lloyd George and Winston Churchill, the government's two most formidable demagogues, echoed the theme, amplifying it with the strident rhetoric of class war. Yet today it seems doubtful that the budget was offered to parliament as a bait, to lure the Lords into a rash and final veto which would enable the Liberals to fight an election on the cry of 'Peers versus People'. The House of Lords after all had not rejected a finance bill for more than 250 years; there was no certainty that it would be unwise enough to do so now. If the issue was taken to the country, the economic picture might still be black, tariff reform could well sustain its popularity and the government might find itself, if returned, dependent upon Irish support, giving the opposition a chance to use the Union, which history had shown to be dangerously effective, as a rallying point.

Balfour fought the budget in the House of Commons. A series of by-elections held during the early summer were largely inconclusive, both sides finding reasons for optimism. Then on 30 July, Lloyd George delivered his celebrated Limehouse speech, adding a new intensity to the battle, depicting the class divide in extraordinarily effective emotional terms. From the beginning Tory opposition had been crude; Dukes appeared from the backwoods to defend themselves, fulminating in tones reminiscent of moribund feudalism.

Balfour, desperate to draw his party together, decided upon rejection by the Lords because he believed, in the face of the Liberal onslaught, there was no other way to enter the next election united. Rejection would provide the much needed standard around which the faithful could gather, fiscal quarrels at last forgotten. Acland-Hood, in a letter to Sandars on 8 August doubted the wisdom of this. He wrote of Unionist discontent, partly attributable to 'the idea that in the House we have been fighting the battle of the big landlords . . . only', also 'the temporary eclipse of Tariff Reform by the campaign against the Budget'. Hood believed that 'for much of all this the Budget Protest League is to blame. In the attempt to catch Liberal and free trade votes they have shut themselves off from advocating tariff reform as the alternative.' The remedy should be in the House of Commons, to defend 'the small landowners rather than the Dukes'. Hood ended by declaring: 'I have had many letters, all in the same strain – the universal experience of all speakers is that the Budget excites little attention one way or the other, Tariff Reform wakes up the audience once more.'[54]

In parliament, Balfour justified his strong opposition by claiming Lloyd George's budget was not a finance bill, therefore had been introduced under false pretences. 'I defy any constitutional lawyer in this house', he said, 'to say it is legitimate for the House of Commons to introduce into its Finance Bill great measures of valuation and compulsory registration. . . . How dare you describe it as a Finance Bill? By your own admission it is not a Finance Bill. It is a compulsory Registration bill.'[5] In the country the party was rallied by a strong speech at Bingley Hall in September in which Balfour anticipated an election, but some Unionists were not so sanguine. St. Loe Strachey, editor of the *Spectator,* had grave doubts about the wisdom of rejection by the Lords, as did Lord St. Aldwyn. The latter (formerly Sir Michael Hicks-Beach) wrote to Balfour on 20 September that 'no doubt, the brewers and many keen Unionists would be much disappointed if we passed it and abuse the Lords. That has happened before – e.g. on the Irish Church – and soon passed away. But if we reject it – that means a fight in which I feel we must be beaten. The "interference of the Lords with taxation" will give the Government the very cry they want, and deprive us of the chance of success we should have had without it.'[6] Even Lansdowne, in the midst of rejection, observed to Sandars of the Liberals 'surely their trump card will be "obstruction by the H. of L." and why should they not play it?'[7]

Circumstances were not altogether favourable to an early election. Trade had revived during the summer of 1909, and the economic depression was lifting. On 30 November the Lords threw out the budget; on 3 December Asquith dissolved parliament. The Unionist party, although pacified by Arthur Balfour's new energy, still had its element of discontent. 'Of course Balfour being leader but without dominating power', J. L. Garvin told Leo Maxse on 22 December, 'is depressing our people to a very disadvantageous extent.'[8] During the election Balfour made plain his affinity with tariff reform by declaring in favour of a proposed corn duty, but the budget and the House of Lords dominated the campaign.

The result was unsatisfactory for both Liberals and Unionists. The distraction of the budget and an intransigent House of Lords seemed to have arrested the opposition's advance of the previous two years; Balfour's party gained over a hundred seats but did not obtain a majority. The new House of Commons was made up of 275 Liberals, 273 Unionists, eighty-two Irish Nationalists and forty members of the Labour party. Thus the Irish held the balance of power, insisting upon a limitation of the powers of the House of Lords, wrecker of earlier Home Rule legislation. The Asquith government set about drawing up a Parliament bill.

Balfour had always entertained a strong respect for hereditary legislators and the concept of supposedly disinterested incorruptible patrician public service. In February 1908 he too had strongly advised that hereditary peers should be included in any Unionist proposals for House of Lords reform, perhaps by means of themselves electing their representatives to a new second chamber. Balfour favoured life peers and a corresponding reduction in the hereditary element in the house; to achieve this he recommended the system of election as 'it would almost certainly exclude the idlest and most incompetent and the least reputable, but it would avoid all the fancy franchise, and the fatal admission that the ancient ground of hereditary qualification was insufficient to qualify for the Upper House. If it is not a sufficient qualification, it is no qualification at all, and your reform of the House of Lords, based upon the hybrid principle, would, in my opinion, only be a half-way house to its abolition.'[9]

But such proposals were soon out-distanced by the pace of the crisis. Before the first election of 1910, Asquith had consulted King Edward VII about the creation of enough new peers to override the House of Lords veto. The precedent of 1832, and the

Reform Bill was there as an example, but the King said that he could not take such a step after one election; there would have to be another before he would agree. On 14 February 1910, Sandars saw the King, who proposed that the opposition and the government should try to solve the impasse together.

Sandars, speaking for Balfour, took a hard line. 'I said quite emphatically', he later told his master, 'that two considerations arose: 1) that the Government's failure to carry the budget would be a complete justification of the action of the House of Lords in December last in referring the finance bill to the constituencies, and that it would be exceedingly difficult to deprive the second chamber of the value of such a proof that the course they had taken was justified by the results. More especially was this the case when the second chamber was threatened with the deprivation of those very powers, the exercise of which had produced this obvious vindication of their decision. 2) that Mr Balfour would probably consider that it was quite impossible for him to volunteer any offer of assistance, and that he could only entertain the question if an appeal came to him from the Prime Minister.'

The King told Sandars that Asquith 'appeared to be by no means disinclined' to all-party talks. A final matter for report was that Winston Churchill, perhaps the government's most vituperative campaigner, especially loathed by the Unionists for his supposed class treachery, 'goes to the Home Office. This statement was accompanied by an assurance that in the future we shall find him much more moderate in his public utterances. I professed myself as incredulous, and I think that the King does not attach much importance to the assurance.'[10] Balfour's response to the King was guarded. He declared his complete opposition to the budget but admitted that 'no final or satisfactory solution of this constitutional issue could be obtained except through the cooperation of both parties in the state. Whether the times are yet right for such a solution may be doubtful; but one thing seems clear, namely, that the Unionist party could never consent to any modification of our present constitution which would practically put legislation of the United Kingdom entirely in the hands of one chamber. For all plans there may be something to be said, but this plan seems wholly inadmissable.'[11]

Balfour was being urged by his supporters to come forward

with some positive proposals for the reform of the House of Lords. 'Evidence comes to hand', Sandars wrote on 1 March, 'day by day and week by week from Scotland, north of England, Lancashire and other parts, that unless the Unionist leaders are ready with a bold and positive scheme of House of Lords reform, there is little hope for the Unionist candidates in the constituencies.'[12] None of the prospective schemes awakened any enthusiasm in Balfour and, characteristically, in March when the battle was beginning, he left for a holiday in the south of France, supposedly for reasons of health. 'What is in Arthur's mind I do not know', Lord Salisbury wrote to Lord Selborne on 19 March. 'He is more and more of a problem. I do not think he went abroad because he was really ill. He is delicate it is true, but his last doctor has pronounced him organically sound. But I think he expects very hard work (perhaps in office) – that is cheering.'[13]

At Cannes, Balfour played golf and indulged his taste for baccarat. He told Lady Elcho that he was in the habit of spending an hour or so in the casino after dinner, before going to bed but 'I don't for a moment suppose that I shall lose more than old Haldane spends annually upon tobacco!'[14] There was one difficult encounter. Joseph Chamberlain, permanently crippled by his stroke of 1906, was staying in the town. 'He looked well', Balfour told Sandars after a visit, 'and I don't think there is any failing of brain power, but it was one of his bad days for speech, and I literally could not understand one word of what he said. It was a painful scene, more so because I could not effectively carry it off by doing all the talking myself.'[15] The meeting must have awakened memories of their old partnership and the tragedy of its dissolution.

Balfour returned to an atmosphere of rising tension. 'This country', Sandars wrote to Leo Maxse on 17 April, 'is threatened with a Revolution.'[16] Asquith, at the start of the new parliament of 21 February, had revealed he had received no guarantee from the King with regard to the creation of peers; he also, falsely, stated that one had never been sought. Resolutions, passed by the House of Commons before the introduction of the Parliament Bill, limited the Lords veto; as the result of these, the budget was passed by both houses at the end of April, the Lords allowing it through without a divison. Asquith declared on 14 April that if the Parliament Bill was rejected by the peers there would be another election, entered into with the government certain that 'the judgement of the people, as expressed in the election' could be 'carried into law'. This could only mean a curbing of the Lords' powers, if necessary by the creation of peers. At Lambeth Palace on 27 April, Arthur Balfour told Lord Esher, Sir Francis Knollys and the Archbishop of Canterbury, that if the King refused Asquith's eventual request for a dissolution with such guarantees he would be willing to form a government. The result of such a move would have been to have brought the crown into the arena of party politics, possibly with dire consequences for the monarchy.

On 6 May King Edward died, the victim of a fatal heart attack. The new King's lack of experience and the deepening crisis led Balfour to agree to the calling of a constitutional conference. At this the Unionists were represented by Lord Lansdowne, Lord Cawdor, Austen Chamberlain and Balfour himself; and the government delegation consisted of Asquith, Lloyd George, Augustine Birrell and Lord Crewe. The meetings began in June and lasted until early November. The Unionists agreed to give up the Lords' power to veto Money bills as long as other measures were not attached to these bills; they also called for the establishment of a committee of members of both houses to help the Speaker, whom the government wished to adjudicate as to what constituted a Money bill, with his new responsibility. If the House of Lords rejected ordinary legislation twice, the Unionists wished this legislation to be submitted to a joint session of the two Houses of Parliament. They also suggested that constitutional questions, such as the Union of Britain and Ireland, should be submitted to a national referendum if the two houses could not agree on them. The Liberals had put forward their proposals in the Parliament Bill. Under its terms the House of Commons was to be supreme over Money bills and the Lords veto over other measures was reduced to the power to delay for two years.

The conference began on 17 June in 10 Downing Street and met twenty-two times. In August Balfour escaped to Bad Gastein for a holiday. It was suggested that the conferees should renew their deliberations in September at Crewe Hall, as guests of Lord

Crewe, but Lansdowne had objected, believing that an impression of frivolity would result. Lady Desborough had already been enrolled by Crewe to assist in the entertainment; on 19 August, from Bad Gastein, Balfour wrote a characteristic letter to her about Lansdowne's doubts. 'His fear seems to be that if the 8 conciliators meet in a country house, conciliation will be regarded by the public as a sort of a cheerful interlude designed to fill up the time between shooting and bridge – a "letter game" in short of rather a pretentious kind. These arguments don't happen greatly to appeal to me. If I remember rightly all the most scandalous negotiations in European politics have (in our time) run their course at watering places; and I really do not see why Crewe Hall should be regarded as an unfavourable theatre for similar operations or why life there should be considered more frivolous than life at Emms or Gastein. Certainly it cannot be more frivolous than *my* life at Gastein, which if you leave out reading or writing, has no serious element in it at all, except for sitting for twenty minutes in a warm bath, and keeping reporters and German Jews at a reasonable distance.'[17] The offer of Crewe Hall was not taken up.

Progress was poor, to Balfour's disappointment. 'Your report of AJB's frame of mind interests me very much', Lansdowne wrote to Lord Salisbury on 11 September. 'I did not know he was so keen for the success of the conference – I think Crewe and Asquith would like to arrive at a settlement. Lloyd George, though very civil and pleasant, would I fancy prefer a breakdown and Birrell is cynical and not at all helpful.'[18] Lord Salisbury told Lord Selborne on 26 September that Balfour's 'main attitude is of course that of an optimist – that we and the government can come to terms except for one or two difficulties'.[19]

This optimism was not shared by the rank and file, many of whom, perhaps bewildered by the secrecy of the conference (no communiqués or reports were issued of its deliberations), felt the need for direction. Acland-Hood wrote to Balfour suggesting that he might make a fighting speech; but Balfour was doubtful. He asked Austen Chamberlain's advice, saying that he thought 'our men rather unreasonable in wanting a "lead" in the same direction and upon the same points every two months'. Balfour wrote 'of course I should make not the most distant illusion to the "constitutional question"; but, even with this limitation, I hesitate . . .'. His hesitation had been confirmed by information that 'the King thinks of nothing else but the conference, and hopes for nothing so much as its success. I cannot conceive how he is to be gratified. But if the thing is to break down – as I fear it must – it becomes doubly important that the breakdown should not be attributed to us.'[20]

Chamberlain did not share Balfour's fears. 'I entirely agree with Hood', he wrote on 22 September, 'that it is most desirable that you should repeat your "lead" to the party. Political memories are aggravatingly short and a repetition cannot be too frequent. I do not think that the conference included any restraint on us except on one subject.'[21] There was no clarion call; and in October an extraordinary move by Lloyd George briefly brought the parties closer, despite the apparent deadlock.

Lloyd George respected Balfour's flexible and ingenious intellect, particularly when contrasted with the obstinate unfertile minds of other Unionists. 'I could work with Balfour', he told Sir George Riddell in 1908, before the budget debacle, 'but his underlying sense of class superiority is the trouble with him. He is kind and courteous, but makes you feel that he believes he is a member of a superior class.'[22] In 1910 they were conferring as equals, and Balfour's much-vaunted charm was at its most persuasive in the intimacy of small groups. It has been said that Lloyd George 'fell in love'[23] with his opponent in 1910 when the Chancellor of the Exchequer's coalition proposals brought them into close discussion for the first time.

The Unionist to whom Lloyd George first showed his ideas was F. E. Smith. Smith informed Balfour who visited Lloyd George at 11 Downing Street on 11 October. On ·10 October, aware that a new departure was in the offing, Acland-Hood had told Sandars, 'the important point is, on what the conference is to break down. I rather think we can trust the chief to beat Lloyd George on this, and throw the onus on them.'[24] Lloyd George and Balfour had several meetings over the next few days; their conversations 'were of the most informal character possible, and ranged casually over a very large number of topics, political and personal'. But the substance of the talks, conducted with the knowledge of Asquith and senior Liberals, was the possible formation of a coalition government, with offices equally divided. Asquith would remain Prime Minister but go to the House of Lords while Arthur Balfour would lead the House of Commons, enabling a programme 'to be carried through by the joint forces of the two parties, in defiance of the extremists on either side'.

Lloyd George argued that the approximately equal state of the parties showed no sign of disappearing. He declared that 'it was not probable that a general election occurring early in 1911, would give a decisive advantage to either side. That being so it was clear that the Unionist party would not be strong enough to carry out any policy at all, while the policy of the radical party must, from the nature of the case, be largely moulded so as to secure the support of the Irish and Labour—Socialist—wing.' The proposals discussed for a common programme, although vague, included the maintenance of a strong navy; compulsory military service 'probably on the Swiss, or six months, pattern;' Colonial Preference and 'an enquiry into our fiscal system'; Welsh disestablishment 'on general terms'; social measures concerning the Poor Law, housing, education and temperance; a resolution of the House of Lords problem; and 'an attempt to deal with the Irish problem by some form of national councils, subordinate to the Imperial parliament',[25] or resuscitation of Joseph Chamberlain's old schemes for Irish local control.

Lloyd George's approach received support from J. L. Garvin, influential editor of Lord Northcliffe's *Observer*, and an old adherent of Joseph Chamberlain. Garvin, despite past doubts, saw Balfour as the only possible hope for the Unionist cause. 'For Heaven's sake', he had told Leo Maxse on 6 October, 'don't revive at present the movement against him. I am as sensible as you are of his deficiencies but there is nobody else'.[26] On 17 October Garvin wrote to Balfour urging a federal solution to the Irish question (in the form of a federal constitution for the United Kingdom) and a breaking of the impasse.

Balfour's reply, sent on 22 October, gave the principal reason for the failure of Lloyd George's coalition initiative. The problems discussed, and the tentative attempts at their solution, show how far both men were prepared to compromise on social questions, tariffs, Welsh disestablishment and defence; but for

Balfour there could be no tampering with the Union. Any scheme of devolution for Scotland and Wales must be doomed for 'in such cases incomplete concessions (and provincial powers are necessarily incomplete) only increase the appetites they are intended to satisfy, while they provide new instruments for extorting more'. As for Ireland, the lessons of Grattan's Parliament, ended in 1782, were 'somewhat disquieting'. 'It took advantage of England's misfortunes to turn it into an "independent Parliament". And why? Because, said Grattan and Flood, anything less than this is inconsistent with Irish freedom. This was the argument of Loyalists and protestants 140 years ago: is it going to be forgotten by Nationalists and Roman Catholics, merely because Redmond, in order to obtain an instalment of what he considers England's debt to Ireland, promised on behalf of posterity that the instalment shall be forever accepted in full?'

Balfour's objections proliferated. How was a recalcitrant Irish government to be coerced; 'they will have money, police and organisation: in Ireland the imperial parliament will have none of these'? Will Ireland form 'one province or two? If you prefer the latter will any nationalist, of any type, accept this administrative solution? And if not, why not?' Federalism in the United States, Canada, Australia and the Cape, quoted by federalists as examples of their system's success, 'is a stage in the progress from separation towards unification; while Federalism in the United Kingdom would be a step from unification towards separation'. Furthermore, 'is the history of Federalism in the United States of America calculated to reassure us? One civil war, and endless recurrent difficulties show how hard it is to reconcile the claim of Central and Local authorities, even when there is no "national" sentiment to be reckoned with.' Lastly 'how are you going to deal with England? Is there to be an English as well as a British Parliament at Westminster? An English as well as a British executive at Whitehall? Or are Ireland, Wales and Scotland to be undivided "nations" while England is cut up into administrative districts?'

Balfour told Garvin he disliked raising objections to a federal solution. 'It seems', he admitted, 'at first sight to make for peace and goodwill, but the difficulties and dangers of the time; the balance of parties, ominous of revolutionary change, make wise men look with friendly eyes on any scheme which promises to give increased power to moderate opinion, and offers some hope of safe-guarding great imperial interests. And yet—?'[27] Lloyd George later blamed Akers-Douglas, the former Unionist chief whip whom Balfour consulted to obtain the feeling of the party, for the rejection of his plan. But Balfour's response to Garvin surely shows that Ireland, and his own strong perception of the difficulties inherent in any form of devolution, moved him to intransigence. In addition there was his old fear of a party split; the spectre of Sir Robert Peel had been raised again. The coalition offer was dead.

During the conference itself, Ireland was one of the chief causes of disagreement. The government refused to include Home Rule in the category of constitutional legislation which, in the event of deadlock between the two houses of parliament, should be submitted to a national referendum. Another matter of contention was the composition of the proposed joint sittings of both houses; the Liberals agreed that the Lords contingent should contain a Unionist majority of forty-five, but this was not large enough for the opposition. On 10 November, the conference broke down without agreement, Acland-Hood fearing that the unsatisfactory outcome would be blamed on the Unionists and lead to electoral catastrophe. The Prime Minister wrote to Margot 'we all agree that A.J.B. is head and shoulders above his colleagues. I had a rather intimate talk with him before the conference this morning. He is very pessimistic about the future and evidently sees nothing for himself but chagrin and a possible private life.'[28]

Asquith went to the King for a guarantee that, after a government electoral victory, enough peers would be created to enable the passing of the Parliament Bill in the event of another deadlock between Lords and Commons. At Sandringham on 11 and 12 November, George V seems to have misunderstood the Prime Minister, imagining that he was not asking for any guarantee to be given, at least until after the election. Some days later, Knollys reported to his master that the promise was sought now; the King, furious, was advised by Sir Arthur Bigge, his other private secretary, to refuse although Knollys, despite his knowledge to the contrary (gained from their conversation at Lambeth in

April), said that Balfour was not prepared to form a government under the present circumstances, therefore there was no alternative to compliance with Asquith's wishes. On 16 November, the Prime Minister obtained the guarantees, to be kept secret until they were needed. Knollys's advice had been accepted at the expense of truth but a minority Unionist government could only have exacerbated the crisis.

The Unionists, emerging from the temporary party truce, were not strongly placed; and Balfour's inability to supply a strong lead was again criticized, Lady Gwendolen Cecil reflecting upon 'the party mischief which these foolish newspapers have done; – quite negligible I agree if we had a leader to put things right, but we are for all practical purposes an unorganised mob now at the mercy of every wind of talk or opinion'.[29] During the election campaign the major new departure was Balfour's pledge, delivered in a speech at the Albert Hall on 30 November, to submit tariff reform to a referendum. Lansdowne, Garvin, F. E. Smith and Curzon supported this; Bonar Law also viewed it favourably, perhaps as a way of securing a similar pledge from the Liberals with regard to Home Rule. Free traders like the Cecils and Lord Cromer were delighted by the possibility of burying the fiscal quarrel; but Austen Chamberlain and other tariff reformers saw the referendum as a serious divergence from the journey mapped out by his father. When it became clear the ploy had failed, Chamberlainite bitterness increased with dire consequences for Balfour's leadership.

The opposition's other electoral theme was Ireland, particularly the influence of American money on the Home Rule movement. Redmond was termed 'the dollar dictator' and Unionists thundered against the government's 'subservience' to 'his republican cash'. The Liberals again played the House of Lords card, with Lloyd George off-setting Asquith's gravity with a combination of knockabout and radical intensity. The election result was a stalemate similar to that of January. The government and the Unionists had 272 seats each, the Irish eighty-four and Labour forty-two. The poll was down, not through apathy but because of an out-of-date register and a large number of uncontested seats.

Balfour in the midst of this stayed calm and still had his

admirers. 'A.J.B. was the only great figure during the election, except Asquith', Esher wrote to Sandars on 27 December. 'No one but these two gladiators were in the running. Of course there will be much criticism of Arthur's tactics, but after all is said and done, the Radical estimate is that he saved the Unionist party at least twenty seats by his speech at the Albert Hall'.[30]

After the election, Balfour and the Unionists faced the prospects of the Parliament Bill. A knowledge that there was likely to be a new creation of peers should the Lords prove recalcitrant cast grave doubts in Balfour's eyes on a policy of no surrender. J. L. Garvin of the *Observer*, who was moving towards advocation of the bill's rejection, was told, through Sandars, some reasons for this. 'In the first place', Balfour wrote on 28 December 1910, 'I think the social prestige of the peerage cannot fail to be permanently injured by the immense number of titles which will be going begging, and by the very indifferent quality of some of those who would get them. I don't know exactly what degree of importance to attach to this consideration, but if we are to have hereditary honours at all I do not want to see them made ridiculous.'[31] Other worries were the transformation by the massive new creation of the House of Lords from an overwhelmingly Unionist assembly into one which would pass a Home Rule bill in one session, leaving no time for the opposition to assert itself in the country as a whole; also that any reform of the Lords satisfactory to the Unionists would be more difficult if there were more peers. The election of December had resulted in the majority against the Lords veto power, therefore the Unionists must be blamed for any further constitutional upheaval.

'I do not suggest that these arguments outweigh those on the other side,' Balfour told Sandars. 'I rather think they do not; but they cannot be ignored.' He also wrote to Lansdowne to say that the election showed there was no alternative to the Asquith government. On 10 January, a dinner took place at the Marlborough Club, with Balfour, Sandars and Esher as guests of Knollys, the King's private secretary. In the course of the evening, Balfour, still ignorant of George V's November pledge to Asquith concerning the creation of peers, informed Knollys in answer to the latter's questions that 'if he were the King and if he were asked by Mr Asquith in the near future to promise the creation of peers in sufficient numbers to pass the Parliament Bill through parliament at some later period, he would make a strong remonstrance, but he would not feel in the position to give a definite refusal'. He also said that had the King sent for him in December, he would have 'felt constrained' to take office, dissolving parliament in January, but that such a course 'would have been imprudent and unwise' as far as the monarchy was concerned. Balfour observed that 'the whole situation is governed by the fact that there is no alternative ministry possible at the present time'.[32]

It is important to remember that Balfour did not learn until July that pledges had been obtained from the King in November 1910. Knollys, at the Marlborough Club, made no mention of this; he also did not tell his guests until the end of the evening that, as Balfour wrote to Lord Stamfordham (formerly Sir Arthur Bigge), 'the dinner had been held with the knowledge and approval of the Prime Minister, and that presumably, therefore, everything I said in the freedom of friendly conversation was to be repeated to him'. Balfour later regarded Knollys's secrecy and the private secretary's effort 'to extract in the course of unbuttoned conversation *obiter dicta* to be used when the occasion arose' as 'one of the most singular examples of domestic diplomacy of which I have ever heard.'[33] Balfour in September claimed to Walter Long that 'had I been consulted in November with that knowledge of the issue which we were only permitted to have in July, there is not the slightest doubt we should have taken office, dissolving in January, and I believe, carried the country with us'.[34]

But would a Unionist government in November have been a possible alternative for the King to the granting of the guarantees? Knollys had not disclosed Balfour's preparedness to take office; probably this was wise. A Unionist administration, appointed by George V, would have faced an electoral contest with the Lords veto as the main issue between the parties, the King perhaps associated in the public mind with the Unionist cause. The constitutional situation was precarious enough without putting the Crown in jeopardy as well. If Balfour was serious in his letter to Long, it demonstrated a grave misreading of the crisis; more accurate were his observations to Knollys on

10 January that there was no alternative to Asquith's ministry.

In the early months of 1911 the cordiality that generally existed between rival politicians outside the political arena became strained. Unionists, incensed by the demagoguery of Lloyd George and Churchill, hardened; and even Balfour was not aloof from this. At the start of Winston Churchill's political career, during the early battles between tariff reform and free trade, Balfour had regarded the son of his old ally with amused, tolerant affection. In the House of Commons, he was adept at dealing with Churchill's carefully prepared oratory, often subtly altering the course of the debate to render his opponent's heavy artillery both inaccurate and obsolete. But in March, Balfour refused to appear with Churchill at the Albert Hall on a neutral platform to open a conference on the prevention of destitution. 'He had overlooked his speeches for a long time, for he liked him', Lady Rayleigh noted, 'but now he really was angry, and his party was so furious that it would have been hard to resist them, even if he had not been stirred himself.'[35]

Despite such feelings, the social round continued. On 24 May Lord Winterton and F. E. Smith gave a fancy dress ball at Claridges, with Balfour and Asquith present in plain clothes. Waldorf Astor, a Unionist member of parliament, came in peer's robes with the figure '499' stuck on one side of his coronet and 'still one more vacancy' on the other in reference to the five hundred new peers supposedly needed to swamp the Unionist majority in the Lords. Later a letter protesting against the frivolity of such a gathering appeared in *The Times* signed by 'A Peer'. Unionist spirits were in need of an uplift. 'The country is amazingly apathetic about this parliament bill either way', Lord Selborne had told his wife in April. 'I can't make out what has come over it; and Arthur's ideas of leadership out of the House of Commons are as scanty as his power of leadership in the House is wonderful.'[36] On 22 June George V's coronation took place, the full splendour of the ancient ceremonial providing romantic and recalcitrant Tory peers with a shining vision of an historic role, perhaps all the more potent for its contrast with contemporary reality.

Balfour, despite Unionist amending of the Parliament Bill in committee, had prepared himself for its passing. Walter Long and

Curzon, previously adherents of rejection, also saw the cause was hopeless. On 4 July Balfour explained his reasons to Lord Rayleigh. 'If it were done now, it would become a precedent', he said. 'I ask your attention to this as it weighs strongly with Lansdowne. – Whenever the House of Lords tries to do anything the government would create 25 peers and the House of Lords would become useless. You can't answer that. I talked it over with Garvin for three quarters of an hour and he was almost in tears, but he could not answer me. It is an impasse now, and we cannot remain in it and the people who are for holding out have not really thought it out. For more than a generation the accepted theory has been that the House of Lords yield when the will of the people has been made clear as it has I believe in this case.'[37]

On 18 July, Lloyd George informed Balfour and Lansdowne that the King intended, if need be, to create enough peers to allow the Parliament Bill to pass without amendment. On 20 July, at the bill's third reading, Lansdowne insisted on amendments which largely echoed the Unionist point of view put forward at the constitutional conference of 1910 but qualified his insistence by the phrase 'so long as we are free agents'. On 21 July two meetings took place which revealed the divide among Unionists. At Carlton Gardens, Balfour presided over the shadow cabinet; a split developed between Balfour, Lansdowne, Curzon, Long, Lord Midleton (formerly St. John Brodrick) and others who favoured the passing of the bill and eight members who were for resistance until the end. Those eight were Austen Chamberlain, George Wyndham, F. E. Smith, Carson, Lord Balcarres, and Lords Salisbury, Selborne and Halsbury. Acland-Hood and Akers-Douglas had supported Balfour out of loyalty although they were by inclination with the resisters. The other gathering was at Lansdowne House where Lord Lansdowne assembled the Unionist peers and fatally failed to supply a strong lead, asking for expressions of individual opinion. The diehards might have carried the meeting had not Curzon supplied the missing direction. Similarly, it was Curzon who dissuaded Balfour from sending out a dangerously equivocal memorandum which tried, characteristically, to satisfy both camps.[38]

The rejectionists' attitude Balfour here described as being

'essentially theatrical', declaring that all 'military metaphors which liken the action of the "fighting" peers to Leonidas at Thermopylae seemed to me purely for Music Hall consumption'. He continued 'I grant that the Music Hall attitude of mind is too widespread to be negligible. By all means play up to it, if the performance is not too expensive';[39] and then observed that he was indifferent to the creation of fifty or a hundred new peers and only cared if a new creation swamped the House of Lords. Both Curzon and Lansdowne were appalled by this; and Balfour agreed not to circulate it. Finally on 25 July, again in response to pressure from Curzon, Balfour wrote to Lord Newton, a neutral peer, advising acceptance of the bill. 'I agree with the advice Lord Lansdowne has given to his friends; with Lord Lansdowne I stand; with Lord Lansdowne, I am ready, if need be, to fall'.[40] The letter, published in *The Times*, ended with a strong appeal for party unity.

The divisions, however, were deepening. On 24 July there had been an extraordinary scene in the House of Commons when Asquith was shouted down by the clamour of diehard Unionists led by Lord Hugh Cecil. Discontent had disrupted old loyalties. By June a no-surrender movement, known as 'the ditchers' was under way; among its members were Lord Halsbury (Lord Chancellor in the previous Unionist government and now aged eighty-four), Willoughby de Broke (a fox-hunting landowner), Salisbury, Lords Hugh Cecil, Robert Cecil and Selborne; also George Wyndham and Austen Chamberlain. The group was united by a sense of frustration, a feeling that extremism was justified by the supposedly revolutionary climate. Some of its aristocratic members possessed a vision of a lost England, the country of their youth, where contentment emanated from the strength of a rigidly structured society with firm rural roots. In fact such a structure had been slowly disappearing since the dawn of the industrial revolution, but to landed Tories, secure in the isolation of their estates, this progress had been almost invisible. A series of strikes and urban violence, coinciding with the constitutional crisis, strengthened both their resolve and their nostalgia.

Lord Willoughby de Broke, as a potentate in Warwickshire, had such feelings; so did George Wyndham, who allowed his disappointment and emotional instability to drive him into opaque prognostications about 'cosmopolitan finance', 'Levantine levies',[41] contaminating the mythical purity of old English stock. The Cecils were more preoccupied with the threat to the church, offered by Liberal proposals for Welsh disestablishment, and of course the immutable Union. Austen Chamberlain and the ardent tariff reformers were still smarting from Balfour's referendum pledge. On 26 July these dissidents gathered to give a dinner for Lord Halsbury at the Hotel Cecil. Six hundred people attended; there were fiery speeches by Selborne, Lord Milner, Wyndham, Austen Chamberlain, Salisbury, Carson and F. E. Smith, and a message of support from Joseph Chamberlain, once a scourge of the aristocracy, was read out.

The muddle caused by Balfour's apparent equivocations is shown in the doubts of Willie Bridgeman, a young Unionist member of parliament. On 26 July he noted in his diary 'the Whips were told by Balcarres that they themselves could go to the Halsbury dinner if they liked, and that it would not break Balfour's heart if the creation of 100 or 150 peers were necessary. This was not an easy one to carry out as everyone wanted to know what "standing or falling by Lansdowne" meant, if Balfour did not regard it as the duty of the party to abstain from the Halsbury dinner. Balcarres himself advised us not to go, and Jack Sandars actually asked me why I had not gone.[42] Two months later, Balcarres told Gerald Balfour that he, by inclination 'a ditcher', had asked Arthur Balfour 'if he minded his followers going to the Halsbury dinner'. Balfour had replied 'of course not' and then, in Gerald's words, 'showing how little he minded he told Balcarres himself he was free to go and all the party Whips'.[43] In the event neither Balcarres, the Commons Whips nor Bridgeman attended the dinner, although all the Lords Whips were there, two of them later voting with the diehards in the last division of the Parliament Bill.

This took place on 10 August in one of the hottest summers for years. Lansdowne, urged on by Curzon, realized that a creation of peers could be avoided only if some Unionists voted with the government. Balfour, equivocal to the end, had expressed himself on 7 August, the day he moved a vote of censure against the government in the House of Commons, at a meeting with

Lansdowne, Curzon, Balcarres and others 'by no means disinclined to see a small creation of peers'.[44] On 9 August Sandars saw the Duke of Norfolk, who was uncertain as to how he was to vote and relayed Balfour's opinion 'that primarily the matter was a House of Lords one, that Lord Lansdowne was really the determining voice, and that the Duke ought to be guided by his representations; but Mr Balfour said that I could inform the Duke that in his judgement Lord Lansdowne ought to condemn with sufficient strength the action of Unionist peers who might be disposed to vote for the bill'.[45] Lansdowne advised his followers to abstain, adding no condemnation of those who might be prepared to vote for the government. The division, at 11 p.m. on 11 August was saved for the Liberals by thirty-seven Unionists who did exactly this. There was a government majority vote of 131 to 114, with a large abstention, thirteen bishops voting for the bill. That morning Balfour had escaped to Bad Gastein. George Wyndham exemplified the extraordinary hysteria of the moment when he wrote: 'When the King wants loyal men, he will find us ready to die for him. He may want us. For the House of Lords today – though they did not know it – voted for revolution.'[46]

14

On the Brink

'Politics have been to me quite unusually odious', Arthur Balfour wrote to Lady Elcho on 10 August from Paris on his way to Bad Gastein. 'I am not going into the subject; but I have, as a matter of fact, felt the situation more acutely than any in my public life – I mean from the personal point of view. As you know I am very easy going, not given to brooding over my wrongs. But last Friday and Saturday – I could think of nothing else: – a thing which has not happened to me since I was unjustly "complained of" at Eton more than forty years ago!'[1]

The crisis had further disrupted Balfour's personal friendships. Among the 'ditchers' were the Cecils, George Wyndham, and his brother-in-law Lord Rayleigh; and the political atmosphere had been soured by an acrimony later exacerbated by the Home Rule struggles of the next three years. 'Margot has, it seems, been wilder than ever,' Balfour told Lady Elcho, 'and has written some unbelievable letters to Etty etc., on the situation generally and the Cecil family in particular. I should do injustice to these gems if I tried to reproduce them: – but when I inform you that she described Linky as a shrill voiced eunuch, you will agree that my description of her correspondence is not over-coloured.'[2] Lansdowne told Sandars on 20 August, 'I hear incredible stories of the violence of the ditchers and their friends'.[3] Of Balfour's social circle, Lady Desborough had preached resistance to the end and Lady Elcho's eldest son told a friend 'I was a frantic diehard'.[4]

Before leaving for Bad Gastein, Balfour had an unusually frank discussion with Sandars in the library at Carlton Gardens. He lamented the refusal of 'a minority' to accept 'my advice which commanded a majority of votes at the shadow cabinet, and the dissentient members have gone out into the world proclaiming their differences and have embarked upon a policy of active resistance. I confess to feeling I have been badly treated. I have no wish to lead the party under these humiliating conditions.' Sandars later noted, 'I have rarely heard him speak with more vigour or with more intensity of feeling. I felt at the time that his words were pregnant of meaning, and they foreshadowed the possibility of a decisive step.'[5]

The 'hedgers' or supporters of Unionist abstention in the Lords debate, were also angry. 'AJB is as usual the chief scapegoat', Lord Midleton told Lady Elcho, 'and both sides feel a good deal, as he was with us and then let people go to Halsbury's dinner and evidently felt a mass of peers, if they were not actually a swamp, did not much signify.'[6] The Unionist press was critical as well. Garvin of the *Observer* had been opposed to any compromise and Leo Maxse of the *National Review* included at the bottom of a page in his September issue the letters B.M.G., representing the slogan Balfour Must Go. Maxse was a friend of Balfour; indeed they continued to play tennis together despite his periodical's caustic campaign.

Leo Maxse was not taken altogether seriously and in July, Gwynne of the *Morning Post* had warned him that Balfour 'is, as you know, one of the most obstinate men in the world and a systematized attack would only have the effect of closing up the ranks of the sycophants and the orthodox supporters'.[7] Maxse's diatribes were also marred by repetition; in addition to B.M.G., he pressed the slogan A.M.G. (Asquith Must Go), C.M.G. (Curzon Must Go) and G.M.G. (Grey Must Go), until even his allies called for a rest.

In September Balfour returned to Whittingehame to be disquieted by a long memorandum from Arthur Steel-Maitland, head of the Unionist organization, which spoke of party discontent and 'the necessity of drastic efforts being made by Mr Balfour to bring his colleagues in the party into line'. This, Sandars wrote, 'had the effect of confirming Mr Balfour's dissatisfaction with his position as leader of the party'.[8] Balfour was still furious with Lord Knollys for persuading the King to give the Liberals guarantees in November, before the second elec-

tion, and in misrepresenting their January meeting at the
Marlborough Club. There was a cold exchange of letters and an
explosive encounter between Knollys and Sandars in the House
of Commons where the latter noted, 'I brought the interview to a
close as quickly as I could, for he was hardly in a frame of mind to
do himself justice'.[9] All this boded ill for their encounter at
Balmoral where Balfour went from Whittingehame in the middle
of September, but a truce was 'patched up'.[10]

Lloyd George and Edward Grey, the Foreign Secretary, were
also at Balmoral. To them Balfour spoke of the Agadir crisis,
which had blown up in June when the Kaiser had sent a gunboat
to the Moroccan port to challenge the French interest there. In
July Lloyd George made a speech at the Mansion House, warning Germany that Britain could not stand idly by in the face of
such international provocation; in September, although the
Germans had denied an interest in Morocco, matters were still
unsettled between Germany and France. Balfour told Sandars on
21 September, after Balmoral, that Lloyd George 'thought war
must come and – this is the best time for fighting. He showed me
two or three dispatches, and at the end of our conversation I said
to him "for my own part I earnestly hope that there will not be
war, but, if come it must, the opposition will certainly not cause
you any embarrassment". To which he replied "if it comes you
will have to join us".'

At Balmoral, Balfour also heard from George V, 'a long and
very detailed account of what occurred last November', in other
words, the granting to Asquith of the guarantees for the creation
of enough peers to pass the Parliament Bill. 'I could not tell him',
Sandars was informed, 'that the course he took was the only
course open to him: but I could, and did, tell him that I thought
he had been monstrously ill-used; and that everybody knew that
he acted with a single eye to the public good.'[11] Balfour still
believed the King had been duped by his ministers; 'the real difficulty, of course, was that neither the King nor his entourage
knew enough about politics to be able to anticipate
contingencies', he told Lord Salisbury in October. 'If they had,
they would never have acquiesced in November.'[12]

On 30 September at Whittingehame, Balfour had a long conversation about his future with Lord Balcarres and Arthur Steel-

Maitland. 'I am coming to the conclusion that it would not be at all a bad thing for the party if I were to resign my leadership', he declared. He said his decision was not final but he enumerated his reasons; these included age, health, a good time for a change before the inevitable battles of next year over Home Rule and the disestablishment of the Welsh church; the 'many symptoms of disquiet in the party' and the press. As to his possible successor, Balfour's remarks were characteristically barbed. 'The faculty for readiness in debate is not one which the country necessarily demands in the leader. W. H. Smith lacked it. A slower brain would often be welcome to the Party as a whole. I see all the factors in a situation. Perhaps this entails want of decision. Some people do not like the qualifications in my speeches. They are not expressed to save myself, but to protect my party in the future when statements of leaders are recalled to injure the party. F. E. Smith contradicts himself once a week.'

A suitable man was difficult to find; the Unionist front bench was not strong and Balfour had dominated his team in the House of Commons. The choice seemed to lie between Austen Chamberlain and Walter Long. Balfour suggested 'Austen in the Commons, Curzon in the Lords. Long is too discursive, too quick-tempered, too changeable and too complimentary. The compliments which he pays to his opponents are the only features in his speeches I ever recall.' Balfour said he himself would retain his seat in parliament and on the front bench, and would 'cooperate zealously with his party', occasionally taking public meetings. His listeners noted 'these observations were marked by force and at times by fervour. Every objection was met by cold analysis. No arguments against his view seemed to be influential'.[13]

On the next day, 1 October, a long critical letter, threatening resignation from the Unionist front bench, arrived from Walter Long. Balfour declared of this intervention from 'my professed friend' that 'nothing of the diehards could be compared with this for what is called disloyalty. But I do not think he can have thought of slipping into my shoes, otherwise he would not have proceeded by such methods.' The letter, for which Long was to apologize two years later, caused a brief flare-up of pugnacity. 'I know I cannot be evicted from the leadership,' Balfour said, 'and if I resigned I should make trouble, which of course is absurd; but Long asks me to change and I cannot change'.[14] Balfour's confidants were furious with Long, Lord Chilston (formerly Akers-Douglas) telling Sandars that the letter 'is brutal and cruel and I join with you in saying that I can never forget or forgive it'.[15] But Balcarres observed that 'it made a considerable and I fancy a lasting impression on his [A.J.B.'s] mind'.[16]

On 7 October, the Halsbury Club, an outgrowth of the diehard movement of August, was formed. On 14 October, Lord Salisbury resigned from this, ostensibly out of loyalty to Lansdowne but also from affection for Balfour. His brother, Lord Robert Cecil, tried to persuade him to remain, declaring 'we are all agreed that we do not wish to turn A.J.B. out, still less Lansdowne', but continued, showing a division in his personal and political loyalties, 'if the Unionist party is to be a force in the country he will have to go'. According to Balfour, the Halsbury Club 'could not be ignored';[17] his mind was made up. He told Lady Elcho on 20 October that he planned to announce his resignation at the National Union's conference at Leeds on 16 November but had not yet talked the matter over with Lansdowne. 'I am afraid', he wrote, 'people have begun to chatter about it at the clubs – which makes it a little more difficult to carry out: – for it looks like yielding to attack. However I am not going to be frightened by the charge of being afraid: and I shall be really vexed if any sound reason is brought forward to make me modify my much desired policy.'[18]

Balfour gave no public sign of his intention. He spoke at Glasgow and Edinburgh, then came south for the new parliamentary session which began on 24 October. For some protesters, the Halsbury Club's attack was too restrained. 'The ostensible reason for the establishment of the club was to make a protest against the leadership of A.J.B.,' Gwynne told Maxse on 23 October. 'Each member now seems to be vying with the other in proclaiming from the housetops his intense loyalty.'[19] Gwynne need not have worried. At the end of October, Balfour informed his closest colleagues of his intention. Lansdowne and Curzon tried to dissuade him and on 2 November, Austen Chamberlain wrote: 'I am confident that the whole party in the House of Commons will regard your retirement at this juncture as a grave misfortune, perhaps even as a disaster.'[20]

On the morning of 6 November, at Sandars' suggestion, Austen Chamberlain persuaded the Halsbury Club to pass a motion expressing confidence in Balfour. This was only possible after Chamberlain had assured F. E. Smith and George Wyndham of their leader's impending retirement, also threatened with Lord Halsbury to resign unless the motion was adopted. That evening, Balfour made 'a brilliant speech' at the Nonconformist Unionists' dinner. After this, Sandars returned with him to Carlton Gardens and they sat together talking into the night, Balfour rejoicing 'in more than one sentence at the fact that this was his last political speech as the leader of the party'.[21] On 7 November he communicated his news in a letter to George V, officially announcing his resignation to a meeting of the City of London Conservative Association the next afternoon. Then on the evening of 8 November he visited the King at Buckingham Palace, before departing from London for his brother Gerald's house at Woking. Earlier in the day Balfour had observed, 'I really think I must ask Leo Maxse to dinner tonight, for we are probably the two happiest men in London'.[22]

Arthur Balfour had led his party in the House of Commons since 1891, and even his critics realized the enormity of the change. Lord Selborne called on his leader and 'seemed wholly at a loss what to say', eventually declaring 'the whole difficulty of the situation had been brought about by the iniquity of Lord Knollys'.[23] Walter Long 'appeared to be much upset and concerned';[24] and after the resignation there came a great outpouring of regret from all sides of political life. Leo Maxse, rising at the National Union's conference at Leeds later in November to withdraw a motion critical of Balfour's leadership, was jeered for ten minutes. Alfred Lyttelton wrote to Balfour of his bitterness 'at the way you have been treated by some upon whose behalf you have lavished your intellect and help and powers. I doubt whether I shall be able to conceal it. But yet I loved the noble generosity and elevation above all personal things which you unconsciously display. And I am proud – though very very angry.'[25] George Wyndham declared, 'you are that sole star of fortitude and radiance in the nightfall that has overtaken our country;'[26] and Lord Robert Cecil wrote: 'I should like just to grasp your hand and tell you what I hope you know that you still are and always will be to me the Arthur of my youth whose visits to Hatfield were keenly looked forward to and long remembered.'[27]

There were also tributes from the government side. Winston Churchill wrote 'fate or whatever it is has condemned me to be constantly, during the ten years I have been in parliament, in an antagonistic and disagreeable political relation to you: and no doubt my own force of character and manner have necessarily aggravated this evil state of things. But you know quite well that I have always been a sincere admirer, and that some of the talks that we have had have been among the most pleasant and memorable experiences of my life.'[28] Margot Asquith told Balfour that her husband had observed of the Unionists: 'it served them d—d right – now if they don't all perceive it the whole world will – the vast gap that separated Arthur from all his colleagues in everything – prestige, intellect, charm, brilliance, etc'; Margot continued (describing Lloyd George's reaction) 'little L.G. who is devoted to you said "well we shall see how he will dwarf them".'[29] But Balfour's public life had not ended. Within four years he was to hold office, this time in the government presided over by his old opponents, and to be considered again as a possible Prime Minister.

Throughout the upheavals of these last months, Lady Elcho had offered consolation. 'I realize', she wrote on 14 August, 'that you have been through I fear a great deal of mental suffering. I feel it is perhaps almost tactless of me even to refer to it for I know well how strenuously you always keep away from you the image of past, present or future pain. . . . I thought your letter quite horribly touching! I longed and long to be able to come and comfort you – not by talking over the situation but by quite other means – a good smacking would brace you up I think!'[30] At the beginning of October Balfour informed her of his impending resignation. 'You will have to promise me one thing', she wrote on 10 October, 'and that is – if yr country needs you . . . if you can help later on you will *have* to come back like Cincinnatus from the Plough!'[31]

Lady Elcho told her brother George Wyndham the news and in London in November Balfour wanted to know of his reaction.

Wyndham was a member of the Halsbury Club and his personal affection mingled with political bitterness. 'I felt far away from you somehow,' Lady Elcho wrote to Balfour on 7 November, ' – or you far away from me – and when we got up to the door I got suddenly frightened when you said "What did he say".' Wyndham had 'begged' his sister 'to give you his very best love and he certainly does love you. What he said showed it in so many ways and he asked me to thank you for letting him know – that was all. The rest is quite impossible for me to cope with and somehow the talk shattered me a good deal.'[32] Within their circle there was sadness. 'I hardly realised how great is the hold you have on people's imagination and affection', Lady Elcho wrote on 10 November. 'It's lucky I'm in the world to keep you in yr proper place'.[33]

Arthur Balfour now had more time for interests outside politics. He had never neglected these, even during the most testing crises, and foremost among them was philosophy. In 1900 the death, tragically young, of Henry Sidgwick led Balfour to propose the disbanding of the Synthetic Society. This was rejected in favour of suspension for a year and the Synthetic lasted until 1908. Balfour himself continued to produce philosophical essays and papers, delivering the Sidgwick Memorial lecture (in memory of his brother-in-law) at Cambridge in 1908 on the theme of 'Decadence' and the Romanes Memorial lecture at Oxford in 1909 on 'Beauty: and the Criticism of Beauty'.

'Decadence' was not a cry of despair for Western society but rather an offering of cautious hope for the future. Balfour believed that 'Progress is with the West – with communities of the European type'; there were no 'untried races competent to construct out of the ruined fragments of our civilisation a new and better habitation for the spirit of man'. Should the modern world suffer the same fate of ancient Rome, there would be no eventual renaissance, for the 'barbaric flood' would be 'like that which in Asia submerged for ever the last traces of Hellenic culture'. To guard against this, there were the saving qualities of science and industry, intelligently and ethically used, in other words combined with the ethical restraints of Christianity. Without this, chaos beckoned; with it 'though time has brought perhaps new causes of disquiet, it has also brought new grounds for hope; and that whatever be the perils in front of us, there are, so far, no symptoms either of pause or of regression in the onward movement for more than a thousand years has been characteristic of western civilisation'.[34]

In 'Beauty: and the Criticism of Beauty' Balfour turned to aesthetics, taking great trouble to read deeply around his subject beforehand but, characteristically, relying only on a few scribbled notes on the back of an envelope as an aid to the lecture's delivery. Balfour believed that the relationship between a work of art and an individual was essentially unique; there could be no accepted body of aesthetic doctrine justifying admiration or distaste, no elitist theory of artistic acceptability. 'Does not', he asked, 'the direct appeal made to uncultivated receptivity by what critics would describe as very indifferent art sometimes produce aesthetic emotion which, measured by its intensity, might be envied by the most delicate connoisseur?' Here the schoolboy engrossed in his adventure story is as content as the most cultivated aesthete.

To Balfour, Ruskin's intertwining of aesthetics and morality is thus unsatisfactory; if 'for myself I admit that I require a mystical supplement to that strictly critical view of beauty and art with which I am now concerned' this again was personal taste rather than aesthetic standard. Art may be educational, even crusading, but it should be judged not only by its moral effect but its own intrinsic isolated beauty as well. Such beauty – selfsufficing and contemplative – cannot be governed by abstract principles. This it shares with the highest state of 'active' (as opposed to contemplative) feeling: love. 'Why', Balfour asks, 'should we be impatient because we can give no account of the characteristics common to all that is beautiful, when we can give no account of the characteristics common to all that is lovable?' His conclusion is: 'Let us, then, be content, since we can do no better, that our admirations should be even as our loves.'[35]

In 1911, while staying at Bad Gastein, he worked on a long critical essay on Bergson's *Creative Evolution*, a work he admired, with certain reservations. This piece appeared in the 25th anniversary number of the *Hibbert Journal*, its composition providing welcome relief from the constitutional crisis, and Bergson, whom Balfour met in London in 1911, became a friend

and guest at Whittingehame. In January and February 1914
Balfour delivered the Gifford lectures at the University of
Glasgow. These were divided into two parts: the first, entitled
'Theism and Humanism', given in 1914, and the second,
originally planned for 1915 but delayed until 1922, called
'Theism and Thought'.

In 'Theism and Humanism' he returned to his old theme: a
Theistic as opposed to a Naturalistic world. The effect of his argument, he hoped, would be 'to link up a belief in God with all that
is, or seems, most assured in knowledge, all that is, or seems,
most beautiful in art or nature, and all that is, or seems, most
noble in morality'.[36] Humanism without Theism was, Balfour
believed, almost valueless. For him beliefs about the world and
God were interdependent and if there was much about God that
was 'unknowable', human intellect, designed only for primitive
man, should not baulk at this. Balfour again emphasizes the impossibility of a final philosophy, 'rationalised throughout', resting
nothing 'on faith or probability'.[37] His own faith in God, at any
rate, is intact at the end. 'And', he declares rhetorically, 'as it is
only in a theistic setting that beauty can retain its deepest meaning, and love its brightest lustre, so these great truths of
aesthetics and ethics are but half-truths, isolated and imperfect,
unless we add to them yet a third. We must hold that reason and
works of reason have their source in God; that from Him they
draw their inspiration; and that if they repudiate their origin, by
this very act they proclaim their own insufficiency.'[38]

Balfour's religious observations are often expressed with a
rhapsodic intensity as if attempting to evoke some inexplicably
splendid but mysterious vision. A part of his understanding of
this vision was the certainty of life after death and his letters, particularly those written during the First War to friends who lost
sons in the trenches, repeat this theme. From his early youth,
Balfour had been associated with the Society for Psychical
Research and in 1911 some remarkable developments took place
involving him, his relatives and communications passed through
mediums. After his defeat in the election of 1906, Gerald Balfour
devoted himself almost permanently to the affairs of the society
and psychical investigation. He was assisted by his sister Mrs
Sidgwick and various others, including his great friend John

George Piddington, Sir Oliver Lodge and Alice Johnson. These investigators continued the work begun in the last century by Edmund Gurney, F. W. H. Myers and Sidgwick himself.

Arthur Balfour, although more sceptical than his brother, occasionally attended seances. At one held sometime before the war while the Unionists were out of office, the 'communicator' was Henry Sidgwick who had died in 1900. Balfour wrote down the words supposedly transmitted through the medium. 'We from our place have a vision not for today but for the future', the message to him ran. 'You must not hesitate. We consent in high tariff, women's suffrage & freedom – the revolutionary spirit is all over England much stronger than you realise & will unless you redouble your efforts come under control of lawyers. I will come to your own home & give you sign of my power. The revolution spirit is so strong, will aim at crown if Conservatives don't come in. Ireland not ready for freedom, but you will have to give her more privileges. If you stand firm Conservatives will get in – if not, Revolutionary spirit will attack Crown, India. Few years you will be a spirit – Must do what you can before you come over. Heart filled with love for you and England as well.'[39]

In 1911 another more personal series of communications began. After resigning the Unionist leadership in November, Balfour drove down to Fisher's Hill, his brother Gerald's house at Woking. At the end of his visit, as he was departing, he encountered the medium Mrs Willett briefly in the hall. Mrs Willett then informed the Gerald Balfours that she had had a vivid dream the night before Arthur Balfour's resignation had appeared in the newspapers in which 'she felt she had seen right through into his soul'.[40] In 1912, at seances held on Palm Sunday and subsequently, Mrs Willett seemed to Gerald Balfour to be communicating, in the form of automatic writing and speaking in trances, messages from May Lyttelton to Arthur Balfour, described as her 'faithful knight'. That year Balfour, as was his custom, spent Palm Sunday with Edmund Talbot (now Bishop of Winchester) and his wife Lavinia (May's sister), keeping alive memories of the old attachment. In April Mrs Sidgwick informed him of Mrs Willett's activities; he was apparently incredulous and said 'but all that happened nearly forty years ago'.[41]

Mrs Willett and other mediums were also said to be in touch

with Frank Balfour (killed in the Alps in 1882), Henry Sidgwick, Edmund Gurney and F. W. H. Myers; but it was May Lyttelton who seems to have been the most insistent communicator as far as Arthur Balfour was concerned. In July 1912 Gerald Balfour obtained from his brother a message to read out during a seance; the message ran: 'The Loyal Knight wishes her to know that he understands.'[42] This was delivered, with Mrs Willett causing a 'very dramatic' scene, both in speech and frenzied writing. The communications continued and in April 1915 a sitting was held in the Long Room at Carlton Gardens, Arthur Balfour present for the first time. It has been said of this occasion that 'A.J.B. was not an experienced sitter, and was no doubt, though deeply interested, also a little embarrassed'.[43] The messages were inconclusive. However in June 1916, also at Carlton Gardens, Mrs Willett performed again with Balfour present. This time communications were clearer and he asked, 'Has May any message for Arthur?' Mrs Willett then wrote:

> The May blossom has never ceased to bloom unfading there sweet-scented as in the meadows near her home.
> She sends the word through a poem Remember –
> And through another sonnet –
>   'And if God will
>   I shall but love thee better after Death'.[44]

The medium, after the writing ceased, spoke, still in a trance, producing details of Balfour's life purportedly unknown to her as if to prove her reliability. Balfour tried to extract more about May's spiritual presence, to receive other messages, but Mrs. Willett 'seemed to wake up further and recognise me, but asked if I were a picture or a real man, not seeming sure, and asked also where she was. After this she soon became quite herself again.'[45]

How much Balfour was moved or convinced by these psychical experiences remains doubtful. Mrs Willett was a persistent intermediary. When she attended the Geneva conference in 1922 as a delegate, she was so perturbed by the presence of Arthur Balfour, who was there to lead the British delegation to the League of Nations, that she began to produce automatic writing, with communications from May and others, during some of the speeches. Then in 1929 there were psychical experiments at Fisher's Hill, with the dying Balfour a passive but interested participant. However Gerald Balfour, who had a firm belief in the psychic powers of others, noted that his brother was 'as impervious and unpsychic as myself'.[46] Arthur Balfour's curiosity was deeply stirred, but although always a champion of psychical research he never claimed to have received firm proof of satisfactory communication and could laugh at other people's efforts. In July 1911 Mrs Annie Besant came to dinner at Carlton Gardens to explain the spiritualist activities of herself and other Theosophists. Balfour told Lady Elcho of the soul of 'a choleric and somewhat blustering Major' whom the Theosophists contacted and who was clearly out of his element. To Mrs Besant 'the astral Major' burst out with the following commentary on his position. 'If this is Hell it has been greatly exaggerated; if it is Heaven I don't think much of it!'[47]

Philosophy and politics were sometimes mixed. In 1908 Theodore Roosevelt, President of the United States, wrote to Balfour about his lecture on 'Decadence'. Roosevelt agreed with Balfour's view of the danger to Western civilization of an invasion of alien cultures, and the necessity of strengthening against this. In 1909, Balfour seems to have had a hand in a document called 'The Possibility of an Anglo-Saxon Confederation', ostensibly for Roosevelt's eyes although the President may never have received it. This paper proposed a federation of the British Empire and the United States, to take its place in a future world dominated by similar federations. Among these would be a Russia extending from Vladivostock to Germany (perhaps also including Scandinavia), a Germany dominating central Europe and a 'Latin' federation composed of France, Italy, Spain, Portugal, Belgium, French Switzerland and Greece. Asia would be left to either China or Japan.

The paper depicts Britain, her empire and America together as being 'practically unassailable', protected by the strength of the Anglo-American navy.[48] The scheme was far-sighted, pointing the way towards future trans-Atlantic co-operation, but took no account of the disparate roots of the United States' population or the stern isolationist sentiment prevalent in parts of that country. For the Irish or German Americans, significant groups in American society, to contemplate an equal partnership with Great Britain was too much to hope; and in the mid-west particulary elections were still won by 'twisting the lion's tail'. The ideas reflect, in the same way as Balfour's attitude towards Indians and Africans within the empire, a certainty of Anglo-Saxon racial superiority and the determination to preserve it. On such matters Arthur Balfour was not a progressive, at least by the standards of today.

Balfour's successor as leader of the Unionist party was Andrew Bonar Law, born in Canada of Ulster and Scottish ancestry, the son of a Presbyterian minister. Law, after becoming a partner in a firm of Glasgow iron merchants, had entered the House of Commons in 1900, making a reputation as a determined if somewhat colourless performer. Austen Chamberlain and Walter Long, perceiving that neither could hope for a clear victory, had stood down and Law emerged as a suitable substitute. Law and Balfour were vastly different, in background and temperament, Law possessing a dour antipathy to pleasure and social enjoyment. He was in awe of his predecessor's reputation and experience, a feeling strengthened by Balfour's courteous but lofty manner towards him. 'No one realises more strongly than I how impossible it is for me to fill your place', Bonar Law wrote to Balfour on 11 November, 'but I know that you will help me.'[49] Law remarked in 1913 that he considered Balfour to be 'the greatest figure of our time';[50] but in 1916 informed C. P. Scott that 'much as he was attached to Balfour, he never could feel intimate with him'.[51]

It has been observed that Balfour's attitude towards his successor was correct rather than helpful. On 19 December he advised Law to dictate letters for, 'I do not believe it is possible for a man with all the burden of work which now falls upon your shoulders to spend time and tissue in autographed correspondence'. He also observed that 'you seem to me to have done quite admirably since you took the reins, and I look forward with perfect confidence to the future'.[52] But what was Balfour's future? Three days after his retirement, Sandars and Balcarres wondered about this, fearing that if he continued to be active on the opposition front bench, Bonar Law would feel inhibited. In March 1912, Balfour returned to the House of Commons for the first time since his retirement and moved, at Law's request, the rejection of a bill to fix a minimum wage offered in response to a serious coal miner's strike. His speech was 'in his most vigorous style'[53] and Balcarres noted that inevitable comparisons were being drawn, to Law's detriment. Lord Hugh Cecil also observed of Bonar Law on 26 March that 'the presence of Arthur makes him feel his immeasureable inferiority, which is not what you desire in a leader'.[54]

Lord Hugh was under-estimating Law. In the House of Commons and on political platforms the new Unionist leader attacked the government in a more simplistic aggressive way. 'Bonar Law's style was like the hammering of a skilled riveter', Leo Amery wrote, 'every blow hitting the nail on the head. Balfour's was more that of a virtuoso on a violin discursively developing an unexpected but intriguing theme.'[55] The years immediately before the First War saw a heightening of political bitterness and civil strife. The suffragette campaign, the great industrial strikes, the battles over Home Rule and Welsh Disestablishment: these took the country to the brink of domestic disaster. Balfour's role, although advisory, showed how strongly he clung to his old beliefs.

On votes for women, he remained by his old support for this, although informing Curzon in March that he was 'no passionate advocate of the cause'[56] and regretted the extreme violence of some of its supporters. Within the Balfour family, his sisters-in-law, Lady Betty and Lady Frances Balfour, were both suffragettes, and exerted strong pressure on him to which he willingly acceded. To Welsh Disestablishment and Irish Home Rule, however, his resistance was strong, fortified by his determination to cause no questioning of his support for his new leader.

The bills to introduce Irish Home Rule and disestablish the Welsh church were both introduced by Asquith in April. The Home Rule debate quickly took on extra-parliamentary dimensions, fuelled by diehard Unionists still smarting from their defeat of 1911. In September, the Ulster Covenant was drawn up and signed by half a million people pledged to maintain the Union. Balfour sent a message of support. Sir Edward Carson led the Orange campaign, but Bonar Law, with his Ulster roots, was in full agreement. At the beginning of 1913, Asquith announced that he would use the Parliament Act to force the Home Rule and Welsh Disestablishment bills through the House of Lords. In Ulster, Carson and his supporters prepared for armed resistance.

In June the political atmosphere was thickened by the Marconi scandal. Lloyd George, the Master of Elibank and Rufus Isaacs (respectively Chancellor of the Exchequer, Government Chief Whip and Attorney-General) had dealt in shares of an American offshoot of the Marconi company at a time when the company was being awarded lucrative government contracts for 'an Imperial wireless chain'. The Liberal majority of a select committee of the House of Commons acquitted the ministers of any impropriety; the Unionists were not content with the verdict nor the lame and late apologies of the accused. Balfour suggested to Law that the party should accept 'a full apology'[57] but Law pressed a critical amendment which was rejected by the government majority, the Commons voting on party lines. The Liberal Charles Hobhouse noted in his diary that Balfour's conciliatory speech 'was excellent, but marred in deliverance by hesitation and repetition' but Law's performance one of 'a repulsive party hack'.[58] The Unionists were infuriated when Asquith appointed Rufus-Isaacs Lord Chief Justice, Kipling's scathing poem 'Gehazi' reflecting their impotent anger.

In October Lloyd George attempted to involve Balfour in a similar charge over the London and Globe Finance Corporation, owned by the speculator Whittaker Wright. This concern had gone bankrupt at the turn of the century, and, despite rumours of dishonesty, the Unionist Attorney-General had not investigated its affairs because, Lloyd George suggested, of the involvement of senior ministers. Lord Robert Cecil suggested Balfour should set his lawyers on to the accusation, saying, 'I know how indifferent you are to personal abuse – no doubt George relied on that in making his charge'.[59] Balfour however was unperturbed and his reaction shows his extraordinary financial vagueness. 'Mr Short tells me', Balfour informed Lord Robert, 'that it is quite true (although I had altogether forgotten the fact) that I invested, and lost, a small sum of money in the Whittaker Wright smash. But what this private misfortune has to do with public duty I am utterly unable to understand.'[60] In 1899 Balfour owned a thousand ordinary shares worth £1 in the company, a considerable sum in those days. But as his income from investments and salary for the year 1900 stood at £15,284 with an annual expenditure of £7,058,[61] perhaps such absent-mindedness is understandable.

Balfour's contribution to the increasingly desperate Home Rule battle was a strange mixture of the partisan and the placatory. Asquith refused to advise the King to dissolve parliament over the issue; the Unionists called for a dissolution, Balfour suggesting in a letter to Sandars in September an alternative government, above party concerns, under Rosebery and himself until a new parliament was returned. If Rosebery refused 'to act, either alone or with me, I should not hesitate, in the circumstances I have indicated, to become sole minister'.[62] Sandars doubted the wisdom of willingness to play the elder statesman for 'it would be an advertisement of your political demise – a matter of grave disappointment to many men in these latter days'.[63] The proposals went no further. Later in the month, while staying with George V at Balmoral, Balfour spoke of a compromise in the event of the King's refusal to call an election whereby Home Rule might be granted to the south of Ireland with Ulster excluded. Writing to Law he saw terrible difficulties in convincing the southern Unionists or Home Rulers of this but wondered if it was not 'the least calamitous of all the calamitous politics which still remain open to us'.

Balfour realized the precarious state of the country. 'I look with much misgiving upon the general loosening of the ordinary ties of social obligation', he wrote. 'The behaviour of suffragettes and syndicalists are symptoms of this malady, and the government in its criminal folly is apparently prepared to add to these a rebellion in Ulster. The loss of life and property which this may entail is in itself sufficiently serious, but I do not think the mischief would end there. Expeditions of armed Orangemen from Scotland, from Lancashire, from Canada; resignations by officers of their commissions in the Army and Navy; the certainty that Ulster tactics will find nationalist imitators in Munster and Connaught, must surely go far to shake the whole foundations on which orderly society rests.'[64] He believed that the Ulster armed resistance, while justified, should be employed with caution, yet informed Wilfrid Ward that 'when you get extreme cases it is impossible to apply rigid rules which remain absolutely unbroken in ordinary life',[65] again blaming Asquith's persistent refusal to call an election.

In 1913 personal loss contributed towards this change from the more temperate political climate of the past. George Wyndham died in June, not yet fifty, exhausted by drink and disappointment. Balfour attended the funeral at Clouds, moved to tears by the simple ceremony and the ghost of their lasting friendship. In July, Alfred Lyttelton died of a burst appendix. On the evening of Lyttelton's death, he sent for Balfour who came immediately for a painful conversation at the end of which 'I utterly lost my self-control'.[66] Balfour went from Lyttelton's London house to Lady Elcho's residence in Cadogan Square, but, to her great regret, his old friend was not there to receive him. 'I should so have loved to see him just then', she later wrote, 'when he needed sympathy, some comfort, he loved Alfred and was utterly broken by seeing him dying.'[67]

The Irish deadlock continued. In October and November Asquith and Bonar Law met secretly at Sir Max Aitken's house in Surrey to discuss the exclusion of Ulster from the Home Rule scheme. In November Balfour told Bonar Law that he doubted if such a proposal would be acceptable either to Unionists or Irish Nationalists and believed the opposition should still press for an immediate election. In December Asquith suggested Ulster's exclusion for only a certain number of years, at the end of which the province should atomatically come under full Home Rule. Law rejected this. In January 1914 Asquith proposed to Carson an even less conciliatory plan which included Ulster in the new Ireland, giving her special veto powers in the Home Rule parliament. Carson refused this, with the support of Law and later agreement of Balfour. The latter, however, baulked at the Unionist idea that the House of Lords should amend the annual Army Act to stipulate that the military could not be used in Ulster until after an election, thereby blocking any possible coercion of the province. Lansdowne also had serious doubts, and the proposal was dropped.

By March it was clear that such an amendment was unnecessary. Officers at the Curragh suspected that there were moves afoot to initiate immediate military coercion of Ulster. Led by Brigadier-General Hubert Gough, fifty-seven officers resigned their commission rather than take part in such an operation. Gough, after bargaining with the War Office, was given a written assurance that the army would not be used 'to crush political opposition to the policy of principles of the Home Rule bill'.[68] On 24 April thirty thousand rifles and three million rounds of ammunition were landed by the Protestant Ulster Volunteers at Larne.

Balfour continued his balancing act between obduracy and compromise. After the Curragh 'mutiny', he accused the government of intending to use troops in Ulster, then, by taking fright, calling into question parliamentary control of the army. He spoke of the possibility of some measure of agreed devolution, yet called for an election, addressing Unionist demonstrations against Home Rule and demanding a complete exclusion of Ulster. Asquith agreed to accept Ulster's exclusion, again with a time limit. This amendment to the Home Rule bill, introduced by the Liberals in the Lords in June, was wrecked by the Unionists who voted out the time limit and the government's proposal for an Ulster plebiscite to decide between immediate inclusion or a wait of six years. Balfour had suggested Unionist abstention and the introduction of only one change in the measure: that a general election or referendum be held as soon as the Home Rule bill was passed. Lansdowne and Law saw this as too obviously obstructive, Law writing: 'if we are to retain the strong position which we hold in the country now, we must I think avoid the appearance of being unreasonable, and continue the attitude which we have adopted up till now – that much as we dislike Home Rule in any form we dread civil war more and are prepared to make great sacrifices to avoid it.'[69]

Others had seen Arthur Balfour as a possible moderating influence. In March, after the Curragh incident, Maurice Hankey, secretary of the Committee for the Imperial Defence, wrote suggesting Balfour might 'talk privately with Asquith or Lord Haldane – approaching the question solely from the point of view of Imperial defence', and also 'discuss the question with Mr Bonar Law from the same point of view'. Hankey feared that, if quick action was not taken, 'the Army would be destroyed and perhaps the Navy also'.[70] Balfour immediately told Bonar Law of this, declaring of Hankey 'he seemed to think, poor dear, that if I saw Haldane something might be done toward effecting an arrangement. I gave him no encouragement. . . .'[71] Hankey also wrote to Haldane who then communicated with Balfour, receiving a frigid reply. 'You doubtless know all that has passed between Asquith and Bonar Law, and between Asquith and Carson,' Balfour wrote on 31 March. 'You also know that other communications have passed. I feel strongly that to introduce two new negotiators into this tangled affair would make confusion worse compounded – even though the negotiators were you and I.'[72] The proposed meetings never took place.

Asquith had not the same view of Balfour's flexibility, knowing the strength and subtlety of his opponent's Unionism. In July, at the King's instigation, an all-party conference took place at Buckingham Palace to try to find a way out of the Irish maze. The Prime Minister refused Balfour as a delegate, for 'A.J.B. is in this matter a real wrecker'.[73] The conference broke down after three days. The Unionists had entered it with few expectations; there was no basis for agreement as to how much of Ulster should be excluded and this was the ostensible cause of the conference's failure, but the divide between the parties was too wide, the positions of the Irish Nationalists and the Ulster Unionists too entrenched, for rational discussion. On 26 July, the Nationalist volunteers landed arms at Howth, outside Dublin. Soldiers and police intervened, but the Nationalists rescued most of their cargo. Returning to Dublin, the troops, stoned by an angry crowd, fired on their assailants, killing three civilians and injuring thirty-eight more. Civil conflict seemed inevitable; then Irish considerations receded before a new and terrible European War.

Law and Carson have been blamed for their obduracy over Ireland. To accept this is to forget the depth of Conservative passions. Law and Carson were prepared to speak of accepting a scheme of Home Rule with the exclusion of Ulster; the Cecils, Walter Long and Lord Lansdowne detested even this small surrender. The Conservative victories of Lord Salisbury's prime were founded upon the failure of Gladstonian Home Rule; older Tories had been nurtured on these and Liberal Unionists, such as Lansdowne, based their early politics on the inviolability of the Union. Balfour too was of this generation. More ingenious, more subtle, more personally pleasing than his party's new leadership,

B S

he perhaps seemed a contrast to its graceless obstinacy. The evidence shows otherwise. Like Law and Carson, he saw the difficulty of leading the party away from diehard resistance towards even the smallest compromise and was determined to avoid complicating Law's task. The result was a mere postponement of the problem; some sixty years later, the search for its solution continues.

15

The First Lord

'Your own position is a unique one', Hankey wrote to Balfour on
27 March 1914. 'I myself can testify from personal knowledge,
to the remarkable respect and regard which many members of
the government have for you. . . .'[1] Hankey's letter bears out
Balfour's remarkable double role: on the one hand strongly op-
posing much of the government's domestic and Irish programme,
on the other assisting and advising on defence and foreign policy.
Winston Churchill, appointed First Lord of the Admiralty in
1911, frequently corresponded with Balfour and took him to
naval exercises as his guest; Hankey communicated details of
the proceedings of the Committee of Imperial Defence, with
Asquith's full approval.

Balfour himself composed memoranda for ministers' atten-
tions, keeping Bonar Law somewhat cursorily informed of his
actions. In June 1912 he sent one of these to Sir Edward Grey at
the Foreign Office, after Churchill had proposed he put his ideas
about Anglo-French relations on paper. Balfour suggested ex-
changing the looseness of *Entente* for an actual defensive alliance.
'An *Entente*', he wrote, 'is the natural prey of every diplomatic
intriguer – and it could hardly be doubted that the immediate
effect of an Anglo-French alliance would be to relieve international strain rather than to aggravate it.' There was one difficulty. 'There are many people in this country (I am one of
them), who would do everything in their power to save France
from destruction, but have no mind to be dragged at her heels
into a war for the recovery of Alsace and Lorraine.' To avoid this
he suggested that, if either France or Britain called on its ally for
help, a condition of this being granted was an agreement to

'submit the points in dispute to arbitration'.[2] No such treaty was entered into, but by 1912 the *Entente* had developed far beyond the vague understandings of 1902.

Balfour disagreed with Lord Roberts's campaign for National Service. Roberts had resigned from the Committee of Imperial Defence in the last months of Balfour's government in order to pursue this. Lord Milner supported him but Balfour saw conscription as unnecessary and expensive, repeating these views to the Committee of Imperial Defence's Sub-Committee on Invasion which he was asked by Asquith to join in March 1913. It is a mark of British defence planning's weakness before 1914 that this subject, supposedly settled by Balfour himself in 1905 and again by Asquith in 1908, was still being debated, with the same conclusions as those reached on the two previous occasions. However Hankey was impressed when, in March 1914, Balfour arrived late at one of its meetings after addressing a large anti-Home Rule rally in the City. 'Suddenly the door opened and Balfour's tall, loose figure sauntered into the room and sat down beside the Prime Minister', Hankey later wrote. 'Almost immediately he grasped the points at issue, and there and then, with inimitable skill, he drafted paragraphs which brought the whole sub-committee together.' Afterwards Balfour told Hankey, 'I spent the first part of the afternoon in abusing the government in the City, and the second part in solving their difficulties at the House of Commons'.[3] The irony evidently pleased him.

At Whittingehame in the spring of 1914, Balfour erected a pair of handsome wrought-iron gates, paid for by the fees from the Gifford lectures. The year was worthy of commemoration, for the outbreak of war and its political effect marked the beginning of his progress back towards office. On Wednesday, 29 July Balfour met Admiral Lord Fisher, the First Sea Lord, in Cockspur Street and Fisher said that 'Winston had ordered the Fleet up the Channel'.[4] Over the following weekend, Winston Churchill came to Carlton Gardens, communicating accounts of cabinet dissension and possible resignations. Only Lord Morley and John Burns finally resigned, John Simon and Lord Beauchamp drawing back after Asquith had spoken of coalition. In September Balfour was to tell his sister Lady Rayleigh that 'it would have been disastrous if the war had had to be carried on by a coalition

Government',[5] but he informed Churchill that, if necessary, he felt the opposition would join the Liberals in office. Churchill later wrote of Balfour as 'a veritable rock in times like these'.[6]

The Unionists, despite the bitter political atmosphere of the past months, offered a party truce and Bonar Law wrote to Asquith accordingly. Balfour, at the urging of Austen Chamberlain, told Haldane (now the Lord Chancellor) that on 4 August a British expeditionary force should be sent to France and either to 'keep out of the conflict altogether or to strike quickly and strike with your whole strength'.[7] He was delighed when Asquith appointed Kitchener to be Secretary of State for War, moving Haldane to be Lord Chancellor. Over Ireland, however, Balfour believed that the Liberals, by pursuing the Home Rule bill, were taking sly advantage of the Unionists' peace-making, and in the House of Commons he objected strongly. On 2 September Lloyd George wrote to Austen Chamberlain that Balfour's speech was 'angry, petulant and shrewish'. He declared 'Mr Balfour is an ex-Premier who has even now great Imperial responsibilities, and no speech from Redmond could have justified the rather truculent zeal with which Mr Balfour advertised our differences to the enemy at a moment of supreme crisis in our fate.'[8]

On 15 September it was announced that both Home Rule and Welsh Church disestablishment were to be put on the statute book, their operation suspended until after the war. Asquith assured the House of Commons that armed coercion of Ulster was 'an absolutely unthinkable thing', but the Unionists, at the end of Bonar Law's speech denouncing the Prime Minister, walked out of the House in a body to show their indignation. The supposed party truce had suffered, and the issue of Ireland was yet again postponed.

Balfour did not baulk at the prospect of war, but had a clear understanding of its probable consequences. As the tension built up, at the end of July and the beginning of August, he went calmly about his business. During these days Lady Elcho (now the Countess of Wemyss after the death of her father-in-law) exclaimed to him, as if he still had supreme power, 'don't go to war'; to which he snapped 'There, you see, you shriek out at first and then get frightened'.[9] Her fear was justified, for she later lost two sons. But Balfour, underneath his carefully constructed

cynicism, was almost unreasonably patriotic; he seemed satisfied
that the struggle was just and his country right to take the field
against the German aim of 'the universal domination of
Europe'.[10] He knew of course the risk of agonizing personal loss.
On 11 August he drove to Blackdown camp to say good-bye to
his nephew, Oswald Balfour, who was to depart that evening for
France as a young officer in the 60th Rifles. On the way back to
London he burst into uncontrollable tears, then was silent for the
rest of the journey, perhaps pondering the responsibility of suc-
cessive politicians for the impending holocaust. 'I was so much
touched by your telling me how you cried about the war' Lady
Wemyss later wrote. 'I wouldn't have missed your telling me that
for worlds.'[11]

Balfour's war work began by his accepting at the King's request a position on the administrative committee of the Prince of
Wales fund for the relief of distress. More than a million pounds
was raised by this in its first days of operation although Seebohm
Rowntree, the cocoa magnate and social reformer, described the
fund's administration as 'a national disaster'.[12] Asquith then invited Balfour to become a full member of the Committee of Imperial Defence and on 7 October he attended his first meeting.
From November he became even more closely involved when the
committee evolved into a small War Council, to direct war planning. Law and other Unionists remained outside this, Balfour
again assuming a role above party politics. On 26 September he
had informed his leader 'how depressed I am about the new
Army'.[13]

Kitchener was a disappointment. At the time of the Field
Marshal's appointment to the War Office, Balfour remarked that
Kitchener was 'no organiser, but he had energy and personality
and the nation trusted him'[14] and had applauded Asquith's move.
In 1929, according to Lady Gwendolen Cecil, he 'spoke of
Kitchener as being hopelessly incapable of facing the greatness of
the crisis. In the first months, during the retreat from Mons, he
[Balfour] dined alone with Kitchener and Fitzgerald (K's private
secretary). K. was consternated at the appalling expenditure of
ammunition and talked of sending out men "to collect the shells"
as a way of meeting the difficulty.'[15] Yet Balfour admitted the
War Minister had 'intuitions of genius',[16] and his immense

prestige was a formidable rallying point, both for recruiting and patriotic sentiment.

Balfour's activities on the War Council were varied. He and Hankey, its secretary, consulted local authorities while planning the defence of the south and east coasts from German raids. He advocated an overseas naval base nearer German ports, to inhibit enemy movement or attempts at invasion, and emphasized the importance of domestic economic strength, believing hostilities would be long and drawn out, advising against recruiting for the forces workers in essential industries. Christmas in 1914 was spent at Whittingehame from where he visited, at the invitation of Admiral Sir David Beatty, a battle cruiser squadron lying in the Firth of Forth, taking along several nephews and nieces to lunch in Lady Beatty's yacht, conveniently anchored off Rosyth. Beatty spoke of the German submarine menace; some five months later this was to confront Balfour at the Admiralty.

The year had ended with another propitious encounter. On 12 December 1914 Chaim Weizmann came to Carlton Gardens to have his first conversation with Arthur Balfour since 1906. Balfour, according to Weizmann, 'remembered everything we had discussed eight years ago, and this made it superfluous for me to repeat my exposition of the Jewish problem and its national aspect'. Speaking of Palestine, he told the Zionist, 'you may get your things done much more quickly after the war' but, as if to test Weizmann, said that he was in agreement with many of Cosima Wagner's 'anti-Semitic postulates' expounded to him at Bayreuth. Her notion of the Jews as a subversive influence in German society, profiting but nationally distinct, combining financial power with foreign cultural and racial loyalties, had been promulgated by both Wagner and the British philosopher Houston Stewart Chamberlain. Weizmann admitted that 'Germans of the Mosaic persuasion were an undesirable and demoralising phenomenon' although he rejected the hypotheses of Wagner and Chamberlain. For him, the sin of these Jewish Germans had been their desertion of the Jewish race. Although they had contributed much to Germany, this had been 'at the cost of the Jewish people as a whole, whose sufferings increased in proportion to its desertion by its most active elements and their absorption by their milieu, while the same milieu later criticises us on account of this very absorption and reacts in the form of anti-Semitism'.

Weizmann told a friend that Balfour listened for a long time and was 'most deeply moved – to the point of tears'. He asked if the Zionists wanted anything practical now, to which Weizmann answered that he only wished to explain 'how vast and deep was the Jewish tragedy, and that I would like to see him again, if he agreed, when the thunder of the guns had ceased'. At the end of the interview Balfour said 'mind you come again to see me. I am deeply moved and interested. It is not a dream. It is a great cause and I understand it.'

They met once more in March 1915 and in September Weizmann became technical adviser to the Admiralty on acetone supplies while Balfour was First Lord. Some time in 1916 there was another long talk at Carlton Gardens about Palestine. Weizmann detested Russia's treatment of its Jewish population; Russia, however, was Britain's ally. The degradation of the Czarist progroms, the perpetual harrassing of Jews in Eastern Europe, would not have happened but for 'their peculiar homelessness'. Could not Britain sponsor the idea of a Jewish national home in Palestine? Weizmann saw this as desirable from the British point of view for 'both material and idealistic motives'. Balfour replied that the United States would be a preferable sponsor, as England 'would be suspected of seeking territorial aggrandizement'. If this failed, Britain and America might undertake the task together but he 'strongly objected to strategic or rather opportunist considerations being brought forward as an argument for assuming the responsibility for Palestine'. Balfour, in 1917, was to show that grand strategy and idealism could work together.[17]

In January 1915, when the government's conduct of the war came under parliamentary attack from the Unionists, the difficulties of Balfour's role became apparent. He told Lansdowne on 9 January that his position on the War Council was both physically exhausting and politically awkward but 'Hankey, of the Defence Committee, with whom I have worked a good deal on very intimate terms, is almost passionately anxious that I should remain; and, so far, I do not think anything has occurred which could possibly put me in any difficulty'. Also, 'if I can be of any use, I do not see how I can refuse my services. I am too old to fight, this is all I can do for the general cause.'[18] Through his presence at the centre, he became involved in the planning and execution of the ill-fated Dardanelles expedition.

Winston Churchill, who was to be haunted by this failure, had initially favoured an attack on Germany's northern flank, through the Baltic or the North Sea. Then, after receiving favourable reports from the naval commander on the spot, he adopted the plan for an assault on Turkey through the Dardanelles. On the War Council, Hankey and later Kitchener had advocated a movement against Turkey, an ally of Germany since October. Balfour's line was, to begin with, strangely contradictory. He expressed doubts to Hankey in a letter of 2 January about 'your proposals for attacking the enemy elsewhere than in the North of Europe'.[19] Then at the War Council on 28 January he observed that a successful attack on the Dardanelles would cut the Turkish army in two; 'Put Constantinople under our control'; open up supplies of Russian wheat and ease her ability to export; and provide a passage to the Danube. Altogether, Balfour said: 'It was difficult to imagine a more helpful operation.'[20]

On 28 January a naval attack on the Dardanelles was agreed. Kitchener at first said troops could not be spared; then dithered, agreeing on 10 March to send a division. On 24 February Balfour stated in a memorandum 'We must send as many troops as may be required to make the Bosphorus operation, to which we are now committed, a success';[21] on 26 February he hoped, with Kitchener, that 'a purely naval operation',[22] without troops, would be enough. On 8 April, after troops had been despatched, Balfour wrote to Churchill: 'As you know, I cannot help being very anxious about the fate of any military attempts on the Peninsula. Nobody was so keen as myself upon forcing the Straits as long as there seemed a reasonable prospect of doing it by means of the fleet alone: – even though the operation might cost us a few antiquated battleships. But a military attack upon a position so inherently difficult and so carefully prepared is a different proposition. . . .'[23] On 25 April, after a naval attack of 18 March had failed to force the Straits, British and Australian troops landed at Gallipoli, to be pinned down by the Turks. On 14 May the War Council decided to send more ships and troops; on 15 May Lord Fisher, Churchill's First Sea Lord, resigned in protest at these ships taken from what he regarded as the vital theatre in the North Sea. On 17 May Asquith formed a coalition government, bringing Balfour in as First Lord of the Admiralty to replace Churchill, who was demoted to Chancellor of the Duchy of Lancaster.

At the time there was gossip and speculation about Balfour's role in the political crisis of May 1915. Asquith, on 21 March, informed Venetia Stanley, his favourite correspondent, that Edwin Montagu, then Chancellor of the Duchy of Lancaster, 'was a good deal exercised by the ascendancy which he thinks A.J.B. is gaining over L.G. as well as Winston. He regards A.J.B. as secretly but genuinely hostile to me.' Montagu suggested that Lloyd George and Churchill confided in Balfour, voicing their dissatisfaction; Churchill indeed had apparently wished 'that he (A.J.B.) could be put in charge of the Foreign Office when Grey goes next week for his fishing holiday!' Asquith, angry at this, told Margot that Balfour had 'a futile feminine brain'; when the Unionist party needed him in 1911 he 'takes his hat off, says he is ill and leaves his unfortunate friends to be led by a man of fifth rate quality like Bonar Law'.[24]

Frances Stevenson, Lloyd George's secretary and mistress, noted on 25 March in her diary that Balfour and the Chancellor of the Exchequer 'are very friendly just now. I am not sure whether there is anything behind Balfour's friendliness . . . at any rate Balfour says that C. is the only man in the cabinet who can do anything – the others just talk'.[25] Churchill and Balfour were also close. Before the war Balfour had always contrived to keep his intense opposition to Churchill's domestic politics apart from their general accord on naval strategy. The First Lord used Balfour as a sounding board for some of his ideas, knowing he could always be sure of the latter's reflective judgement and, perhaps more important, ability to listen.

In the first months of 1915 disillusion had set in. The war, supposed at one stage to be over by Christmas, was dragging on with no sign of an early victory. Balfour, as a politician of experience and a patriot, could not be satisfied with its conduct. In March he had been appointed, with Lloyd George, to the new War Munitions Committee and therefore knew of the War Office's lamentable performance under Kitchener in the supply of munitions for the front. If others complained to him, he could hardly be expected to disagree. On 29 April Jack Sandars told Leo Maxse that Balfour's position 'is really impossible. He is presumed to have knowledge and responsibility: in truth he has little of one and none of the other. I don't suppose any statesman in history has ever been associated with so much of the conduct of political issues when he was neither a director in his own party nor a Minister in the cabinet of his nominal opponents.'[26]

Balfour was, in fact, a participant in the War Council and ministerial activity, but a participant from the outside, un-hampered by Liberal party loyalties or competition. Members of the government thus felt they could use him as a confidant who could provide balanced advice and disinterested mediation. In April he gave a clear picture of his role's advantages and dis-advantages to Lord Robert Cecil, declaring 'I am in very low spirits about the way things have been done. I spent two hours with K. yesterday, whose conversation was at times quite incred-ible in its folly, and who was very angry with Lloyd George. Then after Bonar Law's meeting I spent an hour with Haldane, who begged me to do what I could (privately) to smooth down Von Donop[Major General Sir Stanley Von Donop, Master-General of Ordnance], whose incapacity, in my opinion, is one of the chief causes of our present mess. In consequence of this I shall have to go and spend an hour, I presume, with Von Donop this morning at the War Office; after I left Haldane I spent three quarters of an hour talking over the situation with Winston. Peace makers may be "blessed" – in the long run, but they certainly are not "blessed" while they are making their efforts.'[27]

Outside the cabinet, his lofty position and reputation render-ing him independent and unaccountable, Balfour's role in the first months of the war was bound to attract speculation. Charles Hobhouse wrote of a plot to unseat Asquith, involving Churchill, Lloyd George and Balfour;[28] Gwynne of the *Morning Post* sup-posed there was a similar conspiracy;[29] and Frances Stevenson reported, on 18 May, that Balfour and Bonar Law had suggested to Lloyd George that he should be Prime Minister.[30] Bonar Law even proposed to Lloyd George that Balfour should succeed Asquith.[31] What is certain is that Balfour, dissatisfied with the conduct of the war, was receptive to the dissatisfaction of others.

He believed Lloyd George's remarkable powers of energy and organization should be more widely used and was doubtful of Asquith's capacity for war leadership, telling Lady Rayleigh on 24 March 'it is not in Asquith's nature to speed up things' and that Lloyd George was 'the only member of the government with any drive in him'.[32]

The forming of the coalition was rapid. The shell shortage had provoked Unionist criticism and Fisher's resignation led Bonar Law to tell Lloyd George that if Churchill, still detested by the Tories, remained at the Admiralty he could not prevent an opposition outcry. Lloyd George and Bonar Law saw Asquith together and the Prime Minister, anxious to avoid party conflict and a possible election, also perhaps softened by the upset of Venetia Stanley's engagement to Edwin Montagu, agreed. On 17 May Balfour contemplated his chances of office. 'In reflection I am convinced that you had better say nothing to L.G.' he wrote to Lord Robert Cecil, with whom he had also presumably searched for some satisfactory alternative to the present. 'He might regard the whole scheme as an intrigue. This would be grossly unjust; but it would also be extremely disastrous. It would lower the whole novel level of the reconstructed government. In any case do not assume that I could take any part. I know more of the inside workings of the existing machine than you do – and unpleasant though my present work is, it may be the most useful I can do.'[33] Later that week Asquith appointed him to the Admiralty.

Lady Wemyss visited the new First Lord of the Admiralty in his first days of office. 'I was sad about him that eve', she wrote. 'I thought he looked so tired. It seemed such irony to think of Winston, keen, young, full of energy and love of power, fallen, turned out and chiefly through lack of character and tact and broken-hearted at going; and A.J.B. so weary, reluctantly obliged to shoulder a heavy burden because all the nation trusts him and the Ministry on both sides want him.'[34] Churchill had pressed the appointment, partly because Balfour had argued against Fisher and the evacuation of the Dardanelles. The Admiralty officials also favoured it, realizing the political stature of their new chief; but others were doubtful, Lloyd George later writing in his memoirs that Balfour 'lacked the physical energy, the fertility of resource and untiring industry for the administration of the Admiralty during the great war'.[35] Leo Maxse declared that the appointment 'at any rate places the Navy under a gentleman, and to that extent will soothe a sorely tried service'.[36] Maxse, one of the promoters of an ugly campaign against Haldane's supposed German sympathies, had another reason for satisfaction, for Asquith, bowing to Law's pressure, left Haldane out of the new government. Balfour, knowing the injustice behind the charges, was privately indignant, but, reluctant to disrupt his party's leadership, offered no public support to his old friend. 'I shall loathe Bonar Law', Margot Asquith wrote to Haldane's mother, 'and never care for Arthur Balfour as much again.'[37]

Balfour held the most senior post of the Unionists in the coalition, Asquith having contrived to place Bonar Law, whom he despised, at the Colonial Office. On entering the government Balfour turned to his two trusted servants of the past years: Jack Sandars and Wilfrid Short. Short, who had never left him, moved to the Admiralty with pleasure, but after Balfour's resignation from the Conservative leadership in 1911 Jack Sandars had more or less abandoned the political scene. Appointed a Privy Councillor and awarded the C.V.O., he asked Balfour in 1912 to help him obtain a directorship of an insurance company and became curiously embittered about politics, writing acid letters to his friend Leo Maxse to encourage the persecution of Haldane. Like many Tories, Sandars reserved his especial loathing for Winston Churchill, referring to 'the Churchill microbe'[38] and delighting in the failure of the Antwerp expedition in 1914.

Churchill was the cause of Sandars's break with Balfour. When the latter asked him to come to the Admiralty, Sandars was shocked to hear that Balfour had permitted Churchill, with his young family, to continue to live in Admiralty House, even to maintain an office there. Sandars argued strongly against this arrangement, quoting Churchill's reputation for intrigue; he also said that his personal feelings for Churchill made it impossible to work under such conditions. Balfour would not retract, so Sandars left him, his bitterness exacerbated. Henceforth his references to his old chief were almost entirely deprecatory and, in 1916, he refused an invitation to lunch, addressing his curt answer 'Dear Mr Balfour'. The anger lasted until his death in 1934.

Arthur Balfour took to office easily. 'You asked me how he is', Short wrote to Lady Wemyss in August. 'I can only reply "better than ever", and I am persuaded to think that, if you wish him to reach eighty still with the buoyancy and virility of mind and spirit which he at present possesses, you will hope that he may remain a cabinet minister for many years to come!' Short believed war conditions suited his chief because 'politics has no place'.[39] Balfour's service staff was headed by the new First Sea Lord, Admiral Sir Henry Jackson; and James Masterton-Smith continued as private secretary. On 21 May Hankey and Masterton-Smith had advised the Prime Minister on the 'most suitable arrangement at Admiralty viz. Balfour to be First Lord, and either Sir Arthur Wilson or Sir Henry Jackson as First Sea Lord'. Wilson refused to serve under anyone but Churchill, and Hankey noted 'I find that Masterton-Smith still hankers after Churchill as First Lord, owing to his great power and capacity for work'.[40]

The new regime changed the pace. 'In Winston's time one felt the whole machine pulsating', Sir George Riddell noted on 11 June. 'Today a marked calm pervaded the First Lord's room'.[41] Jackson, an able but academic sailor, lacked his predecessor's ferocious, almost manic drive; and Fisher did not ease Balfour's task. Their relationship had previously been generally amicable, Balfour even contriving to remain trusted by both Fisher and Lord Charles Beresford during their wrangles over naval policy; but now the Admiral deprecated the new First Lord's involvement in his predecessor's eastern venture. In November Fisher informed a receptive Sandars, who repeated it in a letter to Carson whom he was congratulating on his resignation, that 'it was only Balfour's resource and skill in argument'[42] which had enabled Churchill to carry the Dardanelles scheme. Balfour was prepared to use Fisher, despite all this. He appointed the ex-First Sea Lord Chairman of his new Admiralty Board of Invention and Research which began work in July.

This Board was one of the achievements of a chequered period in Balfour's career. Perhaps the chief concern he had inherited from Churchill was the Dardanelles operation and his silence in cabinet began to worry some of its supporters. In June Curzon wrote, after a discussion on this, that 'some of us were stating the Dardanelles case (as I thought) so badly, that I longed for you to come in and in a few sentences rectify our errors and make up for our deficiencies'.[43] Balfour's reassurance was lukewarm. 'Whether we shall in the end curse, or bless, the late government for having embarked us in this expedition is "on the knees of the Gods"; but that the policy of retirement is impossible must be manifest to the meanest intelligence.'[44] By November Curzon was informing Churchill, who had left the government for the front, that 'Balfour is as usual an inscrutable factor, sitting silent and detached as though he were a spectator on Mars, observing through a powerful telescope a fight between the astral inhabitants of Saturn'.[45] Lloyd George and Bonar Law and the new C.I.G.S. Sir William Robertson pushed for a withdrawal; Balfour on 19 November urged against this, believing it would be an irreparable blow to British prestige, but the others carried the day. In December the evacuation of Gallipoli began.

Another challenge, less easily met, was the German U-boat campaign. In August 1915, bowing to American pressure, the Germans had relaxed the blockade. In the autumn of 1916, however, the campaign began again. Balfour and his officials produced no effective riposte; the convoy system was rejected and a general impression of lassitude and defeatism emanated from the Admiralty. 'Even the woeful tale of increasing sinkings of our ships by German submarines and the apparent impotence of the Admirals to stop the disastrous process did not daunt him,' Lloyd George wrote. 'His one comment after hearing the Admirals read out the list of sinkings for the previous day was: "It is very tiresome. These Germans are intolerable".' He had no notion how the German attack on our shipping could be circumvented. He only assumed that sooner or later it would be done.'[46] Critics pointed also to the unreliable enforcement of the blockade of the enemy, although here the Foreign Office fear of offending neutral countries was equally to blame. The Zeppelin raids, involving the civilian population in war for the first time, created further demands for a more effective defence of British shores.

Fisher took advantage of the discontent. He corresponded with Sir John Jellicoe, the Commander-in-Chief of the Grand Fleet, and threatened to reveal Jellicoe's criticisms of naval administration and strategy in the House of Lords. On 16 February Sir Francis Hopwood, the Additional Civil Lord of the Admir-

alty, saw Fisher. Fisher told Hopwood, who was acting as
Balfour's emissary, that 'he would undertake any work if it car-
ried responsibility. He would not accept any consultative or advisory position'. The old Admiral saw himself as 'Joint First Sea
Lord. He to be responsible for programme, ships, output & c.
The other for policy & c.' Hopwood declared this was impossible, for the two were interdependent and 'two First Sea
Lords with the proposed delimitation of functions could not live
together for a day'.[47] In the press, C. P. Scott of the *Manchester
Guardian* and J. L. Garvin of the *Observer* took up Fisher's
cause. On 18 February Balfour saw Scott, admitted that Fisher
possessed 'hustle' but declared 'well, if he came back I think I
should have to go'.[48] Balfour, however, could rely on the support
of Fisher's enemies. The *Morning Post*, the *National Review* and
the *Daily Express* were among these; and on 18 February Admiral George Ballard wrote 'as for this agitation for get Fisher
back, the whole service are dead against it'. Ballard praised
Balfour as First Lord because 'he does not override the opinions
of sailors at the Admiralty' which was 'Winston Churchill's
besetting fault'.[49]

The question surfaced in the House of Commons where
Balfour introduced the naval estimates on 7 March. Fisher was
sitting in the peer's gallery and listened to the First Lord's com-
mendation of his department; but the most dramatic moment
came when Winston Churchill rose to speak. Churchill, on
special leave from the front where he was now serving as a
Lieutenant-Colonel, made an impassioned attack on Balfour's
regime. He enumerated the poor supply of ships and weapons,
the increasing failure to counteract the submarine menace (which
Balfour's speech had glossed over) and the Zeppelin attacks, the
inadequacy of the naval building programme. It was a devastating
onslaught, ruined by its conclusion; for at the end Churchill
delivered an astonishing appeal for the return of Fisher, with
whom he had supposedly irrevocably quarrelled, to replace
Jackson as First Sea Lord. Balfour, replying on 8 March, was able
to concentrate on this rather than attempt a convincing answer to
Churchill's other criticisms; and as Christopher Addison noted,
the First Lord 'took the gloves off in a most astonishing way'.[50]

Balfour did not spare Churchill, who had declared he had

reached his state of mind after 'calm meditation' at the front. 'The great ancestor of my right honourable friend, the First Duke of Marlborough', Balfour observed, 'was always supposed to be more cool, more collected, more master of himself, more clear in thought amid the din of battle than he was in the calmer occupations of peace, and perhaps my right honourable friend shares this hereditary peculiarity. I venture to suggest that that clearness of thought which we all desiderate is bought at a rather costly figure if it involves a European war in order to obtain it.' He also remembered Churchill's former sharp criticism of Fisher's role as his First Sea Lord, declaring that 'the right honourable gentleman, who could not get on with Lord Fisher – I will not say that, but with whom Lord Fisher could not get on – says that Lord Fisher . . . is nevertheless the man who ought to be given as a supporter and a guide to anybody who happens to hold at this moment the responsible position of First Lord of the Admiralty. It is a paradox of the wildest and most extravagant kind.' Churchill, humiliated, admitted that Balfour was 'a master of parliamentary sword play and of every dialectical art'.[51] The rout was complete but, as Christopher Addison wrote, did not 'leave the House satisfied with the Admiralty';[52] and Jack Sandars, despite his loathing of Churchill, spoke of a 'mere debating display'.[53]

Such dissatisfaction was increased by Balfour's handling of the communiqué announcing news of the Battle of Jutland. This great naval engagement took place on 31 May. On 1 June Balfour, using information received from Jellicoe, the commander on the spot, issued a spare statement to an anxious public, stating the number of ships lost, offering no relief or hope. In fact the German fleet, although suffering less losses than the British, had been forced to retire, emerging only once more, and then inconclusively, during the rest of the war. Public opinion, brought up on stories of the invincible Navy, was shocked by Balfour's message. 'Never was a thing so badly handled', H. A. Gwynne of the *Morning Post* wrote to Sandars and blamed Masterton-Smith rather than Balfour, who was said to depend on his secretary's advice. Gwynne declared: 'I know that the sailors were furious at the form of the communiqué especially as Jellicoe's message – from which the communiqué was formed –

was undoubtedly an optimistic one.'[54]

Balfour accepted the blame. He issued a second statement, this time drafted by Churchill, whose willingness to assist showed the unresentful nature of both men, to try to rectify the damage, and defended himself in the House of Commons, saying 'If my candour, if my desire immediately to let the people know the best and the worst that I knew, was in any way responsible for that result, I can only express my regret. But confidence in the desire of the Admiralty to deal straightly and fairly with the British public will be increased by what has occurred and if that be so there is nothing to regret.'[55] Later he told Admiral Beatty that, from the strategic point of view, Jutland had been a 'missed opportunity'.[56] The criticized communiqué was succeeded, in June by Balfour's acceptance of the Order of Merit from George V. Sandars noted acerbically in a magazine article: 'in earlier days Mr Balfour's aversion to titles and honorific distinctions was widely known, and it was believed that, like Pitt and Canning, Peel and Gladstone, he desired to enjoy and bequeath the fine lustre of an undecorated name. It is, however, unbecoming to express more than surprise.'[57]

Balfour's contributions to the deliberations of the cabinet were, for some, also insufficiently galvanic. 'In cabinet, all faults which he showed as P.M. in the 1900 government were accentuated', wrote Lord Selborne, the coalition President of the Board of Agriculture. 'He yearned for decisions just as heartily as the P.M. loathed them; yet he never did anything to obtain them. He seldom spoke (comparatively to his status, second in the cabinet) and when he did it was critically and destructively and not constructively. He showed the same splendid staying power and absence of nerves as the P.M., but he had no more driving force than the P.M. He had the vision the P.M. lacked, but it led to nothing. Philosophy is the worst possible training for politics.'[58] Balfour was a member of the Select Dardanelles Committee, set up in June 1915, and the later War Committee which took its place. These were the innermost councils of Asquith's government and Balfour's role, together with the respect Asquith was known to have for him, led Haldane to observe in July 1915, 'the country is governed by three men: Balfour, Kitchener and Lloyd George, and Balfour is the real Prime

Minister'.[59] In September 1915 Lord Robert Cecil suggested that a War Council under Balfour's Chairmanship should take over 'all questions directly connected with the war which do not require legislation';[60] and in 1916 a group of Lord Milner's admirers known as the Monday Night Cabal discussed seriously the possibility of replacing Asquith with Balfour.[61]

In fact, Balfour's power was great and his contributions various. He attended allied war conferences in France, crossing the Channel invariably in an agony of seasickness, once observing to Hankey 'a mine was the one thing I was praying for'.[62] His fascination with technical invention was also given free rein. From Churchill he had inherited the first stages of the investigations into the development of the tank. At first, according to Christopher Addison, the new First Lord 'did not take kindly to "Winston's fad" and the officers and men attached to it were transferred to the Ministry of Munitions';[63] but in February 1916 trials were held at Hatfield in front of Balfour, Lloyd George, Kitchener and high-ranking naval and military officials. 'Mr Balfour's delight was as great as my own', Lloyd George wrote, 'and it was only with difficulty that some of us persuaded him to disembark from H. M. Landship, while she crossed the last test, a trench several feet wide.'[64] In September the tanks were first used in France.

In the debate over strategy, Balfour began to doubt the wisdom of the 'Westerners' or supporters of the huge offensives in France. He continued to oppose the introduction of conscription, for either the army or industry, fearing a diversion of vital manpower to the slaughter on the Western front. Here he was out of tune with his Unionist colleagues and Lloyd George, but in agreement with Asquith and the Liberals. In the autumn of 1915 Lord Derby's 'scheme' was introduced as a palliative; but in January 1916 Asquith submitted, introducing the Military-Service Act which compelled unmarried men between the ages of eighteen and forty-one to enlist. Balfour approved, speaking in favour of the measure in the House of Commons; only one Liberal (Sir John Simon) resigned from the cabinet.

Ireland was another threat. In April 1916 the Easter rising took place in Dublin, followed by the fatal execution of its leaders by the British. Asquith saw the need for a quick settlement and turned to Lloyd George, who negotiated with Redmond and Carson an agreement whereby the twenty-six counties of the south were to receive immediate Home Rule with Ulster excluded until after the war when an imperial conference would look at the question. Bonar Law, Carson, F. E. Smith and Balfour accepted this, seeing no alternative in the middle of war and concerned about the effect of British intransigence on international opinion. Balfour also believed that a Home Rule government under Redmond stood a much greater chance than the British of quelling the Sinn Fein and Irish pro-German groups. Diehard Unionists, however, like Lansdowne and Walter Long, baulked; and Law, seeing his party was not with him, withdrew. Redmond and the Irish Nationalists would not accept Lansdowne's proposed amendments to the scheme which then foundered. A new Chief Secretary was installed in Dublin Castle and British rule continued.

In 1916, so far as departmental responsibilities were concerned, antagonism surfaced in the dialectical duel between Balfour and Curzon over co-ordination of the air services. Curzon, as president of the Air Board, objected to the Admiralty's refusal to surrender any of its authority over the naval air service and in a series of memoranda did battle with the First Lord, offering the bludgeon to Balfour's rapier. These exchanges, Christopher Addison wrote, provided 'the most elegant and delightful reading of any series of cabinet papers that I have any knowledge of. It was like the next instalment of a novel to wait for Balfour's reply, or Curzon's rejoinder.'[65] On 23 October Curzon produced the first report of his presidency; Balfour described this as being 'of formidable proportions, eloquently written, consisting of thirty folio pages, mostly filled with attacks on the Admiralty'. He knew well how to bait Curzon. 'I do not suppose that in the whole history of the country any government department has ever indulged so recklessly in the luxury of inter-departmental criticism', Balfour wrote. 'The temptation no doubt has often existed but hitherto it has been more or less successfully resisted. In the case of the Air Board, however, the ardour of youth and the consciousness of superior abilities have completely broken through the barriers of official self-control.'[66]

This was all very well, and, as Christopher Addison noted,

'would have been entertaining enough did we not know all the time that things were really getting no "forrader".'[67] Hankey, in November, wrote 'This rotten Air Board question is purely academic'[68] and criticized Asquith for allowing it to continue. There was a curious epilogue in July 1923 when a sub-committee of the Committee of Imperial Defence under Balfour's chairmanship reported on the possible co-ordination of the services and generally favoured the Air Ministry at the Admiralty's expense. However in 1916 the contest merely seemed to emphasize the procrastinatory regime at the Admiralty. In November, bowing to pressure from Sir Edward Grey and others, Balfour accepted Jackson's resignation, appointing Jellicoe First Sea Lord and changing other commands. But, in the press and among politicians, the demand for a more dynamic First Lord continued, fuelled by a resurgence of the U-boat threat. Asquith, however, made no change until one was forced upon him in December.

The toppling of Asquith was gradual. On 5 June 1916 the *Hampshire*, carrying Kitchener to Russia, struck a mine and went down. Kitchener was drowned. There was doubt as to who would be his successor at the War Office, the military commanders pressing for the pliable Lord Derby. 'The important thing is that, whoever the new man may be, he should not interfere with Robertson and the general staff', Balfour wrote to Lord Salisbury on 17 June. 'All this part of the machine is now working fairly well; and what is wanted is somebody who would run the administrative machine, as K. was quite incapable of running it in the past, and as, I fear L.G. would be quite incapable of running it in the future.' Salisbury seems to have put forward Milner's name, but Balfour knew there was no chance of Asquith making this appointment. He also told Salisbury: 'I have kept out of the business altogether, but one piece of information (of, I think, a very unpleasant kind) has come to my knowledge – it is that A was thinking of putting Austen (Chamberlain) at the War Office, and that B.L. [Law] intervened on the grounds that this would be a slight to himself.'[69] Lloyd George, supported by Bonar Law, became the new War Minister.

Lloyd George's appointment coincided with the terrible Somme offensive in July. With the failure of this, and the increasingly effective German attacks on British shipping, the outlook darkened. In November 1916 Runciman, the President of the Board of Trade, produced a deeply pessimistic report on shipping losses, prophesying British economic collapse by the summer of 1917; in the same month Lloyd George told Hankey 'we are going to lose this war'.[70] Criticism of the Admiralty, led in the press by Lord Northcliffe and Garvin, mounted. It was in these circumstances that Lloyd George faced up to Asquith, riding on the back of Unionist discontent. Bonar Law, challenged in the House of Commons and his party by Carson (who had resigned from the government in December 1915) saw that if he was to survive as leader he must act and, assisted on the way by Max Aitken, was drawn to Lloyd George.

The essence of Law and Lloyd George's proposals was that a small war council of three or four members under Lloyd George's chairmanship should take control of the war. Asquith would remain as Prime Minister but not in charge of the council's direction. Lloyd George insisted that Balfour leave the Admiralty and should not be a member of the war council; 'the only reason he gave for this was "too much wool" ', Hankey noted in his diary for 3 December 'but in my opinion he wants to be virtually "dictator" and Balfour is too strong and dialectally too skilful to allow this'. Both Law and Asquith objected to this demand, Asquith protesting that, when Jellicoe had been substituted for Jackson, he had 'added his strong wish that Balfour should remain in office'.[71] Law declared of his old chief that 'nothing would justify me in treating him in such a way after the more than generous treatment I have received from him since the time he ceased to be leader of our Party'.[72]

But what of Balfour's role in the crisis? In April 1916 he had told Salisbury, who was pressing for the removal of Asquith, 'I think the destruction of the present government an unjustifiable gamble. Something better might come of it; but the odds are the other way';[73] but by the end of the year his respect for Lloyd George, and perception of Asquith's fatal dilatoriness, had grown. Balfour believed that, since the war began, Lloyd George had done 'two things – he alone could have done them':[74] the first was the setting up of the Ministry of Munitions; the second, the War Office reorganization of the transport in France under

Geddes, against the soldiers' wishes. On 30 November, Balfour attended the meeting of Unionist ministers at which Bonar Law informed his colleagues of his proposals to Asquith, adding that he was prepared to resign if the Prime Minister rejected these. The Unionists, while agreeing that some change was essential, objected to the possible paramountcy of Lloyd George. Balfour, aware of the dissatisfaction with himself, was prepared to resign, although determined that the Admiralty be represented on the new war council. That night he was taken ill and had to retire to bed, keeping in touch with events through his cousin Lord Robert Cecil and Masterton-Smith.

Asquith wavered, bolstered by the support of his Liberal colleagues and three senior Unionists (Curzon, Austen Chamberlain and Lord Robert Cecil). Having rejected the scheme of 4 December, to be confronted by Lloyd George's resignation and the probability of Bonar Law's too, he was visited by the three senior Unionists on 5 December who reversed their previous judgement, informing the Prime Minister that their resignations must follow as well; they had apparently taken fright at the thought of Law, Lloyd George and Carson in opposition, supported by the Tory press and perhaps the majority of the party. The same day Balfour sent his own resignation to Asquith, advocating a trial of the war council, under Lloyd George's chairmanship and recognizing Lloyd George's view that 'this council would work more satisfactorily if the Admiralty were not represented by me'.[75] Asquith immediately replied, asking Balfour to reconsider and enclosing a copy of his letter to Lloyd George which declared that Balfour as First Lord of the Admiralty must be a member of the war council. Balfour thereupon reiterated the views of his first letter; the experiment of giving Lloyd George a 'free hand with the day to day work of the War Committee was still worth trying' for 'we cannot, I think, go on in the old way'.[76] Asquith resigned, in the hope that neither Law nor Lloyd George would be able to form a government.

Both sides recognized the importance of Balfour's position. His prestige and experience were vital. Asquith had striven to maintain these; on 6 December the opposition, in the form of Lloyd George, Bonar Law and Carson came to Balfour's sick room and it was agreed that 'the best thing would be to form a government in which L.G. should be Chairman of the War Committee and in which Asquith should be included'.[77] That afternoon there was a conference at Buckingham Palace, with Asquith, Bonar Law, Lloyd George, Arthur Henderson (the Labour leader) and Balfour present. George V invited Balfour to come half an hour early to advise; Balfour spoke to the King of the necessity for a change to a division between the direction of the war on the one hand and the Prime Ministership and leadership of the House of Commons on the other. Asquith refused to serve under anyone else; neither Balfour, Law nor Lloyd George were acceptable as far as he was concerned. Law saw that a government headed by him and including Lloyd George would inevitably be dominated by the latter. Thus he advised the King to send for Lloyd George. On the evening of 6 December the War Minister accepted the task of trying to form a government in which Asquith and most of his Liberal cabinet ministers wanted no part.

Asquith still hoped. He knew that the majority of the Liberal cabinet had refused to serve in the new administration and Curzon, despite his and his colleagues' change of mind on 5 December, had assured him that no Unionist except Law would join it. Late in the evening of 6 December, at about half past nine, Bonar Law visited Carlton Gardens where he found Balfour sitting in his bedroom wearing a dressing gown. Law offered him the Foreign Office, at which Balfour, according to Lord Beaverbrook, jumped up declaring: 'Well, you hold a pistol to my head – I must accept.'[78] On the evening of 7 December, Lloyd George kissed hands as Prime Minister, his administration formed. The Labour party had backed him, also the Unionists and the vast majority of the back-bench Liberals. Curzon, Lord Robert Cecil and Austen Chamberlain joined the cabinet, on the condition that Haig remained Commander-in-Chief and both Lord Northcliffe and Winston Churchill were excluded. Of the prominent Unionists, only Lord Lansdowne stayed out.

Law had told Balfour when persuading him to accept the Foreign Secretaryship, that, in Balfour's words, 'if I consented, it would, in the view both of L.G. and himself, greatly help with the rest of our Unionist colleagues'.[79] The importance of Balfour's role was undoubted. 'Under all circumstances, I think that the part played by him was the biggest part played in the crisis', Law later wrote, remarking that, although Balfour was tired of office, aware of Lloyd George's dissatisfaction with his direction of the Admiralty and the uncertainty as to whether the proposed new government could ever be formed, 'he took his decision without a moment's hesitation, and he did it, as he explained to me afterwards, for this reason – that unless the new Government succeeded then the only alternative was to return to the old situation where the conditions, if possible, were even worse than before.'[80]

Balfour had not wished for the complete overthrow of Asquith. 'I am sorry Asquith is not still P.M.', he wrote on 30 December. 'That was what I wanted. But I was all for Lloyd George being given a free hand.'[81] He knew the need for desperate measures and earlier, on being informed that Lloyd George 'wants to be dictator' had remarked: 'Let him be. If he thinks he can win the war, I am all for him having a try.'[82] The Asquiths were furious at what they saw as Balfour's treachery. Asquith felt particularly angry that his determination to retain Balfour in the Admiralty should have been 'rewarded by his being, two days after, the first of the Tories to go over to LL.G., for whom he has jackalled ever since';[83] and Margot launched a series of hysterical letters and wild conversations. In January 1917 Balfour and she met and he reported her 'quite mad. She seemed to think the only use of the war was to keep Asquith in power. Since it had failed in that, what was the good of it!'[84] Some years later Margot told Mrs Dugdale 'between you and me this is what hurt my husband more than anything else. That LL.G. (a Welshman!) should betray him he . . . could understand but that Arthur should join his enemy (LL.G.) and help to ruin him (Henry) he never understood.'[85] Asquith never held office again; but for Balfour a remarkable period had begun.

16

'An Ideal Man for the Foreign Office'

The Great War brought tragedy and change to almost every family in the belligerent nations. Arthur Balfour, although without children or grandchildren, was also touched by this. He had relations serving in the forces and his nephew Oswald was wounded several times at the front. His friends endured more, Lady Wemyss and Lady Desborough both losing two sons; and to them he offered his conviction of an after-life perhaps more satisfactory than any existence on earth. 'The unbalanced evil of death is separation', he told Lady Wemyss in 1915, after the death of her son Ivo. 'There is no other. We have no reason to mourn because those who die young leave so much of life's fresh joys: – for we have no reason to doubt that their change of state may be a gain.'[1] To Lady Desborough he wrote: 'for myself I entertain no doubt whatever about a future life. I deem it at least as certain as any of the hundred and one truths by which I, and all mankind, direct our daily actions.'[2]

When Julian Grenfell, the Desborough's son, was killed, Balfour told Grenfell's mother that 'the noblest of deaths in the greatest of causes he would have deemed no ill-fortune for others, and would have gladly welcomed for himself. For he was cast in a heroic mould: deeply moved by noble causes, loving peril for itself, and glorying in battle. To live greatly and to die soon is a lot which all must admire and some of us envy: indeed to my mind it cannot be bettered.'[3] Such sentiments have today an historical ring, different from the angry exhausted poetry of Sassoon and Owen. Balfour was a politician, and a politician of his time.

For politicians individual experience, even collective horror, are often sacrificed to an idea of the common good; these were exceptional times, demanding exceptional sacrifices. Balfour, convinced of the German threat to Europe, believed the demands on his people to be just.

As at the Irish Office, his combative spirit, once roused, marched almost blindly forward, although now his pace was slower. At the Admiralty, he lacked that perpetual driving force needed to control a great fighting department in time of war. He could be coolly constructive but not convulsively determined; for both age and temperament were against him. With Balfour, procrastination in the face of attack had, since the debacle of 1906, become a weapon to be relied upon more and more. Perhaps, after the accumulating defeats of the last eight years in opposition, this is scarcely surprising. The old fertility of ideas, the remarkable powers of disquisition and assimilation, were still there but not the elemental force so necessary for their expression.

The Foreign Office was a more appropriate post. 'Clearly he was not a man to stimulate and organise the activity of the Navy in a crisis', Lloyd George wrote later. 'But he was an ideal man for the Foreign Office and to assist the cabinet on big issues.'[4] Lloyd George was now his chief and their relationship, previously one of guarded but mutual admiration, entered a new phase. Balfour knew that 'the little man', as he called the Prime Minister, was irreplaceable. His dynamic energy, his power alternatively to force and to conciliate, his extraordinary ability to move and drive his fellow men: these made Balfour sure, as he told Lord Robert Cecil in September 1917, that 'the most patriotic course appears to me to provide the man whom we do not wish to replace with all the guidance and help in our power'.[5] In 1919 Balfour wrote to Bonar Law on the Prime Minister, 'our friend is, I think, the most remarkable single figure produced by the Great War'.[6]

Lloyd George was intensely aware of the usefulness of Balfour's prestige to his government; but what of his personal feelings towards his Foreign Secretary? These at times were almost reverential, particularly when he remembered his first days in the House of Commons as a young Welsh solicitor fascinated by the reality of Gladstone, Balfour and Chamberlain, the great parliamentary figures of their time. In November 1915 Lloyd George told Frances Stevenson after Balfour had asked his advice on the front bench during a debate 'that it sometimes comes to him in flashes how far he has come along the political road', for in the early days he would have considered 'a word or nod from such a great personage as a great event' but 'now here he was sitting by Balfour's side and Balfour was turning to him for advice:'[7] Lloyd George could be exasperated by Balfour's weaknesses; yet he also understood the power of that reflective disinterested intelligence, soaring occasionally above momentary considerations to reach some elementary but previously imperceptible grand conclusion. Harold Nicolson visited Lloyd George in 1932, and there was a photograph of Balfour on the writing table at Churt.

The new War Cabinet was much smaller than its predecessor, having only five members. These were Lloyd George, Bonar Law (Chancellor of the Exchequer), Curzon (Lord President of the Council), Henderson and Lord Milner as Ministers without Portfolio. Lord Derby became War Minister and Carson First Lord of the Admiralty, but neither had the right to attend the War Cabinet unless summoned. Balfour, as Foreign Secretary, was present always when foreign affairs were being discussed and also, alone among the Ministers, had enough authority to be sure that his views would receive a formal or informal hearing. Lloyd George's method of conducting business was occasionally irksome. He operated through a private secretariat, known as the Garden Suburb because it was housed in a number of huts in the garden of 10 Downing Street. The Garden Suburb inevitably challenged the regular government departments, creating an impression of arrogant independence. Curzon, when Foreign Secretary, fretted over this, and Balfour also remarked 'we all unfortunately suffer from the P.M's method, or lack of method, of doing business – and must keep our tempers as best we can'.[8] Balfour, less prickly than Curzon, kept in touch with the central control through Sir Maurice Hankey, the War Cabinet's permanent secretary. He also, as Mrs Dugdale notes, attended three hundred meetings of the new War Cabinet out of some five hundred held; Lord Robert Cecil, his deputy, being present at over a hundred more.

Balfour and Cecil worked well together, despite their earlier tensions over tariff reform. Balfour had admired his cousin's handling of the Ministry of Blockade and felt able to retire almost immediately after his appointment to rest at Eastbourne for most of December. On 18 December the new regime at the Foreign Office faced its first test when Walter Page, the American Ambassador, presented to Lord Robert Cecil a German note proposing peace negotiations, followed the next day by a message from President Wilson appealing for a cessation of hostilities as the aims of both sides appeared 'virtually the same as stated in general terms to their own peoples and to the world'.[9]

Balfour had previously been concerned with peace possibilities. In February 1916 he, together with Asquith, Lloyd George and Grey, had met Colonel House President Wilson's emissary, and listened to House's proposals for bringing the European belligerents together. Balfour and Grey encouraged these after House agreed to the suggestion that America should enter the war on the side of the allies if Germany rejected the American offer; but President Wilson felt unable to guarantee this. In the autumn of 1916 Asquith asked for the War Committee's opinion on the chances of a negotiated peace and Balfour supplied a long memorandum in November starting from the premise, extremely optimistic at this stage of the war, that Germany would have terms imposed on her by the victorious allies. He did not share Lord Lansdowne's opinion, presented to the cabinet in the same month, that to strive for an overall victory was both economically dangerous and tragically destructive.

President Wilson's message of December 1916, initially a reply to the German Chancellor Bethmann-Hollweg's vague peace proposals, was sent without Colonel House's knowledge, and House realized that to equate the war aims of the allies with those of the central powers was to invite immediate rejection. The Germans were aware of their military strength and the invitation to negotiate was in reality a diplomatic ploy aimed at neutral opinion. In January, Balfour sent a note to Sir Cecil Spring-Rice, the British Ambassador in Washington, to supplement the official response to Wilson prepared in consultation with the French. The note declared 'though the people of this country share to the full the desire of the President for peace, they do not believe that peace can be durable if it be not based on the success of the Allied cause'. It emphasized 'the aggressive aims and unscrupulous methods of the central powers' and called for 'some form of international sanction . . . which would give pause to the hardiest aggressor',[10] perhaps an embryonic league of nations. Wilson was more impressed by the allied response, even though it held out little hope for peace by negotiation, than the unbending German refusal to consider the American suggestions. Spring-Rice also told Balfour 'your note strikes a theme that has been deep in the President's thoughts for many months, and namely, the plan of a Court of International Sanction, which would have the force of preventing wars . . . .'.[11]

The United States was, despite isolationist sentiment in Congress, pushed gradually into the European holocaust. On 31 January 1917 Germany announced a resumption of unrestricted submarine warfare; two days later the German Ambassador in Washington was sent back. In February Balfour presented Walter Page with the Zimmerman telegram, intercepted in January, which revealed a German plot to incite Mexico to join the central powers should America enter the war on the side of the allies. This scene with Page was, Balfour later declared, 'as dramatic a moment as I remember in all my life'.[12] German attacks on American shipping further inflamed opinion in the United States. Finally on 2 April Wilson asked Congress for a declaration of war with Germany.

In February Balfour had informed Walter Page that one of his chief intellectual pleasures 'had long been contemplation of the United States as it is, and even more, as its influence in the world will broaden'; thus when Page suggested that one reason for British unpopularity in America was that 'our official people on both sides steadfastly refuse to visit one another and become acquainted', he volunteered to cross the Atlantic 'if you are perfectly sure my going would be agreeable to the President'.[13] Such a mission had been contemplated by the War Cabinet in March; with America in the war its advantages were even more obvious. House advised Wilson to accept Balfour's proposal, although the President feared charges of susceptibility to British intrigue and influence. On 9 April Wilson cabled his acceptance, suggesting the mission should be diplomatic rather than military.

Balfour embarked from Euston Station with some twenty-five companions. These included Lord Cunliffe (the Governor of the Bank of England), General Tom Bridges and Admiral de Chair (the two service representatives), an emissary from the Ministry of Munitions and assorted Civil servants. Sir Eric Drummond was his chief Foreign Office aide and Sir Ian Malcolm his personal private secretary. Malcolm, a lively former Unionist member of parliament, was to remain with Balfour until after the Versailles peace conference; he, in Mrs Dugdale's words, 'took the burden of the important small things which make so much difference in the daily life of a public man,'[14] although critics later remarked that Sir Ian was apt to exhaust his chief with energetic and inappropriate diversions.

Secrecy was vital, given the threat of German submarines. The mission passed the night in the Station Hotel, Dumfries, on the way to embarkation at Greenock; as it left Dumfries Sir Eric Drummond observed to Balfour, 'Thank goodness we are all clear without anyone finding out you were there',[15] to which the Foreign Secretary replied that this was incorrect for he had given his autograph to the lift boy. At midnight they left Greenock in the *Olympic*, accompanied by some three thousand other passengers, to begin one of those long sea voyages that were generally an agony of sickness for Balfour. This time, after spending the first stormy twenty four hours in his room, he had little trouble and never missed a meal or failed to preside over one of the mission's conferences, taking an hour's exercise every day in the ship's gymnasium, apparently oblivious of the U-boat threat. 'As for the dangers that surrounded us', Malcolm later wrote, 'he never gave them a moment's thought; he spurned the curious life-preserving one piece suit made up of india-rubber which had been thoughtfully provided and laid out for him in his cabin, saying that on the whole he would prefer to drown in his nightshirt.'[16]

The *Olympic* arrived in Halifax harbour on the morning of 20 April. For the first time since his early tour with Spencer Lyttelton, Balfour was back in North America and, in the special train sent to convey him to Washington, Malcolm remembered his chief as 'radiantly happy; to be on land again, and to be in a country and among a people for which he had always had great sympathy'.[17] On Sunday, 22 April, they reached Washington and drove, amid cheering crowds and streets decorated with Stars and Stripes and the Union Jacks, to the large private house of Mr Breckenridge Long, which the American government had provided for the visit.

The next morning Balfour went to the White House to meet President Wilson. During his four weeks in Washington they had several discussions, often with Colonel House in attendance. Wilson and Balfour, both intellectuals in politics, were naturally in sympathy with each other, but Mrs Dugdale has written: 'I never heard him really 'let himself go' on the character of the President, a fact in itself significant. I never heard anything but praise, genuine certainly, but always expressed in carefully chosen phrases.'[18] After the peace conference the phrases were apt to be less 'carefully chosen', for Balfour came to share European exasperation with the world's self-appointed saviour. On 30 April, after an intimate dinner at the White House, Balfour disclosed to Wilson and House the so-called 'secret treaties' apportioning territory in the event of an allied victory. In 1919 Wilson denied having knowledge of these before he went to the Paris Peace Conference and Balfour diplomatically told Mrs Dugdale that 'quite likely he did forget. I can quite understand that.'[19]

While the possibilities of collaboration were being discussed by the various experts of the two countries, Balfour set about spreading goodwill. The main obstacle was the antagonism of the Irish Americans and it was feared that there might be opposition from these to Balfour's projected address to Congress. In fact this speech, significantly the first by any visiting British statesman since Parnell in 1880, was a success, Wilson himself attending and coming down into the chamber at its end to shake Balfour's hand with the other legislators. The constant speech-making of the trip was its chief ordeal, especially as this had an aura of competition with a French mission engaged in a similar exercise. The French were led by their Prime Minister, Monsieur Viviani, whose oratory was often highly emotional, so much so in Chicago that Marshall Joffre, the military representative, embraced him in floods of tears at the end of one harangue. Balfour, told of this by Malcolm on his way to address the Senate, said, 'Ian, whatever I say this morning or whatever I do, I count on you to prevent Tom Bridges from kissing me'.[20]

As always, Balfour shone in personal contact. Malcolm wrote of 'the men's dinner parties which he attended night after night to meet politicians and experts from all over the country. I can see him now, when dinner was over, lying back in a comfortable chair, with ten or a dozen men around him and plying him with every conceivable question about the war, advancing new theories, criticising old ones. . . .'[21] The British Ambassador to Washington, Sir Cecil Spring-Rice, declared that 'Mr Balfour's personal influence has been an asset of immense importance';[22] Balfour, however, told Lloyd George by cable in May that, though Spring-Rice had done 'excellent work', he should be replaced by someone of greater stature, perhaps Grey, for the effect of Grey's presence 'would be, to quote House's confidential observation, that we could go to sleep over the future relations of the two countries'.[23] Later in May Lord Northcliffe was appointed to head a special mission to Washington, against the opposition of Balfour and Spring-Rice, both of whom had suffered from the Northcliffe press. Balfour's protest became known to the Asquith family and the newspapers, much to Lloyd George's anger; the Foreign Secretary did not see Lord Northcliffe as a worthy successor to himself.

Leaving Washington, the mission visited New York, where Balfour again met his old friends, Mr Choate, once American Ambassador in London, and Theodore Roosevelt. After attending a morning service in the Cathedral with the Foreign Secretary, Choate died that night to Balfour's deep regret; but at Oyster Bay Roosevelt provided a characteristically ebullient welcome, although on the way back to New York the escorting police neatly foiled a maverick attack by a single car on the British motor cavalcade. The meetings with Choate and Roosevelt rejuvenated Balfour, who was finding the constant round of talks and welcomes tiring. In New York he was shown a massive skyscraper and, informed the building was entirely fireproof, observed 'What a pity'. Eventually, after similar visits to Boston, Ottawa, Toronto and Quebec, the mission again boarded the *Olympic* which docked at Liverpool on 9 June.

Sir Ian Malcolm claimed that Balfour in the United States
'had gained for us (in all but name) an ally whose sympathy
sprang not only from the head but now from the heart'.[24] For the
rest of the war and the beginning of the peace, the Foreign
Secretary strove for more practical gains in the way of material
assistance. Britain, pressed by the U-boat campaign and food
shortages, needed all the help she could obtain from America.
Walter Page, the anglophile American Ambassador, worked
closely with Balfour and came to admire him; but Wilson and his
administration were careful in their dealings with Britain,
responding slowly to requests for naval aid, rejecting in
December 1917 a treaty of mutual assistance because of an old
distrust of European alliances and Britain's treaty with Japan.
During the Balfour mission, Britain's debts to American banks
had been discussed and loans arranged from the United States
government. On Balfour's return the financial position became
desperate and rapid help was called for, with the result that
Britain, already creditor to most of her allies on a vast scale, owed
approximately £850,000,000 to the United States at the end of
the War.[25]

The Foreign Office responded well to the relaxed but determined mood of its new chief. Harold Nicolson, a young diplomat,
remembered Balfour as 'one of the few men I have met who were
immensely impressive without being in the least alarming' with
'that modesty of a man who feels himself to be immensely
superior to other men, but who is great enough to feel at the
same time that we are all equal in the eyes of God'. To Nicolson
the secret of Balfour's charm was not his kindness, for this was
'impersonal and aloof', but 'the fact that he was seriously and
sincerely interested in humanity'.[26] Yet he was occasionally the
despair of his staff; first because of his habit of re-drafting minutes
and despatches with an expertise which could shame their author
and second through his apparent indecisiveness. The office, having once failed to extract an important decision from him, sent up
a memorandum stating that there were two alternative courses
open on the matter and asking for instructions. Balfour simply
wrote 'Yes', initialling his comment and when asked what he had
meant, remarked: 'When I wrote the word "Yes", I merely
meant that I had agreed that there were only two courses open. I

still agree with that proposition.'[27] On another occasion, presented with an account of some fierce bureaucratic quarrel, he simply wrote 'Oh dear, oh dear, oh dear'.[28] One Sunday he dictated into his dictaphone for several hours; the next day a secretary found the tapes blank because Balfour had forgotten to turn the machine on.[29]

The conditions of war did not disturb the celebrated nonchalance. On the ground floor of the Foreign Office there was a padded bomb-proof room, for use during air raids, which was ignored by Balfour; indeed Malcolm remembers that on the occasion of a raid warning, 'A.J.B. picked up his hat and stick and wandered unconcernedly across the Horse Guards Parade to get on with his work at his home in Carlton Gardens'.[30] As always, official duties mingled with family life and Walter Page told President Wilson of lunches at Carlton Gardens with Lady Rayleigh and Alice Balfour present, remarking that 'either of these two ladies could rule this empire'. Page wrote: 'At his "family" luncheon, I found Lord Milner or Lord Lansdowne, or some literary man who had come in to find out from Lady Rayleigh how to conduct the empire or to write a great book; and the modest old chemical Lord sits silent most of the time and now and then breaks loose to confound them all with a pat joke. This is a vigorous family, these Balfours.'[31] When Page departed in 1918, a frail invalid who had to be helped into a railway carriage at Waterloo Station, both the Foreign Secretary and Lord Robert Cecil were there to bid him farewell. 'I loved that man', Balfour later told an American friend. 'I almost wept when he left England.'[32]

As always, there was steel beneath the gentle amiability. Balfour, in all his posts, attracted the loyalty of his staff chiefly because they realized that, over matters of importance, he would fight. The head of the Foreign Office in 1917 was Lord Hardinge, lately returned from being Viceroy of India. Hardinge, after the publication of a critical report by the commission enquiring into the disastrous Mesopotamia campaign which had occurred during his Viceroyalty, considered resigning his office along with Sir Austen Chamberlain, the Secretary of State for India. Balfour dissuaded him, also sanctioning Hardinge's speech in the House of Lords on the issue, a rare and much criticized public intervention by a civil servant. Without his chief's support, Hardinge might have become a useful scapegoat. Christopher Addison wrote on 17 July, after a conversation with Lloyd George: 'Balfour was also kicking over Mesopotamia, and insisted that if Hardinge were dismissed, he would resign, which certainly could not be afforded. LL.G. was in deep waters and he knew it.'[33] Later Hardinge told Balfour, 'I realise that but for you my career at the F.O. would have been ended'.[34] Balfour also took the field against Lord Beaverbrook, the new Minister of Information, and complained to Lloyd George about the Ministry's supposed trespassing on Foreign Office territory. Beaverbrook and Balfour were never to be friends.

In the Middle East Balfour faced the climax of his relations with Dr Weizmann and the Zionists. With the Turkish armies in retreat, European diplomacy was active. In October 1915 Sir Henry McMahon, British High Commissioner to Egypt, had encouraged Arab nationalism by giving support to Arab claims at the expense of the Ottoman empire in correspondence with Sherif Hussein, the Emir of Mecca. In 1916 the secret Sykes-Picot agreement, concluded by the young English Arabist, Sir Mark Sykes and the French diplomat François-Georges Picot, divided the Ottoman Middle East in a scheme of future partition. Britain marked out southern Mesopotamia and the ports of Haifa and Acre on the Palestine coast; the French took much of Syria and the Lebanon, together with a slice of northern Palestine. The remainder of Palestine was to be an 'international zone', administered after consultation with Russia and other allies (including the Sherif of Mecca). Outside these areas an independent Arab state, or confederation was to be established; but again divided up into British and French spheres of influence.

Weizmann and the Zionists, hearing of this settlement in April 1917 through their sympathizer C. P. Scott who had obtained the information from a French source, did not like the idea of Palestine under joint control. By this date too they had another powerful friend. Sir Mark Sykes, previously no admirer of the Jews, was converted to their cause first by Herbert Samuel and then by the realization that Zionism could well assist in furthering British ambitions and influence in the Middle East. Zionists had, since the offer of a settlement in East Africa, believed that there was more to hope for from British goodwill than from the other powers. Weizmann, by his scientific services, had established himself in government circles with access to Lloyd George and, of course, Balfour. In one of their conversations at the Admiralty, Weizmann told Balfour that while the Jews of Eastern Europe, often oppressed and separate from the rest of the community, regarded Palestine as 'a hope, an article of faith', many Western Jews thought little of it. 'But why should they oppose it?' Balfour asked. 'Why can I afford to be a Zionist, and not they?' Weizmann answered that no-one would challenge Balfour, but a Jew expressing such sentiments would be courting anti-Semitic suspicion for 'however good an Englishman a Jew might be, he was constantly challenged'.[35]

Zionism was international. The Berlin Zionist executive was in touch with the German Foreign Office; indeed initially Germany, as the enemy of Russia, seemed a natural ally. In the United States, Jewish influence was strong. During his visit to Washington in May 1917, Arthur Balfour met Louis Brandeis, the eminent American jurist and Zionist, who pressed upon the Foreign Secretary 'the ethical purposes and practicalities of Zionism and the popular strength among Jewry in America of the desire for the Jewish homeland'. Balfour was impressed by Brandeis's moral conviction and, according to his secretary Felix Frankfurter, Brandeis realized 'Balfour's keen understanding of the Jewish problem and said that the whole long discussion with Balfour was pithily summed up by Balfour's quietly emphatic remark: "I am a Zionist".'[36]

Wherever Balfour's personal sympathies may have lain, the declaration of November 1917, giving British government support to the idea of a Jewish national home, was founded upon hard strategic considerations as well as sentiment. The allies had a great, perhaps exaggerated, respect for international Jewish influence, particularly in the United States. The Zionists, assisted by the Russian revolution and consequent uncertainty of Russia's position in the Western alliance, pressed their case. In March Weizmann saw Balfour who spoke of the potential difficulties of the French and British claims in Palestine, further complicated after the winter of 1916 by Italian requests for an interest in the area. He suggested involving the United States, with some

possibility of an Anglo-American protectorate, to which Weizmann observed that two masters were a danger 'and we do not
know yet how far the Americans would agree with the British on
general principles of administration'. Weizmann put forward the
importance of Palestine 'from a British point of view',[37] an aspect
he believed to be new to Balfour.

This importance grew through 1917. Jewish opinion in
Russia, it was thought, could be won over by the allies by support
for Zionist aspirations and then used to subvert the drift towards
Bolshevism and a break with the allies. In June the French
signified their cautious support for a Jewish presence in Palestine,
and in the same month Balfour saw Lord Rothschild and Weizmann at the Foreign Office, who asked for definite declaration of
support. He told them to draft one which was considered by the
War Cabinet on 3 September with Balfour and Lloyd George,
both of whom looked upon it with favour, absent. Meanwhile
opposition had come, from within. Edwin Montagu, the Jewish
Secretary of State for India, submitted a memorandum entitled
'The Anti-Semitism of the Present Government' which fiercely
opposed any concession to Zionist aspirations. Montagu, supported by various prominent British Jews, argued that a Jewish
national homeland would jeopardize the position of Jews already
assimilated into the life and society of their adopted countries.
Their loyalties and national identity would be hopelessly split,
not only for themselves but in the eyes of the community as well,
creating a climate of alienation and suspicion. In the face of this
the War Cabinet postponed its decision.

Activity continued on both sides. At first the American
government's attitude had been cautious, but Brandeis succeeded
in extracting a more enthusiastic response from Wilson. Weizmann saw Lloyd George, emphasizing the strategic advantage of
Palestine to the British Empire. The opportunist reasons for a
quick decision were pressing: the Germans were known to be
contemplating a gesture of friendship towards Zionism, the
uncertainty in Russia was mounting, and a Jewish presence in
Palestine under British protection would be at the expense of
French claims in the area. Curzon, in the War Cabinet, opposed
the declaration, doubting the chances of Arab-Jewish co-
existence, speaking of the poor natural resources of Palestine and

its unsuitability for religious and agricultural reasons as an area for Jewish settlement. The rights of Arabs and Christians must be maintained; indeed perhaps the most that could be done was to give to the Jews 'but not to the Jews alone'[38] equal rights with the rest of the area's population for land purchase and settlement.

Balfour's answer was that the moment was propitious, diplomatically and politically. He told the cabinet that 'the vast majority of Jews in Russia and America, as, indeed, all over the world, now appeared to be favourable to Zionism. If we could make a declaration favourable to such an ideal we should be able to carry on an extremely useful propaganda both in Russia and America.' To this Curzon replied that he 'admitted the force of the diplomatic arguments in favour of expressing sympathy', and recognized 'that some expression of sympathy with Jewish aspirations would be a valuable adjunct to our propaganda' though he thought that 'we should be guarded in the language used in giving expression to such sympathy'.[39] Of the War Cabinet Lloyd George and Smuts were with Balfour; Lord Milner and Balfour had both worked on drafts of the declaration, based on the Zionist draft of July and the final text was produced by Leo Amery, then assistant secretary of the War Cabinet. This, on 2 November, was sent by Arthur Balfour in the form of a letter to Lord Rothschild.

The declaration had been carefully phrased to provide Jewish encouragement without arousing Arab fears. The phrase 'national home' Balfour understood to mean 'some sort of British, American, or other protectorate', and 'did not necessarily involve the early establishment of an independent Jewish state, which was a matter for gradual development in accordance with the ordinary laws of political evolution'.[40] But in February 1918 he told Colonel Meinertzhagen 'my personal hope is that the Jews will make good in Palestine and eventually found a Jewish state'.[41] To Lady Rayleigh he remarked in July of the same year: 'The Jews were too great a race not to count and they ought to have a place where those who had strong racial idealism could develop on their lines as a nation and govern themselves.' Balfour added that he was convinced 'that nothing but the Holy Land would satisfy their aspirations'. When his sister remarked that 'Captain George Lloyd says the Arabs will make difficulties: they say the land is theirs, they are three to one of the Jews'; he replied, 'George Lloyd is quite right, but there are difficulties in whatever you do'.[42] In August 1919 he wrote: 'Zionism, be it right or wrong, good or bad, is rooted in age-long traditions, in present need, in future hopes, of far profounder importance than the desires and prejudices of the seven hundred thousand Arabs who now inhabit that ancient land.'[43]

For Balfour, diplomatic opportunism and personal idealism came together in the declaration. In Weizmann he had met an inspirational articulator of a message which took him back to the stern Old Testament tenets of his mother's low church faith and the Presbyterianism of the Scottish Lowlands. Mrs Dugdale wrote: 'Near the end of his days he said to me that on the whole he felt that what he had been able to do for the Jews had been the thing he looked back upon as the most worth his doing.'[44] In Palestine, European decisions led to local conflict. At the peace conference and afterwards Balfour defended the Zionist cause; and was henceforth looked upon as one of its greatest allies.

In November 1917, the Lansdowne peace letter also had a deep personal concern for Balfour, this time leading to imputations of dishonour. The failure of the Nivelle offensive in April and the terrible losses of the summer and autumn at Ypres and Passchendaele showed the bloody impasse on the Western front. Balfour seemed to maintain an outward confidence in the generals; in October Sir William Robertson told Haig of Lloyd George's effort to change the High Command, but that 'Milner, Carson, Curzon, Cecil, Balfour have each in turn spoken to me separately about his intolerable conduct . . . and have said they are behind us'.[45] Earlier there had been the possibility of an Austrian peace initiative, Hankey recording that Balfour was 'very sniffy'[46] about Lloyd George's efforts to promote this, and in September a German approach was made through Spain. Balfour informed the allied ambassadors of this last move in October, after Lloyd George had discussed it with the French whom he found, with the exception of Briand, suspicious and reluctant.

Lord Lansdowne's second son had been killed in France in the first year of the war. In the winter of 1916 Lansdowne submitted a memorandum to the cabinet, exploring the possibility of a negotiated peace, which Balfour had opposed. At the beginning of November 1917 Lansdowne saw Balfour, discussed this again and on 16 November submitted a long memorandum to his old friend, writing of the futility of the continuing human and economic devastation, also the evidence of increasing 'war weariness' on both sides. To relieve this, or show that the will to relieve it was there, Lansdowne suggested a statement of allied 'war aims' to show 'annihilation'[47] of the enemy was not among these. He proposed to ask a question in parliament to elicit such a statement.

On the same day Balfour spoke at the Mansion House, later informing Lansdowne that during this speech 'I had our conversation in mind'.[48] He told his audience 'the destruction of the German empire has never been the aim of the entente powers. The destruction or injury of German trade is not a war end; it is a war measure, and a most legitimate war measure. We recognise fully that each nation should be allowed to make for itself the government which suits its history, its character and its ideals.'[49] However, in a letter to Lansdowne on 22 November, Balfour wrote 'I do not know that this is a very suitable time for discussing peace matters. I rather think not.' He went on to say that he did 'not desire the destruction or dismemberment of Germany', but that neither Alsace Lorraine nor 'historic Poland' could be included in that 'part of central Europe which probably belongs to the German people'; however, 'the Germans think differently'.[50] On 26 November Lansdowne met Balfour outside St Margaret's, Westminster. He agreed not to ask a question in the Lords but said 'I therefore propose to put my own view before the public in the form of a letter'. Lansdowne later wrote 'He did not dissuade me'. When asked to look at a draft of the public communication, Balfour replied that he was leaving for France that evening but did not object to Lansdowne seeing his Permanent Under-Secretary for, 'Hardinge knows my thoughts'. Next day Hardinge saw the letter, made 'one or two suggestions not touching questions of principle' and observed it was 'statesmanlike' and would 'do good'.[51]

Geoffrey Robinson (later Dawson) of *The Times* refused to publish the letter but Lord Burnham, proprietor of the *Daily Telegraph*, agreed to do so on 29 November. The letter called for 'a co-ordination' of allied war aims to encourage 'the peace party in Germany' and thus make possible a negotiated peace, averting further human suffering and 'ruin to the civilized world'.[52] The press reaction, led by Lord Northcliffe, went violently against Lansdowne, and Bonar Law officially disassociated the Unionist party from his message. On 1 December a government communiqué in *The Times* stated: 'Lord Lansdowne in his letter spoke only for himself. Before writing it he did not consult, nor indeed has he been in communication with any member of the government, His Majesty's Ministers reading it with as much surprise as did everyone else.'[53] Viewed in the context of Balfour's communication, this seems less than fair to Lord Lansdowne.

After the great tirade of personal abuse which haunted the last years of Lansdowne's life, some of his friends, and his son, came to think that Balfour, by not denying *The Times* statement, had neglected to salvage at least a part of his old colleague's reputation. In December 1917 Hardinge wrote to Lord Lansdowne 'to express my sympathy and detestation of the horrible attacks made upon you'. He also declared that, when asked by Lord Robert Cecil if Lord Burnham's statement to him that Balfour and Hardinge knew about the letter was true, 'I said it was so in the main, and that it was on the understanding that Mr Balfour approved of my doing so but I criticised some points in the letter chiefly on technical grounds'.[54] Lansdowne, always chivalrous, wrote back: 'Your responsibility for the letter was, as you point out, strictly limited and infinitesimal. Balfour was not responsible at all.'[55]

Balfour certainly did not see the letter, even in draft, until its appearance in the *Daily Telegraph*; neither did he see *The Times* communiqué until he returned to London, although Mrs Dugdale's suggestion that he remained always unaware of this is surely too unkind both to his staff at the Foreign Office and himself. What probably occurred was an example of Balfour's ability to put unpleasant and emotionally complex matters behind him almost as soon as they had taken place. Lord Newton, then attached to the Foreign Office, wrote to Lansdowne's son, 'my own impression is that A.J.B. paid little or no attention to your father, and made no attempt to stop him'.[56] According to Newton, Lord Lansdowne 'was misled by the attitude and remarks of A.J.B. and Hardinge. I think myself that both of them (especially the latter) treated him badly. The fact that they both appeared to approve is easily explained by their respect and friendship for him.'[57] Some years afterwards Lord Lansdowne's daughter, the Duchess of Devonshire, spoke to Balfour and reported the conversation to her brother. 'I don't believe Arthur B. ever did face the question of publication', she wrote. 'He so seldom faced anything, and would be inclined to agree with Father as to the substance of the memorandum to save himself trouble.'[58]

After the publication of the letter, Balfour made plain his opposition. As the vilification of Lansdowne continued, it was clear that there was little national support for his message. Balfour moved on, leaving the dead idea behind. 'How long is it since we have met, and are we going to meet again?' Lansdowne wrote to him in February 1918. 'I hope so, although I suppose I must be reckoned among the infidels.'[59] After the war they renewed their friendship, for Lansdowne bore no grudges.

In November 1917 the Bolshevik seizure of power in Russia and the offer of a separate peace with Germany brought the war into an even more anxious phase. Lenin began negotiations for an armistice. Balfour was reluctant to force a complete break with Russia's new rulers, if only because allied antipathy would be likely to drive them into German hands. In a famous memorandum to the War Cabinet on 9 December he wrote: 'If, for the moment the Bolsheviks show peculiar virulence in dealing with the British Empire, it is probably because they think that the British Empire is the great obstacle to immediate peace; but they are fanatics to whom the constitution of every state, whether monarchical or republican, is equally odious. Their appeal is to every revolutionary force, economic, social, racial or religious, which can be used to upset the existing political organisation of mankind.' To Balfour the Bolsheviks were 'dangerous dreamers' but, while not advocating recognition of the new regime, Britain should 'avoid, as long as possible, an open breach with this crazy system'. He declared 'if this be drifting, then I am a drifter by deliberate policy'.[60]

Lord Robert Cecil and Winston Churchill were more bellicose. On 8 February 1918, at the War Cabinet, it was decided that Robert Bruce Lockhart, the unofficial British representative to the Bolsheviks, should become the government's official agent in Petrograd. The debate became heated, with Lloyd George, described by Hankey as 'half a Bolshevist himself', calling for closer ties and Lord Robert Cecil very much against. Hankey noted: 'Balfour, as usual, rather on the hedge between these. The discussions got rather hot at one time, as they were getting to fundamentals, the rights of property owners, etc., when I hastily intervened, and brought them back to business'.[61]

Lloyd George was thinking of a change at the Foreign Office. The Northcliffe press had been attacking Balfour's supposed dilatoriness, and there was also his age. In January 1918, Milner told Bruce Lockhart that Balfour was 'a harmless old gentleman' and that 'he would have liked to see Lord Robert Cecil as Foreign Secretary, with Sir Eyre Crowe as his assistant'.[62] Lloyd George remarked to Christopher Addison: 'Balfour is seedy and not in the mood to do much himself. What about Balfour coming into the War Cabinet and Smuts going to the Foreign Office?'[63] Nothing came of this, but there was other criticism of the Foreign Office, particularly with regard to Balfour and Cecil's 'Ultra-caution'[64] over the possibilities of a separate peace with Austria. However the Prime Minister in February 1918 could count on the support of Balfour in his battle against the generals. Sir William Robertson's obstinacy over the Supreme Allied War Council at Versailles made Balfour realize that political control over the military was threatened unless Lloyd George was obeyed.

In February the Russian government repudiated its foreign debts and signed the Treaty of Brest-Litovsk with Germany. On the Western front, the German army, strengthened by troops from the East, launched a great offensive in March. The allies were beaten back, almost disastrously. It was decided, despite President Wilson's reluctance, to aid anti-German forces in Russia with a view to re-opening the war on Germany's Eastern flank. This was a military decision, which Balfour backed with diplomatic activity involving the United States and Japan. He did not however look back with nostalgia to pre-revolutionary times. 'A restored Tsardom would be more dangerous to British interests than the Tsardom which has just vanished: for it would almost certainly be dependent upon German support', Balfour wrote to Lloyd George on 13 July. 'However violent be the re-action caused by the folly and incompetence of the various Governments which have attempted to rule Russia since the Revolution, I cannot believe that Russia will ever be content merely to revert to an outworn despotism.'[65] In June he advised against the Prime Minister seeing Kerensky, believing this could make difficulties with the Bolsheviks.

Allied troops landed at Archangel and Murmansk in August. After an assassination attempt on Lenin in Petrograd, a mob attacked the British Embassy; a British officer was killed and other officials taken prisoner. Balfour sent a protest and Litvinov, the Bolshevik representative in London, was imprisoned with other Russians; later they were exchanged for the British prisoners. One of these was Robert Bruce Lockhart who saw Balfour at the Foreign Office in October when the Foreign Secretary, rather than talk about the Russian situation, concentrated on refuting the Marxist arguments of Lenin's regime. Lockhart prepared a report, advising either whole-hearted military intervention against the Bolsheviks or a decision to come to terms with them. In Russia, the Allied forces, there against Lenin's wishes, inevitably came to be identified with the 'White' counter-revolutionary groups, their allies in the attempt to re-open the Eastern front. After the collapse of the Germans in Western Europe these forces lost their original reason for existence.

This last point was made by Balfour to the War Cabinet on 18 October but on 14 November, at another War Cabinet meeting, the decision was taken to continue support for the 'White' groups where possible, without launching a concerted attack on the Bolsheviks. Balfour felt that the newly independent Polish, Ukrainian and Baltic provinces of Russia should not be allowed 'to be overwhelmed by central Russia, as these states contained populations of different race, language and religion, and were, on the whole, more civilised and cultivated than the Great Russians'.[66] Balfour also thought that old allies should not be abandoned, stating in a memorandum on 29 November that, although 'it is for the Russians to choose their own form of government' and 'we have no desire to intervene in their affairs', he believed 'recent events have created obligations which last beyond the occasion which gave them birth'.[67] By the end of

1918 more than 180,000 foreign troops were aiding, with manpower and arms, some 300,000 'White' Russian forces in the
civil war; and British intervention, originally entered into reluctantly by Balfour, was an accomplished fact.

17

Peacemaking

The German offensive in the west had petered out in July;
in August and September the allied armies, augmented by
American troops, attacked. In the German rear, the Turks
collapsed and the Bulgarians surrendered. Allenby entered
Damascus in September, destroying Ottoman power in the
Middle East. Peace negotiations began in October between
the German government and President Wilson, based on the
earlier declaration of Wilson's fourteen points through which
he hoped to inject a new idealism into the international community. The British were doubtful about these. To an American
acquaintance, Balfour remarked that he hoped Wilson would
not come to the treaty negotiations 'for he thought he was not
sound on the "freedom of the seas", or depriving Germany of
her colonies. He wanted to be kind to all nations,' even those
manifestly 'untrustworthy'.[1]

In October Balfour observed to the cabinet: 'I don't want to
go beyond making Germany impotent to renew the war, and obtaining compensation. I don't want to trample her in the mud.'[2]
In the same month however the German sinking of the Irish Mail
Leinster off Kingston, drowning 450 passengers including many
women and children, caused him to remark of the defeated
enemy 'Brutes they were, and brutes they remain'.[3]

The Paris peace conference did not begin until January
1919. Before then Lloyd George held a general election, the
first since 1910. To maintain the Unionists in his coalition, the
Prime Minister told Bonar Law he was prepared to accept a
measure of imperial preference and the exclusion of Ulster from
Irish Home Rule, and to re-consider the financial terms, but not

the principle, of Welsh church disestablishment. Balfour agreed
with Law that a return to pre-war party controversy should be
avoided, for national unity was desperately needed to re-construct
the country. In December the poll resulted in a massive victory
for the coalition, with 339 coalition Tories and 136 coalition
Liberals facing 26 Asquithian Liberals and 59 Labour members;
both the Asquithians and Labour had previously rejected the
Prime Minister's offer of inclusion in his forces. From Ireland,
there were 73 Sinn Feiners who refused to take their seats at
Westminster, forming a self-constituted parliament in Dublin.
Balfour was re-elected with a large majority from the City of
London and continued in office as Foreign Secretary.

Lloyd George and Balfour both went to Paris for the peace
conference and were housed in apartments in the Rue Nitot,
the British delegation's staff operating from the Hotel Majestic
and the Hotel Astoria. The night before he left London, Balfour had dinner with Lord and Lady Wemyss and observed 'As
I have always told you, it is not so much the war as the peace
that I have always dreaded';[4] to another he remarked that
the conference was going to be 'a rough and tumble affair'.[5]
Curzon, the Lord President of the Council, was deputed to
look after the Foreign Office while the Foreign Secretary was in
Paris; and Balfour took along Ian Malcolm as one of his private
secretaries.

Balfour was now aged 71, and there were doubts about his
powers. Lord Robert Cecil, dining with his cousin in Paris on the
evening of 13 January, noted 'A.J.B. was very exhausted at the
beginning of dinner, though he cheered up a little at the end. Still
I should say that he was alarmingly tired.'[6] Three days later Cecil
found Balfour 'in the last stage of exhaustion' and blamed Ian
Malcolm who, 'very foolishly takes him about to music halls
and things when he ought to save up every ounce of his
strength'.[7] Malcolm would organize nights out in Paris, once
taking in a boxing match, and Balfour himself enjoyed long walks
in Montmartre and Montparnasse where he was accosted by a
journalist who offered him 100,000 dollars for his memoirs.
Sometimes, in the Rue Nitot, there were musical evenings; at one
of these the singer asked if anybody objected to German songs, to
which Balfour answered: 'I don't; I will take them as part of the

reparations that they owe us.'[8]

In Paris Balfour again evinced that remarkable oscillation between physical strength and weakness, and by 18 January Lord Robert Cecil, who had resigned from the government over Welsh disestablishment but was assisting in the drafting of the League of Nations covenant, was writing of his 'wonderful power of recovery'.[9] At first Lloyd George led the delegation, until the signing of the treaty with Germany in June; then from June until September the Foreign Ministers took over the complete task of peace-making with Germany's allies. To observers and participants, the British Foreign Secretary constituted one of the fascinations and exasperations of the conference. Clemenceau, the French Prime Minister, once remarked after a Balfourian summary of a case 'very well—are you for or against?', Hankey calling this 'a very shrewd commentary on Balfour's character',[10] and later referred to him as *'cette vieille fille'*. To Ray Stannard Baker, director of Wilson's press bureau, Balfour was 'the arch conspirator' against the President's idealism, or the representative of 'the philosophy of doubt' as opposed to 'the philosophy of faith'.[11] But Harold Nicolson noted in his diary of a meeting of allied Foreign Ministers in May: 'A.J.B. then rouses himself. He launches off into a really brilliant analysis of our guiding principles. It is crushing in its logic. When he *does* consent to intervene he is a whale among minnows.'[12]

Later Balfour was to be accused of lethargy in Paris; Lord Selborne, his old cabinet colleague writing 'I never could make out that he took any important part at all'.[13] This is unfair, for Balfour was still capable of constructive, if intermittent, activity. In February he was involved in an attempt to arrange a meeting between Bolshevik representatives and their enemies, on the island of Prinkipo. When this failed, he tried to dilute Winston Churchill's plans for increased military intervention against the Bolsheviks which Lloyd George also deprecated, fearful of its effects on labour unrest in Britain. The result was continued support for the 'White' forces but not enough to ensure their victory. A year later Balfour told his sister that 'it was impossible for us to do any good in Russia' for 'the people were not against the Bolsheviks'; indeed there was something to be said for the view 'that the Bolshevik government was the best Russia has ever had'.[14] He remained however in speeches and writings a strong articulator of Bolshevism's absolute unsuitability to his own country.

From the middle of February until the beginning of March Lloyd George, Wilson and Clemenceau were away from the conference: the first two on domestic business in Britain and the United States and the last a victim of a failed assassination attempt. During this period Balfour deputized for Lloyd George and attempted to separate the military, naval and air clauses of the German treaty, proposing the ratifications of these before the more complex political and economic deliberations. This was defeated, but his second proposal, that the reports of the expert committees on frontiers, finance and economic relations with Germany should be ready by 8 March, was accepted. On 8 March Lloyd George returned from London; President Wilson was back on 14 March and the heads of the respective allied national delegations took over the negotiations. Balfour insisted on receiving the minutes of these meetings and occasionally attended. He also took trouble to maintain a close liaison with the delegation's representatives from India and the self-governing dominions.

The conference itself often took on a chaotic air. President Wilson's rather foggy idealism accorded ill with European colonial and diplomatic aims. On 24 April Orlando, the Italian Prime Minister, left Paris in an emotional protest against the refusal to grant Fiume to Italy. Agreements and clauses were patched up rapidly, often ignorantly. Harold Nicolson, writing of the discussion on the Austro-Hungarian empire in May by the Foreign Ministers at the Quai D'Orsay, declared: 'Hungary is partitioned by these five distinguished gentlemen – indolently, irresponsibly partitioned – while water sprinkles on the lilac outside – while experts watch anxiously – while A.J.B. in the intervals of dialectics on secondary points, relapses into somnolence . . .'[15]

Balfour, however somnolent, at least expressed private dissatisfaction. Lord Robert Cecil saw him on 1 May and found the evening uncomfortable 'partly due to the fact that A.J.B. is I think thoroughly dissatisfied with the course of the negotiations. He thinks they are being grossly mismanaged – which as far as I can see is quite true – and he has doubts whether he ought not to interfere but cannot quite bring himself to do so.'[16] Balfour made no public protest. He supported the allied opposition to French proposals for the break-up of Germany and an independent Rhineland state but spoke against sympathy for German lamentations, believing 'the Germans were responsible for the tragedy of the whole world'. To him Germany was 'no unhappy victim of circumstances, she was suffering, and ought to suffer, for her crimes';[17] in other words full reparations were a just demand. Yet he believed in German industrial regeneration, if only to enable payment of reparations, and allowing Germany armed protection of her frontiers.

Throughout the deliberations, Balfour maintained his habitual courtesy. In May, when the German plenipotentiaries received the draft treaty, he suggested the allied delegates should stand at their entry until the Germans were seated. When the German Foreign Minister, Count Brockdorff Rantzau, caused offence by remaining in his chair while replying to Clemenceau, Balfour, questioned afterwards about the incident, remarked: 'Didn't he stand up? I failed to notice. I make it a rule never to stare at people when they are in obvious distress.' Harold Nicolson noted 'A.J.B. makes the whole of Paris seem vulgar'.[18]

On 28 June the Treaty of Versailles was signed. Lloyd George and Wilson then departed from Paris, leaving Clemenceau and the allied Foreign Ministers to conclude treaties with Austria, Turkey, Bulgaria and Hungary. This is not the place for a detailed exposition or justification of these agreements, much debated at the time and since. To obtain a consensus as to the diverse aims and concerns of the allies was difficult enough: to achieve a geographically and economically satisfactory one for every territory almost inconceivable. Austria was established as a separate state, Bela Kun's Bolshevik regime was unseated in Hungary and assistance given to the new independent Russian states in the Baltic. The old Hapsburg empire disappeared.

By August Balfour was exhausted. He wrote to Curzon saying that his doctors insisted he should take a holiday and Curzon characteristically replied with evidence of his own industry, nevertheless agreeing to take Balfour's place in Paris. In September Balfour saw Lloyd George at Trouville and repeated his wishes, both to leave the Foreign Office and to take a rest. The Prime Minister persuaded him to delay his departure until a more propitious moment for a cabinet re-organization. On 10 September Balfour signed the Treaty of Saint Germain with Austria, leaving Paris the next day; and on 24 October Lloyd George announced a reconstituted peace cabinet with Curzon as Foreign Secretary and Balfour Lord President of the Council.

'You have held up the whole nation even as you have held up the hearts of your friends', Lady Desborough wrote to Arthur Balfour in November 1918. 'It is in very great pride that our affection is laid at your feet.'[19] After the war, Balfour continued with his old attachments. Both Lady Desborough and Lady Wemyss compiled books of remembrances of their lost sons, linking letters and accounts of family life with commemorative commentary. Lady Desborough told Balfour of her book, writing that 'above all people on earth I wanted you to have it'.[20] She declared: 'You do not know what a great Idea you were in the boys' lives, as well as a most-beloved presence. They most truly adored you, and in the strangest way you guided them – all unknown to yourself – as you do all of us who love you.'[21]

Lady Wemyss's children had grown up with Balfour constantly at Stanway where they christened him 'Mr Rabbit'. For Lady Cynthia Asquith, the Wemyss's daughter who had married Herbert Asquith, Balfour was 'in a class quite, quite, alone', yet in 1915 she felt 'oddly enough, in spite of his divine amiability and sweetness and easiness, I should still feel shy alone in a room with him', although 'I can imagine how intoxicating he must be to meet on one's own grown-up'.[22] By this date Lord Wemyss's affairs had simplified themselves into a liaison with the formidable Lady Angela Forbes who ran canteens for the troops at Boulogne and Etaples during the war until dismissed for swearing in front of a visiting clergyman and washing her hair in a canteen kitchen. The military authorities attempted to ban her from France before Balfour intervened to allow a triumphant return. Later Lady Angela wrote of Balfour: 'He had charm of manner, but the manner was cold, even to his great friends'. To her he was too 'polished' for 'charm without qualification should have something physical. There should be force behind the speaker, some shadow of barbarism glittering through the veneer of brains.'[23]

'I sat in my room last night sorting and tearing old letters', Lady Wemyss told Balfour in 1915. 'I tore up millions of what were really love letters – but I kept yours – which are not!'[24] Three years before, she had set out their differences of temperament, writing 'were I to go a thousand miles into my lover's arms I'd think the labour well spent and count the distance as nought! To me the Hellespont would be a mere ditch—a Rubicon to be leapt over with laughter – though possibly with irretrievable results – to you (faint heart!) the Hellespont would spell the unplumbed salt-estranging sea!' However she added 'although you have only loved me a little yet I must admit you have loved me long'.[25] Balfour continued gently to tease her, writing in 1916: 'at dinner tonight (I was dining at the Athenaeum) I read the life of the Chevalier du Boufflers – a charming narration of eighteenth century France which centres round two brilliant lovers, who loved each other till death parted them at a great age. It would interest you.'[26]

In 1919 there was a move to suggest Balfour for the Mastership of Trinity College, Cambridge, after the death of Dr H. M. Butler, and Lady Wemyss was asked to consult him; but this came to nothing, probably through his own reluctance. However in October of the same year Balfour was appointed Chancellor of Cambridge University in succession to his brother-in-law Lord Rayleigh who had recently died. At first he had refused, then, under pressure, accepted. 'He asked me about expenses as now he was a poor man',[27] Lady Rayleigh noted in her diary. Since 1895 Balfour had been Chancellor of the University of Edinburgh. He devoted time and care to the responsibilities which went with these two honours, assisting in 1928 in securing a benefaction of £700,000 from the Rockefeller Foundation for the new Cambridge University library.

In 1919 two other notable distinctions came his way. He was elected, at the instigation of Henri Bergson, an *'Associé Etranger'* of the French *Académie des Sciences Morales et Politiques* and delivered an address contrasting the contemporary intellectual climate, where 'nothing remains unquestioned' and 'everything is now permissible, even orthodoxy',[28] with the supposed certainties of the past. Then on 4 June, at Eton, he un-

veiled a portrait of himself by G. Fiddes Watt, presented to the
school by the Old Etonian Association. On the same day in 1918
he had presided over an Old Etonian lunch in Paris, making, in
Lord Robert Cecil's words, 'an extraordinarily suitable speech,
full of old Etonian sentiment, with most of which I profoundly
disagreed'.[29]

As he descended into old age, Balfour became a remarkable
landmark in British and international politics, representing both
a grand, leisured past and a comfortable reassuring present. To
his friends the unique combination of objective sympathy and
gentle brilliance persisted, Sir Edmund Gosse telling Evan
Charteris 'I spent an evening in his company last week, he scin-
tillated and glowed by turns'.[30] For the younger generation this
was enlivened by curiosity and engaging frankness, sometimes
bordering on the eccentric. When Harold Nicolson came to
Balfour during the Peace Conference to ask if he might leave
Paris for a few days to recover from overwork, he was given a pile
of detective novels and told to return to the Hotel Majestic for
the weekend. Nicolson read the books and returned refreshed on
Monday, to Balfour's delight. Away from Paris, supposedly
resting, the young diplomat would not have been able to forget
the pressing negotiations; but a detective novel was a 'counter-
irritant' which 'sets other lobes aflame: and these draw the blood
from your congested regions. The cure is not merely, as you have
seen, immediate: it is complete.'[31]

Balfour seemed destined to pass an agreeable and serene few
final years. A devoted family, national and international respect,
a mind still alert and interested: these were great gifts for old age;
yet there was one cloud: money. This was never previously a
worry; the great inheritance, both in property and investments,
had taken care of all material considerations. Balfour's financial
planning, if it existed, had room for houses, journeys, servants,
purchases of books and occasionally pictures, the endowment of
concerts and philosophical lectures: also the maintenance of
Whittingehame as a great family gathering place, equipped for
the full panoply of Edwardian country house life. Such an abundance led to careless management. Although Alice Balfour was a
painstaking housekeeper her brother took risks at a higher level.
Balfour's doubts about the Chancellor of Cambridge University's

expenses reflect the cost of these risks, and shortly after this he wrote to Bonar Law to complain about his salary as Lord President of the Council, also telling Lady Rayleigh in 1921 'he was not paid nearly enough for the work he was doing'.[32]

Balfour was excited by gambling and financial speculation. At Cannes, he enjoyed the Casino and Lloyd George tried to embarrass him in 1913 by revealing details of Stock Exchange transactions in doubtful companies. Lord Beaverbrook recorded Balfour's thrill 'with the tale of a big coup in the market place', and his admiration for 'the successful promoter', particularly new American millionaires of whom 'the late E. H. Harriman was his hero'.[33] In 1911 Beaverbrook went to see Balfour for political advice and wrote 'he would talk of nothing but the stock markets, with special reference to the chances of making a big killing on the New York stock exchange'.[34]

One of Balfour's speculations was an investment in Wet Carbonising Limited, a company set up in 1912 to exploit a Swedish process for the utilization of peat as an industrial fuel. The inventor of this was a Dr Ekenberg, a Swede who had become so involved in this scheme that, having moved to England in the early years of the century, he tried to send parcel bombs to its Swedish critics. For this he was arrested, dying in Brixton Prison in 1909 while awaiting extradition, and his assistant, Mr Nils Testrup, took over the scientific research. On the company's launching in 1912, Balfour was its largest shareholder, having 57,323 £1 preference shares and 8052 shilling ordinary shares out of a total paid-up company capital of £468,456. Other shareholders included Gerald Balfour, the Marchioness of Crewe and Lord d'Abernon (formerly Sir Edgar Vincent), the politician, diplomat and financier who had brought the process to Balfour's attention.[35]

Despite the setting up of large plant near Dumfries, the promised early success was not forthcoming, although Balfour remained optimistic. 'The family fortunes are critical', he told Lady Wemyss in January 1915. 'But it is a real satisfaction to know that the process is now an assured success: and that whoever reaps the money profit the world is richer by the discovery which will prove of immense economic importance'.[36] Certainly by the end of 1915, these profits were not reaching the Balfours for the initial share capital had disappeared, leaving liabilities of some £300,000 with a further £119,000 contingent liabilities in subsidiary companies. By January 1917 Lord d'Abernon had resigned from the board and, ominously, Mr Testrup's own holdings decreased while those of the Balfour brothers increased. In the same year the government provided financial assistance for the possibility of a factory in France to aid fuel problems at the front. This, given the directors and the past failure of the company to prove the process's practicability, came in for press criticism, the *Saturday Review* remarking 'the mere fact that Mr Gerald Balfour is the Chairman of Wet Carbonising, and that Mr Arthur Balfour is the largest shareholder, ought to make government officials particularly careful in their dealings with it'.[37]

Despite this help, there was still no breakthrough, and after the war the drain on the Balfour finances continued, now in support of a company called 'Peco' set up to advance the process further. As failure became evident, so Balfour's reaction to criticism of his original investment grew increasingly testy. He would not, perhaps could not afford to, withdraw. At his death in 1930 this, coupled with the financial depression, left the family seriously in debt; and his last years were be-devilled by worries about money. The exact size of the damage is unknown, but, given his large inheritance, it must have been extensive and was exacerbated by his neglect of the potentially rich agricultural property around Whittingehame.

Such matters were not allowed to disrupt the adoring family circle. Nephew and nieces, children of Balfour's brothers and sisters, became the most devoted section of this, one later recording that in childhood she had believed 'Arthur's Seat' outside Edinburgh to have been named as a consequence of her uncle's extraordinary eminence.[38] Eustace and Lady Frances Balfour's two daughters were attached to him in different ways: Joan, who married Edward Lascelles, believing that the Zionists had deluded her beloved 'Nunkie' into unnecessary effort and controversy and Blanche, or 'Baffy', becoming a dedicated Zionist herself. Of the young, perhaps Blanche, or Mrs Edgar Dugdale, was closest to Balfour; partly through her passionate Zionism and work for the League of Nations Union, also her interest in past and present politics. Towards the end of his life, she helped with his memoirs and kept alive his attachment to the Zionist cause, working closely with Dr Weizmann towards the establishment of the state of Israel.

'It was *Eretz Israel* (the Land of Israel) which converted A.J.B.'[39] Mrs Dugdale later wrote. There was a mystical element in Balfour's Zionism, encouraged by the messianic faith of Weizmann. Sir Robert Vansittart remarked 'I have never known A.J.B. care for anything but Zionism',[40] and Balfour came to relish his role as protector of the Jews, even writing to golf clubs in the Home Counties in an attempt to remove their ban on Jewish membership. Politically the declaration of 1917 had been only the beginning. After the war the opposition to Jewish ambitions in Palestine continued. In August 1919 Curzon wrote to Balfour complaining of claims by 'that astute but aspiring person' Weizmann 'to advise us as to the principal politico-military appointments to be made in Palestine, to criticise sharply the conduct of any such officers who do not fall on the neck of the Zionists (a most unattractive resting place) and to acquaint us with the "type of man" who we ought or ought not to send'. To Curzon it seemed that 'Doctor Weizmann will be a scourge on the back of the unlucky mandatory; and I often wish you could drop a few globules of cold water on his heated and extravagant pretensions'.[41]

Despite cabinet opposition from both Curzon and Edwin Montagu, the government obtained a British mandate over Palestine, Lloyd George being particularly moved by the land's biblical associations and the prestige of Jerusalem. Balfour was determined to achieve strong foundations for the Zionist enterprise there. 'Our Jewish friends, who are not always easy to deal with, sometimes get dreadfully perturbed over the matters of comparatively small moment', he told Lord Hardinge on 29 September 1920. 'But the question of frontiers is really vital, because it affects the economic possibilities of developing Palestine; and on these economic possibilities depends the success or failure of Zionism. The experiment is, in any case, a bold and rather hazardous one, though, in my opinion, well worth attempting. But it must be given a fair chance'.[42]

In July 1921, at a meeting in Carlton Gardens, Churchill, Balfour and Lloyd George told Weizmann 'that by the Declar-

ation they had always meant an eventual Jewish state'.[43] For
Balfour the Arabs – 'A great, an interesting, and an attractive
race' as he told a Zionist audience in July 1920 – should
remember that Britain 'has freed them, the Arab race, from the
tyranny of their brutal conqueror', the Turk; therefore he hoped
they would not grudge 'that small notch in what are now Arab
territories being given to the people who for all these hundreds of
years have been separated from it'. Indeed he was sure that such a
difficulty 'can be got over and will be got over, by mutual goodwill'.[44] In June 1922, after Balfour had been made an Earl, a
debate in the House of Lords initiated by Lord Islington led to
further examination of the local difficulties. Jewish involvement
in Bolshevism and revolutionary activity was causing an upsurge
of anti-Semitism throughout Europe. Lord Sydenham of Coombe,
once, as Sir George Clarke, secretary to Balfour's Committee of
Imperial Defence, declared 'the Jews have no more valid claim to
Palestine than the descendants of the ancient Romans have to
this country'. Sydenham feared the influx of Jewish settlers, for at
least 'the Arabs would have kept the Holy Land clear from
Bolshevism'.[45]

Balfour's defence of the mandate, after stating his belief that
Jew and Arab could co-exist in Palestine under the aegis of the
League of Nations and the British government, mentioned the
prosperity that must come to the country from the resources of
Jewish capital and 'the enthusiasm of the Jewish communities
throughout the world'. He ended by declaring 'it may fail: I do
not deny that this is an adventure. Are we never to have adventure? Are we never to try new experiments?' To Balfour 'surely
it is in order that we may send a message to every land where the
Jewish race has been scattered, a message which will tell them
that Christendom is not oblivious of their faith, is not unmindful
of the service they have rendered to the great religions of the
world, and that we desire to the best of our ability to give them an
opportunity of developing, in peace and quietness, under British
rule, those great gifts which hitherto they have been compelled to
bring to fruition in countries which know not their language, and
belong not to their race?'[46]

To Balfour and others, the Palestine Arabs appeared but a
small part of a vast race, easily accommodated to Jewish aims.

He misunderstood the extent of their religious and nationalistic feeling, also the impasse that must develop when the Jews acquired their own nationalistic attachment to the new Israel, again fortified by intense historic religious sentiment. The adventure had begun; but 'the peace and quietness of British rule' was to prove a forlorn hope.

In October 1919, Balfour wrote to Curzon about his position as Lord President of the Council. Home Rule was again a dominant issue with Ireland once more in a state of violent protest. 'As regards Ireland', he told Curzon, 'I shall wish to give an independent support to the Government whatever they decide on, for I think their continuance in office at the present time is of the utmost importance to the country.' However he worried that the official line might be one for which 'I should hardly care to make myself responsible as a Cabinet Minister'. In 1919 George V proposed that Balfour be given a peerage, but this was declined, Balfour telling Curzon 'in no circumstances, as I understand the situation, would it be either possible or desirable that I should lead the House of Lords. I cannot imagine a position less congenial to my taste, or less in harmony with the schemes which I have planned for the remains of my active life.'[47]

A task which Balfour shared with Curzon was British representation at the new League of Nations. It is difficult to know exactly what he made of the League; certainly his enthusiasm waned with the American Senate's rejection of United States membership and the Versailles Treaty, followed by Wilson's defeat in the Presidential election in 1920. He was never a passionate advocate of the League of Nations, yet deplored the pessimistic attitude of Hankey, who had refused to become its Secretary-General, and others, telling Hankey in January 1921, after civil service protests at the cost of a permanent office in Geneva, 'what I do object to is the dislike that certain departments have to the whole idea and spirit of the League, and their obvious satisfaction in putting a spoke in its wheel'.[48]

Balfour hoped that the League of Nations would possess moral force, for use of concerted military power was clearly out of the question. To Lady Rayleigh he observed: 'his great hope from it was publicity. He thought iniquitous things against weaker nations would not be done if they were openly discussed first.

The government which wished to do them would not be supported by their own people: public opinion would stop them. The boycott was the only actual weapon of the League. You could not compel the nations belonging to it to mobilise their forces.[49] Although not at the first meeting of the League's council of eight in Paris in January 1920, Balfour attended the second in London in February and the first international assembly in November at Geneva. Among the League's business during its first years of operation were international health control, drug trafficking, also difficult political questions arising from the Treaty of Versailles. On the Council, Balfour's relations with his French equivalent, Leon Bourgeois, were good and in August 1921 he told his sister Alice that 'the extremely friendly relations which personally exist between the members of the council is an immense blessing, and I think is particularly due to the personal qualities of Bourgeois and myself!'[50] Such qualities were needed in abundance in August and September 1921 when the Upper Silesian frontier between Poland and Germany was settled by the League after a deadlock between the French and English governments.

Balfour remained loyal to Lloyd George, although in February 1920 he told the Prime Minister he was doubtful about a paper from H. A. L. Fisher proposing detailed grounds for the union of the Conservatives and coalition Liberals. He called the underlying principle 'admirable' but went on: 'I greatly doubt the expediency of a concrete list of changes, such as Proportional Representation, the extension of Women's Suffrage, Home Rule for Scotland and Wales, detailed purposes for Labour legislation and Labour grievances . . . I think you will get into trouble if you condescend too much to particulars.'[51] In March Balfour drafted a letter to Lord Aldenham, his constituency Chairman, proposing an amalgamation of party organizations, and showed it to Bonar Law who consulted Lloyd George. The Prime Minister found his coalition Liberal ministers on the whole unfavourable and 'frightened at the idea of losing their identity as Liberals'. Law too was dubious, writing to Balfour: 'I do not like the idea of complete fusion if it can be avoided, but I had come to think, as you had also, that it was really inevitable if the coalition were to continue. But it always seemed to me more important from L.G.'s point of view than from ours.'[52] Balfour's letter was never sent.

Balfour renewed his old association with the Committee of Imperial Defence which met in June 1920 for the first time since February 1915. Its functions devolved on to a new 'Standing Defence Sub-committee' at which Balfour took the chair. Here Hankey 'despaired of Mr Balfour'[53] because of his age and frequent absences, but some decisions were made including, in June 1921, the important recommendation that the Singapore base would be developed 'as funds become available'.[54] This was approved by the cabinet and announced to the Imperial Conference later in the same month. Then in November 1921 he made another journey to America, to represent Britain at the Washington Naval Conference.

The conference, proposed by President Harding of the United States, was aimed at limiting the growth of naval armaments. Balfour led the British Empire delegation supported by Lord Lee (First Lord of the Admiralty); Sir Auckland Geddes (British Ambassador in Washington); representatives of Australia, New Zealand and Canada; and the service experts under Admirals Beatty and Chatfield, with Hankey as the delegation's secretary and general adviser. For Lord Lee, Balfour was 'our leader in every sense of the word. Apart from his immense experience and authority, his personal prestige with the Americans became almost legendary.'[55] From Washington Balfour told Lloyd George that he believed the aim of his delegation was 'to secure the largest possible limitation of armaments consistent with the safety of the British Empire'.[56] Within this there were complications: growing naval competition with the United States, now launched on a great programme of naval expansion; American and Dominion distrust of the Anglo-Japanese alliance which Balfour himself had been so anxious to renew in 1905; and Japanese intentions in the Pacific.

Italy, France and Japan were represented at the conference, with China, Holland and Belgium invited to participate in the eastern and Pacific discussions because of their interests in the area. On 12 November the conference was addressed by the American Secretary of State, Charles Evans Hughes. In a dramatic speech, he proposed that there should be no replacement of capital ships for ten years, also a scrapping of older capital ships and a parity of strength on the basis of existing relative

naval power. During Hughes's speech, Balfour made notes on an
envelope and, to the newspaper proprietor Lord Riddell, looked
'rather old and frail, and it was obvious that the Americans
thought poor old Britain was going to make a feeble show'.[57] At
the end of Hughes's address, the main points of which had been a
carefully kept secret, Lee became excited and passed a note to his
chief urging immediate acceptance of the proposals. Balfour said
nothing, waiting to reply at the next session, two days later.

On 15 November Balfour's answer, written from the briefest
of notes on his customary envelope, was, according to Hankey
'perfect in structure'[58] and Lord Riddell wrote 'we all felt very
proud of him',[59] although Lee, who wanted a grand gesture,
found the speech 'embarrassed in spirit and halting in form. He
was obviously ill at ease, and the audience, which in any case was
unfamiliar with his style and personality, hardly knew what to
make of it.'[60] What is certain is that his extemporary, almost conversational manner contrasted, perhaps strangely, with what
Hankey termed 'the raucous voices and unctuous oratory'[61] of the
American delegates. Balfour accepted the principle of the
American proposal, with qualifications involving more cruisers
and destroyers for the British. The Japanese put in a demand for
a higher level for their own navy and the French were not content with their quota.

Britain accepted parity with the United States on capital ships
and aircraft carriers, the Japanese accepting inferiority on a five
to three basis. The naval limitation treaty was signed, Italy and
France joining these three signatories; and in the east the
Japanese alliance was replaced by a four-power pact including
France and the United States. Balfour, on 9 December told his
sister 'on the whole the conference has prospered beyond
anybody's expectations; and so far a very good spirit prevails
among the various delegations'.[62] Yet its achievements were
overcast by unsettled business. Anglo-American rivalry was
limited, at a time when the British economic position made competition impossibly expensive, but outside the capital ship class
the unrestricted building of cruisers, destroyers and submarines
continued, despite Balfour's efforts to put a ceiling on this. In the
east the British and the United States gave Japan an advantage
by agreeing not to fortify certain Pacific bases, Singapore being an

exception. Chinese independence was guaranteed, Japan giving up the Shantung Peninsula and Britain the lease of Wei-hai-Wei, which had been Balfour's responsibility at the Foreign Office in 1898.

For Balfour there had been a long round of official engagements, but Lord Riddell noted 'I have never seen him so enthusiastic and alert as he is just now'.[63] At Christmas he issued a message to the American people, declaring 'if this be the season which above all others suggests thoughts of peace on earth and good will towards men, surely there are no two nations between whom that peace should be more secure and that good will more ardent than the two great peoples of English speech'.[64] The American press was not always complimentary, the anglophobic Hearst journals declaring that Balfour 'comes from a family which has been doing this class of work for England since the time of Queen Elizabeth' and as a consequence of such well-practised deception 'Britain always comes out top and walks off with the goods'.[65]

Yet in February 1922 the formal leave-taking of the British delegation at the White House was extremely cordial. Balfour made a felicitous speech, hoping that President Harding had not been tired by the conference, to which Harding replied that his feelings could be compared to a man on whose lap a very fat girl had been sitting for an hour and a half. Leaving the ceremony Balfour asked Lee to tell him the point of the story as 'I fear I must have missed its precise application', but the second telling failed to produce a flicker of a smile at humour 'so foreign to his own'.[66] In London the Prime Minister and the cabinet were at Waterloo to meet him; outside, a large crowd cheered and the rewards were completed by the award of the Order of the Garter by George V followed in May by an Earldom and a Viscountcy.

18

'The Most Distinguished Figure in the World'

Jack Sandars did not approve of his old master's preferment, writing in an anonymous article that his fellow countrymen had previously thought of Mr Balfour 'as they thought of the august unadornment of Mr Pitt, Mr Canning and Mr Gladstone'.[1] Sandars remembered Balfour's old scorn for honours and those who chased after them: his disdain for political parade and ostentation. Balfour himself had doubts about a peerage, but soon found that the leisured pace of the House of Lords was suited to an old age divided between politics, philosophy and his family. Gerald Balfour, and Gerald's heirs, were appointed to succeed to the Earldom; and after the fall of Lloyd George in October Balfour was writing to Lady Wemyss, in connection with the second instalment of his Gifford lectures; 'What a blessing that I took a Peerage! It seemed disagreeable at the time, but it makes the whole difference now.'[2]

During his absence in Washington, the Irish treaty was signed in December. Some of Balfour's old colleagues remembered his life-long devotion to the Union, his early political triumphs in its defence. 'Nor could I ever understand how after the war he could remain a member of Lloyd George's cabinet when Lloyd George sold the pass in Ireland',[3] wrote Lord Selborne, who had resigned in 1916 as a protest over an earlier attempt at Irish conciliation. In July 1921 Frances Stevenson noted Lloyd George's report of the cabinet discussion on the terms to be sent to De Valera: 'He says Balfour squirmed at the Cabinet when the terms were discussed preliminary to sending them to De V. They were so contrary to all the views the old man had ever held on Ireland. But he gave in gracefully. . . .'[4] On the insistence of Bonar Law, Ulster was given the right to opt out of the new Ireland, which she immediately did.

In 1929 Balfour was reading the concluding volume of Churchill's *The World Crisis* (which he described as 'Winston's brilliant Autobiography, disguised as a history of the universe'). He remarked to Mrs Dugdale: 'The Irish had owed their success to crime. Winston practically admitted it. They had defied British rule, – and British rule had given in to them. How could such a state of things be said to fit in with the scheme of the Empire'.[5] It was in this empire that Balfour had wished to include a contented Irish Free State. After the war Balfour had supported coercion which, although militarily successful, was politically hard to sustain. He knew the strength of international, particularly American, feeling on the Irish question. He was old and tired. The alternative to the treaty was more bloodshed; the alternative to Balfour's acceptance of it, opposition to a Prime Minister whom he had stood by through the terrible years of the war and resignation from a government he believed the most suited to his country's present needs. Thus he relaxed the rigidity of the past.

After his return from the United States, Balfour again resumed his responsibilities at the League of Nations. In July, to his satisfaction, the League confirmed the British mandate in Palestine and in August he was involved in the economic resuscitation of Austria, then in the throes of starvation and impending bankruptcy. Balfour had helped negotiate the Treaty of Saint Germain in 1919 and in 1922 was appointed chairman of the League's Austrian Committee which imposed international supervision of the country's economy in return for loans from the allies and cancellation of war reparations. Complete collapse was avoided and later the Austrian Chancellor, Monsignor Seipel, told Mrs Dugdale 'Your dear uncle saved my country'.[6] The salvation was to prove temporary.

For part of the summer of 1922, Curzon was abroad, recovering from an illness, and Balfour took charge of the Foreign Office. From here, in August, there issued the celebrated 'Balfour Note', calling for a cancellation of allied war debts but announcing that, as the United States was demanding repayment, Britain would only collect from her European debtors enough to pay her debt to America. This would leave Britain out of pocket, but settle a vexatious problem. After the war it was estimated that the British government owed about £850 million to America, out of some £1340 million of debts to Britain's allies, being owed in its turn approximately £1825 million by these allies.[7] Sir Auckland Geddes, British Ambassador to Washington, hoped that Balfour's great standing in the United States would influence American opinion, but the note went unheeded. Other allied governments were also concerned that it might adversely affect their claims for German reparations. In December 1922 a scheme for British repayment of the full American debt was arranged, while Balfour was out of government.

Balfour had returned from Washington to find Lloyd George in trouble. The Prime Minister was dependent on Conservative support and the Tories were doubtful about his Irish settlement and increasingly high-handed leadership, exemplified by the reckless sale of honours to often unworthy recipients. By-elections were going against the government; the great miracle of domestic reconstruction promised in the 1918 election had not materialized. In February Lord Riddell told Lloyd George that Balfour had the power to rally the Conservatives, to which the Prime Minister replied: 'It will be interesting to know what line he is going to take. He may wish to become Prime Minister. If he does I shall support him. . . .' Sir Laming Worthington-Evans, coalition Minister without Portfolio, remarked of the Conservative leadership (from which Law had retired because of ill health in 1921, to be succeeded by Austen Chamberlain, backed by Balfour) 'If A.J.B. would take the position, the Party would rally round him to a man'.[8]

Balfour stood by Lloyd George. He refused to become indignant over the sale of honours, perhaps because when leader he had always regarded patronage with bored scorn. He also supported the Greeks against the Turks in the near-east, observing to Lady Rayleigh in July 1921 that the only friends the Greeks had in the cabinet 'were himself and the Prime Minister.'[9] In August 1922 the Turks captured Smyrna and advanced on Chanak, held by a small British force as part of the Straits' neutral zone. Lloyd George spoke of war and appealed to France, Italy and the Dominions for support, only to receive cold answers, except from New Zealand and Newfoundland. In Britain the feeling was overwhelmingly against such an adventure.

In September Balfour was in Geneva at the League of Nations. On his return on 5 October he supported the decision to negotiate with the Turks and on 11 October Kemal consented to respect the neutral zone until the treaty was concluded. On 10 October the cabinet agreed to fight a general election as a coalition. Only Stanley Baldwin, President of the Board of Trade, opposed the decision, but in the Conservative organization both Sir Leslie Wilson, the Chief Whip, and Sir George Younger, party chairman, were equally against it. Among back benchers and junior ministers, the feeling against Lloyd George was strong.

Austen Chamberlain called a meeting of the parliamentary party at the Carlton Club on 19 October to settle criticism. Balfour, Chamberlain and Birkenhead, all coalitionists, hoped to rally the rank and file; but they were wrong. Law was persuaded, largely by Beaverbrook, to leave retirement and lead the critics. Curzon resigned, angered by the Prime Minister's treatment of him at the Foreign Office. Balfour, at a dinner at 10 Downing Street of Lloyd George's supporters, lost his temper when told of this, pounding the table with his fist and shouting, perhaps aroused by his old irritation with Curzon's scheming, 'I say, fight them, fight them, fight them! This thing is wrong. The Conservative Party has always acted on the advice of its leaders. Is the lead of Law and Curzon to count as everything, and the advice of the rest of us as nothing? This is a revolt and it should be crushed.' An observer noted: 'Nothing could have been less like the dreamy Balfour of tradition.'[10]

Balfour was almost late for the Carlton Club meeting, having searched in vain in Carlton Gardens for a newspaper to learn the result of the Newport by-election. On reaching the club, he must have heard that the independent Conservative had defeated both the coalition Liberal and Labour candidates, thus damaging Austen Chamberlain's theory that the coalition must remain intact because the Conservatives alone would allow Labour the advantage of a split vote. At the meeting Chamberlain, Balfour and Birkenhead spoke for the coalition: Baldwin and Law against. The result was a majority of 187 to 87 for fighting the

next election as an independent party and that afternoon Lloyd
George resigned. Balfour's speech was, by all accounts, lamen-
tably uninspiring; he was presumably as ignorant of party feeling
in 1922 as in the years of his own leadership.

'Bonar, poor man, is trying to make a Government', Balfour
told Lady Wemyss on 21 October, 'and no doubt will find plenty
of material, though what its quality will be is perhaps more
doubtful.' He remarked that his secretary Miss Bliss, who had
succeeded Wilfrid Short in 1920, had informed him 'that the
most outstanding figures as yet mentioned are chiefly Marquises
and Earls!'; indeed Law's cabinet was heavily trimmed with
ermine. On the new Prime Minister, Balfour was gently condescending, observing 'there does not, oddly enough, seem to be
anyone available in the House of Commons except himself who
has yet won any reputation as a speaker and debater';[11] and he
assured Balcarres that 'it was an advantage to have a leader who
was not intellectually much superior to the rest of the party he
led'.[12] Of Baldwin's conduct, in taking the lead in cabinet against
Lloyd George and speaking out at the Carlton Club, Balfour
simply remarked: 'It is the sort of thing gentlemen don't do.'[13]

Balfour was now out of the cabinet, yet still, in his seventy-
fourth year, alert. In 1922 he saw a doctor who had examined
him during his premiership some twenty years ago, and was told
that his heart and health were in better condition now than then.
The only debilitation was increasing deafness which Lady Rayleigh noted he concealed 'with extraordinary skill, letting the
conversation pass him by if he does not hear and joining in again
when he catches it. He never says "what" unless he is driven
to it by a direct question which he has not caught.'[14] In spite of
this, and his age, some coalitionists considered him as a possible
alternative to Lloyd George in October as Prime Minister.[15]

At the end of October, during the election, Lloyd George,
Birkenhead and Sir Robert Horne visited Whittingehame. They
too were with Balfour in the wilderness and at a bibulous dinner
discussed their circumstances, Joan Lascelles noting 'the disap-
pearance of many glasses of brandy down Lord Birkenhead's
throat' and Lloyd George's wonderful mimicry of Curzon.
Balfour observed that Law's conduct had 'not been pretty' and
the rest concluded he 'was an ambitious man and that even to be

P.M. for three weeks would mean much to him'. When Lloyd George and Birkenhead damned Curzon for his supposed treachery, Balfour 'pleaded he was clever', but remarked of the new cabinet, whose declared aim was a return to calm, 'Fancy going to a die-hard Government for a rest'. The next morning Sir Robert Horne told a delighted Mrs Lascelles 'that LL. G., Lord B. and he talked over Nunk, and agreed that taking it all round he was at this moment the most distinguished figure in the world'.[16] The result of the election was a decisive victory for Law and the Conservatives who gained a majority of seventy-seven over the other parties.

Despite exclusion from the cabinet, his work at the League of Nations continued. On 22 December, ostensibly to discuss the announcement of this to the newspapers, Bonar Law visited Whittingehame on his way to Glasgow. The meeting might have been awkward but, according to Balfour, 'we immediately got upon our old footing', Law being especially anxious to show that his disposal of Lloyd George had not been for reasons of personal aggrandisement, but an unavoidable course dictated by party discontent. 'He was, and remained, clearly of the opinion', Balfour noted, 'that since neither Lloyd George nor Austen were prepared to make any attempt to liquidate the situation, the time had come when he must either leave politics or take action himself.' Law cited Lloyd George's readiness to accept the miners' proposals for coal nationalization as an example of his incomprehension of Conservative opinion; also a suggestion, made at a dinner party at 10 Downing Street with Carson and Law among the guests, that Ulster might be coerced. To Law's objection that this must break up the Unionist party, Lloyd George had apparently replied that 'on the contrary, both Austen and F. E. Smith were prepared to agree'.[17]

The conversation seems to have impressed Law for, at the end of December, he remarked to Hankey, who had heard from Sir Eric Drummond that Balfour was willing to join the government for a year, that 'he would sooner have Balfour than all the rest [of the dissident Conservatives] put together.'[18] This, however, did not come about. In the new year Balfour attended a meeting of the League council in Paris, at which the French occupation of the Ruhr was discussed. Concerted League action was impossible although Balfour disapproved of the French move. Then in February he told Law he could not continue as British representative, giving age, deafness, fatigue caused by the constant travel and the need for the position to be held by a cabinet minister as his reasons. The earlier rumour that he wished to join Law's administration seemed to be dead; perhaps it had merely been a hint that a transfer from League affairs would be welcome.

On 22 March Balfour attended a dinner given by Birkenhead for the coalition Conservatives. It may have seemed now that only a few more years of quiescent distinction were left to Balfour: a gentle descent towards peace and oblivion. Indeed he described the House of Lords as 'like talking to a lot of tombstones';[19] but in May, with the retirement of Bonar Law after his doctors had diagnosed cancer of the throat, he was called to advise George V on Law's successor.

From Sheringham in Norfolk, where he was laid up with phlebitis during a Whitsun golfing holiday, Balfour kept in touch with events. Visited by old friends, entertained by the Wemysses, Evan Charteris, Lady Desborough and Lord d'Abernon, his convalescence was congenial, interrupted only by a message from the King on 20 May asking him to come to London the next day. There were two candidates: Stanley Baldwin (the Chancellor of the Exchequer) and the vastly more experienced Lord Curzon (the Foreign Secretary). Lord Stamfordham, George V's private secretary, came to Carlton Gardens on the afternoon of 21 May and received advice which, Balfour said, came 'regardless of the individuals in question, for whereas, on the one side, his opinion of Lord Curzon is based upon an intimate life-long friendship, and the recognition of his exceptional qualifications; on the other, his knowledge of Mr Baldwin is slight and, so far, his public career has been more or less uneventful and without any special gifts or exceptional ability'.[20]

Balfour told Stamfordham he believed Baldwin should be chosen, for it was now impossible to have a Prime Minister in the House of Lords. Amplifying his reasons he remarked on the large number of peers already in the cabinet, and 'to put, in addition to the existing Secretaries of State, a Prime Minister in the Upper House would certainly be resented'; also '(though I did not mention this) the present Opposition were the Labour Party, who had no representative in the House of Lords at all. I understood from Stamfordham that these views were probably in very close conformity with those already held by His Majesty.'[21] Law too had advised against Curzon. The next day the latter journeyed from Montacute, confident of his accession to the premiership after receiving Stamfordham's telegraphed request for an interview, only to suffer terrible disappointment on his arrival in London. On Balfour's return to Sheringham he was asked by a member of the coterie 'And will dear George be chosen?' He answered: 'No, dear George will not.'[22]

Balfour's advice was supposedly not based on personal character; yet he had experienced the tribulations of working with Curzon, and even in one whose reactions were subjected to such meticulous control these memories cannot have been entirely absent that May afternoon. For a final view, there is a conversation with Mrs Dugdale in the last year of his life, when Balfour remembered his cousin Lord Salisbury's 'most interesting view' that 'George was a very able, ambitious man but always conscious that he was second-rate. I rather think he [Curzon] was, but I'm not sure it wasn't a second-ratedness that amounts to first ratedness. In all the things which George was second-rate, I was even more second-rate.' Inevitably Mrs Dugdale protested; but Balfour went on: 'I hadn't George's ambitions any more than his capacities – and his powers of speech were extraordinary. He told me he was never at a loss for a word.' Concluding the faint praise, Balfour admitted: 'I daresay my powers of debate, such as they were, were of a more original kind. My arguments were perhaps of a less commonplace kind.'[23]

In May there had come a disagreement with Lord Robert Cecil, caused by his article in *The Times* criticizing the reaction of the British delegation at the Paris peace conference towards President Wilson's idealistic proposals. Lord Robert, at the League of Nations, had already been openly critical of France's conduct over the Ruhr occupation, to the chagrin of Balfour who preferred a more discreet diplomatic approach. *The Times* article led to Balfour's resignation from his Vice-Presidency of the League of Nations Union, of which Lord Robert was Chairman. Lord Robert himself threatened to resign and Balfour wrote on 4 June: 'I think it seriously worth considering whether your

resignation does not supply a fitting occasion for bringing its
labour to an honourable close, though I fear Baffy would burst
into tears if I told her so.' Cecil drew back. Baldwin appointed
Lord Robert Lord Privy Seal, with responsibility for League of
Nations' affairs, which Balfour, already somewhat disenchanted
with the League, welcomed, declaring: 'I am delighted you have
joined the Government for many reasons; – but not least because
it will be you and not I who will spend September in Geneva.'[24]

Cecil and Balfour were in agreement about the error of
Baldwin's decision to enter the elections of December with a
policy of tariffs to protect British industry. The vote resulted in
the Conservatives being unable to form a majority government in
the new parliament, although they were still the largest party.
Mrs Dugdale remembered that Balfour commented sparingly,
'contenting himself with throwing up his hands and casting his
eyes to the ceiling'; but she was wrong to suggest that 'his
attitude to politics was rather detached at this time'.[25]

Others certainly doubted his detachment. After the election,
the question was whether Baldwin should resign immediately or
face parliament. Willie Bridgeman, Conservative Home Secretary
and confidant of Baldwin, was visited by Sir Samuel Hoare, the
Secretary for Air, to be told of 'a great intrigue afoot to bustle
Baldwin out', led by Rothermere and Beaverbrook ('the cussed
newspaper millionaires') with 'Birkenhead, Austen Chamberlain,
Derby, Worthington-Evans and Joynson-Hicks and Balfour said
to be assisting'.[26] The idea seemed to be to persuade the King to
send for another Conservative leader, perhaps Derby or Austen
Chamberlain, who might form another coalition, thus keeping a
Labour government out. On 8 December, indeed, Balfour, in his
role as elder statesman, saw Lord Stamfordham and lamented the
ending of the coalition in 1922. He thought that George V
'would naturally turn to someone else in the Party to form a new
Administration in the event of Mr Baldwin's resignation';[27] and
avoided a definite refusal to be considered as an alternative Prime
Minister.

But by 9 December, when Balfour was called upon to advise
the King himself, it was clear that there was little support within
the party for 'the Birkenhead plot'. George V told Balfour of his
'brainwave' to decline to receive Baldwin's resignation 'and say

that the present Government should meet Parliament'. Balfour later noted 'I told him that my impression was that, in spite of the fiasco of the Election, Mr Baldwin was popular with his Party, more popular indeed than any possible substitute. In these circumstances it was very important that he should not resign the Leadership'; and Baldwin must continue as Prime Minister 'until a combination of hostile forces turned him out'. George V 'saw no reason to change the view'[28] previously expressed to him by Balfour that the Prime Minister must be a member of the Commons. Of the other contenders, Balfour recommended Neville Chamberlain rather than Austen or Sir Robert Horne if Baldwin resigned.

On 11 December Birkenhead, excluded from the cabinet since October 1922, wrote to Balfour urging that Stanley Baldwin resign immediately so that 'the King can send for another Conservative acceptable unlike B. to the Liberals and not tarred by the election folly', for if Baldwin was defeated in parliament 'the King would be bound to send for Ramsay Macdonald who had defeated him. The disastrous results of this are apparent.'[29] Balfour's answer showed his doubts. First he stated an assumption 'that it would be a national disaster if Labour came in now, even for a brief period. It would give, so the City firmly believed, a shock to our tottering credit and might have serious electoral consequences'; then he put forward joint action, short of coalition, on the part of the Liberals and the Conservatives to keep Labour out. The Conservative party would not, Balfour believed, have Austen Chamberlain as leader, although he himself saw Chamberlain as 'incomparably the superior' in political and personal attributes to any rival. Thus the only alternative appeared to be Baldwin, supported by Asquith's Liberals, even though Asquith had declared 'nothing would induce him to keep in office any man so stupid as Baldwin'. Balfour wrote: 'Of course it would be much better that the Liberals should be "in" with Unionist support, than that the Unionists should be "in" with Liberal support. But I see no possible way of securing the first of these arrangements, while the second may perhaps be within our reach.'[30]

Neither Baldwin nor Asquith could agree to such an arrangement, and Balfour castigated the Liberal's obstinacy. In January the Conservatives were defeated in parliament and George V asked Ramsay Macdonald to form the first Labour government. On 4 February Baldwin saw Balfour and received a sharp answer to his comparison of January 1906 with January 1924. 'The Election of 1906 was not my act in the sense that the Election of 1923 was his,' Balfour noted. 'Undoubtedly he was in a somewhat peculiar position, because he had committed himself to the two propositions that the great pressing problem for British statesmanship at the present moment was Unemployment, and that the only way to deal with Unemployment was by Tariff Reform.'[31]

Balfour's advice was to allow the coalition ministers, even the distrusted Birkenhead, to rejoin the party. On 7 February he attended a meeting of the shadow cabinet to which the old coalitionists, including Birkenhead, were invited, and in the same month Baldwin dropped protection. The Conservatives seemed united in defeat; yet in March there was trouble over Winston Churchill's candidature in the Westminster Abbey by-election as an independent anti-socialist. Baldwin wrote in support of the Conservative candidate. Balfour sent a letter of support to Churchill which, despite Baldwin's initial attempts to stop it, was published. The Conservative won, by forty-three votes. Churchill, however, was headed for a post in the next Tory cabinet.

In November the Conservatives returned to power with a large majority after scares of Labour's supposed Communist sympathies. The Liberals were annihilated in the election, losing 100 seats, among them Asquith's. Balfour wrote of this rout that 'the causes of it are doubtless manifold; but the most obvious of them is the policy Asquith pursued in first placing the Socialists in power and then trying to guide their policy. He failed and deserved to fail.'[32] Stanley Baldwin was again Prime Minister. Of the old coalitionists, Austen Chamberlain was given the Foreign Office, Birkenhead became Secretary of State for India and Winston Churchill Chancellor of the Exchequer; but Balfour was excluded, perhaps partly because Baldwin had felt 'a certain sense of gaucheness and inferiority'[33] in his presence since the Carlton Club meeting.

Baldwin asked Balfour to join the Committee of Imperial Defense which, he told his sister, 'exactly suits me, – no pay and no responsibility, except for the work I actually do and the advice I actually give'.[34] This post did not preclude a visit, in March 1925, to Palestine, in the company of Dr and Mrs Weizmann and his niece Mrs Edward Lascelles and her husband, for the opening of the Hebrew University in Jerusalem.

'In six weeks time, I hope we shall be able to compare our Eastern experiences!'[35] Balfour told Lady Wemyss, referring no doubt to her old adventure in the desert with Wilfrid Scawen Blunt. His trip was entirely different. Arriving at Alexandria, the party received an enthusiastic welcome from a great Jewish crowd before proceeding to Cairo to stay briefly with Lord Allenby at the Residency. Then came the tour of Palestine itself, arranged by the Zionist Organisation but conducted against a background of Arab protest. In Tel Aviv Balfour attended a gala performance of the third act of *Samson and Delilah*. In Jerusalem Handel's *Belshazzar* was sung for him in Hebrew and on the slopes of Mount Scopus he opened the university, dressed in the scarlet robes of the Chancellor of Cambridge, before a crowd of some ten thousand people. Also present were Allenby, Jerusalem's conqueror, and Sir Herbert Samuel, the British High Commissioner, together with other religious and academic dignitaries. Balfour declared: 'A great cultural effort within Palestine which came to an end many hundreds of years ago is going to be resumed in the ancient home of the people.'[36]

An Arab one-day strike was backed up by demonstrations. In Syria, where Balfour visited Baalbec, the hostility increased, with riots in Damascus forcing the party to spend the last three days on their ship in Beirut harbour. To the Jews Balfour seemed a saviour, to the Arabs an insult to their religion and nationality. Mrs Lascelles, always opposed to Zionism, later wrote: 'Of course Nunk's visit to Palestine was an awful mistake – and it was driven home to him many times during his stay – and two or three times my diary records him saying "I suppose I ought not to have come".'[37] According to her, the Zionists had tried to hide the controversy and were using Balfour's reputation to dignify their own activities. But Balfour told Weizmann how impressed he was with 'the flourishing Jewish settlements which testify to the soundness and strength of the growing National Home'. When asked about the rioting, he remarked, 'Oh, I wouldn't worry about that – nothing compared with what I went through in Ireland!'[38]

In March, after Curzon's death, Baldwin asked Balfour, now aged seventy-six, to join his cabinet as Lord President of the Council. The post gave him a chance to develop one of his longest-lived enthusiasms: government encouragement of scientific research. At the Admiralty he had launched the Board of Invention and Research; in 1919 his War Cabinet Research Committee led to the construction of the Admiralty Research Laboratory at Teddington and in 1920 he set up the Committee for the Co-ordination of Research in Government Departments. During this time Balfour also had responsibility for the Advisory Council of the Department of Scientific and Industrial Research. In 1924 he became chairman of the Medical Research Council, for which, as Lord President in 1925, he came to have departmental responsibility as well.

In April 1925 a parliamentary commission's report on East Africa showed the need for further government centralization of scientific and industrial research, at least in the colonial context. Baldwin asked his Lord President for an administrative scheme. The result, making use of an idea left over from Macdonald's government, was the Committee of Civil Research, organized along the lines of the Committee of Imperial Defence, to aid both domestic industry and colonial development. In 1926 Balfour, worried lest Treasury economies should affect the committee, asked Hankey, a supporter of its aims, 'Can we afford not to spend the sums on research which the general economic policy of the government and our national position among world producers seem to require?'[39] In 1930 the Committee of Civil Research evolved into the Economic Advisory Council, but before then among the topics considered by it and its subcommittees were Heavy Industries, Dyestuffs, the tsetse fly, the Severn barrage, Agricultural Training in the Empire, the Co-ordination of Research in Government Departments, Radium and Locust Control.[40]

Balfour retained his great interest in defence. He supported the First Lord of the Admiralty, Willie Bridgeman, in his battle with Churchill and the Treasury over cuts in naval expenditure and the decision to reverse the previous government's scrapping of the Singapore base, here again encountering Churchill's protestations. In November 1925 he argued for a naval base at Rosyth, rather than in the Thames estuary, to impress the French, and hailed the Treaty of Locarno, which attempted to guarantee Germany's Western frontier, as a diplomatic triumph.

At home, the General Strike of May 1926 challenged Baldwin's government. Thomas Jones, Deputy Secretary to the cabinet, lunched at Carlton Gardens to persuade Balfour that proposed Trade Union legislation should not be rushed through parliament as it might 'profoundly change the quite peaceful temper of the men now on strike'. Jones found 'all the family male relatives seem to have joined up as Special Constables but were kicking their heels because they had nothing to do'.[41] Balfour reluctantly agreed with Jones, but remained firm in his support for the legislation, also decrying Soviet Russian influence on the strikers. Then in October of the same year, he embarked upon perhaps his last great achievement: the chairing of the Inter-Imperial Relations Committee at the Imperial Conference.

Originally it had seemed as if Baldwin would be chairman of this vital committee, and Leo Amery imagined that Balfour would head the special subcommittee on Research. However Amery seems to have advised that the Prime Minister's workload was too heavy and that Balfour should take his place. Amery knew the Lord President was 'entirely in sympathy with the newer conception of Commonwealth equality, while his immense personal authority would not only hold the Committee together, but commend its conclusions to the British Cabinet where, I felt, the greatest difficulty might have to be encountered'.[42] Balfour had long realized the Dominions' wishes for greater autonomy. At the Paris Peace Conference and the League of Nations he had dealt with their separate diplomatic representatives; and the treaties of Lausanne and Locarno had led to Dominion refusal to be committed in the name of the Empire to British foreign policy.

At the conference of 1926, both General Hertzog, Afrikaner Prime Minister of South Africa and old Boer enemy of the British, and Mackenzie King of Canada, were determined to see a clear definition of further constitutional independence for their countries. From the new Irish Free State came similar demands, but Balfour was convinced that the Crown was still the strongest

and most effective unifying influence for the Empire. Therefore
he was delighted when, at the first meeting of the Inter-Imperial
Relations Committee, Hertzog coupled a call for the Dominions
to be 'equal in status and separately entitled to international
recognition' with a declaration of allegiance to the Crown from a
free association of 'The British Commonwealth of Nations'.[43] In
July, before the conference, Balfour himself had spoken in the
House of Lords in favour of Dominion equality for 'None of us
conceive that of this conglomeration of free states one is above
the other'.[44]

In the report of the conference Balfour drafted an extension of
these beliefs, the product of his committee's deliberations. The
report declared: 'The rapid evolution of the Overseas Dominions
during the last fifty years has involved many complicated ad-
justments of old political machinery to changing conditions. The
tendency towards equality of status was both right and inevitable.
Geographical and other conditions made this impossible of attain-
ment by way of federation. The only alternative was by way of
autonomy; and along this road it has been steadily sought. Every
self-governing member of the Empire is now the master of its
destiny'.[45]

Lord Esher told Balfour that this was 'a crowning achievement',[46] and in 1931 the Statute of Westminster established the
new Commonwealth relationship. For the colonies of White
Settlement and South Africa, unity and autonomy were brought
together. Once again the Empire's peoples who were not of European stock were neglected, India remaining unchanged. Balfour
could be satisfied with his role.

19

'A Fitting End'

Balfour's political life continued gently for another two years. In January 1927 he advocated a blockade of Canton harbour to protect British interests from the new Nationalist regime and in the summer became involved in controversy over the Geneva disarmament conference at which the Americans demanded that Britain reduce its maximum of cruisers. The conference broke down and Balfour's cousin Lord Cecil of Chelwood (formerly Lord Robert Cecil) resigned from the cabinet over the Admiralty's intransigence. Balfour believed the American demands were too great and did his best to soften Cecil's resignation announcement, playing his accustomed conciliatory role.

Baldwin, always in awe of Balfour, was undemanding of the cabinet's oldest member. 'As Prime Minister (who is ever grateful to you for serving in his Cabinet)', he wrote on 31 May 1927, 'I desire that you go to Epsom tomorrow to attend the Derby, and that you report to the Cabinet at its next subsequent meeting your impressions.'[1] In October 1928, when Balfour's health was failing, the Prime Minister assured him that cabinet meetings need not be attended for 'your main care (tedious as it is) must be to look after your bodily health, for your own sake and for the sake of those who hold you in such high regard and affection'.[2]

In December 1925 Balfour delivered his last philosophical discourse, to the British Academy of which he was President. Entitled 'Familiar Beliefs and Transcendent Reason' it covered the familiar ground of the inadequacies of a purely scientific, or 'naturalistic', belief. But the decline was perceptibly hastening and the deafness grew worse. In the House of Lords it was partially conquered by the amplifiers, installed in 1925, causing one of the Whips to warn Balfour that 'his asides to Lord Salisbury were being heard all over the Chamber – much to the amusement of the reporters in the Press Gallery!'[3] At Whittingehame, in February 1927, Lady Rayleigh wrote of her brother: 'He is very deaf, could not hear the sermon at all in Church and general conversation gets more difficult. Still he is the life of the party: plays lawn tennis with the children and evidently fascinates them.'[4]

Inevitably the chief fascination was now the past. In the new year of 1928 Balfour fell ill at Whittingehame with the circulatory failure from which he was to die. At the end of 1927 he had had most of his teeth removed after suspected gum poisoning and was congratulated on this by Lady Oxford (formerly Margot Asquith) who believed that the roots of most diseases lay either here or in the bowels. In March 1928 he suffered a mild stroke while staying with the Desboroughs at Taplow, but recovered in time to visit Stanway and Lady Wemyss. To her he had once remarked 'I don't hold with all this fuss about death';[5] now it was obvious that the end of all the years they had known each other 'fairly well'[6] was not far away. She dreaded a tragic farewell, imagining talk, how 'They would say – How pathetic to see Arthur Balfour and Mary Wemyss. How sad is the end of life – the necessary onslaught of illness and old age. How sad to outlive Romance. I believe they were lovers once – tho' nobody knows – no-one ever knew the truth about these things.' Yet she was able to tell him 'Stanway was not a failure & I have delicious memories' of Balfour with her grandchildren, 'so serene and patient . . . no one could have been more delightful'.[7]

In July there came his 80th birthday. The day before, the British Academy gave a lunch in his honour, with his health proposed by the Prince of Wales, and on 25 July, the anniversary itself, both Houses of Parliament presented Balfour with a Rolls Royce motor car. He thought his speech of thanks inadequate, but Winston Churchill called for 'Three Cheers for A.J.B.' At the end of the summer at Whittingehame his health was worse and the doctors would not allow him to return to London and politics. Balfour offered to resign, but Baldwin refused, so he came south, to his brother Gerald's house of Fisher's Hill at

Woking, to be available for consultation, never to see Whittingehame again.

He pressed on with his memoirs, reminiscing to Mrs Dugdale who was charged with drawing the different strands together. In February 1928 a contract had been signed with the publishers Cassell, for two volumes of not less than 200,000 words, along the lines of Lord Grey's *Twenty Five Years*. 'I shall now expect the money to come flowing in', Miss Bliss, who supervised his finances, wrote to Mrs Dugdale. 'I need it badly!'[8] Peco had left its terrible mark. 'Money is at the bottom of all our difficulties', Alice Balfour told Lady Wemyss in June 1928. 'I can only leave Arthur to put his mind to the matter or not, as he likes.'[9] Balfour's mind, however, was ranging more freely, from his visit to Paris after the Commune in 1871, with the ruins of the Tuileries and the devastated Bois du Boulogne, through the Congress of Berlin, the fall of Parnell, Chamberlain's brash imperialism, the great partnership with Lord Salisbury, Lloyd George, Clemenceau, Lord Randolph Churchill and his son: early encounters with Charles Darwin and Gladstone, later friendships with Bergson and Chaim Weizmann. It had been a long life, full of great opportunities, some wasted and perplexing, others triumphantly realized and understood.

Wherever he was, solitude was out of the question. It was easy to come down from London to Fisher's Hill and the devoted circle enjoyed the journey. 'Time, Death, Eternity cannot efface the past', wrote Lady Wemyss, '& you have been a wonderful friend, some people might almost have said a lover but that might be excessive.'[10] In May, after the general election had produced MacDonald's second Labour government, Balfour travelled to Bognor, where George V was also convalescing, to surrender his seals of office as Lord President of the Council, 'a fitting end', he told Lady Wemyss, 'to my political & official career; which I thought I had concluded some time in November 1911'.[11] The next day he woke with a harsher pain in his leg, marking a new, more serious onslaught of phlebitis, and from then onwards was confined to his rooms at Fisher's Hill.

To these rooms, throughout the summer of 1929, came Hankey, Lloyd George, Baldwin, Austen Chamberlain, Philip Snowden, Ladies Desborough and Wemyss and many others, to talk and listen. Winston Churchill, in June, told Mrs Dugdale as he left 'What a combination we might have been. All my fighting strength behind him, and his judgement behind me.'[12] Lord Salisbury told Lord Selborne 'Of course he gets easily tired, but till then in conversation he is quite his old fascinating self'.[13] A conspicuous absentee was Jack Sandars. After his old master's death, he was to refuse sharply to assist Mrs Dugdale with her biography.

By the late summer, the sickness was clearly growing worse, although the mental faculties still showed little sign of wear. Lady Betty Balfour wrote to Lady Desborough in July of 'his graciousness over anything done for him – his deep love for all his friends – & the never failing humour which makes any moment spent with him such a joy – and yet & yet I have begun to wish him released'.[14] In October Mrs Willett, the medium, came to Balfour's sitting room with assorted spirits in her wake. As the gramophone played Beethoven's Trio in B Flat, she conjured up contact with May Lyttelton. Two days later Mrs Willett again visited him, this time going into a trance, communicating messages from May, Alfred Lyttelton and Frank Balfour, suddenly crying out from May 'Tell him he gives me Joy', at which Balfour clutched her hand fiercely, afterwards declaring 'he was most profoundly impressed'. No other comment is recorded of the experience, other than that it made him 'very happy'.[15]

Balfour wrote to congratulate Baldwin in November on his speech on the future of India. In the new year Baldwin came to Fisher's Hill again and was amused when Balfour asked Mrs Dugdale 'Baffy, was I a Protectionist or a Free Trader in 1903?' She answered: 'That is what all the country wanted to find out.'[16] In March 1930 his strength began to run out. Dr Weizmann came a few days before the end, to bid a silent farewell, remembering perhaps that one of Balfour's last political interventions had been to support a British government loan to the Zionists in Palestine which the cabinet turned down in 1928. Then on 17 March, Lady Wemyss, in the south of France, noted in her diary 'I had baddish dreams on Sunday night & woke up feeling very nervous and depressed, in fact I fell into floods of tears after breakfast'.[17]

Balfour died on 19 March, in the early hours of the morning, holding the hands of his brother Gerald and his sister Mrs Sidgwick. Lady Wemyss received a telegram from the family. She wrote: 'I chiefly felt a sense of overwhelming fatigue and sadness blended with relief to know that the struggle & distress, helplessness and discomfort are now over – but I cannot yet realize how great the blank will be – but can only feel grateful to have had such a friend for fifty years.'[18]

Westminster Abbey was offered as a burial place, but Balfour had always wished to lie at Whittingehame beside his mother and brothers. The coffin was carried on a cart drawn by Clydesdale horses, followed by two more carts overflowing with a vast array of bright wreaths. Telegrams from Jewish communities and expressions of regret were sent from all over the world. Only the family's flowers were thrown into the grave, together with a small bunch of thyme and rosemary gathered by Lady Wemyss at Hyères. Then the mourners dispersed into the early spring day, under the Lowland hills whose tops were covered with a late fall of snow.

'He will be just like the scent on a pocket handkerchief',[19] Lloyd George once remarked of Balfour's place in history. Yet the record, stretching back into the nineteenth century, is remarkable. His constructive work in Ireland, the Education Act, the Committee of Imperial Defence, the Declaration of 1917, the support for scientific research, the Washington Naval Treaty, the Balfour Note on war debts, the preparation for the Statute of Westminster: all these are indelibly associated with Balfour's name and reputation. His conservatism could be obstructive, as over Ireland before the First War, but also flexible, as with his later perception that Irish coercion was an impossible battle. Balfour would fight, and fight fiercely, where victory was possible: not for a chimerical vision of the unattainable.

His energy and passions were intermittent. He pursued education, defence reform and constructive Unionism with vigour; on tariffs and at the Admiralty he failed to provide an invigorating lead. His triumphs were generally administrative rather than political: the triumphs of rational perception as opposed to inspirational guidance. A ruthless practitioner of power in the defence of what he saw as his country's interests, Balfour believed in the fragility of order. He wished to preserve structures which seemed to contribute to this order and feared quickly conceived change. In religion, the ethical framework of Christianity, fashioned over centuries of thought and belief, should live alongside contemporary science and reason; in politics, radical social and constitutional reform should be distrusted.

Balfour often seemed strangely ornamental. His circle of meretricious admirers and adoring relations, the dandified appearance and languid manner, contributed to this impression. There appeared to be no earthiness or domestic solidity in his subdued, inexpressible nature, and this put him apart from other men. His philosophical works show how much he valued love, beauty, the lofty abstractions of spiritual needs; and he cherished his friendships, dreading their destruction by death or disease. Balfour's control, however, extended to his emotions. If he seemed, by the standards of others, neither openly passionate nor emotionally incautious, he did not wish it otherwise.

His greatest work had been, he felt, in Ireland and with the Jews. In one he had fought what he conceived to be an anarchic threat to civilization; with the other his Old Testament religion, originally imbibed from his mother's strength in the early days at Whittingehame, had led to an understanding of the Jewish predicament. There was nothing ornamental about these, and each touched the core of his beliefs. The beliefs changed little, from an early manhood as Lord Salisbury's protegé to the last days only a decade before the Second World War. As with other men Balfour's strengths lay here: and his weaknesses also.

APPENDIX

From Chapter I of *The Foundations of Belief*

Man, so far as natural science by itself is able to teach us, is no longer the final cause of the universe, the Heaven-descended heir of all the ages. His very existence is an accident, his story a brief and transitory episode in the life of one of the meanest of the planets. Of the combination of causes which first converted a dead organic compound into the living progenitors of humanity, science, indeed, as yet knows nothing. It is enough that from such beginnings famine, disease, and mutual slaugher, fit nurses of the future lords of creation, have gradually evolved, after infinite travail, a race with conscience enough to feel that it is vile, and intelligence enough to know that it is insignificant. We survey the past, and see that its history is of blood and tears, of helpless blundering, of wild revolt, of stupid acquiescence, of empty aspirations. We sound the future, and learn that after a period, long compared with the individual life, but short indeed compared with the divisions of time open to our investigation, the energies of our system will decay, the glory of the sun will be dimmed, and the earth, tideless and inert, will no longer tolerate the race which has for a moment disturbed its solitude. Man will go down into the pit, and all his thoughts will perish. The uneasy consciousness, which in this obscure corner has for a brief space broken the contented silence of the universe, will be at rest. Matter will know itself no longer. 'Imperishable monuments' and 'immortal deeds', death itself, and love stronger than death will be as though they had never been. Nor will anything that *is* be better or worse for all that the labour, genius, devotion, and suffering of man have striven through countless generations to effect.

MANUSCRIPT SOURCES

The main sources for any biography of Arthur Balfour are his papers in the British Museum and at Whittingehame, his old home in East Lothian. Of these two collections, the one in the British Museum is by far the larger, but the Whittingehame archive contains many documents of personal and political significance. An additional source is the papers of Balfour's secretary, J. S. Sandars, in the Bodleian Library, Oxford. These, only made recently available (this is the first life of Balfour to make use of them), contain many of Balfour's own papers, including copies of his cabinet letters and reports to Edward VII. I have also consulted cabinet and government documents in the Public Record Office and the Scottish Record Office. A list of personal papers used comprises:

The Balfour papers (The British Museum).
The Balfour papers (Whittingehame).
The Gerald Balfour papers (Whittingehame).
The Diary of the 1st Viscount Bridgeman (Viscount Bridgeman).
The Balfour–Wemyss correspondence (the Earl of Wemyss).
The Arnold–Forster papers (The British Museum).
The Wilfrid Scawen Blunt papers (The Fitzwilliam Museum, Cambridge).
The Viscount Cecil (Lord Robert Cecil) of Chelwood papers (The British Museum).
Lady Gwendolen Cecil's papers (Hatfield).
The Desborough papers (Hertford County Record Office).
The Grosvenor papers (George Wyndham's papers in the Grosvenor Estate Office).
The Hagley (Lyttelton) papers (Viscount Cobham).
Sir Edward Hamilton's Diary (The British Museum).
The Lansdowne papers (Bowood).
The Lloyd George papers (House of Lords Record Office).
Bernard Mallet's diary (Mr Philip Mallet).
The Maxse papers (West Sussex County Record Office).

Lord Quickswood's (Lord Hugh Cecil) papers (Hatfield).
Lady Rayleigh's Diary and Recollections (Lord Rayleigh and the Hon: Charles Strutt).
The 3rd Marquis of Salisbury's papers (Hatfield).
The 4th Marquis of Salisbury's papers (Hatfield).
The Sandars papers (Bodleian Library, Oxford).
The 2nd Earl of Selborne's papers (Bodleian Library, Oxford).

BIBLIOGRAPHY

ADDISON, CHRISTOPHER. *Four and a Half Years* (London 1934)
   My Political Life. 2 vols (London 1953)
ADELSON, ROGER. *Mark Sykes* (London 1975)
ALDERSON, BERNARD. *Arthur James Balfour* (London 1903)
AMERY, LEO. *My Political Life.* 2 vols (London 1953)
ASKWITH, BETTY. *The Lytteltons* (London 1975)
ASQUITH, LADY CYNTHIA. *Diaries* (London 1968)
   Haply I May Remember (London 1950)
   Remember and be Glad (London 1952)
ASQUITH, H.H. *H.H.A., Letters of the Earl of Oxford* and
   Asquith to a Friend (London 1933)
ASQUITH, MARGOT. *Autobiography I & II* (London 1920 and
   1922)
   More Memories (London 1933)
   Off the Record (as Countess of Oxford. London 1943)
BALFOUR, ARTHUR JAMES. *Chapters of Autobiography* (London
   1930)
   A Defence of Philosophic Doubt (London 1879)
   Economic Notes on Insular Free Trade (London 1903)
   Essays and Addresses (Edinburgh 1893 and 1905)
   Essays Speculative and Political (London 1920)
   Familiar Beliefs and Transcendent Reason (London 1925)
   Fiscal Reform Speeches (London 1906)
   The Foundations of Belief (London 1895)
   Nationality and Home Rule (London 1913)
   Opinions and Arguments (London 1927)
   Speeches on Zionism (London 1928)
   Theism and Humanism (London 1914)
   Theism and Thought (London 1924)
BALFOUR, LADY EVE. My Uncle – A.J. Balfour (*The Listener*
   1956)
BALFOUR, LADY FRANCES. *Ne Obliviscaris.* 2 vols (London 1930)

BALFOUR, JEAN COUNTESS OF. The Palm Sunday Case (*S.P.R. Proceedings* 1960)

BARNETT, CORRELLI. *Britain and Her Army* (London 1970)

BEAVERBROOK, LORD. *The Decline and Fall of Lloyd George* (London 1963)
Men and Power (London 1956)
Politicians and the War (London 1960 edition)

BIRRELL, AUGUSTINE. *Things Past Redress* (London 1937)

BLAKE, ROBERT. *The Conservative Party from Peel to Churchill* (London paperback edition 1972)
Disraeli (London 1966)
The Private Papers of Douglas Haig (London 1952)
The Unknown Prime Minister. The Life and Times of Andrew Bonar Law (London 1955)

BLEWETT, NEAL. Free Fooders, Balfourites, Whole Hoggers. Factionalism within the Unionist Party 1906–1910 (*Historical Journal* 1968)
The Peers, the Parties and the People (London 1972)

BLUNT, WILFRID SCAWEN. *The Land War in Ireland* (London 1912)
My Diaries. 2 vols (London 1919, 1920)

BROWN, A.W. *The Metaphysical Society* (New York 1947)

BROWNING, OSCAR. *Memories of Sixty Years* (London 1910)

BUCHAN, JOHN. *A Lodge in the Wilderness* (London 1906)

CECIL, VISCOUNT. *All the Way* (London 1949)

CECIL, LADY GWENDOLEN. *Life of Robert, Marquis of Salisbury.* 4 vols (London 1921–31)

CECIL, HUGH. Lord Robert Cecil (*History Today* 1975)

CHAMBERLAIN, AUSTEN. *Down the Years* (London 1935)
Politics from Inside (London 1936)

CHARTERIS, EVAN. *Life and Letters of Sir Edmund Gosse* (London 1931)

CHILSTON, VISCOUNT. *Chief Whip* (London 1961)

CHURCHILL, RANDOLPH. *Winston Churchill.* 2 vols (London 1966–7)
Lord Derby (London 1959)

CHURCHILL, WINSTON. *Lord Randolph Churchill* (London 1951 edition)
Great Contemporaries (London 1937)
The World Crisis. 5 vols (London 1923–9)

COWLING, MAURICE. *The Impact of Labour* (Cambridge 1971)

CURTIS, L.P. *Coercion and Conciliation* (Princeton 1963)

DANGERFIELD, GEORGE. *The Strange Death of Liberal England* (London 1970 edition)

DESBOROUGH, LADY. *Pages from a Family Journal* (Privately printed 1916)

The Dictionary of National Biography

DILKS, DAVID. *Curzon in India.* 2 vols (London 1969–70)

DUGDALE, BLANCHE. *Baffy. Diaries.* Ed: N. Rose (London 1973)
Arthur James Balfour. 2 vols (London 1936)
Family Homespun (London 1940)

DUNRAVEN, THE EARL OF. *Past times and Pastimes.* 2 vols (London 1922)

EGREMONT, MAX. *The Cousins* (London 1977)

ENSOR, R.C.K. *English History 1870–1914* (Oxford 1936)

ERSKINE, LADY ANGELA ST: CLAIR. *Fore and Aft* (London 1932)

ESHER, REGINALD BRETT, VISCOUNT. *Cloud Capp'd Towers* (London 1927)
Journals and Letters. 4 vols. Ed: Oliver Viscount Esher (London 1933–8)

FITZROY, SIR ALMERIC. *Memoirs.* 2 vols (London N.D.)

FRASER, PETER. Unionism and Tariff Reform: The crisis of 1906 (*Historical Journal* 1962)
The Unionist Debacle of 1911 and Balfour's Retirement (*Journal of Modern History* 1963)

GARDINER, A.G. *Prophets, Priests and Kings* (London 1908)

GARVIN, J.L. and AMERY, J. *Joseph Chamberlain.* 6 vols (London 1932–69)

GATTY, CHARLES. *Recognita* (London 1917)

GILBERT, MARTIN. *Winston Churchill.* Vols 3–5 (London 1971–6)
Exile and Return (London 1978)

GOLLIN, A. *Balfour's Burden* (London 1965)
Proconsul in Politics: A Study of Lord Milner (London 1964)
The Observer and J.L. Garvin (London 1960)

GOOCH, G.P. and TEMPERLEY, H.W.V. *British Documents on the Origins of the War* (London 1927 on)

GRENVILLE, J.A.S. *Lord Salisbury and Foreign Policy* (London 1970 edition)

GRIGG, JOHN. *Lloyd George. The People's Champion* (London 1978)

GWYNN, STEPHEN. *The Letters and Friendships of Sir Cecil Spring-Rice.* 2 vols (London 1929)

HALEVY, ELIE. *A History of the English People in the 19th Century.* Vol 5. *Imperialism and the Rise of Labour* (London 1929) Vol 6. *The Rule of Democracy* (London 1934)

HAMILTON, LORD GEORGE. *Parliamentary Reminiscences.* 2 vols (London 1922)

HANHAM, H.J. The Creation of the Scottish Office (*Juridical Review* 1965)

HANKEY, LORD. *The Supreme Command.* 2 vols (London 1963) *The Supreme Control* (London 1963)

HARDINGE OF PENSHURST, LORD. *Old Diplomacy* (London 1947)

HAZLEHURST, CAMERON. *Politicians and the War* (London 1971)

HENDRICK, BURTON J.· *Life and Letters of Walter Page.* 2 vols (London 1930 edition)

HOBHOUSE, CHARLES. *Inside Asquith's Cabinet.* Ed: Edward David (London 1977)

HUNTER, JAMES. *The Making of the Crofting Community* (Edinburgh 1976)

JAMES, ROBERT RHODES. *Churchill. A Study in Failure* (London 1970)

JENKINS, ROY. *Asquith* (London 1964) *Mr Balfour's Poodle* (London 1954)

JOHNSON, F.A. *Defence by Committee* (Princeton 1960)

JOLLY, W.P. *Sir Oliver Lodge* (London 1974)

JONES, THOMAS. *Lloyd George* (London 1951) *Whitehall Diary.* 2 vols (London 1969)

JUDD, D. *Balfour and the British Empire* (London 1968) *Radical Joe* (London 1977)

KEDOURIE, E. *England and the Middle East* (Cambridge 1956) *Into the Anglo-Arab Labyrinth* (Cambridge 1976)

KOSS, STEPHEN. *Asquith* (London 1976) The Destruction of Britain's Last Liberal Government (*Journal of Modern History* 1968) *Lord Haldane. Scapegoat for Liberalism* (New York 1969)

KURTZ, HAROLD. The Lansdowne Letter (*History Today* 1968)

LEE, VISCOUNT. *A Good Innings.* Ed: Alan Clark (London 1974)

LEE, SIR SIDNEY. *King Edward VII.* 2 vols (London 1925–7)

LESLIE, SHANE. *The End of a Chapter* (London 1916)

LEVESON-GOWER, SIR GEORGE. *Years of Endeavour* (London 1942)

LEWIS, MICHAEL. *Ancestors* (London 1966)

LLOYD GEORGE, DAVID. *The Truth about the Peace Treaties.* 2
vols (London 1938)
War Memoirs. 2 vols (London 1938 edition)
LOCKHART, ROBERT BRUCE. *Giants Cast Long Shadows* (London
1960)
LUCY, HENRY W. *A Diary of the Salisbury Parliament* (London
1892)
A Diary of the Home Rule Parliament (London 1896)
A Diary of the Unionist Parliament (London 1901)
The Balfourian Parliament (London 1906)
LUTYENS, LADY EMILY. *A Blessed Girl* (London 1953)
LYONS, F.S.L. *John Dillon* (London 1968)
Ireland Since the Famine (London 1971)
Charles Stewart Parnell (London 1977)

MACKAIL, J. and WYNDHAM, G. *The Life and Letters of George
Wyndham.* 2 vols (London 1925)
MACKINTOSH, J.P. The Role of the Committee of Imperial Defence
Before 1914 (*English Historical Review* 1962)
MACLEOD, ROY and ANDREWS, E. KAY. The Committee of Civil
Research. Scientific Advice for Economic Development 1925–30
(*Minerva* 1969)
MAGNUS, PHILIP. *King Edward VII* (London 1964)
Gladstone (London 1954)
Kitchener (London 1958)
MALCOLM, IAN. *Lord Balfour* (London 1930)
MALLET, VICTOR. *Life with Queen Victoria* (London 1968)
MANSERGH, NICHOLAS. *The Irish Question* (London 1965)
MARDER, ARTHUR. *From the Dreadnought to Scapa Flow.* 5 vols
(London 1961–70)
MARJORIBANKS, E. and COLVIN, I. *Life of Lord Carson.* 3 vols
(London 1932–6)
MASTERMAN, LUCY. *Mary Gladstone. Diaries and Letters* (London
1930)
MEINERTZHAGEN, RICHARD. *Middle East Diary* (London 1959)
MIDDLEMAS, KEITH and BARNES, JOHN. *Baldwin* (London 1969)
MIDLETON, EARL OF. *Records and Reactions* (London 1939)
MILNER, VISCOUNTESS. *My Picture Gallery* (London 1951)
MORLEY, VISCOUNT. *Recollections.* 2 vols (London 1917)
MOSLEY, NICHOLAS. *Julian Grenfell* (London 1976)
MUNSON, J.E.B. The Unionist Coalition and Education (*Historical
Journal* 1977)

NEWTON, LORD. *Lord Lansdowne* (London 1929)
Retrospection (London 1941)
NICOLSON, HAROLD. *Curzon. The Last Phase* (London 1934)
King George V (London 1952)
Peacemaking 1919 (London 1933)
People and Things (London 1931)
Small Talk (London 1937)
O'BROIN, LEON. *The Prime Informer* (London 1971)
O'CONNOR, T.P. *Memoirs of an Old Parliamentarian.* 2 vols (London 1929)
OWEN, FRANK. *Tempestuous Journey. Lloyd George, His Life and Times* (London 1954)
PETRIE, CHARLES. *Life and Letters of Sir Austen Chamberlain.* 2 vols (London 1939)
Walter Long (London 1936)
The Powers Behind the Prime Ministers (London 1959)
PONSONBY, A. *Henry Ponsonby* (London 1942)
PONSONBY, SIR FREDERICK. *Recollections of 3 Reigns* (London 1951)
RAYLEIGH, LORD. *Lord Balfour in His Relation to Science* (Cambridge 1930)
RAYMOND, E.T. *Mr Balfour* (London 1920)
RIDDELL, LORD. *Intimate Diary of the Peace Conference and After* (London 1933)
More Pages From My Diary 1908–1914 (London 1934)
War Diary 1914–1918 (London 1933)
ROBERTSON, DR JAMES. *Lady Blanche Balfour* (London 1897)
ROSE, KENNETH. *The Later Cecils* (London 1975)
Superior Person (London 1969)
ROSKILL, STEPHEN. *Hankey. Man of Secrets.* Vols 1 and 2 (London 1970, 1972)
Naval Policy between the Wars. Vol 1 (London 1968)
RYAN, A.P. *Mutiny at The Curragh* (London 1956)
SALVIDGE, S. *Salvidge of Liverpool* (London 1934)
SANDARS, J.S. *Studies of Yesterday by A Privy Councillor* (London 1928)
SCOTT, C.P. *Political Diaries.* Ed: Trevor Wilson (London 1970)
SHORT, WILFRID. *The Mind of Arthur James Balfour* (New York 1918)
SIDGWICK, A. and MRS E.M. *Henry Sidgwick* (London 1906)
SMITH, JANET ADAM. *John Buchan* (London 1965)
STEIN, LEONARD. *The Balfour Declaration* (London 1961)

STEVENSON, FRANCES. *Lloyd George. A Diary.* Ed: A.J.P. Taylor (London 1971)

STORRS, RONALD. *Orientations* (London 1937)

SYDENHAM, LORD. *My Working Life* (London 1927)

TAYLOR, A.J.P. *Beaverbrook* (London paperback edition 1974)
English History 1914–1945 (Oxford 1965)

TAYLOR, ROBERT. *Lord Salisbury* (London 1975)

THOROLD, ALGAR. *Life of Henry Labouchere* (London 1913)

ULLMANN, RICHARD. *Anglo-Soviet Relations.* 2 vols (Princeton 1961–8)

VICTORIA, QUEEN. *Letters. 2nd series.* 2 vols (London 1926)
Letters. 3rd series. 3 vols (London 1931)

WARD, MAISIE. *The Wilfrid Wards and The Transition.* 2 vols (London 1934–7)

WEBB, BEATRICE. *My Apprenticeship* (London 1926)
Our Partnership (London 1948)
Diaries 1914–1917 (London 1952)

WEIZMANN, CHAIM. *Trial and Error* (London 1949)

WELLS, H.G. *Experiment in Autobiography* (London 1934)
Men Like Gods (London 1923)
The New Machiavelli (London 1911)

WEMYSS, THE COUNTESS OF. *A Family Record* (Privately Printed 1932)

WILLOUGHBY DE BROKE, LORD. *The Passing Years* (London 1924)

WILSON, ANGUS. *The Strange Ride of Rudyard Kipling* (London 1977)

WILSON, JOHN. *C-B. A Life of Sir Henry Campbell-Bannerman* (London 1973)

WINTERTON, EARL. *Fifty Tumultuous Years* (London 1955)
Pre-War (London 1932)

WOODWARD, E.L., BUTLER, R. and BURY, J.P.T. *Documents on British Foreign Policy* (London 1946 on)

YOUNG, KENNETH. *Balfour* (London 1963)

ZEBEL, SYDNEY. *Balfour. A Political Biography* (Cambridge 1973)

NOTES

CHAPTER 1

p13   1. Balfour. Whitt: 133.
p13   2. Lewis. *Ancestors,* p41.
p14   3. I am indebted to Sir John Balfour: *Notes on the Balfour Family History.*
p15   4. Lady Rayleigh: *Traditions of the Balfours of Whittingehame & Recollections,* p2.
p15   5. Chapters of Autobiography, p3.
p15   6. Dugdale. *Balfour I,* p18.
p15   7. Balfour. Whitt: 138.
p16   8. Balfour. Whitt: 144.
p16   9. Robertson. *Lady Blanche Balfour,* p19.
p17 10. For her family's memories of Lady Blanche, see Balfour. Whitt: 145; also Rayleigh 'Traditions'.
p17 11. Dugdale. I, p19.
p18 12. Balfour. Whitt: 157.
p18 13. Robertson. *Op. cit.* p20.
p18 14. Dugdale. I. p18.
p19 15. Robertson. *Op. cit.* p26.
p19 16. *Ibid.* p25.
p20 17. Balfour. Whitt: 195.
p21 18. Chapters of Autobiography, p6.
p21 19. Balfour. Whitt: 195.
p22 20. Chapters of Autobiography, p7.
p22 21. Malcolm, *Lord Balfour,* p15.
p22 22. For Eton housemaster letters see Balfour. Whitt: 239.
p23 23. Chapters of Autobiography, p33–4.
p23 24. *Ibid.* p xii.
p24 25. *Ibid.* p56.
p25 26. A. & E. M. Sidgwick. *Henry Sidgwick,* p347.
p25 27. *Ibid.* p348.
p25 28. Balfour. Whitt: 195.
p26 29. Dugdale I, p28.
p26 30. *Ibid. I,* p19.
p26 31. Chapters of Autobiography, p60.

CHAPTER 2

p27   1. Balfour. B.M. Add. mss. 49839. F.51–2.
p27   2. Balfour. Whitt: 266.
p27   3. Balfour. Whitt: 195.
p28   4. Malcolm. *Lord Balfour,* p104.
p28   5. Browning. *Memories of Sixty Years,* p164.

p29   6. Hatfield. *Class E.*
p29   7. Dugdale. *Family Home-spun,* p92.
p31   8. Short. *The Mind of Arthur James Balfour,* p216.
p31   9. Balfour. Essays & Addresses. ('Handel', p111–184).
p31 10. Masterman. *Mary Gladstone,* p54.
p32 11. Mary Gladstone. Recollections of A. J. B. Balfour Whitt: 80, p3–4.
p32 12. *Ibid.* p23.
p32 13. *Ibid.* p19.
p33 14. *Ibid.* p5.
p33 15. *Ibid.* p47.
p33 16. Balfour. Whitt: 138.
p33 17. Balfour. Whitt: 80. p27.
p34 18. Askwith. *The Lytteltons,* p175.
p34 19. Hagley Papers. May Lyttelton's Diary 12.6.1870.
p34 20. *Ibid.* 18.5.1870.
p34 21. *Ibid.* 26.10.1870.

p34 22. *Ibid.* 11.9.1872.
p34 23. Askwith. *Op. cit.* p177.
p34 24. *Ibid.* p178.
p35 25. Hagley Papers. May's Diary 11.12.1870.
p35 26. *Ibid.* 6–8.1.1871.
p35 27. *Ibid.* 11.3.1871.
p35 28. *Ibid.* 19–20.3.1871.
p35 29. *Ibid.* 20.6.1871.
p36 30. *Ibid.* 30.6.1871.
p36 31. *Ibid.* 30.8.1873.
p36 32. *Ibid.* 1.9.1873.
p36 33. Askwith. *Op. cit.* p180.
p37 34. Hagley Papers. May's Diary. 15–23.12.1874.
p37 35. Hagley Papers. Lavinia Talbot's notes.
p37 36. *Ibid.*
p37 37. *Ibid.*
p37 38. *Ibid.*
p38 39. Masterman. *Mary Gladstone,* p93.
p38 40. Hagley Papers. Lavinia Talbot's notes.
p39 41. Balfour. Whitt: 80, p34–36.

CHAPTER 3

p40   1. Balfour. Whitt: 217.
p41   2. Cecil. *Salisbury I.* p59.
p41   3. *Ibid. I,* p86.
p42   4. Balfour. Whitt: 195.
p42   5. Chapters of Autobiography, p22–23.
p42   6. *Ibid.* p85.
p42   7. Balfour. B.M. Add. mss. 49688 F.5.
p43   8. Chapters of Autobiography, p89.
p43   9. Balfour. Whitt: 80, p32.
p44 10. Chapters of Autobiography, p91
p44 11. *Ibid.* p94.

p44 12. Dugdale I, p45.
p44 13. Chapters of Autobiography, p120.
p45 14. A. J. B. to Alice Balfour, 15.6.1878 (letter in possession of Frances, Lady Fergusson).
p45 15. A. J. B. to Alice Balfour, 10.7.1878 (letter in possession of Frances, Lady Fergusson). See also Chapters of Autobiography, p110.

p46 16. Chapters of Auto-
biography, p110.

p46 17. Chapters of Auto-
biography, p108.

p46 18. A. J. B. to Alice Balfour
to 10.7.1878
(Fergusson).

p46 19. *Ibid.*

p46 20. A. J. B. to Alice
Balfour, 11.7.1878
(Fergusson).

p47 21. Dugdale I, p40.

p48 22. A Defence of Philosophic
Doubt, p302.

p48 23. *Ibid.* p37.

p48 24. *Ibid.* p34.

p49 25. *Ibid.* p37.

p50 26. Hagley Papers. Lavinia
Talbot's Notes.

p50 27. Cecil. *Salisbury I.* p115.

p50 28. *Ibid. I*, p113–4.

p50 29. *Ibid. I*, p113.

p51 30. Masterman. *Mary
Gladstone*, p138.

p51 31. A. J. B. to Alice Balfour
16.3.1880 (Fergusson).

p52 32. Balfour. Whitt: 60.

CHAPTER 4

p54 1. Chapters of Auto-
biography, p123.

p54 2. Balfour. Whitt: 60.

p54 3. Balfour. Whitt: 60.

p55 4. Balfour. B.M. Add. mss.
49688, F.24.

p55 5. Hatfield Class E.

p56 6. Chapters of Auto-
biography, p136.

p56 7. For an account of this
episode, see Magnus,
King Edward VII,
p144–150.

p57 8. Chapters of Auto-
biography, p139.

p57 9. Raymond. *Mr Balfour*,
p25.

p57 10. Dugdale I, p57.

p57 11. *Ibid.* p58.

p57 12. Hatfield Class E.

p58 13. Hatfield Class E.

p58 14. Balfour. B.M. Add. mss.
49791, F.5–6.

p58 15. Chapters of Auto-
biography, p146.

p58 16. Balfour. B.M. Add. mss.
49688, F.33.

p59 17. Balfour. B.M. Add. mss.
49838, F.101–104.

p59 18. Lucy. *A Diary of Two
Parliaments II*, p84–85.

p61 19. Hansard. 3rd series. Vol:
269. Col: 834–7.
See also Lucy, *A Diary
of Two Parliaments II*,
p248–9.

p61 20. Balfour. B.M. Add. mss.
49692, F.5.

p61 21. Balfour. B.M. Add. mss.
49789, F.24–27.

p61 22. Rayleigh. *Traditions*,
p21.

p61 23. *Ibid.* p21.

p62 24. See Frances Balfour, *Ne
Obliviscaris I*, p348–354,
for account of family
reactions to Frank
Balfour's death.

p62 25. Blake. *The Conservative
Party from Peel to
Churchill*, p151.

p63 26. Balfour. *Ne Obliviscaris
I*, p381.

p64 27. Hatfield Class E.

p64 28. Balfour. B.M. Add. mss. 49838, F. 181–2.

p64 29. Hatfield Class E.

p65 30. Chapters of Auto-biography, p173.

CHAPTER 5

p66 1. Balfour. B.M. Add. mss. 49695, F.175–8.

p67 2. M. Asquith. *Auto-biography*, p162.

p68 3. Wemyss, 14.2.1905.

p68 4. Wemyss, 14.2.1905.

p69 5. Midleton, Records and Reactions, p43.

p70 6. Wemyss, 8.5.1886.

p70 7. M. Asquith. *Auto-biography*, p46–51.

p70 8. Wemyss, 17.10.1889.

p71 9. Balfour. Whitt: 28.

p71 10. Balfour. Whitt: 28.

p71 11. Balfour. Whitt: 28.

p72 12. Balfour. Whitt: 74.

p72 13. Balfour. B.M. Add. mss. 49721, F.238–9.

p73 14. Dugdale I, p87.

p73 15. Balfour. *Ne Obliviscaris* I, p380.

p75 16. Chapters Autobiography, p211–212.

p75 17. Balfour. B.M. Add. mss. 49688, F.80.

p75 18. Balfour. Whitt: 64.

p76 19. Dugdale I, p97–102.

p76 20. *Ibid. I*, p101.

p76 21. *Ibid. I*, p104.

p77 22. Wemyss, 27.7.1886.

p77 23. Dugdale I, p107.

p77 24. Balfour. B.M. Add. mss. 49737, F.4.

p77 25. Balfour. B.M. Add. mss. 49757, F.1–3.

p78 26. For a recent account of Highland land agitation, see Hunter, *The Making of the Crofting Community.*

p78 27. Hansard, 3rd series, Vol. 308, col: 995.

p78 28. P.R.O. CAB 37/18/42.

p79 29. Hatfield Class E.

p79 30. Balfour. B.M. Add. mss. 49688, F.128.

p79 31. Balfour. B.M. Add. mss. 49688, F.129.

p79 32. Balfour. *Ne Obliviscaris* II, p85.

p79 33. Hatfield Class E.

p80 34. Balfour. Whitt: 29.

p80 35. Balfour. Whitt: 29.

p80 36. S.R.O. H.H/1/168.

CHAPTER 6

p81 1. Hatfield Class E.

p82 2. Curtis, *Coercion and Conciliation*, p168.

p82 3. *Ibid.* p168–9.

p82 4. *Ibid.* p170.

p82 5. Balfour, Whitt. 66.

p82 6. Wemyss, N.D.

p82 7. Wemyss, 6.3.1887.

p83 8. O'Connor, *Memoirs of an Old Parliamentarian* II, p126.

p83 9. Cecil, *Salisbury III*, p347

p83 10. A. Chamberlain, *Politics From Inside*, p185.

p84 11. *Ibid.* p262.

p84 12. Rayleigh Diary, Introductory note.

p84 13. Curtis, *op. cit.* p182.

p84 14. Rayleigh Diary, Introductory note.

p85 15. Balfour B.M. Add. mss.
49807, F.35–37.

p85 16. Balfour B.M. Add. mss.
49807, F.60–61.

p86 17. Dugdale I, p132.

p86 18. Balfour B.M. Add. mss.
49688, F.147.

p87 19. Dugdale I, p147.

p87 20. Balfour B.M. Add. mss.
49688, F.152.

p87 21. Dugdale I, p147.

p87 22. Balfour B.M. Add. mss.
49688, F.149.

p87 23. Balfour B.M. Add. mss.
49808, F.14–17.

p88 24. Grosvenor Papers,
13.1.1888.

p88 25. Balfour, Whitt: 283.

p88 26. Balfour, Whitt: 165.

p89 27. O'Connor, *op. cit. II,*
p123.

p89 28. Wemyss, 27.10.1887.

p89 29. Blunt, *Land War in
Ireland,* p301.

p89 30. Freeman's Journal,
16.1.1888.

p89 31. Wemyss, 27.10.1887.

p90 32. Wemyss, 24.12.1887.

p90 33. Balfour, B.M. Add. mss.
49688, F.153.

p91 34. Curtis, *op. cit.* p280.

p91 35. Balfour, B.M. Add. mss.
49808, F.142–3. For
further activity against
Parnell, see O'Broin,
The Prime Informer.

p92 36. Dugdale I, p163.

p93 37. Balfour, B.M. Add. mss.
49812, F.187–9.

p93 38. Curtis, *op. cit.* p303.

p93 39. Hatfield, Class E.

p93 40. Dugdale I, p181.

p94 41. Wemyss, 5.1.1889.

p94 42. Dugdale I, p154.

p94 43. Curtis, *op. cit.*
p369–370.

p95 44. Mackail, *Life and Letters
of George Wyndham I,*
p252.

p95 45. Balfour, B.M. Add. mss.
49826. F.300–1.

p95 46. Rayleigh Diary,
4.3.1888.

CHAPTER 7

p97 1. Dugdale I, p185.

p98 2. Balfour, B.M. Add. mss.
49689, F.38.

p98 3. Rayleigh Diary, Introductory note.

p98 4. Balfour, *Ne Obliviscaris
II,* p92.

p98 5. *Ibid. II,* p199.

p99 6. Rayleigh Diary,
9.9.1893.

p99 7. Morley, *Recollections I,*
p228.

p100 8. Balfour, B.M. Add. mss.
49689, F.89.

p100 9. Lord G. Hamilton,
*Parliamentary
Reminiscences II,* p199.

p100 10. Winston Churchill, *Lord
Randolph Churchill,*
p735.

p100 11. Balfour, B.M. Add. mss.
49695, F.186.

p100 12. Balfour, B.M. Add. mss.
49841, F.179–80.

p101 13. Balfour, B.M. Add. mss.
49689, F.132.

p101 14. Balfour, B.M. Add. mss.
49689, F.136.

p101 15. Balfour, B.M. Add. mss. 49689, F.138.
p101 16. Balfour, B.M. Add. mss. 49689, F.140.
p101 17. Balfour, B.M. Add. mss. 49689, F.142.
p101 18. Balfour, B.M. Add. mss. 49689, F.143.
p101 19. Hatfield, Class E.
p102 20. Balfour, B.M. Add. mss. 49812, F.201–2.
p102 21. A. Ponsonby, *Henry Ponsonby*, p273.
p102 22. Sir Frederick Ponsonby, *Recollections of Three Reigns*, p12.
p102 23. A. Ponsonby, *op. cit.* p274.
p102 24. Sir Frederick Ponsonby, *op. cit.* p41.
p102 25. Letters of Queen Victoria, 3rd series, III, p73–4.
p103 26. Magnus, *King Edward VII*, p219.

p103 27. Hatfield, Class E.
p103 28. Hatfield, Class E.
p104 29. Hatfield, Class E.
p104 30. Hatfield, Class E.
p104 31. Hatfield, Class E.
p104 32. Magnus, *King Edward VII*, p221.
p105 33. Lady Emily Lutyens, *A Blessed Girl*, p158–9.
p105 34. Wemyss, 30.10.1903.
p105 35. Dugdale I, p188.
p106 36. Cynthia Asquith, *Remember and be Glad*, p177.
p106 37. Balfour, Whitt: 164.
p106 38. Balfour, Whitt: 164.
p106 39. Wemyss, 21.1.1909.
p106 40. Wemyss N.D.
p106 41. Balfour, Whitt: 164.
p107 42. Lady Emily Lutyens *op. cit.* p160.
p107 43. Balfour, Whitt: 162.
p107 44. Balfour, Whitt: 165.
p107 45. Frances Balfour, *Ne Obliviscaris I*, p450.

CHAPTER 8

p109 1. Blunt, *My Diaries I*, p65.
p109 2. M. Asquith, *Autobiography*, p173.
p110 3. *Ibid.* p177.
p111 4. Cynthia Asquith, *Haply I may Remember*, p51.
p111 5. Wemyss, 5.1.1889.
p111 6. Charles Gatty, *Recognita*, p88.
p112 7. Midleton, *Records and Reactions*, p51.
p113 8. M. Asquith, *More Memories*, p112.
p113 9. Wemyss, N.D.
p113 10. Desborough Papers, 22.8.1910.

p114 11. Wemyss, 16.8.1893.
p114 12. Grosvenor Papers, N.D.
p114 13. Leveson-Gower, *Years of Endeavour*, p276–7.
p114 14. B. Webb, *My Apprenticeship*, p303.
p114 15. Rayleigh Diary, 25.1.1902.
p115 16. Cynthia Asquith, *Remember and be Glad*, p14.
p115 17. Blunt, Fitzwilliam Ms.3, p203.
p115 18. Blunt, Fitzwilliam Ms.3, p203.
p115 19. Balfour, Whitt: 65.

p116 20. Countess of Oxford, *Off The Record*, p52.
p116 21. Wemyss, *January 1904*.
p116 22. Wemyss, N.D.
p117 23. Mosley, *Julian Grenfell*, p30.
p117 24. Wemyss, 14.3.1893.
p117 25. Wemyss, 27.3.1895.
p118 26. Wemyss, 20.9.1904.
p118 27. Wemyss, 12.6.1896.
p118 28. Blunt, Fitzwilliam, Ms.338, 3.9.1887.
p119 29. Blunt, Fitzwilliam, Ms.34, 24.1.1895.
p119 30. Blunt, Fitzwilliam, Ms.35, 20.7.1896.
p119 31. Wemyss, 22.4.1890.
p119 32. Wemyss, 15.3.1889.
p120 33. Wemyss, April 1887.
p120 34. Wemyss, 2.1.1903.
p120 35. Desborough Papers, 3.3.1944.

p120 36. Buchan, *Memory Hold the Door*, p159.
p120 37. Wemyss, 19.1.1894.
p121 38. Wemyss, 23.11.1907.
p121 39. Wemyss, N.D.
p121 40. Viscountess Milner, *My Picture Gallery*, p57.
p121 41. Mackail, *Life and Letters of George Wyndham, I*, p67.
p122 42. Brett, *Journals and Letters of Viscount Esher, I*, p182.
p122 43. Ward, *The Wilfrid Wards and the Transition I*, p347.
p123 44. *Ibid. I*, p373.
p123 45. Rayleigh Diary, 24.9.1899.
p123 46. Ward, *op. cit. I*, p352.
p123 47. Foundations of Belief, p19.
p124 48. *Ibid.* p251.

CHAPTER 9

p126 1. Wemyss, 15.3.1892.
p126 2. Rayleigh Diary, 23.2.1894.
p126 3. Letters of Queen Victoria, 3rd Series, II, p96.
p127 4. Balfour, B.M. Add. mss. 49690, F.55–64.
p127 5. Balfour, B.M. Add. mss. 49690, F.65–6.
p127 6. Rayleigh Diary, 7.6.1898.
p127 7. Hansard, 4th Series, Vol. 58, col. 119–125.
p128 8. Rayleigh Diary, 7.3.1894.
p128 9. Hamilton Diary, B.M. Add. mss. 48679, F.108.

p128 10. Balfour, B.M. Add. mss. 49690, F.137–8.
p129 11. Rayleigh Diary, 14.5.1899.
p129 12. Sandars, Ms. Eng. Hist. c:771:50–51.
p130 13. Sandars, Ms. Eng. Hist. c:771:322.
p130 14. Sandars, Ms. Eng. Hist. c:771:327.
p130 15. Balfour, Whitt: 81, p13.
p131 16. Balfour, Whitt: 81, p6.
p131 17. Wemyss, 10.1.1894.
p131 18. Desborough Papers, 5.2.1917.
p132 19. Hamilton, *Parliamentary Reminiscences II*, p253.
p132 20. Mallet Diary 1896, Prologue.

B – Y*

p132 21. Blunt, Fitzwilliam Ms. 35, 15.7.1896.

p134 22. Rayleigh Diary, 27.10.1894.

p135 23. Balfour, Whitt: 76.

p135 24. For letters see Balfour B.M. Add. mss. 49784, F.89–96.

p135 25. Wilson, C-B, p148.

p135 26. Dugdale I, p226.

p136 27. Sandars, Ms. Eng. Hist. c:728:18.

p136 28. Balfour, B.M. Add. mss. 49852, F,282–3.

p136 29. Wemyss, 16.7.1891.

p136 30. Viscountess Milner, *My Picture Gallery,* p233.

p137 31. Dugdale I, p224.

p137 32. Grenville, *Lord Salisbury and Foreign Policy,* p143.

p138 33. *Ibid.* p144.

p138 34. *Ibid.* p145.

p138 35. Times, 30.4.1898.

p138 36. Grenville, *op. cit.* p154.

p139 37. Balfour, B.M. Add. mss. 49691, F.6–19.

p141 38. P.R.O. Cab. 37/49/29.

p141 39. Wemyss, 27.8.1899.

p141 40. Wemyss, 10.9.1899.

p141 41. Sandars, Ms. Eng. Hist. c:771:331.

p142 42. Balfour, B.M. Add. mss. 49853, F.157.

p142 43. Balfour, B.M. Add. mss. 49853, F.187–190.

p142 44. Mallet Diary, 10.1.1900.

p142 45. Balfour, B.M. Add. mss. 49720, F.74–5.

p143 46. Mallet, Life with Queen Victoria, p206.

p143 47. Balfour, B.M. Add. mss. 49831, F.9–11.

p143 48. Balfour, Whitt: 74.

p143 49. Sandars, Ms. Eng. Hist. c:732:92–3.

p143 50. Balfour, B.M. Add. mss. 49727, F.64–72.

p144 51. Sandars, Ms. Eng. Hist. c:732:79–83.

p144 52. Sandars, Ms. Eng. Hist. c:713:159–60.

p144 53. Memorandum found in Wemyss papers.

p144 54. Sandars, Ms. Eng. Hist. c:732:79–83.

p145 55. Balfour, B.M. Add. mss. 49691, F.110.

p145 56. Balfour, B.M. Add. mss. 49853, F.18–21.

CHAPTER 10

p147 1. Wemyss, 17.7.1902.

p147 2. Hamilton Diary, B.M. Add. mss. 48679, F.127–8.

p147 3. Balfour, Whitt: 281.

p147 4. Hamilton Diary, B.M. Add. mss. 48679, F.127–8.

p148 5. Sandars, Ms. Eng. Hist. c:736:13–19.

p148 6. Sandars, Ms. Eng. Hist. c:736:138–9.

p148 7. Balfour, Whitt: 81, p5.

p148 8. Hamilton Diary, B.M. Add. mss. 48682, F.126.

p148 9. Hamilton Diary, B.M. Add. mss. 48680, F.4.

p148 10. Hamilton Diary, B.M. Add. mss. 48679, F.111.

p148 11. Garvin and Amery, *Joseph Chamberlain* vol: 5, p75.

p148 12. Balfour, B.M. Add. mss. 49730, F.275–6.

p148 13. Lee, *King Edward VII, II,* p47.

p149 14. Hamilton Diary, B.M. Add. mss. 48682, F.32–3.

p149 15. Magnus, *King Edward VII,* p305.

p150 16. Rayleigh Diary, 21.1.1902.

p150 17. Rayleigh Diary, 28.9.1902.

p150 18. Sandars, Ms. Eng. Hist. c:771:324.

p151 19. Dugdale I, p326.

p151 20. Balfour, Whitt: 165.

p151 21. Sandars, Ms. Eng. Hist. c:771:325. The pamphlet is included in Essays and Addresses, p415.

p152 22. Hamilton Diary, B.M. Add. mss. 48680, F.68.

p152 23. Sandars, Ms. Eng. Hist. c:737:165.

p153 24. Sandars, Ms. Eng. Hist. c:725:94–9.

p153 25. Balfour, Whitt: 17.

p154 26. Wemyss, 17.6.1901.

p154 27. Sandars, Ms. Eng. Hist. c:732:125–7.

p154 28. Sandars, Ms. Eng. Hist. c:736:7–8.

p155 29. Rayleigh Diary, 5.2.1897.

p155 30. Sandars, Ms. Eng. Hist. c:738:93 and 93A.

p155 31. Wemyss, 27.2.1903.

p156 32. Selborne, Ms. 3: 212–13.

p156 33. Selborne, Ms. 3: 217.

p156 34. Arnold-Forster Diary, B.M. Add. mss. 50339, F.107–8.

p156 35. Hankey, *The Supreme Command I,* p45.

p157 36. Hansard, 4th Series, Vol: 118, col: 1579.

p157 37. Balfour, B.M. Add. mss. 49722, F.118.

p157 38. Sydenham, *My Working Life,* p169.

p157 39. Sandars, Ms. Eng. Hist. c:716:27–8.

p157 40. Balfour, B.M. Add. mss. 49710, F.51–2.

p158 41. Balfour, B.M. Add. mss. 49761, F.110.

p158 42. Selborne Ms. 1: 20–25.

p158 43. Sandars, Ms. Eng. Hist. c:715:140–4.

p158 44. Sandars, Ms. Eng. Hist. c:719:228–9.

p159 45. Balfour, B.M. Add. mss. 49684, F.76–7.

p159 46. Sandars, Ms. Eng. Hist. c:721:88–90.

p159 47. Brett, *Journals and Letters of Viscount Esher II,* p14.

p160 48. Hamilton Diary, B.M. Add. mss. 48682, F.1–2.

p160 49. Balfour, B.M. Add. mss. 49762, F.198–201.

p160 50. Sandars, Ms. Eng. Hist. c:720:112–115.

p161 51. Arnold-Forster Diary, B.M. Add. mss. 50352, F.193.

p161 52. Sandars, Ms. Eng. Hist. c:721:101.

p161 53. Balfour, B.M. Add. mss. 49685, F.29–30.

p162 54. Hamilton Diary, B.M. Add. mss. 48682, F.1–2.

p162 55. Sandars, Ms. Eng. Hist.
          c:745:184–6.
p163 56. Dugdale notes in posses-
          sion of Frances, Lady
          Fergusson.
p163 57. Sandars, Ms. Eng. Hist.
          c:771:330.
p163 58. Balfour, B.M. Add. mss.
          49691, F.55–74.

p163 59. Balfour, B.M. Add. mss.
          49812, F.296.
p164 60. Balfour, B.M. Add. mss.
          49727, F.159–179.
p165 61. Balfour, B.M. Add. mss.
          49730, F.275–6.
p165 62. Dugdale I, p374.

CHAPTER 11

p167 1. Webb, *Our Partnership*,
          p359.
p167 2. Hamilton Diary, B.M.
          Add. mss. 48680, F.39.
p167 3. Hamilton Diary, B.M.
          Add. mss. 48680,
          F.108–9.
p167 4. G. Hamilton, *Parliamen-
          tary Reminiscences II,*
          p253-4.
p168 5. Judd, *Balfour and the
          British Empire,* p229.
p168 6. Balfour, B.M. Add. mss.
          49732, F.76–82.
p169 7. Balfour, B.M. Add. mss.
          49732, F.106–9.
p169 8. Balfour, B.M. Add. mss.
          49732, F.110–16.
p169 9. Wemyss 13.2.1903.
p170 10. Balfour, B.M. Add. mss.
          49732, F.131–3.
p170 11. Balfour, B.M. Add. mss.
          49720, F.212.
p171 12. Balfour, B.M. Add. mss.
          49732, F.134–5.
p171 13. Balfour, B.M. Add. mss.
          49683, F.164.
p171 14. Midleton, *Records and
          Reactions,* p200–201.
p172 15. Balfour, B.M. Add. mss.
          49729, F.1.
p172 16. Midleton, *op. cit.* p200.
p173 17. Dugdale I, p404.

p173 18. Balfour, B.M. Add. mss.
          49732, F.175–183.
p173 19. Sandars, Ms. Eng. Hist.
          c:717:88–90.
p173 20. Sandars, Ms. Eng. Hist.
          c:717:94–5.
p174 21. Sandars, Ms. Eng. Hist.
          c:717:106–7.
p174 22. Balfour, B.M. Add. mss.
          49733, F.72–8.
p174 23. Mosley, *Julian Grenfell,*
          p104.
p176 24. Hamilton Diary, B.M.
          Add. mss. 48680. F.90.
p176 25. Sandars, Ms. Eng. Hist.
          c:771:60–3.
p177 26. Hamilton Diary, B.M.
          Add. mss. 48680,
          F47–8.
p177 27. Sandars, Ms. Eng. Hist.
          c:738:220–23.
p177 28. Sandars, Ms. Eng. Hist.
          c:715:53–4.
p177 29. Garvin and Amery,
          Joseph Chamberlain. Vol:
          5, p194.
p177 30. *Ibid.* Vol: 5, p193.
p178 31. *Ibid.* Vol: 5, p183.
p178 32. M. Asquith, *Auto-
          biography II,* p53.
p178 33. Judd, *Radical Joe,* p246.
p179 34. Cecil, Lord Robert Cecil,

History To-day. Vol: 25, p121.

p179 35. Balfour, Whitt: 281.

p180 36. Wemyss, 25.8.1903.

p180 37. Balfour, B.M. Add. mss. 49737, F.7–8.

p180 38. Balfour, B.M. Add. mss. 49836, F.181.

p181 39. Sandars, Ms. Eng. Hist. c:742:15.

p182 40. Fitzroy, *Memoirs I,* p15.

p182 41. Sandars, Ms. Eng. Hist. c:771:36.

p182 42. Lansdowne Papers, 11.7.1902.

p182 43. Sandars, Ms. Eng. Hist. c:745:257.

p182 44. Sandars, Ms. Eng. Hist. c:745:260.

p182 45. Sandars, Ms. Eng. Hist. c:745:258.

p183 46. Balfour reported this to Lady Gwendolen Cecil who informed her brother Lord Salisbury, Hatfield S (4) 54:101.

p183 47. Sandars, Ms. Eng. Hist. c:744:108–110.

p183 48. Sandars, Ms. Eng. Hist. c:745:264.

p184 49. Sandars, Ms. Eng. Hist. c:715:140–4.

p184 50. Rayleigh Diary, 16.8.1910.

p184 51. Sandars, Ms. Eng. Hist. c:740:164–8.

p184 52. Sandars, Ms. Eng. Hist. c:715:99–100.

p185 53. Sandars, Ms. Eng. Hist. c:715:125–9.

p185 54. Wemyss, 18.9.1903.

p185 55. Sandars, Ms. Eng. Hist. c:715:148–9.

p185 56. Wemyss, 18.9.1903.

p185 57. Sandars, Ms. Eng. Hist. c:719:228–9.

p186 58. Sandars, Ms. Eng. Hist. c:719: 232–5.

p186 59. Hatfield S (4) 54:25.

p186 60. Hatfield S (4) 54:121.

p187 61. Hatfield S (4) 54:119.

p187 62. Hamilton Diary, B.M. Add. mss. 48681, F.104–5.

p188 63. Hamilton Diary, B.M. Add. mss. 48681, F.123.

p188 64. Hamilton Diary, B.M. Add. mss. 48681, F.131.

p189 65. Arnold-Forster Diary, B.M. Add. mss. 50337, F.48–9.

p189 66. Arnold-Forster Diary, B.M. Add. mss. 50338, F.52.

p190 67. Sandars, Ms. Eng. Hist. c:748:207–210.

p190 68. The Times, 27.9.1904.

p190 69. Dunraven, *Past times and Pastimes II,* p26.

p191 70. Hamilton Diary, B.M. Add. mss. 48682, F.106.

p191 71. Hamilton Diary, B.M. Add. mss. 48682, F.112.

p191 72. Balfour, Whitt: 165.

p191 73. Grosvenor Papers, 23.1.1905.

p191 74. Sandars, Ms. Eng. Hist. c:771:60–3.

p192 75. Wemyss, 24.2.1905.

p192 76. Sandars, Ms. Eng. Hist. c:771:60–3.

p192 77. Wemyss, 4.3.1905.

p192 78. *Ibid.*

p192 79. Selborne, Ms.2, F.35–40.

p192 80. Selborne, Ms.2, F.53.

p193 81. Leslie, *The End of a Chapter,* p138–9.

p193 82. Balfour, B.M. Add. mss. 49805, F.51-2.

p193 83. Balfour, Whitt: 281.

p193 84. Wemyss, N.D. 1905.

p193 85. Balfour, B.M. Add. mss. 49863, F.11-15.

p193 86. Gardiner, *Prophets, Priests and Kings,* p41.

CHAPTER 12

p195 1. Hamilton Diary, B.M. Add. mss. 48682, F.126-7.

p196 2. Rayleigh Diary, 18.5.1905.

p196 3. Hamilton Diary, B.M. Add. mss. 48683, F.49.

p197 4. Sandars, Ms. Eng. Hist. c:749:134.

p197 5. Selborne, Ms. 1, F.66-7.

p197 6. Balfour, B.M. Add. mss. 49764, F.107-8.

p197 7. Selborne, Ms. 2, F.108-12.

p198 8. Sandars, Ms. Eng. Hist. c:750:245-6.

p198 9. Newton, *Retrospection,* p146.

p198 10. Wemyss, 16.1.1906.

p198 11. Wemyss, N.D.

p198 12. Wemyss, 3.12.1895.

p198 13. Wemyss, 9.7.1897.

p199 14. Wemyss, 25.6.1905.

p199 15. Webb, *Our Partnership,* p374.

p199 16. Balfour, 'The Palm Sunday Case' *S. P. R. Proceedings.* Vol: 52, p170.

p199 17. Balfour, Whitt: 81, p33.

p200 18. Wemyss, 4.10.1909.

p201 19. Hatfield, 28.7.1905.

p201 20. Arnold-Forster Diary, B.M. Add. mss. 50342, F.90.

p202 21. Webb, *Our Partnership,* p345.

p202 22. Sandars, Ms. Eng. Hist. c:716:135-7.

p203 23. Malcolm, *Lord Balfour,* p23.

p203 24. Winterton, *Pre-War,* p20.

p203 25. Bridgeman Diary, January 1906.

p203 26. Wemyss, 1905.

p203 27. Churchill, *Great Contemporaries,* p252.

p204 28. Ward, *The Wilfrid Wards and the Transition I,* p399.

p204 29. Malcolm, *op. cit.* p9.

p204 30. Grigg, *Lloyd George, The People's Champion,* p90.

p205 31. Stein, *The Balfour Declaration,* p79.

p205 32. Dugdale I, p433.

p205 33. *Ibid. I,* p435.

p206 34. Bridgeman Diary, 2.2.1906.

p206 35. Balfour, B.M. Add. mss. 49685, F.94.

p206 36. Sandars, Ms. Eng. Hist. c:751:104-5.

p206 37. Sandars, Ms. Eng. Hist. c:751:99

p206 38. Balfour, B.M. Add. mss. 49758, F.95-6.

p207 39. Balfour, B.M. Add. mss. 49729, F.206-7.

p207 40. Balfour, B.M. Add. mss. 49737, F.40-2.

p207 41. Sandars, Ms. Eng. Hist. c:751:108-9.

p208 42. Sandars, Ms. Eng. Hist. c:751:124-6.

p208 43. Maxse Papers, Vol: 455, F.229.
p208 44. Selborne, Ms. 2, F.131–2.
p208 45. Maxse Papers, Vol: 455, F.236.
p209 46. Dugdale II, p28–9.
p209 47. Hatfield 16.2.1906.
p209 48. Lansdowne 15.2.1906.
p209 49. Maxse Papers, Vol: 455, F.263.
p210 50. Webb, *Our Partnership*, p335
p210 51. Wilson, C-B, p497.
p211 52. Balfour, B.M. Add. mss. 49729, F.228–30.
p211 53. Hatfield, 3.8.1906.
p212 54. Birrell, *Things Past Redress*, p191.
p212 55. Selborne, Ms. 2, F.159–162.
p212 56. Balfour, B.M. Add. mss. 49859, F.109.
p212 57. Sandars, Ms. Eng. Hist. c:753:33–6.

p212 58. Balfour, Whitt: 273.
p213 59. Sandars, Ms. Eng. Hist. c:753:51–6.
p213 60. Balfour, B.M. Add. mss. 49859, F.158–9.
p213 61. Balfour, B.M. Add. mss. 49758, F.163–4.
p213 62. Balfour, B.M. Add. mss. 49758, F.167–173.
p214 63. Gardiner, *Prophets, Priests and Kings,* p41.
p214 64. Selborne, Ms. 2, F.181–3.
p214 65. Sandars, Ms. Eng. Hist. c:754:127.
p215 66. Hansard, 4th Series, Vol: 170, col: 1367.
p215 67. Hansard, 4th Series, Vol: 162, col: 798–800. See Judd, *Balfour and the British Empire,* p209.
p215 68. Balfour, B.M. Add. mss. 49765, F.113–14.
p216 69. Sandars, Ms. Eng. Hist. c:756:156–7.

CHAPTER 13

p217 1. Selborne, Ms. 1, F.68–78.
p217 2. Selborne, Ms. 1, F.79–80.
p218 3. Selborne, Ms. 100, F.153–6.
p220 4. Sandars, Ms. Eng. Hist. c:759:74–7.
p220 5. Dugdale II, p56.
p220 6. Balfour, B.M. Add. mss. 49695, F.171–4.
p220 7. Balfour, B.M. Add. mss.49730, F.3–4.
p221 8. Maxse, Vol. 460, F.495.
p221 9. Sandars, Ms. Eng. Hist. c:756:87–90.
p222 10. Sandars, Ms. Eng. Hist. c:760:35–40.

p222 11. Sandars, Ms. Eng. Hist. c:760:47–50.
p223 12. Balfour, B.M. Add. mss. 49766, F.147–51.
p223 13. Selborne, Ms. 6, F.44–6.
p223 14. Wemyss, March 1910.
p223 15. Sandars, Ms. Eng. Hist. c:760:52–3.
p223 16. Maxse, Vol: 461, F.610.
p225 17. Desborough Papers, 19.8.1910.
p225 18. Hatfield S (4) 68:57.
p225 19. Selborne, Ms. 6, F.77–81.
p226 20. Sandars, Ms. Eng. Hist. c:761:101–4.
p226 21. Sandars, Ms. Eng. Hist. c:761:105–6.

p226 22. Riddell, *More Pages from my Diary*, p5.

p226 23. Dugdale II, p183.

p226 24. Sandars, Ms. Eng. Hist. c:761:170–1.

p227 25. Balfour memorandum, Sandars, Ms. Eng. Hist. c:761:176–184.

p227 26. Maxse, Vol: 462, F.727–733.

p229 27. Gollin, The Observer and J. L. Garvin, p215–18. For a copy of Balfour's letter see Sandars, Ms. Eng. Hist. c:761:240–46.

p229 28. Jenkins, *Mr. Balfour's Poodle,* p107.

p230 29. Hatfield, 8.11.1910.

p231 30. Sandars, Ms. Eng. Hist. c:762:238–9.

p231 31. Sandars, Ms. Eng. Hist. c:762:241–245.

p232 32. Balfour, B.M. Add. mss. 49719, F.179–182.

p232 33. Balfour, B.M. Add. mss. 49686, F.66–72.

p232 34. Balfour, B.M. Add. mss. 49777, F.104.

p233 35. Rayleigh Diary, 16.3.1911.

p233 36. Selborne, Ms. 102, F.17–18.

p234 37. Rayleigh Diary, 4.7.1911.

p234 38. See Sandars, Diary of the Parliament Bill, Ms. Eng. Hist. c:763:162–214. Also Balfour B.M. Add. mss. 49767, F.195–270.

p235 39. *Ibid.* p22–23.

p235 40. *Ibid.* p26–29.

p236 41. Egremont, *The Cousins,* p270.

p236 42. Bridgeman Diary, 26.7.1911.

p236 43. Balfour, Whitt: 276.

p237 44. Sandars, *Diary of the Parliament Bill,* p47.

p237 45. *Ibid.* p48.

p237 46. Grosvenor Papers, 11.8.1911.

CHAPTER 14

p238 1. Wemyss, 10.8.1911.

p238 2. Wemyss, 30.7.1911.

p238 3. Sandars, Ms. Eng. Hist. c:763:217–219.

p238 4. Wemyss, A Family Record, p168.

p239 5. Sandars, A Note on the Events Leading to Mr Balfour's Resignation, Ms. Eng. Hist. c:764:157–173, p2–3. Also Balfour, B.M. Add. mss. 49767, F.291–311.

p239 6. Wemyss, 18.8.1911.

p239 7. Maxse, Vol: 463, F.98–101.

p239 8. Sandars 'Note', p3.

p240 9. Sandars 'Diary', p51.

p240 10. Wemyss, 13.9.1911.

p240 11. Sandars, Ms. Eng. Hist. c:764:65A–59A.

p240 12. Hatfield S (4) 71:62.

p241 13. Sandars, 'Note', p3–5.

p242 14. *Ibid.* p6.

p242 15. Sandars, Ms. Eng. Hist. c:764:126. Long's original letter is in the Sandars papers, Ms. Eng. Hist. c:764:128–137.

p242 16. Sandars, Ms. Eng. Hist. c:764:138.

p242 17. Hatfield S (4) 71:59–61.

p242 18. Wemyss, 20.10.1911.

p242 19. Maxse, Vol: 464, F.823.

p243 20. Balfour, B.M. Add. mss. 49736, F.180–88.

p243 21. Sandars 'Note', p12.

p243 22. Dugdale II, p86.

p243 23. Sandars 'Note', p12.

p243 24. *Ibid.* p12.

p243 25. Balfour, B.M. Add. mss. 49775, F.75–79.

p243 26. Balfour, B.M. Add. mss. 49806, F.102–4.

p244 27. Balfour, B.M. Add. mss. 49737, F117.

p244 28. Balfour, B.M. Add. mss. 49694, F.62–3.

p244 29. Balfour, B.M. Add. mss. 49794, F.129–131.

p244 30. Wemyss, 14.8.1911.

p244 31. Wemyss, 10.10.1911.

p245 32. Wemyss, 7.11.1911.

p245 33. Wemyss, 10.11.1911.

p246 34. 'Decadence' in *Essays Speculative and Political,* p1–52.

p246 35. 'Beauty and the Criticism of Beauty', *Essays Speculative and Political,* p103–147.

p247 36. 'Theism and Humanism', p18–19.

p247 37. *Ibid.* p262.

p247 38. *Ibid.* p274.

p248 39. Balfour, B.M. Add. mss. 49832, F119–123.

p248 40. Balfour, 'The Palm Sunday Case', *S.P.R. Proceedings.* Vol: 52, p111.

p248 41. *Ibid.* p121.

p249 42. *Ibid.* p132.

p249 43. *Ibid.* p144.

p249 44. *Ibid.* p156. The last two lines are from Elizabeth Barrett Browning's 'Sonnets from the Portuguese'.

p249 45. *Ibid.* p157.

p250 46. *Ibid.* p163.

p250 47. Wemyss, 30.7.1911.

p250 48. Quoted in Judd, *Balfour and the British Empire,* p315–16.

p251 49. Balfour, B.M. Add. mss. 49693, F.17–8.

p251 50. Salvidge, *Salvidge of Liverpool,* p131.

p251 51. Scott, *Political Diaries,* p183.

p251 52. Balfour, B.M. Add. mss. 49693, F.21–2.

p252 53. Dugdale II, p94.

p252 54. Hatfield S (4) 72:35–8.

p252 55. Amery, *My Political Life I,* p387.

p252 56. Balfour, B.M. Add. mss. 49733, F.147–8.

p253 57. Balfour, B.M. Add. mss. 49693, F.28–9.

p253 58. Hobhouse, *Inside Asquith's Cabinet,* p139–40.

p253 59. Cecil Papers, B.M. Add. mss. 51071, F.25–6.

p253 60. Balfour, B.M. Add. mss. 49737, F.122–3.

p254 61. Balfour, Whitt: 156.

p254 62. Balfour, B.M. Add. mss. 49767, F.48–61.

p254 63. Balfour, B.M. Add. mss. 49767, F.63–65.

p254 64. Balfour, B.M. Add. mss. 49693, F.41–7.

p255 65. Ward, *The Wilfrid Wards and the Transition II,* p411.

p255 66. Wemyss, July 1913.

p255 67. Wemyss, Note.

p256 68. Blake, *The Unknown Prime Minister,* p197–8.

p256 69. Sandars, Ms. Eng. Hist. c:766:133–6.

p256 70. Roskill, *Hankey I,*
p132–3.

p257 71. Balfour, B.M. Add. mss.
49693, F.159–60.

p257 72. Haldane Papers,
Ms.5910, F.182.

p257 73. Jenkins, *Asquith,* p320.

CHAPTER 15

p259 1. Roskill, Hankey I,
p132–3.

p260 2. Balfour, B.M. Add. mss.
49731, F.1–6.

p260 3. Hankey, *The Supreme
Command I,* p150–1.

p260 4. Dugdale II, p113.

p261 5. Rayleigh Diary,
21.9.1914.

p261 6. Churchill, *The World
Crisis I,* p218.

p261 7. Haldane, Ms. 5910,
F.242–250.

p261 8. Petrie, *Life and Letters of
Sir Austen Chamberlain
II,* p3.

p261 9. Wemyss, 1914.

p262 10. Speech to C.I.D. Sub-
Committee on Invasion,
20.5.1908. See Marder,
*From the Dreadnought
to Scapa Flow I,* p121.

p262 11. Wemyss, N.D.

p262 12. Stevenson, Diary, p18.

p262 13. Balfour, B.M. Add. mss.
49683, F.184–5.

p262 14. Rayleigh Diary,
30.9.1914.

p262 15. Balfour, B.M. Add. mss.
49833, F.36.

p262 16. Rayleigh Diary,
30.9.1914.

p264 17. Stein, Balfour Declar-
ation, p154–6. Also see
Weizmann, *Trial and
Error,* p195–7.

p265 18. Balfour, B.M. Add. mss.
49730, F.272–4.

p265 19. Roskill, *Hankey I,* p150.

p265 20. War Council Notes
quoted Gilbert, Churchill
III, p272.

p265 21. Balfour memorandum,
quoted Gilbert III, p305.

p265 22. War Council Notes
quoted Gilbert III, p308.

p265 23. Balfour, B.M. Add. mss.
49694, F105–6.

p266 24. Letters quoted, Gilbert
III, p361.

p266 25. Stevenson, *Diary,* p35.

p267 26. Maxse Papers, Vol: 470,
F.160.

p267 27. Cecil, B.M. Add. mss.
51071, F.31–2.

p267 28. Hobhouse, *Inside
Asquith's Cabinet,*
p237–8.

p267 29. Maxse Papers, Vol: 470,
F.195.

p267 30. Stevenson, *Diary,* p51.

p267 31. See Hazlehurst,
Politicians and the War,
p267.

p268 32. Rayleigh Diary,
24.3.1915.

p268 33. Cecil, B.M. Add. mss.
51071, F.33–4.

p268 34. Wemyss, N.D.

p269 35. Lloyd George, *War
Memoirs I,* p607.

p269 36. National Review, Vol:
65, p516.

p269 37. Haldane Papers, Ms.
6082, F.8

p269 38. Maxse Papers, Vol: 471, F.430.

p270 39. Wemyss, 26.8.1915.

p270 40. Roskill, *op. cit. I*, p175.

p270 41. Riddell, War Diary, p103.

p270 42. Sandars, Ms. Eng. Hist., c:768:93–98.

p271 43. Balfour, B.M. Add. mss. 49734, F.3–74.

p271 44. Balfour, B.M. Add. mss. 49734, F.1–2.

p271 45. Gilbert, *op. cit. III*, p601.

p271 46. Lloyd George, *War Memoirs I*, p607.

p272 47. Balfour, B.M. Add. mss. 49715, F.80–82.

p272 48. Scott, *Diary*, p184.

p272 49. Balfour, Whitt: 75.

p272 50. Addison, Politics from Within I, p191.

p273 51. See Hansard, 5th Series, Vol: 80, cols: 1571–1576.

p273 52. Addison, Four and a Half Years, p180.

p273 53. Sandars, Ms. Eng. Hist. c:769:88–89.

p274 54. Sandars, Ms. Eng. Hist. c:769:144–5.

p274 55. Dugdale II, p162.

p274 56. *Ibid.*

p274 57. Sandars, *Studies of Yesterday*, p203.

p274 58. Selborne, Ms. 80, F.285–290.

p275 59. Webb, Diaries, p42.

p275 60. Balfour, B.M. 49737, F.169–172.

p275 61. Gollin, Milner, p330.

p275 62. Hankey, *The Supreme Command II*, p454.

p275 63. Addison, *Politics from Within I*, p133.

p275 64. Lloyd George, *War Memoirs I*, p283.

p276 65. Addison, *Politics from Within I*, p235.

p276 66. P.R.O. Air 1/2311.

p277 67. Addison, *op. cit. I*, p235.

p277 68. Roskill, *Hankey I*, p321.

p277 69. Hatfield S (4) 77:113.

p278 70. Jones, Lloyd George, p78.

p278 71. Roskill, *Hankey I*, p325.

p278 72. Blake, *The Unknown Prime Minister*, p310.

p278 73. Balfour, B.M. Add. mss. 49758, F.298.

p278 74. Balfour, B.M. Add. mss. 49831, F.250.

p279 75. See Balfour's memorandum containing these letters and others, on 'The Government Crisis', see Balfour, B.M. Add. mss. 49692, F.179–215.

p279 76. *Ibid.* F.193–4.

p280 77. *Ibid.* F.196.

p280 78. Beaverbrook, *Politicians and the War*, p502.

p280 79. Balfour, B.M. Add. mss. 49692, F.209.

p281 80. Beaverbrook, *op. cit.* p503.

p281 81. Balfour, B.M. Add. mss. 59831, F.250.

p281 82. Balfour, B.M. Add. mss. 49831, F.249.

p281 83. Asquith, *Letters to a Friend*, p91.

p281 84. Rayleigh Diary, 31.1.1917.

p281 85. Balfour, B.M. Add. mss. 49833, F.356–357.

CHAPTER 16

p282 1. Wemyss, 28.12.1915.

p282 2. Desborough Papers, 5.8.1915.

p282 3. Desborough Papers, 25.9.1915.

p283 4. Lloyd George, *War Memoirs, I*, p607.

p283 5. Dugdale II, p185.

p283 6. Balfour, B.M. Add. mss. 49693, F.293–4.

p284 7. Stevenson, Diary, p78.

p284 8. Balfour, B.M. Add. mss. 49744, F.9–11.

p285 9. Dugdale II, p188.

p286 10. *Ibid. II*, p188.

p286 11. *Ibid. II*, p190.

p286 12. *Ibid. II*, p191.

p286 13. *Ibid. II*, p193–4.

p287 14. *Ibid. II*, p197.

p287 15. Malcolm, *Lord Balfour*, p44.

p287 16. *Ibid.* p46.

p288 17. *Ibid.* p49.

p288 18. Dugdale II, p200.

p288 19. *Ibid. II*, p201.

p289 20. Malcolm, *op. cit.* p52.

p289 21. *Ibid.* p50.

p289 22. Gwynn, *Letters and Friendships of Sir Cecil Spring-Rice II*, p400.

p289 23. Balfour, B.M. Add. mss. 49692, F.282–3.

p290 24. Malcolm, *op. cit.* p56.

p290 25. Taylor, *English History*, p123.

p290 26. Nicolson, *People and Things*, p10–11.

p291 27. *Ibid.* p13.

p291 28. Balfour, *Book of Bosh;* copy in possession of Frances, Lady Fergusson.

p291 29. Malcolm, *op. cit.* p39.

p291 30. *Ibid.* p38.

p291 31. Hendrick, *Life and Letters of Walter Page II*, p257–8.

p291 32. *Ibid. II*, p403.

p292 33. Addison, *Four and a Half Years*, p412.

p292 34. Balfour, Whitt: 15.

p293 35. Dugdale II, p226.

p293 36. Stein, Balfour Declaration, p428.

p294 37. *Ibid.* p380–1.

p295 38. P.R.O. Cab 24/30.

p295 39. For Balfour-Curzon exchange, see Cabinet paper 'Palestine and the Balfour Declaration, January 1923. Balfour Whitt: 5. Also P.R.O. Cabinet minutes 23/4.

p295 40. P.R.O. Cabinet minutes 23/245.

p295 41. Meinertzhagen, *Middle East Diary*, p8–9.

p296 42. Rayleigh Diary, 29.7.1918.

p296 43. Balfour, B.M. Add. mss. 49752, F.150–250.

p296 44. Dugdale II, p235.

p296 45. Blake, *Private Papers of Douglas Haig*, p259.

p296 46. Roskill, *Hankey I*, p401.

p297 47. See p5–8 of 'The Peace Letter of 1917' by the Marquess of Lansdowne. Pamphlet in Lansdowne papers reprinted from *The Nineteenth Century and After*, Vol: 115, p370–384.

p297 48. *Ibid.* p10.

p297 49. Times, 17.11.1917.

p297 50. Lansdowne pamphlet, *op. cit.* p9.

p297 51. Lansdowne notes. See Times 6.8.1933. Letter from Lord Lansdowne.

p298 52. Daily Telegraph, 29.11.1917.

p298 53. Times, 1.12.1917.

p298 54. Lansdowne Papers, 3.12.1917.

p298 55. Lansdowne Papers, 3.12.1917.

p298 56. Lansdowne Papers, 18.8.1933.

p299 57. Lansdowne Papers, 29.5.1934.

p299 58. Lansdowne Papers, 1.8.1933.

p299 59. Balfour, B.M. Add. mss. 49730, F.300.

p299 60. Lloyd George, *War Memoirs II*, p1545-7.

p300 61. Roskill, *Hankey I*, p494.

p300 62. Lockhart, *Giants Cast Long Shadows*, p13.

p300 63. Addison, *Four and a Half Years*, p465.

p300 64. Roskill, *Hankey I*, p503.

p301 65. Balfour, B.M. Add. mss. 49692, F.295-6.

p301 66. P.R.O. Cab. 23/8.

p301 67. Quoted Roskill, *Naval Policy Between the Wars I*, p132.

CHAPTER 17

p303 1. Rayleigh Diary, 11.11.1918.

p303 2. Jones, Whitehall Diary I, p69.

p303 3. Nicolson, *Peacemaking*, p24.

p304 4. Dugdale II, p263.

p304 5. Nicolson, *op. cit.* p84.

p304 6. Cecil, B.M. Add. mss. 51131, F.13.

p304 7. Cecil, B.M. Add. mss. 51131, F.17.

p305 8. Malcolm, *Lord Balfour*, p67.

p305 9. Cecil, B.M. Add. mss. 51131, F.18.

p305 10. Roskill, Hankey I, p559.

p305 11. Quoted Dugdale II, p264.

p305 12. Nicolson, *op. cit.* p331.

p305 13. Selborne, Ms. 191, F.70.

p306 14. Rayleigh Diary, 11.2.1920.

p306 15. Nicolson, *op. cit.* p329.

p307 16. Cecil, B.M. Add. mss. 51131, F.141.

p307 17. Dugdale II, p.280-1.

p307 18. Nicolson, *op. cit.* p329.

p308 19. Desborough Papers, 11.11.1918.

p308 20. Desborough Papers, 21.8.1916.

p308 21. Desborough Papers, 7.10.1916.

p308 22. Cynthia Asquith, *Diaries*, p14-15.

p309 23. Lady Angela St. Clair Erskine, *Fore and Aft*, p50.

p309 24. Wemyss, 1915.

p309 25. Wemyss, 19.11.1912.

p309 26. Wemyss, 28.4.1916.

p309 27. Rayleigh Diary, 16.9.1919.

p309 28. Dugdale II, p295.

p310 29. Cecil, B.M. Add. mss. 51131, F.93.

p310 30. Charteris, *Life and Letters of Sir Edmund Gosse*, p429.

p310 31. Nicolson, *Small Talk*, p224-9.

p311 32. Rayleigh Diary, 25.7.1921.

p311 33. Beaverbrook, *Politicians and the War,* p33–4.

p311 34. Taylor, Beaverbrook, p93.

p311 35. For details, see 'Wet-carbonising the War Office' in 'Truth', 17.10.1917, p524.

p311 36. Wemyss, 17.1.1915.

p312 37. Quoted in 'Truth', 17.10.1917. For the Balfour family memories of 'Peco' see Young, Balfour, p321–2.

p312 38. See Lady Eve Balfour, 'My Uncle – A. J. Balfour', The Listener, 25.10.1956.

p313 39. Dugdale, *Baffy,* p9.

p313 40. Lockhart, *Giants Cast Long Shadows,* p13.

p313 41. Balfour, B.M. Add. mss. 49734, F.141–3.

p313 42. Balfour, Whitt: 5.

p314 43. Quoted in Gilbert, *Exile and Return,* p136.

p314 44. Balfour, *Opinions and Argument,* p232–3.

p314 45. Hansard (Lords), 5th Series, Vol: 50, col: 1019–1026.

p314 46. *Ibid.* col: 1008–1019.

p315 47. Balfour, B.M. Add. mss. 49734, F.196–200.

p315 48. Balfour, Whitt: 17.

p316 49. Rayleigh Diary, 15.2.1920.

p316 50. Balfour, Whitt: 76.

p316 51. Balfour, Whitt: 1.

p316 52. Blake, *The Unknown Prime Minister,* p416–7.

p317 53. Roskill, *Hankey II,* p156.

p317 54. Roskill, *Naval Policy Between the Wars I,* p291.

p317 55. Lee, A Good Innings, p214.

p317 56. Documents on British Foreign Policy 1919–34, First Series, Vol: 14, 467–9.

p318 57. Riddell, *Intimate Diary,* p335.

p318 58. Roskill, *Hankey II,* p241–2.

p318 59. Riddell, *op. cit.* p335.

p318 60. Lee, *op. cit.* p218.

p318 61. Roskill, *Hankey II,* p242.

p318 62. Balfour, Whitt: 76.

p319 63. Riddell, *op. cit.* p337,

p319 64. Press cutting, Wemyss.

p319 65. Riddell, *op. cit.* p337.

p319 66. Lee, *op. cit.* p221–2.

CHAPTER 18

p320 1. Sandars, *Studies of Yesterday,* p182.

p320 2. Wemyss, 21.10.1922.

p320 3. Selborne, Ms. 191, F.70.

p321 4. Stevenson, Diary, p231.

p321 5. Dugdale II, p337.

p321 6. *Ibid. II,* p354.

p322 7. Taylor, *English History,* p123.

p322 8. Riddell, *Intimate Diary,* p356.

p322 9. Rayleigh Diary, 25.7.1921.

p323 10. Salvidge, *Salvidge of Liverpool,* p239.

p324 11. Wemyss, 21.10.1922.

p324 12. Jones, *Whitehall Diary I,* p222.

p324 13. Stevenson, Diary, p270.

p324 14. Rayleigh Diary, 25.7.1921.

p324 15. Cowling, *The Impact of Labour*, p193.

p325 16. Balfour, Whitt: 76.

p325 17. Balfour, B.M. Add. mss. 49693, F.300–5.

p325 18. Roskill, *Hankey II*, p328.

p326 19. Dugdale II, p358.

p326 20. Nicolson, *King George V*, p376.

p327 21. Balfour, B.M. Add. mss. 49686, F.145–7.

p327 22. Churchill, *Great Contemporaries*, p287.

p327 23. Dugdale notes in possession of Frances, Lady Fergusson.

p328 24. Cecil, B.M. Add. mss. 51071, F.37–41.

p328 25. Dugdale II, p362.

p328 26. Bridgeman Diary, December 1923.

p328 27. Balfour, Whitt: 1.

p329 28. Balfour, Whitt: 21.

p329 29. Balfour, Whitt: 1.

p329 30. Balfour, Whitt: 1.

p330 31. Balfour, Whitt: 19.

p330 32. Wemyss, 1.11.1924.

p330 33. Jones, Whitehall Diary I, p303.

p331 34. Balfour, Whitt: 76.

p331 35. Wemyss, 12.3.1924.

p331 36. Balfour, *Opinions and Argument*, p250.

p331 37. Balfour, Whitt: 166.

p332 38. Weizmann, *Trial and Error*, p400.

p332 39. Balfour, B.M. Add. mss. 49704, F.50–67.

p332 40. See Macleod and Andrews, 'The Committee of Civil Research' in *Minerva*, Vol: 7, No: 4.

p333 41. Jones, *Whitehall Diary II*, p45–6.

p333 42. Amery, *My Political Life II*, p384.

p334 43. Judd, *Balfour and the British Empire*, p330.

p334 44. Hansard (Lords) 5th Series, Vol: 65, col: 286.

p334 45. Judd, *op. cit.* p334–5

p334 46. Balfour, B.M. Add. mss. 49719, F.297.

CHAPTER 19

p335 1. Balfour, Whitt: 19.

p335 2. Balfour, Whitt: 19.

p336 3. Balfour, Whitt: 76.

p336 4. Rayleigh Diary, 19.2.1927.

p336 5. Balfour, Whitt: 229.

p336 6. Balfour, Whitt: 229.

p336 7. Balfour, Whitt: 229.

p337 8. Balfour, Whitt: 3.

p337 9. Wemyss, 28.6.1928.

p337 10. Balfour, Whitt: 229.

p337 11. Wemyss, 7.5.1929.

p338 12. Dugdale notes in the possession of Frances, Lady Fergusson.

p338 13. Selborne, Ms.7, F.203–5.

p338 14. Desborough Papers, 18.7.1929.

p338 15. S.P.R. Proceedings, Vol: 52, p166–7.

p338 16. Jones, Whitehall Diary, II, p244.

p338 17. Wemyss Diary, 17.3.1930.

p339 18. Wemyss Diary, 19.3.1930.

p339 19. Jones, *Whitehall Diary I*, p201.

INDEX